T0400672

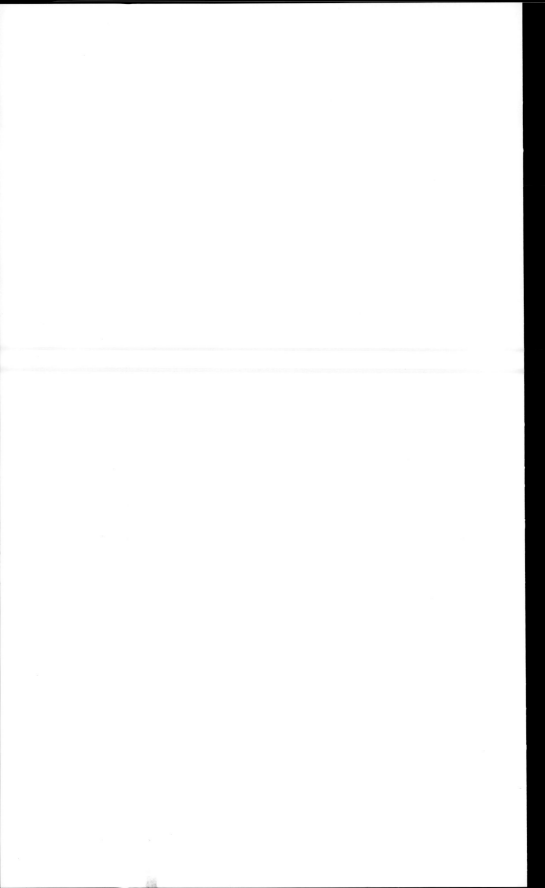

China's Old Churches

Studies in the History of Christianity in East Asia

VOLUME 2

The titles published in this series are listed at *brill.com/hcea*

China's Old Churches

*The History, Architecture, and Legacy of
Catholic Sacred Structures in Beijing, Tianjin,
and Hebei Province*

By

Alan Richard Sweeten

BRILL

LEIDEN | BOSTON

Cover illustration: The South Church at Beijing, Undated Drawing (probably ca 1860s). Source: Courtesy Library of Congress.

Library of Congress Cataloging-in-Publication Data

Names: Sweeten, Alan Richard, author.
Title: China's old churches : the history, architecture, and legacy of
    Catholic sacred structures in Beijing, Tianjin, and Hebei Province / by
    Alan Richard Sweeten.
Description: Leiden ; Boston : Brill, [2020] | Includes bibliographical
    references and index.
Identifiers: LCCN 2019037981 (print) | LCCN 2019037982 (ebook) |
    ISBN 9789004416123 (hardback) | ISBN 9789004416185 (ebook)
Subjects: LCSH: Catholic church buildings—China—Beijing. | Catholic
    church buildings—China—Tianjin. | Catholic church
    buildings—China—Hebei Sheng. | Catholic Church—China—History. |
    Christianity and culture—China—History.
Classification: LCC NA4828 .S94 2020 (print) | LCC NA4828 (ebook) |
    DDC 726.50951/15—dc23
LC record available at https://lccn.loc.gov/2019037981
LC ebook record available at https://lccn.loc.gov/2019037982

Typeface for the Latin, Greek, and Cyrillic scripts: "Brill". See and download: brill.com/brill-typeface.

ISSN 2542-3681
ISBN 978-90-04-41612-3 (hardback)
ISBN 978-90-04-41618-5 (e-book)

Printed by Printforce, the Netherlands

To Bashton Booshehri, my grandson,
and the memory of our trip to China and the old churches
we visited during the summer of 2017

∵

Author and Grandson at the Sacred Heart Cathedral, Guangzhou

Trust in the Lord and do good;
dwell in the land and enjoy safe pasture.
Delight yourself in the Lord
and he will give you the desires of your heart.
Commit your way to the Lord;
trust in him and he will do this.

PSALM 37: 3–5.

Contents

Acknowledgments

Research for my book *Christianity in Rural China* led me to archives in France and Ireland, and the opportunity to peruse reports and letters from missionaries. With notes in hand, I later traveled to China to visit the rural sites where Catholics had long ago built churches, hoping some of them still stood. I will never forget the first time I saw an old church in the countryside. In 1994, as I walked along a dusty, narrow country road that led to an out-of-the-way village in eastern Jiangxi Province, walls and houses blocked my view of the horizon until I rounded a bend and saw in the distance a large, tall building obviously European and Christian in inspiration, although no cross adorned its exterior. I had read that at this place in the early seventeenth century a Vincentian priest had built a small hillside church overlooking the adjoining rural community and its rice fields. More than four hundred years later, the scene looked about the same.

The importance of this remote village to early and later missionaries was already familiar to me, yet at this stage of research I did not comprehend the visual impact that the church's setting and architecture had made on me or, I am sure, others. Only after I had gone to numerous churches in both urban and rural locales in Hebei Province did I begin to have a sense of the rationale behind the various locations selected and what the styles represented to the Vincentian priests who built them and the congregations that worshipped in them. I also began to weigh the impact that the churches of central Beijing and Tianjin, impressive sacred structures with grand architectural lines and long histories, made on Christians and non-Christians alike. I realized that building the Church (the establishment of Catholicism in China) had taken place coterminously with the construction of church structures, and that most studies had chosen to emphasize the former to the neglect of the latter.

I want to acknowledge a few of the many people that have influenced my pursuit of the connections between the Church and its churches. My days at the University of California, Davis, are fondly remembered because Professor Kwang-Ching Liu encouraged me to study matters that pertained to ordinary people and local society. This led me to legal cases involving missionaries and villagers in Jiangxi and then to priests building sacred structures in North China's countryside. Gratifyingly, other researchers have taken to heart varied rural developments, including those involving Christianity. In particular, Professors Ernest (Ernie) P. Young and R.G. (Gary) Tiedemann have done this, setting the bar high and challenging all of us to do the same. I have benefitted from proximity to the University of San Francisco's Ricci Institute, which has an excellent library centered on Christianity in China. The institute's editors, Rev. M. Antoni J. Ucerler, S.J., Ph.D., and Dr. Xiaoxin Wu, have gently guided my project while Mr. Stephen Ford, in his role as editorial assistant, has provided all manner of help with the text and maps. Others in the China studies field, too many for me to properly recognize, continue to redefine the local issues that should concern us.

From figures ranging from Teodorico Pedrini, an eighteenth-century Vincentian priest who established a church in Beijing, to his twentieth-century confreres proselytizing in rural areas, and from modern-day priests of the Congregation of the Mission to Chinese Fathers, come a range of unique documents and materials. Revs. Georges Baldachinno, C.M., and Paul Henzmann, C.M., archivists at their Congregation's motherhouse, deserve recognition for organizing and cataloguing that which ended up in Paris. Paul's role warrants special mention because he intimately knew the files and folders, intuitively understood their historical value, and truly enjoyed helping researchers. Although he rests in peace at the Congregation's crypt at the Montparnasse Cemetery, I want others to be aware of my gratitude for his welcoming manner and friendly guidance. In the U.S., Rev. John Carven, C.M., archivist of the Eastern Province, kindly gave me access to materials housed in Philadelphia, while Rev. Louis Durbin, C.M., did the same for those located in Perryville, Missouri. The latter are now part of the DeAndreis Rosati Memorial Archives at DePaul University Library, Chicago.

I am grateful to the Florence Tan Moeson Fellowship Program, which supported my work at the Asian Division of the Library of Congress. The Vincentian Studies Institute, DePaul University, generously helped me make several trips to domestic and foreign archives as well as undertake field research in China. The institute's Rev. Edward R. Udovic, C.M., Ph.D., while shouldering countless administrative tasks, has not only found the time for his own scholarship but also the energy to cheer on myself and many others. Rev. John E. Rybolt, C.M., Ph.D., a prodigious and prolific scholar, is amazing for his gracious replies to requests for information. Revs. Hugh O'Donnell, C.M., Henk de Cuijper, C.M., and Pawel Wierzbicki, C.M., demonstrate through personal example different ways Vincentians do mission work—and help researchers. Without naming them, for privacy reasons, I must mention the many Chinese priests who opened their church doors to and had conversations with an unannounced and inquisitive stranger. I especially admire the pastors who "inherited" old Catholic churches because they appreciate them and on a daily basis deal with the challenges of the past as well as those of the present. Collectively, they have assisted and inspired me more than I can ever say. Contact with all these people, whether academic or clerical, regrettably has not perfected my scholarship and the errors that may be found here are mine and mine alone

Last, I thank my family for support, especially my wife. Carol intuitively understands what traveling, researching, and writing means to me and accepts (tolerates?) the frequent trips I have taken in the name of various projects and to see firsthand the objects of my interest. I agree with advice given by my older brother, Leonard, that one should try to make good impressions with those whom we have been in contact and leave with them pleasant memories. I think this is particularly true when visiting other countries. To relatives and friends, curious over the years about what I really do with my time and why so much of it has been spent studying China, I can now say, apparently, this book is it.

Cambria, California
"If you're lucky enough to be at the beach, you're lucky enough."
15 June 2019

Maps, Figures and Tables

Maps

Figures

Tables

Special Terms and Acronyms

Boxer Uprising (Boxers)	a popular movement led by so-called Boxers, later joined by Qing forces, that targeted foreigners and Christians, 1899–1900; Western and Japanese military forces suppressed it, forcing the dynasty to agree to a protocol and pay a huge reparation
Christians	usually refers to Catholics; context or source will clarify if it includes Protestants; similarly, Christianity
Church	the Roman Catholic Church
churches	Catholic sacred structures, unless identified as Protestant; "properly stated" churches refer to those of European style
church names	formal names are given in English, followed by *pinyin* on first mention (see glossary for Chinese characters)
C.I.C.M.	Congregation of the Immaculate Heart of Mary; its members—Scheutists
C.M.	Congregation of the Mission; its members—Lazarists, Vincentians
concession (area)	a delimited district within a treaty port that was under the extraterritorial control of a foreign power
C.P.A.	Catholic Patriotic Association, sometimes called the "Official Catholic Church" of China
Cultural Revolution	abbreviated term for the Great Proletarian Cultural Revolution, 1966–1976; its militant supporters—Red Guards
Daughters of Charity	of St. Vincent de Paul; its members referred to as Sisters
"districts" and "residences"	used in Vincentian reports of the early twentieth century as divisions of a vicariate
imperial reign title	an emperor is usually referred to by his reign title and not his personal name; also, regnal years for the recording of time periods
jiao'an	"[Christian] Religious Case(s)," a term for an incident or dispute that involved Christians (usually

	Catholics and priests) adjudicated by Chinese officials and/or foreign diplomats
Legations (Legation Quarter)	foreign diplomatic ministries (and their collective location in Beijing)
Manchus	the Tungusic people of Northeast Asia that founded the Qing dynasty
M.E.P.	Missions Étrangères de Paris (Foreign Missions Society of Paris)
O.F.M.	Order of Friars Minor; its members—Franciscans
Opium War(s)	the first war, 1840–1842, between Britain and China; the second, 1858–1860 (or 1856–1860), also referred to as the Arrow War and the Anglo-French War
Propaganda Fide	the Sacred Congregation for the Propagation of the Faith; formed in 1622 at Rome to administer Church designated mission jurisdictions until they merged into the Church hierarchy as dioceses
Qing dynasty	established in 1636 in the Northeast, moved to Beijing in 1644; its last emperor abdicated the throne in early 1912
Qing empire	the Manchu-ruled territory that included China proper as well as encompassing Mongolia, Tibet, and large parts of Northeast and Central Asia
S.J.	Society of Jesus; its members—Jesuits
tael	commonly used equivalent for an ounce (*liang*) of silver
treaty port	a city opened via unequal treaty to foreign trade and residency
unequal treaties	a term that dates to the early twentieth century; customarily and retrospectively used to describe the accords forced upon China by foreign powers and in effect from 1842–1943
vicariate	an ecclesiastical jurisdiction in mission areas assigned exclusively to a Catholic order, society, or congregation; its vicar held the title of bishop; later, most became a diocese
village(s)	rural communities are identified as *cun, tun*, or *zhuang* to help distinguish from others with a similar name (see glossary for village names in characters)

yamen   refers to the office and residence (a walled
                                   compound) of an official, from local to provincial
                                   levels, including some in the capital

Zongli Yamen   shortened name for Zongli geguo shiwu yamen
                                   (office for the management of general matters for all
                                   countries); the dynasty's office of foreign affairs,
                                   1861–1901

Abbreviations

Annales CM-F	*Annales de la Congrégation de la Mission*
Annales OSE	*Annales de l'Oeuvre de la Sainte-Enfance*
Annals CM-E	*Annals of the Congregation of the Mission*
Annals PF	*Annals of the Propagation of the Faith*
Archives CM, Paris	Congregation of the Mission, (Maison-Mère) Paris, Archives
Archives CM, Philadelphia	Congregation of the Mission, (Eastern Province) Philadelphia, Archives
Archives CM, Chicago	Congregation of the Mission, (Western Province) Chicago, DeAndreis Rosatti Memorial Archives, DePaul University
Cath-M Annals PF	*Catholic Missions and Annals of the Propagation of the Faith*
JWJAD	*Jiaowu jiao'an dang*

MAP 1.1   China proper and part of the northeast, late Qing. Some visual modifications have been made, and some modern place-names provided for convenience.

SOURCES: CHGIS VERSION 6 © FAIRBANK CENTER FOR CHINESE STUDIES AND THE INSTITUTE FOR CHINESE HISTORICAL GEOGRAPHY AT FUDAN UNIVERSITY, DEC 2016

CHAPTER 1

An Introduction to Old Churches

"The material church signifies the spiritual church" (*ecclesia materialis signifi-cat ecclesiam spiritualem*).[1] Theologians of the Middle Ages and Early Modern Europe intuitively understood this statement inspiring them to dream of ever bigger and taller as well as more intricate and complex sacred structures. Over two millennia, as Christianity spread, Catholics creatively found ways to con-struct them, witnessed by the evolution of architectural styles from Roman to Modernist, each expressed with regional or national features. Church buildings reflect time and place, something relatively well known for the West but hardly considered for the East. China's experience deserves examination because of the opportunity presented by a four-hundred-year-long effort to transplant Christianity, one that involved a variety of religious structures.[2] As missionar-ies of various religious organizations made great strides in their work during the nineteenth century's second half, they stressed that churches aided them in the conversion of non-believers.[3] Priests observed that Chinese Catholics had feelings of "inferiority" at places where there were large "magnificent

---

1 Hans Jantzen, *High Gothic: The Classic Cathedrals of Chartres, Reims, and Amiens*, trans. James Palmes (Princeton: Princeton University Press, 1984), 169.

2 The mission period in China starts about 1550 with the arrival of Catholic priests and may be said to end in 1946 when the Church regularized its ecclesiastical hierarchy with the es-tablishment of dioceses (some apostolic prefectures remained mission jurisdictions). An era of "independence" began in 1949 when the new government started expelling Western missionaries. In 1957, the Religious Affairs Bureau was charged with regulating all religions. Since then (and recently) there have been administrative changes; the Catholic Patriotic Association (C.P.A.) continues to be the official organization responsible for Catholicism's churches and their worshippers.

3 Fr. Louis-Gabriel Delaplace, of the Congregation of the Mission (C.M.), wrote from Henan Province in central China that "a place of worship is one of the first requirements in this country where the pagans have the upper hand, and where isolated Christians would soon abate their zeal if they were not mutually encouraged by the united performance of good works." Delaplace letter, 26 August 1848, *Annals of the Propagation of the Faith* 12 (1851): 25. Hereafter, *Annals PF*. A Jesuit missionary in the northern province of Zhili put it this way in 1861: "In order that success may crown our labours, we need churches; we must have chapels to collect the pagans." Leboucq letter, 7 September 1861, *Annals PF* 13 (1862): 112. Two decades later, a C.M. bishop in Jiangxi wrote that peace and buildings for worship would lead to an in-crease in converts. Vic letter, 10 April 1884, *Annales de la Congrégation de la Mission* 50 (1885): 129. Hereafter, *Annales CM-F*.

FIGURE 1.1   Beijing's South Church (rebuilt in 1904) and sacred grotto
SOURCE: PHOTO BY AUTHOR, 2018

temples."[4] Both wanted their religious structures, typically of European style, to visually convey a grand, inspiring image and an ongoing community presence so that they could communally and emotionally support one another. The establishment of churches reinforced devotional practices and boosted

---

4   From the northwestern frontier village (*cun*) of Xiwanzi, a priest of the Congregation of the Immaculate Heart of Mary (C.I.C.M.) noted the sensory impact that established temples, often with lavish furnishing, had on Chinese. Catholics wanted churches to represent the greatness of their religion. Bax letter, 22 November 1872, *Annals PF* 34 (1873): 367–368. From Zhili, a Jesuit reported that "the Chinese ... allow themselves to be influenced by exterior effects; the more you address their eyes, the more you influence their minds." "Vicariate-Apostolic of South-east Pe-tche-ly," *Annals PF* 34 (1873): 73.

worshippers' and priests' morale.[5] In wide-ranging ways, churches represented the first of three types of mission progress.[6]

China's churches, especially the old ones (pre-1949) that remain structurally intact, are at the center of this study because they offer significant historical insights into the spread and state of one religion, while their distinctive, sometimes controversial, architecture hints at its long-term struggle to survive. Chronologically and spatially, they exemplify Christianity's efforts to establish itself and Chinese reaction to this endeavor that, for a variety of reasons, made church buildings themselves one cause for local incidents, regionally based episodes of attack, and even several country-wide mass movements of destruction. Opponents did not eliminate all sacred structures and those left standing in Beijing, Tianjin, and several cities in Hebei (formerly Zhili) Province are pursued because, with notable pasts, a variety of styles, and different restoration work, as well as easy access, they offer important insights into the spiritual vitality of Catholicism.[7] Missionaries built an abundance of churches in Hebei's rustic areas, a surprising number still well preserved. Often off the beaten track, seldom studied or celebrated, these survivors project distinctive qualities of their own that help us understand developments in the countryside.

The highs and lows of Catholicism in China are clearly reflected by its sacred structures. The first four in Beijing, each of European style, stood tall during the early eighteenth century, filled with people drawn to the faith by determined missionaries only to vanish save for the one that remained in use until the late 1830s. After 1860, churches reopened in the capital as Catholicism's comeback began. In the pages that follow, we shall see that those in Beijing inspired the construction of rural ones of a similar architectural style, an influence that continued into the late 1930s. After a fifty-year interregnum, people of the 1980s were drawn back to certain hallowed buildings, most with Western-design

---

5   After the Reformation, church architects in Europe felt that their creations would play a role in "the emotional stimulus to pious devotion." Roloff Beny and Peter Gunn, *The Churches of Rome* (New York: Simon and Schuster, 1981), 161. Missionaries in China agreed. A member of the Foreign Missions Society of Paris (M.E.P.) en route to China said he felt uplifted at the mere sight of a church. Lavigne letter, 6 July 1853, *Annals PF* 16 (1855): 24.

6   Proselytization had one or more physical components. In the mid-nineteenth century the Congregation of the Mission focused on three broad undertakings: 1) conversion of the Chinese and building sacred structures; 2) the formation of Chinese priests and construction of seminaries; and 3) philanthropy, which included educating children in newly built schools and helping the needy by opening foundling homes and hospitals. "Missions of China," *Annals PF* 11 (1850): 14–16. In all cases, churches served as the showpieces of evolving mission compounds filled with infrastructural support.

7   How I refer to the province depends on the era under discussion. For overlapping periods, I use Zhili/Hebei.

FIGURE 1.2   Sacred grotto at Housangyu Village, Beijing Diocese. It is visited
              regularly by local Catholics and every May by many others.
              SOURCE: PHOTO BY AUTHOR, 2009

features. To older Catholics they felt familiar, holding warm memories of baptisms, marriages, and other personal events. Significantly, priests made churches religiously and culturally relevant for worshippers by locating the chancel
in the north side and often reserving the west side for statues or chapels dedicated to Holy Mary. Beginning in the early twentieth century and becoming
very popular eighty years later, Catholics built within church courtyards what
they called "sacred grottoes" (*shengshan*) and pavilions dedicated to Mary, and
in certain places (usually rural) that pilgrims visited annually to pray to her.
Presently, as China's demographics shift and the country becomes statistically
more urban than rural, the strength of the Marian movement remains rooted

in the countryside because of the numerous believers who live near the thousands of sacred structures located in small towns or villages.

1   Contextualizing Churches

One approach to studying churches, and Church history, is to narrow the focal point and concentrate on just one group of Western missionaries and Chinese priests—in this case those of the Congregation of the Mission (called Lazarists and Vincentians), who served in China from the late eighteenth century to the mid-twentieth. Others have narrated their long and rich chronicle, so it is unnecessary to retell it here except as it relates to the confines of this study.[8] In 1785, a handful of Vincentians arrived to assume administration of ecclesiastical areas in Beijing and Zhili from the Society of Jesus (S.J.) due to its dissolution by the pope. That deed placed Vincentians in the country's most important city, the imperial capital, from which they expanded their evangelical activities into villages. For a time, they worked in Mongolia, Hubei, and Henan before withdrawing to concentrate their resources on Zhili and two provinces in China's center. Split between the metropolitan capital and its surrounding province in the north, between agriculturally rich Zhejiang Province and rurally impoverished Jiangxi, Vincentians made progress as manifested in the construction of places of worship, their maps highlighting them with red crosses.

Christianity's growth slowed due to imperial proscription in 1724, reinforced by later decrees that lasted until 1844 when U.S. and French treaties added liberalizing provisions not included in the British settlement of the First Opium War (1840–1842). Treaties allowed missionaries to reside in the five ports

---

8   For a detailed history from a Vincentian perspective, see *Mémoires de la Congrégation de la Mission*, 3 vols. (Paris: La Procure de la Congrégation de la Mission, 1911–1912); and Octave Ferreux, *Histoire de la Congrégation de la Mission en Chine (1699–1950)* (Paris: Congrégation de la Mission, 1963). I treat the latter as a stand-alone publication rather than volume 127, the last of the *Annales CM-F* series. It has been translated into Chinese and published under the title *Qianshihui zai Hua chuanjiao shi* (see the bibliography). Brief biographical information on almost a thousand Vincentians with service in China is in J. [Joseph] Van den Brandt, *Les Lazaristes en Chine, 1697–1935: notes biographiques* (Pei-p'ing [Beijing]: Imprimerie des Lazaristes, 1936). Fr. Octave Ferreux, C.M., and Bro. Joseph Van den Brandt, C.M., served in China and had access to internal records no longer extant. For a recent study, see *The Vincentians: A General History of the Congregation of the Mission*, 6 vols. (Hyde Park, N.Y.: New City Press, 2009–2016). In this series, Rev. John E. Rybolt played a prominent role as editor and author, contributing general treatments of the Vincentians and chapters focusing on their work in China.

opened for trade and Chinese Christians to practice their faith wherever they lived.[9] During the proscribed years, three of Beijing's four churches had been consumed by either fire or politics, the fourth closing due to the death of its sole resident priest. A handful of Vincentians found refuge outside the capital in Zhili, others in Zhejiang and Jiangxi. Although they built more in the countryside of these three provinces, not a single rural sacred structure from this period has survived. In the 1840s, missionary numbers began to increase as they took up residency in coastal treaty ports from which they surreptitiously initiated a slow rural recovery.

With the Second Opium War (1858–1860), Western countries—mainly France—enhanced treaty-imposed rights for missionaries.[10] They proceeded to recover previously owned properties in Beijing, acquire fresh sites, and erect churches, one of the largest situated in the treaty port of Tianjin, seventy-five miles east of the capital. Concomitantly, the country suffered several major social disruptions with armed opponents (Taiping forces being the largest) rampaging through almost every province including Zhili. In Zhejiang and Jiangxi in the 1850s and 1860s, repeated battles between imperial forces and the Taipings meant the utter destruction of many towns with several areas virtually

---

9   Decrees of 1805 and 1811 are relevant: the former for its condemnation of ongoing Christian activities that included publications, and the latter for its emphasis on the eradication of "heresies" that became part of the Qing legal code. Full translations of them may be found in J.J.M. de Groot, *Sectarianism and Religious Persecution in China: A Page in the History of Religions*, 2 vols. (1903–1904; reprint, 2 vols. in 1, Taipei: Literature House, 1963) 2:387–401. The British Treaty of Nanjing, 1842, concerned itself mainly with ways to open China commercially. The U.S. treaty of 1844 added a provision that allowed missionaries to construct churches in the five ports. France's negotiator sought more. He successfully pressured his Chinese counterpart to petition the emperor for a rescript of toleration for Catholicism, which was issued in 1844. The next year another rescript did the same for Protestantism. Jonathan D. Spence, *The Search for Modern China* (New York: W. W. Norton & Co., 1990), 161.

10   In the first treaties of the 1840s, Western countries included the most-favored-nation clause. This meant that if China subsequently agreed to a certain term with one power, others automatically acquired it without the need for treaty revision. All powers therefore shared the provisions in the French treaties of 1858–1860 that helped Catholicism expand. The unequal treaty system, as it became known, is cogently presented in terms of its main features and an evolving Chinese interpretation of them in Dong Wang, *China's Unequal Treaties: Narrating National History* (Lanham, Md.: Lexington Books, 2005), 1–34. France actively used the treaty system to protect missionaries' rights, effectively creating a religious protectorate. A study by Ernest P. Young carefully dissects French actions in this regard with ample attention given to Vincentians. See his *Ecclesiastical Colony: China's Catholic Church and the French Religious Protectorate* (Oxford: Oxford University Press, 2013).

depopulated: Catholic churches and congregations disappeared.[11] After suppressing their militant rivals, a weakened imperial government had only tenuous control of some localities, as evidenced by continued unrest and recurrent attacks on Westerners—a prominent example being the anti-Catholic activity of 1870 that destroyed Tianjin's church. Over the next three decades, tenacious Catholic missionaries proselytized practically everywhere, all the while suffering repeated blows with enormous losses of life and property.

By century's end, Catholics, still a widely scattered minority, endured the waves of attacks and destruction that swept through China proper, collectively referred to as the Boxer Uprising (1899–1900). This populist-inspired antiforeign, anti-Christian movement led to the murder of many missionaries and priests as well as thousands of Chinese Christians, with some of the worst incidents occurring in Zhili. The Qing court joined the clash by declaring war on the treaty powers in June 1900, optimistic it could channel personal-level resentment of Christians (Catholics being the majority) and Westerners into a broad anti-imperialist campaign. The rampage quickly entered its last stage. In the capital, Boxers burned three of the four main Catholic churches and laid siege to the city's Legation Quarter. In Tianjin, they set torches to a landmark church as cohorts sought to do the same to the foreign concession area they had surrounded. And in the countryside, thousands died as hundreds of sacred structures went up in flames. Of all those built between 1844 and 1900, only a handful remain.

It took a joint Western-Japanese military expedition to defeat the Boxer militias and the Qing forces that supported them.[12] The punitive peace accord of 1901 required the dynasty to pay over thirty-nine years (plus interest) a massive reparation in silver, valued at the time at $333 million, with much of France's 15 percent share earmarked by its legation for bishops to use in the reconstruction of lost churches and chapels that priests soon filled with survivors and

---

11   Fr. Antoine Anot, C.M., wrote about the heavy loss of life in Jiangxi and how few people remained in one large central area. Anot letters, 28 September 1856, *Annales CM-F* 23 (1858): 521–524 and 15 July 1859, *Annales CM-F* 25 (1860): 184. British traveling up the Yangtze River to Zhenjiang commented on the number of dead and overall devastation. Robert Bickers, *The Scramble for China: Foreign Devils in the Qing Empire, 1832–1914* (London: Penguin, 2012), 178.

12   The Boxer Uprising is well-studied and the literature voluminous. This is a sampling: Joseph W. Esherick, *The Origins of the Boxer Uprising* (Berkeley: University of California Press, 1987); Paul A. Cohen, *History in Three Keys: The Boxers as Event, Experience, and Myth* (New York: Columbia University Press, 1997); Diana Preston, *The Boxer Rebellion: The Dramatic Story of China's War on Foreigners that Shook the World in the Summer of 1900* (New York: Walker & Company, 2000); and Robert Bickers and R.G. Tiedemann, eds., *The Boxers, China, and the World* (Lanham, Md.: Rowman & Littlefield, 2007).

the recently converted. In many locales, officials collected additional money (the unknown total by no means small) from residents to recompense Chinese Catholics for lives lost and personal property destroyed.[13] Starting then and continuing for thirty plus years, convert numbers skyrocketed in Zhili/Hebei's rural areas and Vincentians embarked on a veritable church building spree to accommodate them.[14] Due to an unprecedented numerical increase in religious structures, it is not surprising that many of them have survived to this day.

Active building stopped during the Sino-Japanese War (1937–1945), with Church efforts turning from expansion to relief work. When that conflict ended the last stage (1945–1949) of the Civil War immediately took center stage, culminating with the creation of the People's Republic of China. During these twelve years of intense fighting, shells frequently and indiscriminately struck many buildings, even sacred structures with roofs painted with large red crosses. Afterwards, circumstances and finances meant there could be neither extensive repairs to surviving churches nor any construction of new ones. From the early-1950s to the mid-1970s, political storms—particularly the Great Cultural Proletarian Revolution (1966–1976)—buffeted the already damaged and weakened buildings. Revolutionary zealots, known as Red Guards, had many prominent targets, among them China's churches—Catholic and Protestant. Destruction by arson proved too quick and easy; instead they sought to humiliate Christians by stripping façades of religious adornments and ripping out altars and pews. Now secularized, the buildings became schools, hospitals, factories, and warehouses. In the late 1970s, China's leaders decided to open the country and implement reforms, one aspect of which meant qualified toleration of publicly practiced religion. The policy course led to the return of former churches (a majority of them though not all) to the Catholic Patriotic Association, a government organ sometimes labeled the "Official Catholic Church," for transfer to dioceses that then eagerly began

---

13   An excellent discussion of the complexities that involved the official Boxer indemnities and those paid out separately and additionally, what may be called "the irregular indemnity," is in Young, *Ecclesiastical Colony*, 79–82.

14   Priests sometimes commented on this. One mentioned that "in the provinces [vicariates] of Beijing and Tianjin there is an extraordinary movement of conversion among the people." Latouche, "A la 'semaine sociale' de Versailles, 1913, ... Interview d'un missionnaire chinois [V. Lebbe]," *Annales CM-F* 79 (1914): 64. For a Protestant view of growth during the twentieth century's first two decades, see Milton T. Stauffer, *The Christian Occupation of China: A General Survey of the Numerical Strength and Geographical Distributon* [sic] *of the Christian Forces in China Made by the Special Committee on Survey and Occupation China Continuation Committee, 1918–1921* (Shanghai: China Continuation Committee, 1922), 32–39.

mobilizing people of various places to restore them.[15] At the same time, additional construction projects began.

In regard to repairs, renovations, and rebuilding, this is not all a recent phenomenon and should not be treated superficially. Consideration should be given to how Catholics engaged in such work in terms of the architectural details of these churches, even though their ever-changing appearance—inside and out, through time and much turmoil—is problematic. The approach taken here emphasizes churches' exteriors because their basic, physical configurations tended to remain intact; opponents might deface façades, but the structural remnants that expressed earlier stylistic choices survived, making possible reconstruction of something closely resembling the original. And, when a congregation restored a façade, one might understand this as a sort of public statement by Catholics about their religion and its architectural place in a locale or, more broadly, in China. No less significant are interior décor and furnishings, yet due to their fragility and portability not one of today's old churches is as originally appointed. In terms of interior layouts, the placement of the altar and side chapels, if any, conform to European Catholic patterns with some details particular to traditional China with its segregation of male and female worshippers. Therefore, some information about interiors is included when germane to understanding architectural designs and Church culture in China.

2   Materials and Documentation

The following highlights the types of materials found most useful for this study. For the earliest sacred edifices in Beijing, there are a few contemporaneous descriptions by missionaries supplemented by a handful of rare sketches and painting—ones that reveal intriguing architectural features and elevations. An abundant source of information about later churches comes from Vincentians then in China. Editors at the Congregation of the Mission's motherhouse in Paris selected letters and reports from priests (later including some from the Daughters of Charity of St. Vincent de Paul), compiling them into annual volumes that they published in French from 1834 to 1963 under the title *Annales de la Congrégation de la Mission*.[16] Rich in first-hand accounts, missionaries

---

15   Those not affiliated with the C.P.A. are considered by it to be "unofficial," "house," or "underground" Christians.

16   The first Daughters of Charity (members known as Sisters) arrived at Macao on 21 June 1848. Thérèse letter, 20 July 1848, *Annales CM-F* 13 (1848): 505. Some moved to Ningbo in

write about their heavy workloads, busy schedules, mission activities, and interactions—in short, about the challenges of proselytization in China. This orientation is not surprising because, after all, they had traveled long distances before arriving in a very different cultural milieu that had so many customs drawing their attention. A careful gleaning is not wasted and brings to light all kinds of information from descriptions of existing or newly built churches that typically reflected their Western tastes to the financing and attendant problems in constructing them. The publication kept readers abreast of Vincentians' worldwide activities as well as indirectly aiding in the solicitation of donations.[17] Likewise, the Society for the Propagation of the Faith, founded at Lyon in 1822, published in French a series that soon became available in several other languages.[18] Editors selected letters from missionaries of various religious orders and congregations, including some from Vincentians. The English version, *Annals of the Propagation of the Faith*, spans the years 1838–1934.[19] Although the publication's inclusiveness provides comparative insights into the difficulties of mission work, it is well to remember that one of its purposes was to elicit donations for the financial support of mission work in progress all over the globe.

Another rich vein is the Lazarist Press (Imprimerie des Lazaristes), situated next door to Beijing's North Church from the late-nineteenth century to the mid-twentieth century. The busy press produced numerous publications ranging from French-language historical accounts of its missions in China and annual statistical series that tracked Vincentian mission growth in China to

---

1852. *Handbook of Christianity in China, Volume Two: 1800 to the Present*, ed. R.G. Tiedemann, *Handbook of Oriental Studies*, vol. 15/2 (Leiden: Brill), 59. More arrived in 1862, first serving in Tianjin and Beijing. J.-M. Planchet [A. Thomas, pseud.], *Histoire de la mission de Pékin*, 2 vols. (Paris: Imprimerie de la Presse Française, 1923–1925), 2:412. The Sisters' work focused on health care through the establishment of dispensaries, hospitals, and foundling homes. The Holy Childhood Society or Association (l'Oeuvre de la Sainte-Enfance), financially supported their work to medically aid and educate abandoned children. To raise funds, the society published reports and letters from priests and Sisters in the field in *Annales de l'Oeuvre de la Sainte-Enfance*. Hereafter, *Annales OSE*. Also, see Chapter 2, note 34.

17   In 1894, the *Annals of the Congregation of the Mission* became available with its contents usually the same as its French counterpart. Hereafter, *Annals CM-E*. By title or abbreviation, I clarify which language edition is cited.

18   Initially entitled *Annales de l'Association de la Propagation de la Foi*, its name was shortened to *Annales de la Propagation de la Foi* in 1837.

19   In January 1924, the title changed to *Catholic Missions and Annals of the Propagation of the Faith*. As an illustrated monthly, most knew it as *Catholic Missions*. Hereafter cited as *Cath-M Annals PF*.

religious tracts in Chinese.[20] Fr. Jean-Marie Planchet, C.M., and Bro. Joseph Van den Brandt, C.M., in particular labored tirelessly, drawing from their respective missionary experiences and in-house records in China to provide accounts of the Congregation of the Mission's work that the press then published.[21] It also printed, mainly for in-house use, limited-run booklets on specific mission districts that offer an inside view of the Church and its infrastructure. Some publications include photographic reproductions of rural sacred structures, originals of which no longer exist. The Lazarist Press's storage room and the North Church's library served as repositories, which authorities shutdown in the 1950s, the holdings dispersed. A few libraries in the West have preserved some of the major French-language publications though not many of its booklets and pamphlets nor materials printed in Chinese. As for the North Church's once extensive collection of rare books, government officials moved most of it to the National Library in Beijing. Access to many old titles is tightly restricted.[22] Other Vincentian libraries did not fare as well, their collections scattered or burned.

Prior to 1949, Vincentians (mostly French) maintained a variety of records at their churches and seminaries and at the same time regularly sent to their superior general at the motherhouse in Paris letters, reports, statistical summaries, photographs, and an assortment of other materials that have been

---

20 A complete list of its publications is needed to gauge the range of subjects treated and their potential influence. Of limited scope is Joseph Van den Brandt, *Catalogue des principaux ouvrages sortis des presses des Lazaristes à Pékin de 1864 à 1930* (Pékin [Beijing]: H. Vetch, 1933). Many of the press's publications became part of the North Church's library. For general information Hubert G. Verhaeren, *Catalogue de la bibliothèque du Pé-t'ang* (1949; reprint, Paris: Belles lettres, 1969).

21 Planchet served from 1896 to 1932 as a priest and historian in the Vicariate of Beijing and Zhili North (formally, an apostolic vicariate). In the early years of its formation, the area was known as the Vicariate of Zhili North, becoming the Vicariate of Beijing in 1924. I will use its later, longer designation for clarity in the pages that follow. Planchet published several books dealing with Vincentian work and summarized Catholic demographics in a series on the missions of China and Japan. Van den Brandt, mentioned in note 8, began his service in Jiangxi in 1903, five years later transferring to Beijing. He managed the Lazarist Press into the 1930s.

22 No detailed pre-1949 catalogue of the North Church's library exists. In the 1950s, the collection went to the National Library with the Ningxia Hui Autonomous Region Library in Yinchuan later obtaining a large portion of it. Liu Qinghua, "The Beitang Collection in Ningxia and the Lazarist Mission Press in the Late Qing Period" in *History of the Catholic Church in China: From Its Beginning to the Scheut Fathers and 20th Century. Unveiling Some Less Known Sources, Sounds and Pictures*, ed. Ferdinand Verbiest Institute (Leuven: Ferdinand Verbiest Institute K.U. Leuven, 2015), 420–421.

preserved.[23] American Vincentians went to China in the early twentieth century, keeping some records at hand while forwarding copies and other materials to the headquarters of the Eastern Province or Western Province. The former's archives are at St. Vincent's Seminary in Philadelphia and the latter's, once in Perryville, Missouri, are now at DePaul University in Chicago. These three archival collections are extremely valuable given that in the 1950s–1970s the Chinese government decommissioned churches, effectively eradicating their records.[24] Surviving primary sources plainly reveal how Catholicism had expanded and how that expansion took the form of religious buildings. As for what they actually looked like, there are archival photographs, some identified and displayed in albums, others without markings and shuffled together in envelopes. The few pre-1900 shots found are of churches in Beijing or Tianjin. From 1900 forward there are more photographs, even some of those in rural areas. When apropos, copies of these visual treasures are reproduced here.[25]

During the last decades of the Qing period, 1860–1912, government authorities dealt with hundreds of what they labeled "[Christian] religious cases" (*jiao'an*), that is, situations (some purely legal disputes and adjudications, others conflict marred by physical violence) that involved one or more of the following: Western missionaries, Chinese priests, and local Christians.[26] Officials investigated and reported on these cases, forwarding a wide variety of materials to the Zongli Yamen (the Qing equivalent of a foreign affairs office, 1861–1901)

---

23   Some of the most valuable include missionaries' unpublished letters, reports, and visual records. Several archivists organized the materials and a catalogue of those relating to China is available online. Georges Baldacchino, "Relevé global des dossiers sur la chine," revised 2013, http://famvin.fr/Congreg_Mission/ARCH_Invent_PDF%2026_08_09/ARCH_Chine%20Mais_Mere.pdf (accessed 10 November 2016).

24   Some materials have, in fact, survived. The Xikai church in Tianjin has many uncatalogued books and records that may be from its former library. Anthony E. Clark, "Vincentian Footprints in China: The Lives and Legacies of François-Régis Clet, C.M. and Jean-Gabriel Perboyre, C.M.," *Vincentian Heritage Journal* 32, no. 1 (Spring 2014). A priest told me that he believes the materials came from the Jesuits' former college at Tianjin. Author's field notes, 26 September 2016. As another example, a few books from the pre-1949 era sit on a church office's shelf at the village (*cun*) of Jiahoutuan, Tongzhou District, Beijing. Author's field notes, 30 September 2011.

25   Photography was expensive and few people in China, Western missionaries included, owned cameras during the mid and late decades of the nineteenth century. Photographs of a general sort are limited in number; photographs of churches even more so until about 1920.

26   From the government's standpoint, and, in a broad sense, *jiao'an* were "sectarian cases." In this study, *jiao'an* are understood as "religious cases," that is, specifically, "[Christian] religious cases." The term "missionary case(s)" is too inclusive, implying only their involvement.

in Beijing for review and instructions on what to do.[27] These records, the most comprehensive available and covering the last six decades of the dynasty, eventually ended up at Academia Sinica in Taiwan; later Institute of Modern History editors organized them by province and photolithographically published everything in twenty-one volumes under the title *Jiaowu jiao'an dang* ([Zongli Yamen] Archives on [Christian] religious cases).[28] Not all documents made it to this Qing-era office in the capital, with some transmitted to other government boards and bureaus; those housed at the First Historical Archives in Beijing have been edited and published under the title *Qingmo jiao'an* (Late Qing [Christian] religious cases).[29] Dispute and conflict oriented *jiao'an* materials have led to monographs with a provincial focus and have proved invaluable in understanding Church activities and Catholic villagers' contact with others at the community level.[30] Here I find them useful for general information about religious structures.

Local, district, and county gazetteers (*difangzhi, quzhi, xianzhi*), both pre-1949 and post-1979 versions are a type of quasi-official material in that government authorities and elites typically involved themselves as sponsors and authors. These materials take us to specific places and provide information about Christianity's arrival and growth in the area. Gazetteers are good for basic information about when and where churches were built, typically providing abbreviated, non-analytical accounts without notation about sources, that is, whether information came from informants, privately held materials, or printed matter. In a more limited way, present-day congregations have created their own gazette-like histories via independently printed, limited-run

27 Archivists and scholars have been sorting and studying these materials for years. In the 1930s–1940s some documents became available in published form as *Qingji jiao'an shiliao* (in 2 parts, Peiping [Beijing]: Gugong wenxiangguan, 1937 and 1941). A general survey of sources soon appeared: Wu Shengde and Chen Zenghui, eds., *Jiao'an shiliao bianmu* (Peiping [Beijing]: Yanjing daxue, 1941).

28 *Jiaowu jiao'an dang*, Series I, 1860–1866, 3 vols.; Series II, 1867–1870, 3 vols.; Series III, 1871–1878, 3 vols.; Series IV, 1879–1886, 3 vols.; Series V, 1887–1895, 4 vols.; Series VI, 1896–1899, 3 vols.; Series VII, 1900–1911, 2 vols. (Taibei: Zhongyang yanjiuyuan jindai shi yanjiusuo, 1974–1981). Hereafter, *JWJAD*. For in-depth comments about this valuable source, see Alan Richard Sweeten, *Christianity in Rural China: Conflict and Accommodation in Jiangxi Province, 1860–1900* (Ann Arbor: Center for Chinese Studies, University of Michigan, 2001), 201–203 n. 44.

29 *Qingmo jiao'an*, ed. Diyi lishi dang'anguan, 3 vols. (Beijing: Zhonghua shuju, 1996–1999). The First Historical Archives has edited some materials related to affairs of the early and mid-Qing under the title: *Qing zhongqianqi Xiyang Tianzhujiao zai Hua huodong dang'an shiliao*, 4 vols. (Beijing: Zhonghua shuju, 2003).

30 Lin Wenhui, *Qingji Fujian jiao'an zhi yanjiu* (Taibei: Taiwan shangwu yinshuguan, 1989); and Sweeten, *Christianity in Rural China*.

books, booklets, and pamphlets—so-called "internal circulation material(s)" (*neibu ziliao*) not publicly disseminated. These give accurate information albeit without references; crosschecking with other sources has been pursued when possible.

As for family-held materials relating to Catholicism, virtually everything disappeared during the political movements of the 1950s–1970s, when participants sought to eradicate all connections, written or otherwise, with imperialist-dominated times that for some included religious connections with the West. Most people took the safe route and burned anything that remotely associated them with Christianity. Needless to say, this included photographs. At the same time that families destroyed their personal records, government authorities generated public ones. In the early 1950s, they inventoried everything from landlords' pots and pans to the Church's extensive property holdings. They deposited the data in county-level government records offices (*difang dang'anguan*). Archives of this sort are seldom open to the public as the government continues to deal with the issue of how to compensate Catholics for previously confiscated Church property, much of which their predecessors adapted for use as schools, hospitals, and housing. In fact, these archives often have the only documentation regarding former property boundaries—those erased by development in the form of the public buildings just mentioned. Officials remain concerned that information on these parcels will complicate negotiations over exactly what the Church once owned, its current valuation, and how to deal with occupants' improvements made to it. From the government's perspective, the less that is known about former churches and their adjacent properties the better, meaning visits to archival offices by local people are discouraged and access by non-Chinese researchers is routinely denied.

The marvel called the Internet has allowed people to contribute information on churches in a variety of ways. Google searches lead to some useful websites, mainly in Western languages and limited in scope. The Baidu search engine provides the opportunity to expand the range of data sought—in Chinese. Two useful ones are Weiji baike (Wikipedia's Chinese version) and Baidu baike (featuring encyclopedia-type articles), which are usually well-written with citations. By simply entering a place-name and church, links will appear.[31] Their reliability varies considerably with verification via other materials a good practice. Another useful resource are blogs and personal posts. They are unique in providing information that individuals have collected from visits to sites to consult with locals and take snapshots. At some blog sites are

31   For example, "Tianzhujiao Xuanhua jiaoqu," http://blog.sina.com.cn/s/blog_87ca2ce 40102v6dh.html (accessed 15 January 2017).

copies of rare photographs of churches that I thought available only at a few mission-oriented Western archives. Occasionally, one finds pictures available nowhere else. These materials, once in the hands of priests or individuals, miraculously escaped destruction during the years following the revolution. In terms of recent photographs, it is useful to find images of unrestored churches or those in the process of being renovated for reopening. Inquisitive and well-traveled individuals are contributing meaningfully, in my opinion, to research of this topic.[32]

The last source to mention is the information that comes from an on-site investigation of surviving old sacred structures. One benefit of seeing them in their community settings is the spatial aspect. Previously built security walls and gates become observable as well as the church's place in its neighborhood. This also allows for ascertaining the church's compass orientation. A second benefit is determining what congregations think is important about their past by having casual conversations with parishioners about old stone monuments displayed on church grounds or finding elderly people willing to share what they remember about their area's history. Or it may involve talking with pastors about the commemorative brochures or simple mimeographed sheets filled with basic information they have composed. As mentioned, twentieth-century politics affected the preservation of materials, so it is astonishing to find that some people were able to hold on to important records. In one of Beijing Municipality's outlying villages a Catholic family kept safe an early twentieth-century book on its locale's experiences during the Boxer Uprising.[33] It is treasured by the family and congregation for what it represents to them— survival and a special history. We can only learn about privately held items and experiences by asking informants. Fieldwork constitutes an integral part of this study.

The availability of the various materials mentioned and the public nature of the churches under study makes it pointless to veil their names or locations, as anthropological and ethnographic studies often do by using pseudo-toponyms. However, I am careful not to cite the names of informants or list the clergy that I have visited or consulted with. On several occasions, once in

---

32 Several blogs and the links they provide reveal that there is a small group of people (mostly Catholics) actively acquiring historical materials and photographs. A man I know in Beijing has visited churches all over China and collected a variety of unique and rare materials about Christianity. For him it is a research and travel hobby, the subject of his blog. He has not published anything in hard copy. Author's field notes, 5 October 2011.

33 Author's field notes, 30 September 2011. The book is actually a chapter in a set that is available in a few Western libraries. This and the place are discussed in Chapter 4 under the heading Jiahoutuan Village.

a whisper, pastors told me that officials closely monitor their activities and do not like them to have contact with foreign visitors. Constrained as such, priests are cautious about sharing too much with an outsider such as myself because it would only attract unnecessarily authorities' attention and generate questions about what I am doing and why they are helping me. Priests also do not want to be seen as nosy about the affairs of other congregations or as having opinions about them. Consequently, information gathered directly from priests is given judiciously to protect them as sources. The churches treated here all are relatively well-known, at least within Catholic circles, and I considered them representative of all those that have survived. Only a few old ones are not discussed because their existence came to my attention too late for me to locate materials on them or allow for a visit.

3   Interpretative Issues

In pre-1949 rural China, village temples—Buddhist and clan—helped establish a socio-historical narrative in which bodies of people built a sense of themselves, that is, a common identity through cultural and religious activities.[34] Missionaries did not understand that temples represented village communities and people had strong feelings about their place and functions. The insertion of a Christian alternative in the form of a sacred building, supported by a congregation backed by outsiders, had to affect everyone's religious lives. The Church (and the church) was an outside agency with ideas and structural symbols that changed local society.[35] In other words, Christianity's long-term expansion can be understood as the formation of an alternative religious identity with integration of churches spatially and architecturally into the cultural landscape, a process termed indigenization and inculturation (dependent somewhat on perspective).

In looking at the process, we must distinguish between the different audiences and how each saw the choices regarding sites, styles, orientations, and other matters. Western missionaries, for their own individual and religious reasons, preferred and built European-style churches, believing they knew

---

34   One detailed study of Beijing "shows how temples became the focus for community-building and identity-defining activities by providing the space to assemble and the occasions for worship that justified doing so." Churches are briefly discussed in this general context. Susan Naquin, *Peking: Temple and City Life, 1400–1900* (Berkeley: University of California Press, 2000), xxxi–xxxii.

35   Charles A. Litzinger, "Temple Community and Village Cultural Integration in North China: Evidence from 'Sectarian Cases' (*chiao-an*) in Chihli, 1862–1895" (Ph.D. dissertation, University of California, Davis, 1983), chapter two.

best what a sacred structure should look like. Control over this basic decision came naturally given they provided most of the funding, drew up the plans, and supervised the construction. That Chinese Catholics worshipped at them implies acceptance yet what do we actually know about their opinions and desires regarding places of worship? Another way to delve into the cultural context is to investigate the perspective of non-Catholics. Those actively opposed to Christianity often focused on church locations that harmed geomancy (*fengshui*), something thought to affect directly the entire community's well-being. Foes from the 1900-era escalated opposition on cultural grounds by concentrating on Christianity's overt foreignness, as did Communists from the 1920s to the 1960s with objections to it in terms of Western imperialism and physical infringement on Chinese cultural and national sovereignty. These same rationales later sanctioned Red Guards' destruction of interior furnishings and defacement of exteriors, both accomplished without affecting the shell. Did this then mean that the church's religious features rather than its profile or shape symbolized imperialism? Whatever cultural or ideological objections governmental or secular circles once entertained have not been sufficient to stop Catholics from restoring old churches as they once looked. Succinctly put, architecture does matter—in intricate and varied ways.

On another level, how do we frame churches in terms of modernization? China's transformation from a tradition-bound society and pre-industrial economy to its current system did not occur without the removal of all manner of objects that arguably might have been in the way or delayed the creation of a modern infrastructure. Rail lines and highways have linked cities together, cutting across farmland and influencing rural development—impacting people's lives. In Beijing, its tall, thick imperial, inner, and outer city walls came down, replaced by wide boulevards; residential areas crisscrossed by narrow lanes (*hutong, xiaoxiang*) have been squashed by mammoth high-rise apartments and office buildings. Sacred edifices, once the centerpieces of large mission compounds that dominated neighborhoods by virtue of area occupied and building size, not to mention profile, have had to adjust to less space and coexist with all types of neighbors. Church settings have become distinctly modern with aesthetic sight lines changed, the visual environment affected if not diminished. In one city, the space directly in front of a church's main entrance, once Catholic property, is a block-long line of shops offering well-known transnational brands of coffee, pastries, and ice cream.[36] Whether a worshipper or non-Catholic shopper, what is the reaction to the meeting of

---

36   This can be looked at in terms of how commercial real estate development represents the goal and ideal of modernity as it emerged in the socialist market economy that has driven China since the early 1980s. Mayfair Mei-hui Yang, "Spatial Struggles: Postcolonial

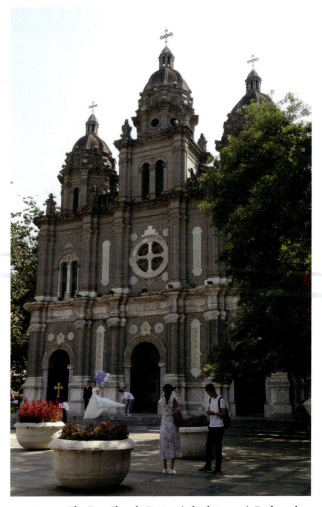

FIGURE 1.3   The East Church, Beijing (rebuilt in 1905). Bride and
groom photo shoot in progress.
SOURCE: PHOTO BY AUTHOR, 2018

old religious and new commercial icons? Is the convergence seamless, an unnoticed part of crowded, modern life?

Implicit in this study's historical and architectural approaches is the notion
that people see various structures, churches included, as more than occupants
of physical space and shadow casters in neighborhoods—they are places of

Complex, State Disenchantment, and Popular Reappropriation of Space in Rural Southeast China," *Journal of Asian Studies* 63, no. 3 (August 2004): 726.

memory (*lieux de mémoire*). Popular in Western Europe, scholars have contemplated how there are accepted official (state) memories and unofficial (community) myths that are equally valid in analyzing the way places of memory have led to constructed identities for various groups of people. For example, churches have simultaneously epitomized religious traditions and secularized representations that are subject to various spatial and temporal interpretations. According to one typology, religious structures in the West can be a mnemonic key that opens for observation personal and sociopolitical doors.[37] It follows that in a Chinese context it is also possible to see how people treat churches as something sacred, or vestiges of imperialistic events, or historic sites, or even as monumental examples of visual and material culture. Simultaneously they can involve individual, familial, and collective memories.

Catholics have naturally found spiritual comfort in churches, going there for baptisms, marriages, and funerals—essential parts of their congregational lives. Non-Catholics tend to view them differently. In the past, many objected to their size, style, directional orientation, and connection to Western powers, believing their existence did more harm than good to neighborhoods and

FIGURE 1.4   "Wedding-business" van at the Xian County church (Zhangjia
             cathedral). Characters on the van read, "preordained and dreamlike
             wedding pictures—the studio provides everything [apparel, site
             access, etc.]."
             SOURCE: PHOTO BY AUTHOR, 2011

37   Pierre Nora, "General Introduction: From *Lieux de mémoire* to *Realms of Memory*," in
     Realms of Memory: Rethinking the French Past, vol. 1, *Conflicts and Divisions*, ed. Pierre
     Nora (New York: Columbia University Press, 1996), xv–xxiv.

communities. They viewed religious structures as the sites of certain incidents with local, regional or even national significance. Older domestic tourists visit them for this and other reasons. Younger people, however, seem minimally concerned with a past filled with cultural and political issues linked to churches. To secular millennials they are picturesque and beautiful, an aesthetic backdrop for pre-wedding photographs. Setting up shoots at them is a flourishing business in urban and rural milieus that church business departments encourage. These couples associate churches with a joyous life moment without emphasis on religious beliefs. Put another way, churches can be diverse places of memory to different people and reflect changing personal and community-level sentiments.

This study's broad themes are historical, architectural, and mnemonic. The commonality linking them comes from the range of materials that elucidate old churches' foundations and developments, appearances and representations, articulated or tacit traditions. According to a Chinese aphorism, "falling leaves settle on the [tree's] roots" (*ye luo gui gen*) or, metaphorically, everything returns to its source. In going to churches' origins, whether of the distant or recent past, it is necessary to deal with accumulated layers of facts and beliefs all of which have been subject to the influence of time and events. Digging into these will require the use of different tools or, if you appreciate interdisciplinary research, keep reading.

Chapter 2 looks at Catholicism's expansion and churches in Beijing, Tianjin, and Zhili/Hebei. Traveling with an early Vincentian missionary across China provides a glimpse of this study's places and topics of interest. Explanations of the various ecclesiastical divisions that changed with time and estimates of Catholic numbers are provided while sacred buildings are looked at in terms of specific categories of information.

The oldest and most famous of Beijing's core urban area are these six: the South, North, East, and West Churches plus one in the former Legation Quarter, that is, St. Michael's, and another located in the neighborhood of Nangangzi, St. Thérèse's. Priests built the first in 1611 and the sixth in 1910. This long history is traced as each building's architecture is examined in Chapter 3.

Next, we look at sacred structures in the outlying area of today's spread-out Beijing Municipality with attention directed to several in the capital's suburbs and ones still in rural locations. Chapter 4's sites are all old but some of the churches have been rebuilt. Their distance from the political center shaped them in variety of ways—perhaps even ensuring their survival.

The discussion in Chapter 5 turns to Tianjin City's three famous churches, one of which opponents torched in 1870 and again in 1900. The other two were in protected locations and fared better. Each is historically and architecturally unique, yet collectively represent a controversial presence in this city. Tianjin's dynamic relationship with Catholicism spilled over into rural areas and is examined.

For Chapter 6 the central subject is old sacred buildings in Zhili/Hebei's lesser-known and once-small cities such as Xuanhua and Baoding. When possible, the spotlight is placed on towns peripheral to the capital and villages deep in the countryside. Each of the churches discussed is important in its own right and illustrate Catholicism's resilient rural presence. They set the stage for the chapter that follows.

Chapter 7 deals exclusively with a rural administrative unit known as Zhuo, which during the Qing period was a department before becoming a Republican-era county. Currently, it is the county-level city of Zhuozhou. It is examined in depth because of unique materials that provide statistical, cartographic, and photographic evidence of the astonishing growth of Catholicism in the early twentieth century. This previously unstudied locale has much to offer.

A consideration of Catholicism's material—and spiritual—legacy in China wraps up the study in Chapter 8. Vincentian missionaries left behind churches in several styles that continue to be favored today, which connect traditional and revolutionary times as well as serving as a link to Christianity's current revitalization. Reflected in these pages is the study's overarching purpose—the composition of a discerning account regarding Catholicism and its churches in an ever-changing China.

Common Missionary Routes

MAP 2.1   Early nineteenth century missionary routes into
China. Missionaries going to Beijing generally followed
north-south sections of the so-called Imperial Way (*yidao*)
and/or rivers from Guangzhou north to Nanchang then
east; from Jiangxi northeast through Zhejiang; from
Hangzhou north via the Grand Canal. Depending on the
destination, some used the Yangtze River and land routes.
SOURCES: CHGIS; BISHOP, *CHINA'S IMPERIAL WAY*; AND
ARCHIVES CM, PARIS

CHAPTER 2

Church Building and Church Buildings

After attempts to propagate Christianity during the Yuan dynasty (1260–1367) stopped due to the scant numbers of missionaries involved and the dangers of the arduous overland or indirect sea routes to China, Catholic priests returned in the mid-sixteenth century as European powers began exploring the world's oceans and establishing coastal outposts in distant lands.[1] The first Jesuits arrived via Portuguese ships on China's southeastern coast at the fast-growing enclave of Macao, a "colony" the Ming dynasty (1368–1643) allowed Portugal to establish because the Chinese wanted to control contact and trade with foreigners. Priests built a hilltop church that they dedicated to St. Paul and from it gazed eagerly at the vast interior's densely populated landscape.[2] Jesuits eventually moved inland and developed a from-the-top-downward conversion strategy that led them to urban areas and China's scholarly elite. Fortunately tolerated by some city-based officials met en route to Beijing, Jesuits eventually arrived there, quickly gaining the attention of imperial authorities and employment by them.

Augustinians, Franciscans, and Dominicans soon followed, clandestinely entering from various ports along the coast before heading to the hinterland's small towns and villages to concentrate on converting ordinary people. The mendicant orders gradually made converts in rural areas and constructed small churches, later-arriving priests finding temporary accommodations and the good company of otherwise isolated confreres at these places. The Qing dynasty (1636–1912), suspicious of all Christian activity, tolerated it off and on during the seventeenth century before proscribing it in 1724, a ban that

---

1 Early missionary efforts in China are discussed in *Handbook of Christianity in China, Volume One: 635–1800*, ed. Nicolas Standaert, *Handbook of Oriental Studies*, vol. 15/1 (Leiden: Brill, 2001), 1–111.

2 At Macao, priests built small, simple chapels followed by an elaborate church dedicated to St. Paul in 1594. It underwent reconstruction in the 1620s and later renovations. Fire destroyed it in 1835 but its façade survived and famously still stands. Its unusual features not reproduced elsewhere in China intrigue scholars. For a detailed interpretation of it, see César Guillén-Nuñez, "The Façade of St. Paul's, Macao: A Retable-Façade?" *Journal of the Hong Kong Branch of the Royal Asiatic Society* 41 (2001): 131–188; Hui-Hung Chen, "Encounters in Peoples, Religions, and Sciences: Jesuit Visual Culture in Seventeenth Century China" (Ph.D. diss., Brown University, 2004), 112–179; and César Guillén-Nuñez, *Macao's Church of Saint Paul: A Glimmer of the Baroque in China* (Hong Kong: Hong Kong University Press, 2009).

© KONINKLIJKE BRILL NV, LEIDEN, 2020 | DOI:10.1163/9789004416185_003

would last for 120 years.[3] To avoid deportation many priests assumed a low
profile in remote hamlets, while a handful of Jesuits remained in Beijing due
to their astronomical, calendrical, and other services to the Qing court. The
first Vincentians sent under the auspices of their Congregation arrived from
Macao via an interior route to replace the Jesuits in 1785.[4] Two more priests
joined them in 1801 after spending five tiring months on the road in China.[5]
A few years later Qing authorities refused to allow more, leaving only about
ten Western priests in Beijing.[6] It would not be until the early 1830s that a
few Vincentian replacements began sailing by junks along the coast to Fujian
and from there to various points, as did Fr. Bernard Laribe, C.M., who in 1832
used a littoral route to get to his assignment in Jiangxi, and Fr. Jean-Gabriel
Perboyre, C.M., who went to Hubei Province four years later.[7] Whether by
land or sea, Western missionaries went incognito, rubbing tea on their faces to

---

3   Manchus founded the dynasty in the Northeast in 1636; eight years later they captured
    Beijing and moved their capital there.
4   The Vincentians Louis-Antoine Appiani and Johann Müllener arrived at Guangzhou in 1699,
    directed by the Sacred Congregation for the Propaganda of the Faith not their Congregation.
5   *The Vincentians*, vol. 3, *Revolution and Restoration (1789–1843)*, 661.
6   Ibid., 667–669.
7   Laribe letter, 30 June 1832, *Annales CM-F* 1 (1834): 195; and Laribe letter, 1 September 1833,
    Annales CM-F 1 (1834): 282–324. Laribe was the third French Vincentian of the nineteenth
    century to arrive at Macao and probably the first to go to Jiangxi via Fujian. Perboyre de-
    scribes his nine-week journey by junk from Macao to Fujian, two-week trip to Jiangxi, and
    other travels on his way to Hubei Province. Perboyre letter, 7 March 1836, *Annals PF*, old series
    (1838): 363–372; and Perboyre letter, no date, 373–382. The second letter is an extract, its full
    version available as Perboyre letter, 10 August 1836, *Annales CM-F* 3 (1837): 217–251. Some mis-
    sionaries had entered China via Fujian in 1630. In the early nineteenth century, Dominicans
    ventured from Macao up the coast to Fujian's ports. Vincentians would have learned of
    this in Macao. The early period is discussed by Eugenio Menegon, "Jesuits, Franciscans and
    Dominicans in Fujian: The Anti-Christian Incidents of 1637–1638," in *"Scholar from the West:"
    Giulio Aleni S.J. (1582–1649) and the Dialogue between Christianity and China*, ed. Tiziana
    Lippiello and Roman Malek (Brescia: Fondazione Civiltà Bresciana, 1997), 224–228.
        The small boats used along the coast sailed from dawn to dusk for safety reasons, the
    major concerns being weather and pirates. Sometimes they only covered short distances in
    one day. Still, missionaries liked going by boat, whether inland or coastal, because compared
    to land routes they encountered fewer people curious about them and, if they had advanced
    warning, could hide in the boat's small compartments or under blankets. Priests found the
    journeys by land hard on the feet and tiresome, fraught with logistical difficulties. Another
    problem for priests was local security personnel such as *dibao* who might report them to
    government officials. In the 1850s, before more treaty ports opened, missionaries sought
    to avoid rapacious custom officers watching for boats carrying goods subject to domestic
    transit fees.

darken the skin, wearing local garb, and staying in the shadows with the help of trusted guides.[8]

At this time, Britain's sale of opium hit record highs as it used the drug to rectify trade imbalances caused by massive purchases of Chinese teas, silks, and porcelains, an economic situation that finally provoked the Qing government into taking measures to interdict the rampant smuggling occurring up and down the coast.[9] The opium scourge had created millions of addicts and contributed to local disorder and inflation, but worst of all hinted at imperial ineptness: the dynasty slowly realized that something had to be done. The emperor consequently appointed Lin Zexu as special commissioner and dispatched him to the southeast in 1839 with power to take whatever steps necessary to halt the further contamination and weakening of China by Western opium smugglers. Ostensibly, due to Lin's almost immediate confiscation of huge quantities of the drug at Guangzhou (Canton), the British took retaliatory military action the next year. War had begun.

With Chinese warships patrolling the sea lanes, missionaries had to resume the use of former routes that entailed frequent transfers between small riverine boats and then tiresome days walking. Illustrative of travel during the Opium War period is Fr. Évariste-Régis Huc, C.M., and his extended trip across China from Macao to Xiwanzi, a secluded community outside the Great Wall about one hundred miles northwest of Beijing. At the time of his arrival in June 1841, this rural area was part of the Vincentian-administered Vicariate of Mongolia.[10] Huc went by junk through the Pearl River delta to the Guangzhou area then by flat-bottomed sampan upriver into Guangdong Province, accompanied by two local guides to help him avoid detection by

---

8   Usually Catholic and native to the province in which they traveled, guides helped in many ways. They carried baggage, bought needed supplies, arranged transport, advised, and translated.

9   The British sold the most opium, with others, notably Americans, participating in the trade.

10   Vicariates served as unofficial dioceses in mission countries because the Church had not been fully and formally established. In the early twentieth century, a high-ranking priest with experience in South China, offered the following explanation of the mission hierarchy in China: "A number of settlements [congregations] depending from a central station from where resides the missionary or native priest, make up the missionary district or parish [in the 1930s termed a 'quasi-parish']. The several districts or parishes constitute the mission, that is the missionary diocese that is presided over by a Bishop having the title of Vicar Apostolic." Archbishop [J.B.] de Guebriant [M.E.P.], "The Church in China," *Cath-M Annals PF* 3, no. 11 (November 1926): 338.) Placed over an extinct see, the bishop was, strictly speaking, titular. This nominal qualification will not be used in the pages that follow. "Apostolic Vicariate," https://en.wikipedia.org/wiki/Apostolic_vicariate (accessed 17 July 2017). Note 53 explains further.

authorities and transit judiciously from one safe place to another.[11] They partially followed known inland paths used by Fr. Joseph-Martial Mouly, C.M., and other priests in the 1830s.[12] Huc recounts how he altered his appearance in order to be less obviously a Westerner.[13]

> Towards six o'clock in the evening [of 20 February 1841] I assumed the Chinese costume: my hair was cut off, with the exception of what I allowed to grow for nearly two years on the top of my head. Other hair was attached to it: the whole was dressed, and I found myself in possession of a magnificent queue that reached to my knees. My complexion, tolerably dark as you know, was still further deepened by a yellow colour; my eyebrows were cut after the manner of the country; long and thick mustaches, that I had allowed to grow for a long time, concealed the European turn of my nose; and, finally, the Chinese habit completed the disguise. A young Mongol Lama, lately converted to the faith, gave me his long robe: the short tunic that is put over it, and which almost resembles a rochet, was a relic of Father [Jean-Gabriel] Perboyre [C.M.], who was martyred last year in the province of Hou-Pé [Hubei].[14] (Here and as the quotation continues below, italics and variant spellings in cited source.)

Wherever possible Huc hired boats for transportation because they afforded him shelter from the elements as well as the public eye, provided relative comfort, and merged inconspicuously with the thousands of other junks plying

---

11   Place-names (except for those of villages) and Qing-era civil administrative divisions used in this study may be found in G.M.H. Playfair, *The Cities and Towns of China: A Geographical Dictionary*, 2nd ed. (1910; reprint, Taipei: Ch'eng Wen Publishing Co., 1971).

12   Fr. Jean-Henri Baldus, C.M., who went by sea to Fujian then to Hubei, mentions that Mouly took the overland route, passing through Hubei on his way north. Baldus letter, 3 August 1835, *Annales CM-F* 2 (1835–1836): 104. Fr. François-Alexis Rameaux, C.M., recorded seeing Mouly in Hubei. Rameaux letter, 19 August 1835, *Annales CM-F* 2 (1835–1836): 128. Other Vincentian priests who went overland into China are Fathers Joseph Ly (Li; Chinese given name unknown) and Pierre Peschaud. Ly letter, 4 April 1836, *Annales CM-F* 3 (1837): 81–87; Peschaud letter, 20 September 1838, *Annales CM-F* 5 (1839): 184; and Peschaud letter, 12 October 1838, *Annales CM-F* 5 (1839): 193–194.

      Apropos names, it was not unusual for Vincentian missionaries to know only Chinese priests' surnames and their Western (usually French) baptismal names. On the other hand, Vincentians took full Chinese names, and were known as such by officials at various levels. Van den Brandt, in *Les Lazaristes*, provides Western and Chinese names for the individuals he cites.

13   A Vincentian father wrote similarly about his trip from Macao via Guangzhou into Jiangxi. Anot letter, 16 May 1844, *Annales CM-F* 10 (1845): 592–599.

14   Huc letter, 2 April 1841, *Annals PF* 4 (1843): 162.

FIGURE 2.1   Junks and a sampan of the type that transported missionaries
in the southeast. Photo ca early twentieth century.
SOURCE: COURTESY LIBRARY OF CONGRESS

the waterways of South China carrying tons of tea and various other cargoes.
When rivers shrank into streams, he disembarked and walked, often offering
an opinion about overland routes and life on the road.[15]

---

15   Another priest complained about overland travel, writing that he had traversed Jiangxi
and been to its borders with Fujian: "Oh, the mountains are high and the rocks hard. My
poor feet." Rameaux letter, *Annales CM-F* 6 (1840): 353. A missionary in Sichuan Province
said little about this aspect of working in his mountainous district, choosing instead to
comment on aspects of daily life. He wrote that "It is to the Chinese manner of eating
and lodging that a European experiences the most difficulty in reconciling himself. In
this country bread is unknown ... [and] the vine is not cultivated." As for habitation, "the
houses are in China, a nook, sometimes a wretched garret." Bertrand letter, 10 August 1840,
Annals PF 3 (1842): 54. Adjusting to China took time and effort. Some Vincentians missed
home and at the village (*cun*) of Jiudu (Youjia), Jiangxi grew greens for salads and built
ovens to bake bread.

FIGURE 2.2   The Imperial Way at Mei Gate (Meiling Pass). Along the
             Imperial Way, parts of which were paved with stones, were
             a series of military-post stations for the conveyance of
             government dispatches, here connecting Guangdong and
             Jiangxi. Many porters and travelers also used it.
             SOURCE: PHOTO BY AUTHOR, 2012

It has also happened to me to become acquainted with the high roads of
the celestial empire. I have travelled during a day upon the most famous
road in the country; they call it the *imperial way*....[16] Although it is paved
from one end to the other, the work has been executed in so irregular a
manner, with sharp stones, that it is not, I assure you for the greatest convenience of foot-passengers....

---

16   Its main purpose was for couriers to convey government documents between officials
     serving in the provinces and the emperor in Beijing. Kevin Bishop, *China's Imperial Way:
     Retracing an Historical and Communications Route from Beijing to Hong Kong* (Hong Kong:
     Odyssey, 1997).

The great advantage which the Chinese roads present is, that from one end to the other, and almost without interruption, they are lined with hotels,... [which] are mere sheds, under which one can repose and sleep without untying his purse....

Upon the top of a difficult, high, and steep mountain, there is raised a great gate [at Meiling Pass], a kind of triumphal arch, which fixes the limits of two provinces, that of Canton [Guangdong] ... and of the province of Kian-Si [Jiangxi], which, with Che-Kian [Zhejiang], forms the vicariate-apostolic recently confided by the Holy See to our [C]ongregation....[17]

Four days after entering Jiangxi, Huc found the first of the congregations and pastors he would encounter along his path to Beijing. Stopping to see a confrere benefited both parties: solitary priests had few Western guests and were happy to hear news of the outside world and receive much needed religious icons and money. Visitors had the opportunity to recuperate, observe how veteran missionaries worked and survived in China, and participate in religious activities.

... I had the joy of landing at one of our Missions [outside of Ganzhou in southern Jiangxi], and of embracing Father [Pierre] Pescaud [C.M.]....[18] The Christians of the neighborhood were immediately informed of the arrival of a European father; they came to salute me in the oriental fashion, saying "May God protect you."

I passed the Sunday amongst them, and offered the holy sacrifice in a very poor chapel, it is true, but embellished by the fervour of these worthy neophytes, and by the prayers that they sung in the two choirs during the Mass....

... [Several weeks later, I found another Vincentian, Fr. Bernard-Vincent Laribe, who] ... wished to give me a welcome. We passed the solemnity of Easter ... in the Christian congregation of Kiou-Tou [Jiudu], a place of peace and solitude, where the Missionary ordinarily resides.[19] In the

---

17   Huc letter, 2 April 1841, *Annals PF* 4 (1843): 169–170.
18   That is, Peschaud.
19   In the English version of the *Annals PF*, the word "congregation" is used in translation for the French term "*chrétienté*." In other volumes, "Christian settlement," "Christian community," and "mission station" are sometimes used as equivalents. In pre-twentieth century materials, when French missionaries in China wrote *chrétienté* they invariably referred to all the Catholics living at one place, a generality that suited many circumstances. In 1919, a Vincentian working in Zhili stated: "We call *chrétienté* a group of Christian families in a village, even if the majority of the village is pagan; certain *chrétientés* have 800,

bosom of a deep valley there is a large [village], the third of whose inhabitants are Christians. Over the village, and upon the top of a charming
hill, crowned with large trees, is raised the house of God, that is, a little
chapel, of great neatness; near it there is a poor dwelling for the priest....
    I found the days I passed at Kiou-Tou very short; it is an oasis that I met
upon my way, where I was enabled to recreate my mind at ease....[20]

In his letters, Huc provides few specifics about his exact route, probably
passing from Jiangxi into Zhejiang, and the known locations of Vincentian confreres. He rested at rural worship places and used available waterways, of which
there were many to choose, to continue northward. Although accumulated silt
had made the Grand Canal impassable for heavy grain barges, light boats continued to use it and were available to take him through Shandong into Zhili—he
then resorted to different modes of land transportation. On occasion he relates
amusing information about the horses, mules, and carts used. Huc notes that as
he approached Beijing the roads improved but his commentary on the capital
city is minimal and he provides no information about the South Church.

Pekin possesses no monument, at least in the sense which you give in
Europe to the term; the houses are low and generally ill built; nothing
rises to the heights of the ramparts [city walls]. The streets are wide, and
almost in a straight line; not being paved, they are excessively miry, and
exhale infection. As it is probable that I shall, hereafter, have the occasion
to return to Pekin, and to sojourn there for some time, I will endeavor
[then] to take the opportunity of *daguerreotyping* for you the city....
    Steep mountains, rocks, cut perpendicularly and bordered with preci-
pices, form the road [of ninety leagues] from Pekin [northward] to Si-Wan
[Xiwanzi]....

1200 Christians, others have 15 or 20." "Vicariate du Tché-ly méridio-occidental: quelques
notes sur un vicariat en Chine par Mgr de Vienne," *Annales CM-F* 84 (1919): 1087. A
study of Sichuan specifies that "most Catholics lived in small communities [of various
sizes], known as *chrétientés* in the writings of French missionaries." Robert Entenmann,
"Chinese Catholic Clergy and Catechists in Eighteenth-Century Szechwan," in *Images de
la Chine: le Contexte Occidental de la Sinologie Naissante*, ed. Edward J. Malatesta and Yves
Raguin (Paris: Institute Ricci—Centre d'Études Chinoises, 1995), 400–401. In numerous
contexts, *chrétienté* was used to mean any number of Catholic individuals or families of
the same local community. I prefer "congregation" (those who gather for worship or a
religious service) as an equivalent of *chrétienté* and use it throughout the text that follows.
    Regarding Youjia, still home to numerous Catholics, refer to Sweeten, *Christianity in
Rural China*, 177–195.
20   Huc letters, 2 April 1841, *Annals PF* 4 (1843): 170; and 11 April 1841, *Annals PF* 4 (1843): 173.

FIGURE 2.3 Vincentian priest traveling by cart, North China, early twentieth century. Huc
would have recognized this cart type, commonly used in Zhili for hundreds
of years.
SOURCE: ARCHIVES CM, PARIS

... I have spent in this expedition about four months of time, a great
deal of sapecs [copper cash], some little of the epidermis of my feet, a
portion of my plumpness, and a quantity of patience....

Si-Wan is a large village, stuck on the side of a mountain. Its population, which is entirely Christian, may amount to eight hundred souls.
The mandarins, great and small, every one, in fact, knows that the village
professes the Gospel; and yet our religion is practiced in it with the greatest freedom. How long this [local] toleration may last no one can tell....[21]

In this hardscrabble frontier zone outside the Great Wall, Huc stayed at
Xiwanzi Village, home to Vincentians who had toiled successfully there for at
least two decades. Religious life for locals had gradually improved due to the efforts of Mouly and other priests as they arrived in the 1830s (Chapter 6 provides
more details). Most of the residents had converted to Catholicism, Huc's statement to the contrary, a fact that helped reduce civil conflict and the lawsuits
that often drew officials' attention. The situation in Beijing stood in stark con-
trast as one aging priest, Fr. Cayetano Pires Pereira, C.M., hung on tenuously

---

21   Huc letter, 15 September 1841, *Annals PF* 4 (1843): 54–56.

at the South Church.[22] Imperial authorities tolerated him due to his advanced age and position with the Directorate of Astronomy (Qintian jian), and because the dwindling number of Catholics did not concern them.[23] When Pires died in late 1838 and the South Church closed, Mouly had already built a large one at Xiwanzi that supported the local faithful and allowed him to maintain a presence not too far from the capital. In recognition of his success, the Holy See had formed for Mongolia a vicariate in 1840 with Mouly as its first titular bishop.[24] He made the Xiwanzi church his episcopal seat, and even after his departure in the mid-1850s it remained the most important Catholic outpost in the border area between northwest Zhili and Mongolian territory.

About one year after Huc arrived at Xiwanzi, the First Opium War ended.[25] He and confreres did not comment in their letters on the war and probably knew little or nothing about the various battles. On the other hand, the treaties initiated a new era for them. At Nanjing in 1842, high Qing officials reluctantly signed an accord with victorious Britain followed two years later by similar ones with the United States and France. Via these Western-dictated treaties, foreigners gained among other provisions the right to reside, for the purpose of trade, in the five port cities that became officially open to them as well as the right to establish extraterritorial enclaves known as the concessions. Missionaries entered these ports as easily as Western merchants, quickly

22   I refer to him as Pires. In various nineteenth-century materials he is called Gaetano (or Caetano) Pirès, the French rendition of his Portuguese name, and, occasionally, as Pereira. Named the bishop of Nanjing Diocese in 1804, he never served there, going instead to Beijing to become a prominent priest in the city. In 1827, he was named administrator of Beijing Diocese, a position he held until his death. Van den Brandt, *Les Lazaristes*, 15; and *The Vincentians*, vol. 3, *Revolution and Restoration (1789–1843)*, 664–665.

23   Charles O. Hucker, *A Dictionary of Official Titles in Imperial China* (1975; reprint, Taipei: SMC Publishing, 1995), 169. In 1645, Fr. Johann Adam Schall von Bell, S.J., became the first missionary to serve on the directorate (sometimes translated as the Imperial Astronomical Bureau) and Pires would be the last.

24   Consecration of Mouly as bishop took place in 1842. Vincentian administration of the vicariate passed to the Congregation of the Immaculate Heart of Mary whose priests arrived in late 1865. Vincentians took assignments in Zhili. Ferreux, *Histoire de la Congrégation*, 112, 118–119, 158–159. Van den Brandt, *Les Lazaristes*, 15, 38; *Handbook of Christianity in China, Volume One*, 351, 720.

25   Huc and his confrere, Fr. Joseph Gabet, C.M., who had been in the Xiwanzi area since 1837, teamed up to explore remote western areas of the Qing empire during a two-year expedition (1844–1846) that took them as far as Lhasa, Tibet. They returned to Macao with Huc going back to North China in 1849. Their detailed records speak to another type of Vincentian missionary experience. Évariste-Régis Huc and Joseph Gabet, *Travels in Tartary, Thibet and China, 1844–1846*, 2 vols., trans. William Hazlitt (New York: Dover Publications, 1987), vi–ix.

FIGURE 2.4 Joseph-Martial Mouly, ca 1860s. He served in
China from 1834 to 1868 and was the first bishop
of the Vicariate of Mongolia in 1840, becoming the
same for Zhili North in 1856.
SOURCE: FAVIER, *PÉKING*, 1897

erecting sacred structures in the concession controlled by their home country.[26]
Proselytization outside its boundaries became possible as officials found it
hard to contain Westerners strictly to the enclaves. At the same time, missionaries wanting to go deeper inland to evangelize found it problematic because
the emperor's removal of the empire-wide ban on Christianity in 1844–1845 did
not give them the unrestricted access to the interior.[27]

---

26   After the establishment of five treaty ports in the early 1840s, missionaries usually went
     by ship to the one nearest their intended inland destination. The treaties of 1858–1860
     opened more treaty ports (e.g., Tianjin), making shipboard travel to them relatively easy.
27   See Chapter 1, note 10.

1   The Study's Geographic Scope

Huc passed through many provinces on his way to Xiwanzi, but this book's geographic range will not be as large, instead limited to areas in North China that
Vincentians administered over the period 1785–1950, that is, Beijing, Tianjin,
and Zhili/Hebei (including some places under Jesuits and other areas not originally within current provincial boundaries). Collectively, these three areas are
where the bulk of Vincentian mission work took place in terms of making converts and building churches. Vincentians also had a strong presence in Jiangxi
and Zhejiang, and information from these two provinces will be weaved into
the narrative as appropriate.[28]

Beijing is of interest because of its status as capital, missionary attention
to it, and its historic churches. Early Jesuits sought permission from the Ming
court to reside there, hoping to begin converting its scholars and officials. This
sociopolitical elite would in turn influence acceptance of Catholicism among
the common people of China's largest city, its population by the early seventeenth century an estimated seven hundred thousand or more.[29] The pioneer-
ing Jesuit, Fr. Matteo Ricci arrived in 1601, worshipping privately at his home
and later establishing two small public chapels, one for men's use and one for
women's. Not until 1610 did he start work on Beijing's first church (Catholics
will later refer to it as the South Church) near Xuanwu, an important city gate
that separated the Inner City, within which were the Imperial and Forbidden
Cities, from the Outer City. Although the Ming dynasty ended in 1643, the
Jesuits established a multifaceted relationship with the Qing serving it in various capacities but most crucially in composing astronomically based accurate
calendars that the emperor relied on for scheduling dates for state rites. With
court connections and status, priests had established four churches in Beijing
by the 1720s.

Through the eighteenth century, Beijing attracted more missionaries than
any other site in China, yet overall Catholic growth waned as officials enforced
the 1724 imperial proscription of Christianity. All of Beijing's churches disappeared by the late 1820s save for the South Church, while the few remaining illegal missionaries and Chinese priests in North China worked clandestinely in
out-of-the-way rural locales such as at the village (*zhuang*) of Anjia southwest

---

28   Vincentians once served in Hubei Province, but withdrew, as they did from Mongolia,
     to focus their attention exclusively on Beijing, Tianjin, Zhili, Jiangxi, and Zhejiang. Their
     nineteenth-century experience in Jiangxi is discussed by Sweeten, *Christianity in Rural
     China*, 17–176.
29   "List of Largest Cities Throughout History," http://en.wikipedia.org/wiki/List_of_largest_
     cities_throughout_history (accessed 29 October 2014).

of Beijing, or in remote places like Xiwanzi.[30] The missionaries' dire situation during the 1830s–1850s did not cause the Second Opium War; unresolved economic and political issues did. A joint Anglo-French naval force fought its way to Tianjin in 1858 and there, only seventy-five miles from the capital, dictated peace terms. Qing negotiators agreed to open additional ports to trade, tacitly permit the importation of opium, and allow Western nations to have a diplomatic presence in Beijing. When the Xianfeng emperor (r. 1851–1861) rejected the Treaties of Tianjin, British and French troops marched into the capital two years later. Such a show of military power forced him to validate the 1858 treaties and their 1860 supplements, the Conventions of Beijing. Article VI of France's convention explicitly benefited Catholic missionaries by allowing them to recover previously confiscated Church property. Additionally, a French priest serving as translator surreptitiously inserted into the Chinese language version of the article wording that gave missionaries the right to rent and purchase properties. The subterfuge implied travel and residency, opening the entirety of China to Catholic (and Protestant) missionaries eager to start proselytizing.[31]

With ink on the agreements still wet, French soldiers quickly spruced up the dilapidated South Church in order that compatriots who had died fighting in North China might have proper funeral rites. With its interior barely made presentable, the bishop, his coadjutor, army chaplains, and over twenty priests participated in services. One chaplain said mass, another gave absolution, and the bishop a sermon. The regimental band played, and everyone sang "*Te Deum*" (Thee, O God, We Praise) in gratitude for the military success that had led to its reopening.[32] Qing authorities soon issued a certificate of restitution (or ownership, equivalent to a deed) for the South Church and each of the capital's three other sites.[33] It did not take long for Catholic infrastructure in Beijing to expand with the construction of chapels, clerical residences, seminaries, orphanages (foundling homes), schools, hospitals, and other buildings.[34]

---

30   Enforcement of the Yongzheng emperor's proscription came in the provinces not Beijing because some missionaries remained employed by the imperial court. Eugenio Menegon, "Yongzheng's Conundrum: The Emperor on Christianity, Religions, and Heterodoxy," in *Rooted in Hope: China—Religion—Christianity*, ed. Barbara Hoster, Dirk Kuhlmann, and Zbigniew Wesolowski (Sankt Augustin: Institut Monumenta Serica, 2017), 311–312.

31   Young, *Ecclesiastical Colony*, 28–34. Most-favored nation clauses gave the same right to other treaty signatories (and thus to Protestants of those countries).

32   Delamare [Delamarre] letter, 18 November 1860, *Annals PF* 12 (1861): 135.

33   Archives, CM, Paris. The "deeds" are filed under "Archives des Lazaristes de Pékin de Centre des Archives Diplomatiques de Nantes," Carton 9, "Petang 1860 Restitution."

34   I use "orphanage" and "foundling home" interchangeably, the former term preferred in the primary sources referred to in this study. Foundling home more accurately describes

Beijing, already sprawling beyond its city walls to accommodate a population in excess of one million people, easily absorbed the increasingly large missionary presence and huge complexes such as the one Vincentians began building at a new site for the North Church in the late 1880s.[35]

No other city in China comes close to Beijing in terms of its historical experiences (good and bad) with Catholicism, the quantity of sacred structures and Church infrastructure (see map 3.1), the famous and not-so-well-known missionaries who worked there—and its extensive Chinese Catholic community, larger than any other in the country. Its vibrant religious past continues into present times, clearly reflected in each of the original four Catholic churches, their current iterations dating to the late nineteenth and early twentieth centuries as well as in two more important churches, one that arose in 1904 (St. Michael's in the Legation Quarter of the Inner City) and one in 1910 (St. Thérèse's in the Outer City). These and others add to the variety and richness of the story.[36]

Tianjin is integral to this study due to its strategic location in north China and devastating events that occurred there. The Dagu Forts situated thirty-seven miles to the east on both sides of the Hai River at its entry point into the Gulf of Zhili (Bo Sea), constituted the city's first line of defense. The walled-city of Tianjin provided additional security as well as guarding the vital junction of the South Grand Canal that brought barges laden with rice grown in central China through Zhili to Tianjin before they turned westward via manmade and natural channels to reach Beijing.[37] By the 1820s, due to the canal's high silt level, rice transport shifted to the coast before using the Hai River to Tianjin

---

the facility that provided care for the infants and young children abandoned by their parents—and constituted most of the so-called orphans. Missionaries observed the widespread plight of poor Chinese children, making the situation commonly known in Europe. In 1843, a bishop in France aware of mission work in China founded the Holy Childhood Society whose goals were "the administration of baptism to children in danger of death and the purchase and adoption of a great many others." The society solicited donations that it forwarded to China (most funds going there) for distribution to the Daughters of Charity (later to other religious sisters as well), who took the lead in operating foundling homes and clinics, such work bringing them in contact with dying children whom they baptized. Young, *Ecclesiastical Colony*, 39–40. Priests, catechists, and "medical practitioner-baptizers" were all actively involved. Sweeten, *Christianity in Rural China*, 187.

35   By 1800, approximately 1.1 million people resided in Beijing. "List of Largest Cities Throughout History."

36   There were two sacred structures outside the city's western wall, each with a cemetery. Everything is now gone, and I will only mention them again in passing.

37   The Bai is one of several rivers that converge near or at Tianjin, flowing to the sea as the Hai River. See Chapter 5, note 1.

and the North Grand Canal as the main route to the capital's grain warehouses.[38] Western military forces destroyed the forts during the Second Opium War, temporarily occupying parts of Tianjin, a sprawling city with several hundred thousand residents. Realizing it best to have a long-term presence, the French constructed a consulate opposite the city wall's northeastern section and across the Hai River near its junction with the Grand Canal. Vincentians built a small chapel next door then replaced it in 1869 with a large church dedicated to Our Lady of Victories.

Grateful missionaries had given it a religiously symbolic name, one that spoke indirectly to the outcome of a war that permitted it. Locals all knew the church's general waterfront location because the Qianlong emperor (r. 1736–1795) stayed there when in the area. For a long time, the housing he used and a nearby well-known temple remained, easily visible from several directions. Now both were gone and, in their place, stood a fortress-like structure that Chinese saw as representing foreign invasion, occupation, and nefarious missionary activities—they called it the Wanghailou jiaotang, the "Tall Church [Building] Overlooking the Hai [River]. In 1870, angry residents torched it, a foundling home, other properties, and the French consulate while killing any Westerner in sight, most of whom were French with connections to the church. Known in the West as the "Tianjin Massacre," it deeply scarred Sino-French relations. Security-conscious France moved its consulate a couple of miles away to the Black Bamboo Grove (Zizhulin) area, a fast-growing treaty concession district reserved for Western use and extraterritorially administered.[39] Vincentians again followed and in 1872 finished a place of worship there that they dedicated to St. Louis—most people referred to it by its locational name, not its formal one. From this church, priests took their message to the surrounding countryside, baptized people, and built many small sacred structures.

In 1899–1900, virulently antiforeign and anti-Christian Chinese known as the "Boxers United in Righteousness" became active near Tianjin, a growing metropolis of an estimated seven hundred fifty thousand to one million people.[40] Boxers first destroyed rural churches and murdered local Catholics

---

38   Jane Kate Leonard, *Controlling from Afar: the Daoguang Emperor's Management of the Grand Canal Crisis, 1824–1826* (Ann Arbor: Center for Chinese Studies, University of Michigan, 1996).

39   Also referred to as the Purple Bamboo Grove, Britain and France demarked it for use as their treaty concession areas in 1860–1861. See Chapter 5's Zizhulin jiaotang section for more details.

40   The lower figure is from Lewis Bernstein, "After the Fall: Tianjin under Foreign Occupation, 1900–1902," in *The Boxers, China, and the World*, eds. Robert Bickers and R.G. Tiedemann (Lanham, Md.: Rowman & Littlefield, 2007), 134. The higher one is from Henri Cordier,

before brazenly entering the urban districts. After burning the Our Lady of Victories Church, rebuilt at the same location as its predecessor in 1897, they laid siege to the concession area; most buildings there survived as did the church at Zizhulin.[41] An international contingent of soldiers soon came to break the siege (and the one in Beijing), restore law and order, and enforce the onerous settlement terms imposed on the Qing dynasty. A third iteration rose quickly, completion coming in 1904. To accommodate Catholicism's fast growth, the Vatican in 1912 made Tianjin the center of a recently formed vicariate that included several adjoining rural counties. The bishop quickly selected a site for a church even before France had controversially annexed it and additional space to the French concession; named for its urban location, his episcopal seat in 1916 became informally known as the Xikai cathedral. Tianjin has grown and flourished economically and is one of China's mega-municipalities. Its religious structures are historically significant and, as will be seen, architecturally unique.

A third geographic focal point is Zhili, the province that surrounded the capital. The name, meaning "directly ruled" by the emperor, indicates its importance. The imperial court considered security of the capital area paramount and consequently garrisoned more Manchu soldiers there than in any other province. Whether military or civil, all officials kept a close watch on the populace for any flickers of trouble, cautiously monitoring heterodox beliefs, Christianity included. In 1793, followers of the White Lotus (Buddhist) sect, had brazenly attacked the Forbidden City. Authorities brutally suppressed them, afterwards increasing security measures particularly when the emperor traveled in the province on his way to either of the two imperial mausoleum parks or on hunting expeditions. Rural Catholics were considered sectarians and lived under a pall of suspicion. Their scant and scattered congregations, mere specks on Zhili's heavily populated landscape (estimated for 1812 at about twenty-eight million) explains how they avoided notice by officials and survived.[42] A few small semi-hidden and so-called "Christian villages" served as havens for a handful of Western and Chinese priests optimistically hoping for a resurgence of conversions among the province's large population. From 1860 to 1900 their numbers increased steadily. The presence of Catholics, missionaries, and sacred structures meant that Boxers had abundant targets to

---

    Histoire des relations de la Chine avec les puissances occidentals, 1860–1900, 3 vols. (1901–1902; reprint, Taipei: Ch'eng-wen Publishing, 1966), 1:348.

41   Esherick, *Origins of the Boxer Uprising*, 290–301.

42   The population figure is from Lillian M. Li, *Fighting Famine in North China: State, Market, and Environmental Decline, 1690s–1990s* (Stanford: Stanford University Press, 2007), 76–77. The 2010 census put Hebei's population at almost eighty million. "Demographics of China," https://en.wikipedia.org/wiki/Demographics_of_China (accessed 13 April 2017).

choose from and that in the background they might draw support from people unsympathetic or hostile to Christianity's growth.[43] Hit hard, Catholicism recovered quickly and added many converts. Among all provinces it had the largest number, a ranking that continues into present times.

Its importance to the dynasty and role in the spread of Christianity aside, several other matters related to Zhili require brief clarification. In 1928, the province's name changed to Hebei, meaning "north of the [Yellow] river." Shortly after the 1949 founding of the People's Republic, the government made boundary adjustments with Shandong Province in the southeast and Henan in the south. In the north and northwest, territorial changes were larger with Chengde and some areas that had once been part of Inner Mongolia or had belonged to short-lived provinces established by the Republic of China's government, shifting to Hebei. Xiwanzi and other villages located north of Zhangjiakou and outside the Great Wall (once in Zhili's frontier zone) belonged to Hebei. Lastly, in 1927, with further adjustments in 1954 and later, the central government made Beijing and Tianjin into two special municipalities, civil units administratively equivalent to provinces in the central government hierarchy. These vast cities stretch over urban and rural landscapes, having greatly reduced Hebei's size and altered its shape.

2   Catholic Ecclesiastical Divisions and Statistics

As civil units, the three geographic areas described above are clear enough, yet source materials often refer to ecclesiastical territories that do not correspond exactly to them or that frequently changed boundaries and names. The following provides a basis for understanding their evolution and impact on Vincentian growth in these areas and illuminates numbers for those residing in the places under discussion.

In 1493, the pope granted Portugal "the right of (royal) patronage" (*padroado*) for missionary work in the New World.[44] About sixty years later the Portuguese king formed the Macao Diocese, which encompassed all of China. By 1663, approximately fifteen thousand Christians lived in Zhili, of which one

---

43   One study has found that "most Boxer violence [in Zhili] was perpetrated by local villagers [who joined with Boxers from other areas] against local Christians." Esherick, *Origins of the Boxer Uprising*, 280. Boxers and locals destroyed virtually everything that belonged to Catholics and Protestants, including their cemeteries.

44   The pope granted the king of Spain the same right for a different part of the world. Thus, the kings of Portugal and Spain had the authority to appoint bishops to dioceses within their respective realms.

to two thousand claimed Beijing as home.[45] In the late seventeenth century, Lisbon and Rome wrangled over jurisdictional authority. In 1690, the former delimited two new dioceses (one for Beijing and one for Nanjing), retaining the right to present priests to the pope for appointment to the sees as bishops, in effect, naming them. The Sacred Congregation for the Propagation of the Faith (referred to here as Propaganda Fide) successfully countered (with Lisbon's acceptance) by appointing a Venetian and Franciscan as the bishop of Beijing.[46] Bernardino Della Chiesa, o.f.m., served as the bishop of Beijing from 1690 to 1721.[47] His diocese encompassed Zhili, Shandong, and Liaodong (a large area to the northeast of Beijing and outside the Great Wall).[48] According to the bishop, in the late seventeenth century there were approximately one hundred thousand Christians in all of China with ten thousand residing in Zhili (including Beijing). By another estimate, the total for the country was two hundred thousand with twenty to thirty thousand residing in the Beijing Diocese, and roughly fifteen to twenty-three thousand living in Zhili (Beijing included).[49]

In 1696, the papacy directly curtailed the scope of the three bishoprics under Portuguese control (via *padroado*) by ordering the establishment of eight vicariates, each taking a different province as its jurisdiction, to which the Holy See rather than Lisbon named apostolic vicars to govern them. Beijing Diocese continued to exist with its area unchanged and with the Catholic total in Zhili in 1765 increasing to about thirty-two thousand, four to five thousand of them residing in the capital.[50] Jesuit priests had worked hard over the span of two centuries to achieve these numbers. Vincentians, who arrived in 1785 and toiled under difficult circumstances, struggled to care for Christians living in the countryside. Even in remote villages, the dark shadow of imperial proscription curtailed religious life and some fragile, small congregations vanished.

---

45   *Handbook of Christianity in China, Volume One,* 385. I extrapolate for Beijing. Priests of the nineteenth century and later only counted baptized and confirmed individuals as Catholics with catechumens enumerated separately. Presumably, those that preceded them did the same in their reports and estimates.

46   The pope created Propaganda Fide in 1622 to bolster the Church's mission duty and resume its direct engagement in apostolic work thereby curtailing the right of patronage. It took many years to do so. Latourette, *History of Christian Missions in China,* 124–126, 241; and *Handbook of Christianity in China, Volume One,* 576–578.

47   Della Chiesa's appointment, which he may not have known about until 1699, led to friction with Portuguese Jesuits who considered Beijing Diocese to be under their king's patronage and expected one of theirs to be in line for the position.

48   He chose not to move to Beijing and continued to reside in Linqing Prefecture, Shandong until his death in 1721. Professor R.G. Tiedemann, email to author, 7 October 2017.

49   Della Chiesa estimated that 10 percent of them were in Beijing and Zhili. *Handbook of Christianity in China, Volume One,* 383, 385.

50   Ibid., 385. Again, I extrapolate for Beijing.

TABLE 2.1   Chinese Catholics, estimates (see Appendix 1 for added information)

Year	China	Zhili/Hebei (entire province)	Beijing
c. 1600	1,000	100	0
c. 1700	200,000	23,000	2,000
c. 1800	200,000	20,000	700
c. 1900	600,000–720,000	126,000–150,000	25,000
c. 1950	3,400,000	800,000	50,000
c. 2000	8,000,000	750,000	50,000
At present	9,000,000–12,000,000	1,000,000–1,500,000	75,000–100,000

TABLE 2.2   Ecclesiastical divisions for Zhili/Hebei, 1690-1946 (see Appendix 2 regarding additional divisions)

Year	Area	Name
1690–1856	Zhili (entire province)	Part of Beijing Diocese
1856	Zhili—northern part	Apostolic Vicariate (A.V.) of Beijing and Zhili N established; named changed to A.V. of Beijing, 1924; divisions made; core part becomes diocese, 1946
1856	Zhili—southwestern part	A.V. of Zhili SW est.; name changed to A.V. of Zhengding, 1924; divisions made; core part becomes diocese, 1946
1856	Zhili—southeastern part	Jesuits' A.V. of Zhili SE est.; named changed to A.V. of Xian County, 1924; divisions made; core part becomes diocese, 1946

In the mid-nineteenth century, the Holy See took the final step to limit *padroado* in China by officially suppressing the dioceses of Beijing and Nanjing. Rome, without the Lisbon complication, exercised full control of jurisdictions and the appointment of apostolic vicars to lead them. Propaganda Fide as the pope's right arm for missionary matters oversaw the formation of vicariates. By the 1850s a stream of illegal missionaries had started flowing into China. As they revitalized the faith of Catholics and made thousands of converts, it became necessary to whittle down the size of the large vicariates. The adjustment allowed for concentrated efforts and a better allocation of finances for their future development.[51] In 1856, the pope created three vicariates for Zhili. A restored Society of Jesus had already returned to Shanghai and Jesuits naturally sought control of the areas previously placed in Vincentian hands. The latter initially refused to relinquish anything, eventually agreeing to give a multi-county section, about one-third of Zhili, back to the Jesuits. It took the name Vicariate of Zhili Southeast. The capital city and the other two-thirds portion stayed under Vincentians' ecclesiastic control, forming the Vicariate of Zhili North and the Vicariate of Zhili Southwest, respectively.

Amply large and heavily populated, the Vincentians' two vicariates remained unchanged until century's end, when Propaganda Fide with input from the Congregation of the Mission decreased their size for the sake of more efficient administration and use of resources. The first modification took place in 1899, when the pope approved the removal of part of Zhili North's eastern section to create the Vicariate of Zhili East with the bishop's cathedral at Yongping. During the first half of the twentieth century no ecclesiastical territory stayed the same size for very long, reflecting a pattern of ever more clergy, funding, and numbers. In 1900, approximately one hundred and seventy-five thousand Catholics lived in the province and its two large cities; by 1950 that number hovered at eight hundred fifty thousand. Almost seven decades later, the Catholic Patriotic Association (C.P.A.) oversees ten active dioceses with over one million "registered" worshippers with estimates that hundreds of thousands more belong to the "unofficial Church" (for which no census exists).

Numerical growth and interest in inculturation led the Church in 1946 to reorganize its vicariates into dioceses with about one-fifth under a Chinese bishop.[52] The dioceses mainly retained the boundaries of the apostolic vicariates and prefectures from which they had been formed.[53] For a short time after the formation of the People's Republic in 1949, the dioceses continued to exist in name only. Over the next thirty years, bishops and priests worked under increasingly intimidating conditions with many arrested and imprisoned.

---

51   Ferreux, *Histoire de la Congrégation*, 148–150.
52   *Handbook of Christianity in China, Volume Two*, 571, 585.
53   Certain areas, typically smaller than vicariates and with fewer Catholics, became apostolic prefectures headed by a prefect. The first one in Hebei was that of Li County in 1924. The Vatican hoped to develop them into vicariates that would someday become dioceses. By the 1940s, most were under Chinese prefects. These ecclesiastical prefectures are not to be confused with those under the civil government prior to 1949. For a detailed explanation of ecclesiastical areas and titles, refer to Joseph de Moidrey, *La hiérarchie Catholique en Chine, en Corée et au Japon (1307–1914)* (Chang-hai [Shanghai]: Imprimerie de l'Orphelinat de T'ou-sé-wé, 1914), 217–222. "Apostolic Prefect," https://en.wikipedia.org/wiki/Apostolic_prefect (accessed 17 July 2017).

Authorities closed churches, seminaries, schools, and foundling homes altering the confiscated buildings for different uses. Lay Catholics survived by hiding their religious affiliation. The nadir for the dioceses came with the ten-year Cultural Revolution that officially ended in 1976. A few years later China's leaders began to open the country to outside contact, reestablishing diplomatic and trade relations with Western nations while domestically releasing religious prisoners and permitting congregations to resume religious services.

Concurrent with China's resumption of contact with the world, the central government began administratively to reorganize itself and its provinces. In Hebei it established in stages eleven civil jurisdictions called prefectural-level municipalities (*diji shi*), each composed of a main urban center that provides the unit's name. These municipalities include county-level cities (*xianji shi*) that are composed of substantial rural areas with numerous townships and villages. To illustrate, in Hebei's northwest corner is the prefectural-level municipality of Zhangjiakou. It encompasses over fourteen hundred square miles with sixteen main subdivisions (six districts and ten counties). The municipality's boundaries are the same as Zhangjiakou Diocese's because authorities require civil and religious units to coincide. Chongli District is one part of the municipality and Xiwanzi, once a remote community in a loosely governed border area, is now a town (*zhen*), adjacent to and an indistinguishable part of the district city and its government offices. Xiwanzi demonstrates how some historically important places have shifted from one civil or ecclesiastical jurisdiction to another.

3   Church Details

The preceding discussion provides the general background in which Catholicism's expansion occurred. Putting a lens on the sacred structures themselves helps clarify them in their Christian and Chinese contexts. The sub-topics that follow are framed by lines of inquiry that will reveal different facets of churches and perspectives regarding them. To start, when a building became a church, how was it named and how did people refer to it? The cost to construct them varied greatly, depending on size and features, but what can be determined about the financial side?[54] Further insight comes from looking at the classifications mentioned in missionaries' reports. The labels used have meaning. This leads in turn to an examination of church types (and sizes) and

---

54   Sources provide figures in various currencies, which are changed to U.S. dollars whenever possible.

their importance. What can be said about the sites where they were built? And why were they built on certain directional axes? Is it possible to track the ever-changing tallies of churches? Do time periods have a bearing on survival numbers? Materials that provide answers tend to be better for those built after the mid-nineteenth century than for earlier periods.

3.1   Names

A building formally became a sacred structure when a bishop (or equivalent) blessed it. Each one had its own title or name that, relying on Catholic canon, derives from one of several religious categories. The most frequently used were those of Christ and Mary (or a variation thereof used in mass) as well as of angels and saints, the latter common in Europe and the U.S.[55] By the early eighteenth century, four important churches existed within Beijing's city walls. Priests dedicated each of them (and others) to a specific Christian figure, the patron, whose name then became that of the church. For example, the one completed in 1651 near Xuanwu Gate to replace the chapel Ricci had erected carried the formal name of the Holy Savior Church (Jiushi tang). Later (1776), it took the name, Church of the Immaculate Conception (Shitai tang). In 1659, St. Joseph's Church (Sheng Ruose tang), arose east of the Forbidden City.[56] Missionaries finished a third one in 1702 to the others' north (with the Holy Savior as patron), and a fourth on the west side twenty-one years later dedicated to Our Lady of Seven Dolors (Qiku Sheng Mu tang).[57]

Chinese Catholics knew their church's formal name with most calling it *tianzhutang*, the romanization of its pronunciation in Mandarin using the *pinyin* system. The term's origin reputedly dates to 1611 when, upon completion

---

55   "Every church to be dedicated must have a titular. This may be: the Blessed Trinity; our Lord Jesus Christ invoked according to a mystery of his life or a title already accepted in the liturgy; the Holy Spirit; the Blessed Virgin Mary, likewise invoked according to some appellation already accepted in the liturgy; one of the angels; or, finally, a saint inscribed in the Roman Martyrology or in a duly approved Appendix. A blessed may not be the titular without an indult of the Apostolic See. A church should have one titular only, unless it is a question of saints who are listed together in the Calendar." Chapter 2, 11.4. *Rite of Dedication of a Church and an Altar.* (n.p.: International Committee on English in the Liturgy, 1978; http://www.liturgyoffice.org.uk/Resources/Rites/RDCA.pdf, accessed 15 June 2018).

56   This source gives the date as 1655. *Handbook of Christianity in China, Volume One,* 583.

57   C.M. missionaries in China seldom dedicated their sacred structures to their founder, St. Vincent de Paul. To my knowledge, the only one graced with his name stood at Jiudu (Youjia), Jiangxi. A priest referred to it as [St.] Vincent['s] Church, "Oui-cen-tsio tang" (Weizengjue tang). Rouger's letter, 8 July 1862, *Annales CM* 30 (1865): 150. It still goes by this name. Author's field notes, 19 July 1994.

of Beijing's first church, the president of the Ming dynasty's Ministry of Rites conferred it. A literal translation is "Hall of the Lord of Heaven."[58] The high official was aware that Jesuits had decided on using "Tianzhu" for (Christianity's) God and his choice of *tang* seems inspired because it had a literary tone and meant an important meeting place, often used in conjunction with buildings within a government compound. Equally significant, neither Buddhists nor Daoists named temple buildings *tang*, thus eliminating nominal confusion. When only one church stood in Beijing, Catholics referred to it as *tianzhu-tang*. Over the next two hundred years, the term simply meant the "church" or "Catholic [Christian] church" since there were no Protestant ones in China until the early nineteenth century. Later a generic expression for church (*jiao-tang*) came into use, context disclosing whether it was Catholic or Protestant.[59]

Missionaries did not see a need to put on the façades of the four earliest churches any writing to identify them. The North Church, dating to its first construction, did have above its main entrance a small vertical plaque (*biandou*) with the characters *chijian tianzhutang* "[Catholic] church built by imperial order." When Catholics constructed one at a different location in 1887–1888, they placed something similar with the same wording directly over the central doorway (a version of it is mounted in the same place today), but here it should be interpreted to mean "[Catholic] church built with imperial permission"— hair splitting that is relevant to its circumstances.[60] The characters were on the South Church's entry gate when it was finished in 1776, but not preserved on the one rebuilt in 1904. The three (St. Joseph's, Our Lady of Seven Dolors', and St. Michael's) built during the imperial period are all devoid of this imperial

---

58   Paul Bornet, "Les anciennes églises de Pékin: notes d'histoire, Nant'ang [part 1]," *Bulletin catholique de Pékin* 31 (1944): 499.

59   In the pages that follow, I use *tianzhutang* to mean "Catholic [Christian] church" or just "church," if the context is clear. Today, some people use *Tianzhujiao tang*, which may be translated the same way or with a slight emphasis on Catholic. Later, to distinguish, Protestant ones were (and still are) called "hall of worship" (*libai tang*) and "gospel hall" (*fuyin tang*), if literally translated. Both terms mean "Protestant [Christian] church" or "church," qualified as needed. Likewise, "all temples, large and small, have some name or inscription," according to a 1936–1937 survey. Frank Wilson Price, *The Rural Church in China: A Survey* (New York: Agricultural Missions, 1948), vii, 29–35, 113. Following this custom, at least in the twentieth century, most Protestant churches had their Chinese name either over the main gate or on the church itself.

60   Although *chijian* is usually translated as "built by imperial order," the emperor was in fact allowing missionaries to build it, not literally ordering them to do so. "Built by imperial permission" seems appropriate in the case of the 1887–1888 North Church, whose situation is discussed in detail in the next chapter. Missionaries liked the first translation because it implied more than the second.

FIGURE 2.5   Replica of the plaque that hung above the third North Church's main
             entrance. It reads, "Church built by imperial order, the thirteenth year of
             Guangxu [1887]." It is in the same location on today's church.
             SOURCE: ARCHIVES CM, PARIS

cachet and the *tianzhutang* designation. In present-day Beijing, of the four earliest, only the West Church has added the characters high up on its steeple.[61]

It is uncertain when the practice of adding *tianzhutang* (either vertically or horizontally) to façades started—given the imperial proscription of Christianity, it probably did not begin until the 1850s–1860s. Gradually, churches in some of Zhili's smaller cities labeled themselves as such without claiming to have an imperial commission. However, all three of Tianjin's important churches were devoid of the characters on their façades. As for post-1860 churches in rural areas of Zhili (Jiangxi and Zhejiang Provinces included because they were Vincentian areas), more and more included the words on either their entry gates or façades or both.[62] From 1900 forward to today, about one-half of the congregations in Zhili/Hebei's countryside posted on the sacred structure's façade the Chinese for *tianzhutang* while most of the other half displayed a

---

61   Drawings and photographs of its earlier iterations do not include the characters.
62   This is derived from my reading of *JWJAD* materials for these three provinces. I venture
     that the same is true for all of China.

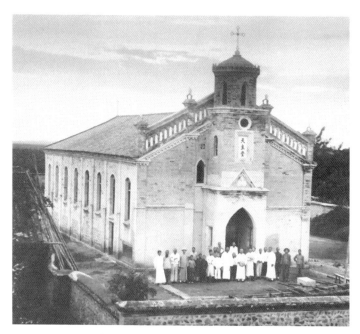

FIGURE 2.6 *"Tianzhutang."* A Chinese priest built the church at Miyun,
Vicariate of Beijing in 1923. On some pre-1949 churches the
characters were mounted horizontally and read right to left.
Since the 1980s, churches have reversed the reading direction.
SOURCE: ARCHIVES CM, PARIS

cross, sometimes including the religious patron's monogram such as "IHS" or
"JHS" (for Jesus), "M" (for Mary), and "SJ" (for St. Joseph). A few have a cross
and a popular inscription.[63]

Beijing's churches also had an informal name based on their positions relative to the first one and each other. Missionaries and local Catholics liked
this for its simplicity and for the locational clarity. With the 1659 completion
of St. Joseph's, to the northeast of Xuanwu Gate, it became the East Church
(Dongtang) whereas its earlier counterpart gained another name. Beijing's
third sacred structure was completed in late 1702. Located almost directly
north of Xuanwu (outside the Forbidden City's Xihua Gate), locals fittingly
nicknamed it the North Church (Beitang) and Canchikou tang after its neighborhood. Thereafter, the one near Xuanwu had its name changed to the South

---

63 The front of the Housangyu church (presented in Chapter 4) has only a cross and the
characters *wan you zhen yuan* (discussed in Chapter 3), read left to right, above the main
entrance. Author's field notes, 25 October 2009.

Church (Nantang). Two decades later, Fr. Teodorico Pedrini, C.M., built the capital's fourth, a small sacred structure in the Inner City's northwest quadrant. It assumed the last compass point available and became known as the West Church.[64] When priests added two important religious edifices to Beijing's skyline in the early twentieth century, rather than complicating their names with directional prefixes locals used, added the neighborhoods as part of their informal names. In 1904, the Legation Quarter gained one dedicated to St. Michael (Sheng Miwei'er jiaotang), which people referred to as the Legation Street church (Dongjiaominxiang tang) due to its placement on the lane of that name. In the 1910s, another one arose in a residential neighborhood of narrow alleyways near the Temple of Heaven that was later dedicated to St. Thérèse of Lisieux (Shengnü Xiaodelan); most everyone knew it as the Nangangzi church. The reader will recall that Tianjin's first three had commonly used names that related to their locations at Wanghailou, Zizhulin, and Xikai.

In pre-twentieth century Zhili's countryside, congregational numbers never warranted more than one Catholic church in a village, it dedicated to and protected by a patron or saint just like its urban counterparts. Clerics of course knew its formal name and ordinary people spoke of it as the such-and-such place's church, for instance, the Anjia Village church (Anjia zhuang tianzhutang). Those living in the vicinity identified it simply as *jiaotang*, no placename prefix needed. Such simplification was the norm in Zhili/Hebei, Jiangxi, and Zhejiang as well as in all areas in China with places of worship. Reference to present-day ones remains similar to that just described with toponym prefixes popular as labels for specific sacred structures, for instance the Pingfang church in suburban Beijing. In some locales, urban growth has turned former rural communities into suburban neighborhoods, though the churches' former village names have stuck. Such names are part of their identity and eliminate confusion over location.

In letters and reports, missionaries succinctly referred to "mission chapels" in rural areas as just chapels. On occasion, they distinguished between "public chapels," where they said mass, and "private chapels" that were actually oratories in homes, not those situated within a mission center reserved exclusively for the use of priests and Sisters. And, due to space and financial considerations, most were not used full time this way, people simply setting the room up as needed for religious services. To most Chinese Catholics, the linguistic distinction between a church and chapel was not architectural; it was nominal. In a large collection of nineteenth century Chinese government documents

---

64   Pedrini served in China under the direction of Propaganda Fide, not the Congregation of the Mission.

FIGURE 2.7   House used as a chapel, Vicariate of Baoding, ca 1920s
                    SOURCE: ARCHIVES CM, PARIS

regarding Christian affairs, both officials and ordinary people used the term
tianzhutang and *jiaotang* for church or *xiao tianzhutang* and *xiao jiaotang* for
chapel.[65] Catholics and non-Catholics alike sometimes used the term *gongsuo*,
that is, a public meeting place, in reference to a "public chapel."

3.2   *Costs*
For the seventeenth and eighteenth centuries, financial information concerning construction expenses is nonexistent except that we know the Kangxi

---

65   Based on my extensive examination of *JWJAD* materials.

emperor (r. 1662–1722) donated ten thousand Chinese ounces (*liang*, referred to as taels) of silver in 1705 for the renovation of the sacred structure in Beijing now known as the South Church.[66] At about that time a priest wrote that one tael was valued at five French *livres*, making the gift worth a total of fifty thousand *livres*.[67] Seventy years later it burned and the Qianlong emperor gifted the same amount of silver for its reconstruction, or the equivalent of seventy-five thousand *livres*.[68] The amount given in 1775, if we may use U.S. dollars exchange rates for 1792, came to about $12,500.[69] No matter the value in foreign currencies, the donations constituted extremely large sums given missionaries' limited financial resources. Records do not specify whether they used the money to subsidize only construction costs (labor and materials) or if some of the donation went for other uses.[70]

No construction in Beijing took place between 1730, when the West Church was rebuilt after an earthquake, and 1867, when three replacements (East, West, and North Churches) arose, their respective costs unknown. Two years later, a Vincentian missionary built Tianjin's first one at Wanghailou

---

66   A Chinese ounce of silver usually contained 37.5 grams. A general explanation of China's monetary system, regional variations, and how foreign silver changed it during the Qing period is provided by Lloyd E. Eastman, *Family, Field, and Ancestors: Constancy and Change in China's Social and Economic History, 1550–1949* (New York: Oxford University Press, 1988), 108–112.

67   The exchange rate information used comes from a letter dated 9 December 1700 as cited by Paul Bornet, "Les anciennes églises de Pékin: notes d'histoire, le Pei-t'ang [part 1]," *Bulletin catholique de Pékin* 32 (1945): 122.

68   A missionary wrote in 1775 that 1.0 Chinese ounce or tael equaled 7.5 French *livres*. Bornet, "Les anciennes églises ... Nant'ang [part 1]," 503. The U.S. dollar made its debut in 1792 and for that year the estimated value of 1.0 tael is $1.25.

69   Not finding a table showing the relative values of Chinese, French, British, and American currencies, I have composed my own. Refer to Appendix 3 for rates and notes on information I have gleaned from sources. The subject of exchange rates is complicated not only because of the dual use of silver taels and copper coins (*qian*, often referred to as cash) but also because foreign traders, beginning in the early 1800s, used large quantities of Mexican silver dollars to pay for tea and luxury goods, which impacted exchange ratios. About two decades later, the opium trade led to an outflow of Chinese silver, causing varying levels of inflation depending on the province. The standard value for one tael of silver was one thousand copper cash, which began to increase. Contemporaneous reports usually provide monetary information using one unit or the other, sometimes equating it to a Western currency (*francs*, pounds, or dollars).

70   To economize, missionaries would have bought materials locally and hired laborers from the area. Even if some Catholics were available to work, they would have not been any more experienced in building European-like churches than others. For missionaries, the main issues would have been cost and quality control.

for $11,840.[71] According to Fr. Alphonse Favier, C.M., construction of the East Church in Beijing in 1884 "cost more than 80,000 dollars" and in 1888 the new cathedral, the North Church, was "over 150,000 dollars."[72] Its elaborate façade and size, built as others were with stone foundations and brick walls, insufficiently explains the bloated amount that at the time made it China's most expensive, even more than the Sacred Heart Cathedral constructed of quarried granite in Guangzhou with much difficulty over the years 1863–1888 at a cost as high as $170,200.[73] The construction of "other large churches" in Beijing that Favier did not name ranged from $10,000 to $20,000.[74]

In the countryside, the situation was quite different. Perboyre commented in the mid-1830s that in Hubei "our church and house [residence] here pass for

71   In taels, it was eight thousand. Also, see Chapter 5, notes 10 and 66.

72   This is the first mention of Favier, whose name appears numerous times in the pages that follow. He worked in China from 1862 until his death in 1905 and was one of the Vincentians' most capable and knowledgeable as well as active and influential priests. He became the bishop of the Vicariate of Beijing and Zhili North in 1899. A brief recapitulation of his career is in Van den Brandt, *Les Lazaristes*, 68–69. Favier designed and supervised the construction of several sacred edifices in China, apparently not influenced by the style of the parish church at his hometown, Marsannay la Côte, in eastern France. He is remembered as "evéque de Pékin," his title displayed on a plaque above the gate to his parent's home; the nearby church bears no resemblance to any I have seen in Beijing and Hebei. Author's field notes, 23 October 2010.

       In regard to costs, Favier stated that the South Church "asked the sum of 40,000 dollars for [its] renovation," implying that it received this amount. Favier letter, 4 October 1899, *Annals CM-E* 7 (1900): 222. In a book published in 1901, the North Church's cost is said to have exceeded $150,000. Favier, *Heart of Pekin*, 5. In Shandong in 1898, the German minister and missionaries forced the Chinese to allow construction of three "atonement" churches at a cost of sixty-six thousand taels ($51,480) each. At each a stone marker had the inscription *chijian tianzhutang*. R.G. Tiedemann, "The Church Militant: Armed Conflicts between Christians and Boxers in North China," in *The Boxers, China, and the World*, ed. Robert Bickers and R.G. Tiedemann (Lanham, Md.: Rowman & Littlefield, 2007), 27–28.

73   The all-stone cathedral in Guangzhou, by one estimate cost four hundred thousand *francs* (using 1870 exchange rates, $118,400 or 80,000 taels). Jean-Paul Wiest, "The Building of the Cathedral of Canton: Politics, Cultural, and Religious Clashes," in *Religion and Culture: Past Approaches, Present Globalisation, Future Challenges—International Symposium Organized by the Macao Ricci Institute* (Macao: Macao Ricci Institute, 2004), 240–242. An Internet source gives a cost of five hundred seventy-five thousand *francs* (the equivalent of $170,200 or 115,000 taels). "Sacred Heart Cathedral (Guangzhou)," http://en.wikipedia.org/wiki/Sacred_Heart_Cathedral_(Guangzhou) (accessed 14 March 2015). For comparison, the Holy Trinity Church in Paris, built from 1861 to 1867, cost about five million *francs* ($1,480,000). "Sainte-Trinité, Paris," http://en.wikipedia.org/wiki/Sainte-Trinit%C3%A9,_Paris (accessed 5 March 2015).

74   Favier letter, 4 October 1899, *Annals CM-E* 7 (1900): 221–222.

palaces, though they are no better than mud huts with an earthen floor, and a thatch covering laid down on the bambou [sic] branches which supply inside the place of ceiling."[75] In other words, the priest occupied a Chinese style rural house with a low cost, perhaps $50 or less each.[76] For the same period, Mouly reported that his church in rural Xiwanzi cost about $1,600 to build, probably including some interior décor.[77] He bragged that it was one of the biggest in China, implying one of the finest. Construction funds came from the pockets of Mouly, locals, and Catholics of nearby communities. Southeast of Beijing at the village (zhuang) of Gaojia in the late 1860s, Favier built one dedicated to St. Peter (Sheng Boduolu tang) for $1,200, its cost sponsored by his home parish, parents, vicariate, and the congregation. Mouly remarked that its façade with a tall tower, built to resemble the West Church, "dominates the entire [rural] area."[78] During the 1870s in southeastern Zhili, Jesuits counted 261 congregations in their vicariate. In thirty of them they had built "little churches, half Chinese, half European, so that they are not at all like the pagodas [Buddhist temples]." Each of the structures had pounded earth walls faced with bricks that were whitewashed with reed roofs over a thin layer of clay to protect the interior. Their dimensions ranged from forty to forty-eight feet long by thirteen to seventeen wide, with the smaller size costing about $538 and the larger $718, a "high price" because of the scarcity of local materials and the cost to transport them from other areas. About one hundred congregations had "little chapels," some jointly owned by the local Catholics, some owned by individuals. Indistinguishable in style from village houses, these chapels had unpainted walls and earthen floors, ranging in size from ten to thirty feet long by ten to

---

75   Perboyre letter, 10 August 1836, *Annals PF*, old series (1838): 381. In another letter, he wrote similarly adding that he had "a table for [an] altar, overhung with a small canopy." *Annals PF* 2 (1841): 98.

76   For comparison, in the early 1860s in Sichuan, oratories ("large rooms") cost $978–1,223 to build. Delamare [Delamarre] letter, 8 April 1861, *Annals PF* 12 (1861): 329. These figures, provided in pounds, must be in error. If taken to be *francs*, they would equal $29–36 and be in line with costs elsewhere.

77   In his currency, eight thousand *francs*, or 1,143 taels. Mouly letter, 6 November 1836, *Annals PF*, old series (1838): 400. Ferreux writes that it cost one thousand taels ($1,400). *Histoire de la Congrégation*, 115.

78   Mouly letter, 28 October 1868, *Annales CM-F* 34 (1869): 278–279, 282. There are several communities by this name in Zhili/Hebei; this one is located midway between Beijing and Tianjin. Favier served as its pastor from 1865 to 1868. In the early 1900s, it constituted an important part of the "Capital South" District. Boxers attacked the village and destroyed the church. The Catholics that survived numbered 282 and worshipped at a recently built chapel. Archives CM, Paris, Folder 163-I, "Vicariatus Apostolicus Pekini et Tche-ly Septentrionalis. Status Missionis, 1904–1905," 12.

fifteen wide. Due to their modest construction from local materials and their size, they cost from $90 to $135 to erect.[79]

By the end of the century, "small churches" (chapels) cost about $1,000 each with one priest hoping to build two each year.[80] Favier quotes the same cost for a chapel as he fished for donations from readers of a mission publication.[81] One report from the 1920s in Jiangxi described some of these places of worship as deplorable.[82] In many villages, priests said mass in "an ordinary room" with worshippers standing in the doorway or outside. Such rooms were part of a Catholic's house, its use free of charge. During the early twentieth century, based on a report written in 1928, churches, chapels, and "residences" (mission centers or complexes) in the Beijing-Xuanhua area had risen to a minimum of $5,000, $800, and $6,000, respectively.[83] Two years later to inspire donations, *Catholic Missions and Annals of the Propagation of the Faith*, prominently displayed a photograph of a solidly brick-built "Mission Chapel" at the village (*zhuang*) of Zhaoge, Hebei that had been constructed for $1,000, the funds provided by an American. By this time, missionaries carefully monitored the quality of the materials used, even custom ordering and inspecting the bricks used—at extra expense. The editor wrote in a brief caption that for the same amount or even half of it a benefactor could endow a similar chapel, designate

79   "Vicariate-Apostolic of South-east Pe-tche-ly," *Annals PF* 34 (1873): 73–74. In the early
      1870s, a Chinese priest built a church in a rural section of northwestern Jiangxi that
      cost three thousand *francs* ($888). His bishop thought it was too expensive. Bray letter,
      10 February 1884, *Annales CM-F* 50 (1885): 120. For one comparison outside of China, in
      1870, the small (twenty-four feet wide by sixty feet long) all-wooden Santa Rosa Church in
      Cambria, California cost $100 to build (plus another $100 for the parcel of land on which
      it sat). Author's field notes, 18 July 2017.

80   "Report of the Missions by Rev. Father Bettemburg [Bettembourg]," *Annals CM-E* 2 (1895):
      372. By this time, the construction quality of ones in rural areas had improved and many,
      if not all, were built of bricks. One in southeastern Zhili is a case in point, a priest boast-
      ing that its sturdiness served to guarantee that this "Christian village" would persevere.
      Émile Becker, *Un demi-siècle d'apostolat en Chine, le Révérend Père Joseph Gonnet de la
      Compagnie de Jésus*, 3rd ed. (Ho-kien-fou: Imprimerie de la Mission, 1916), 129.

81   Favier wrote about the need for donations for chapels (or public oratories) as follows: "Let
      us hope that our readers of the *Catholic Missions* will be happy to share with us the merit
      of all these good works, participating therein by offerings proportioned to their means."
      Favier letter, 4 October 1899, *Annals CM-E* 7 (1900): 220–222.

82   An American Vincentian in southernmost Jiangxi wrote that in one village people wor-
      shipped in a "little chapel," describing it as "a dark, dingy hole." He stated that it would
      cost $500 to build a chapel (that is, something better). McGuillicuddy letter, 29 January
      1922, *Annals CM-E* 29 (1922): 100, 104.

83   Archives CM, Paris, Folder 168-I-a, "État comparative des Vicariats de Pékin et de
      Suanhoafou," 1–3. Also, see note 91 below.

A Lasting Memorial

Endowments are now being sought and obtained by universities and scientific institutes. You may never be able to endow a school of higher learning, one of its departments or even a single chair.

The cost would be prohibitive.

But you can endow a mission activity that will thus endure indefinitely and cause your name to remain in benediction.

SUCH A MEMORIAL WOULD BE

A MISSION CHAPEL
Cost $500 or $1,000

FIGURE 2.8 "A Lasting Memorial." The chapel at Zhaoge village, Vicariate of Beijing.
SOURCE: *CATH-M ANNALS PF*, JANUARY 1930

FIGURE 2.9 Yangjialou Village church, Vicariate of Beijing, ca 1930s
            SOURCE: ARCHIVES CM, PARIS

its "titular saint," then, upon completion, receive photographs of it.[84] Of simple style, with a modest bell tower and gable roof, it had become the preferred style for chapels, as confirmed by a rare photograph of one at the village (*cun*) of Yangjialou.[85] When war started in the late 1930s, church construction stopped (and did not resume until the 1980s).

3.3 Classifications

Preserved in the Vincentians' Parisian archives are several types of statistical reports that China-based missionaries provided, important not just because of data on how their work had progressed but also because of the way they

---

84   Zhaoge's location is not specified. *Cath-M Annals PF* 7, no. 1 (January 1930): inside back cover page and 7, no. 5 (May 1930): inside front cover page. To potential American bene-factors, the cost would probably have seemed low. Catholics in the small rural town of Turlock, California built a well-designed sacred structure with bell tower for $30,000. "First Services Held in Sacred Heart Church," *Turlock Journal*, 31 October 2009, reprint of article in *Turlock Tribune*, 25 October 1929.

85   It was categorized as a chapel (public oratory). Archives CM, Paris, Folder 163-I, "Vicariat Apostolique de Pékin. État de la Mission, du 1ᵉʳ Juillet 1936 au 30 Juin 1937" (Peiping: Imprimerie des Lazaristes, 1937), 86.

FIGURE 2.10   Vincentian missionary inspecting bricks, Wenzhou area, Zhejiang, early
              twentieth century. Priests wanted quality bricks for use in the construction
              of churches and other structures.
              SOURCE: ARCHIVES CM, PARIS

classified it. The earliest extant reports date to the 1820s and 1830s for Jiangxi
and Zhejiang Provinces and provide the number of confessions, communions,
baptisms, deaths, and marriages that occurred over one year.[86] Missionaries
did not bother to count churches or chapels because during this time of imperial proscription few existed and enumeration of them meant less than what
had transpired spiritually among the scant number of Christians. The earliest
use of churches or chapels as a statistical sub-heading that I have found is in an
1840 report for Jiangxi in which the missionary used the term "*capella domes-
tica*" (domestic chapel).[87] Sometimes recorded on small pieces of paper, such
data for Zhili and other provinces may not have made it to Paris or were easily
lost afterwards.[88]

---

86   Archives CM, Paris, Folder 165-I-b, "Catalogus Missionis. Kian-ing et Ou-sy, 1827–8;" and
     "Tche-kiang Catalogus, 1832." Planchet [A. Thomas, pseud.], *Histoire de la mission de
     Pékin*, 1:23–24 mentions that the first Vincentian report on religious life at Beijing dates
     to 1788.
87   Archives CM, Paris, Folder 165-I-b, "Fructus Spirituales, Kiang-si, 1840."
88   Tallies for other areas of this period are scattered among different archival folders.

Beginning in the last quarter of the nineteenth century and reflecting their expansion, Vincentians started specifying what constituted a church in terms of style and size, a classification that came with cost implications. In statistical reports to Paris in French and Rome in Latin, clerics defined what a place of worship was in China. A document for 1878–1879, written in Latin, notes that there were 28 "*majores cum bonâ residentiâ*" (large [churches] with good residences [for priests]), 93 "*minores seu capellæ publicæ*" (small or public chapels) and 109 "*oratoria quæ manent proprietas alicujus familiæ, licet eis utatur communitas christianorum*" (oratories that remain the property of families even if the Christian community [congregation] makes use of them).[89] Another report, a "state of the mission" document for 1885 written in French, gives the same numbers as six years earlier, similarly stating that there were "*grandes avec résidence*" (large [churches] with residence), "*petites ou chapelles publiques*" (small or public chapels), and "*oratoires privés*" (private oratories).[90] It is clear the bishop who filed the report, using data provided by his priests, classified worship places as one of three types and that those in the second category might be a small church or public chapel, "public" meaning owned by the vicariate and available for the common use of the congregation. Individual Catholics privately owned the third type, rooms in their own homes, that they and neighbors used as oratories.

Although in earlier decades of the nineteenth century it appears that a few hundred Catholics might have a modest-sized sacred structure, times changed. By 1894 Fr. Nicolas Bettembourg, C.M., procurator general of the Congregation of the Mission, reported that when an area's worshippers numbered from eight hundred to one thousand, they needed a "small church," several of them costing a total of $1,083.[91] Growth of the Church's spiritual side had created pressure on how to finance the sometimes expensive material side. Bettembourg stated that in the Vicariate of Beijing and Zhili North he counted 460 Catholic "settlements," that is, places with congregations, and categorized places of worship as follows: "churches, large, with residence for the missionaries" that

89   Archives CM, Paris, Folder 168-I-a, "Vicariatus Apostolicus Pekini et Tche-ly Septentrionalis, Fructus Spirituales, a die 15 Aug. 1878 ad diem 14 Aug. 1879."
90   Archives CM, Paris, Folder 168-I-a, "Tche-ly Septentrional, État de la mission en 1885."
91   He based this on information provided by Fr. Jean-Baptiste Sathou, C.M. "Report of the Missions by Rev. Father Bettemburg [Bettembourg]," *Annals CM-E* 2 (1895): 372. I have converted five thousand *francs* to dollars using 1899 exchange rates. In Hubei in the 1920s–1930s, Columban priests built chapels with a maximum capacity of four hundred and distinguished in a report for 1937 between "Sacred Buildings: holding more than 400, [and] holding less." Neil Collins, *The Splendid Cause: The Missionary Society of the St Columban, 1916–1954* (Dublin: The Columban Press, 2009), 97–98.

FIGURE 2.11   Vincentian priest saying mass outside a villager's home, southern Jiangxi,
ca 1930s
SOURCE: ARCHIVES CM, PHILADELPHIA

numbered 25; "churches, small, or public chapels," 160 in number; and "oratories private, but frequented by Christians," totaling 106.[92] Wording differences
between the 1880s and the mid-1890s are not significant.

An important change in describing the first category of worship places occurred in 1896–1897. Now 25 were designated as *majores modo europæo constructæ*, that is, large sacred structures only of European style construction.
In addition, there were 186 small churches or public chapels and 270 private
oratories.[93] One year later Vincentians produced a general report on their work
in North China, classifying places of worship this way: "*Églises proprement
dites*" (churches, properly stated), "*Chapelles publiques*" (public chapels), and

---

92   "Report of the Missions by Rev. Father Bettemburg [Bettembourg]," *Annals CM-E* 2 (1895):
370. Regarding residence, in pre-1860 times, it typically referred to a priest's dwelling. By
the end of the nineteenth century, the word designated this and more. Within a vicariate,
certain areas became known as "districts," a subdivision of which were "residences," that
is, places where churches stood alongside housing for the priest and his staff as well as
other buildings used as clinics, hospitals, schools, and foundling homes. In short, "residence" often denoted a mission center—and the area it served. In the 1930s, terminology
changed (see Chapter 7, note 54).
93   Archives CM, Paris, Folder 168-I-a, "Vicariatus Apostolicus Pekini et Tche-ly Septentrionalis, Fructus Spirituales, a die 15 Augusti 1896 ad diem 14 Augusti 1897." Reports for the
previous three years are not in the archives.

FIGURE 2.12   Room in a residence used as an oratory, Youjia Village,
Jiangxi. On the wall, below the cross is written *wan you*
zhen yuan.
SOURCE: PHOTO BY AUTHOR, 1995

"*Oratoires*" (oratories).[94] It is clear that Vincentians had decided that "properly-stated" churches were those built in European architectural style. Bishop Favier said in 1899 that there were thirty-one "large European [style] Churches many [of which] would compare favorably" with those in the West. He mentioned 216 "of the second rank," no description provided, and oratories that had been "built in the Chinese style."[95] One decade into the twentieth century, a statistical summary of Vincentian work in Zhili North distinguished worship places by type as "European churches, public chapels, and oratories." Terminology varies a bit: another report specifies "Large European churches, smaller churches,

94   Archives CM, Paris, Folder 164-I-b, "Congrégation de la Mission, dite des Lazaristes. Province de Chine. Tableau Général de l'État des Missions et des Résultats obtenus pendant l'Exercice, 1897–1898." In a Latin-language report, usage switched to "*Ecclesiæ propriedictæ; oratoria publica; oratoria private.*" Archives CM, Paris, Folder 168-I-a, "Vicariatus Apostolicus Pekini et Tche-ly Septentrionalis. Fructus Spirituales, 1904–1905."
95   Favier letter, 4 October 1899, *Annals CM-E* 7 (1900): 220–222.

and Chinese oratories."[96] Western missionaries knew exactly what sacred structures were and what they should look like.

3.4 Types (Styles)

Vincentian priests evidently thought in terms of type, depending of course on funding. As noted, those of the first rank were large (and more expensive to build) European looking structures. In general, what urban and rural ones had in common was a distinctive façade that included a cross on the roof's anterior apex or atop its steeple or its bell tower, all distinctive architectural elements of European inspiration, one of which was usually present.[97] Behind the façade was a relatively low-profile building of one to three stories tall with brick walls on a stone foundation covered by a gable roof, constructed by local workers under the supervision of a priest acting as an on-site "general contractor" (in modern terms).[98] Priests conceived of them in Western design terms that began simply and then became more intricate and larger, depending on the era, location, and, once again, funding. Many people (then and now) have labeled these European-style churches as "Gothic style" (gete shi), as did, for example, an 1895 newspaper report stating that the proposed cathedral for the treaty port of Jiujiang, Jiangxi would be built "in the Ogival (Gothic) style."[99]

---

96 Archives CM, Paris, Folder 168-I-a, "Mission de Pékin et Tche-ly Nord, Confiée aux Lazaristes, Fruits Spirituels, du 1er Juillet 1908 au Juin 1909" and "Vicariat Apostolique de Péking et Tche-ly Nord, Tableau Comparatif, 1889–1899." A new vicariate in Zhili/Hebei used two classifications: "Églises proprement dites" and "Chapelles et Oratoires." Archives CM, Paris, Folder 164-I-a, "Congrégation de la Mission, dite des Lazaristes. Vicariate Apostolique de Yungpingfu. Tableau Général de l'État des Missions et des Résultats obtenus du 1er Juillet 1926 au 30 Juin 1927."

97 A Jesuit in Zhili commented that "All our churches are surmounted with a large cross, which can be seen all over the plain. We feel less strange in China since we can, from distance to distance, rest our eyes on the cross of our dear Saviour. It is a sweet consolation, particularly in the infidel countries." "China," Annals PF 28 (1867): 328. The psychological role of crosses as a morale booster to Western missionaries must not be ignored. In this regard, the voice of Chinese Catholics is seldom heard. At present, individuals display crosses inside homes to show their faith and do not hide it from kith and kin. Cross pendants have become popular, worn to demonstrate publicly one's religious affiliation.

98 Missionaries occasionally commented that the Chinese workers employed in building churches had no skill in stone working or implementing designs unfamiliar to them, implying that this limited grandiose architectural projects. In Hunan, the bishop commented in the mid-1860s that Fr. Pascal Capezzuto, o.f.m., had directed a church's erection and that "he was obliged to handle both hammer and sculptor's chisel while teaching the labourers, who had no idea of this kind of building." Navarro letter, 16 February 1866, Annals PF 28 (1867): 85.

99 These details are notable: first, Fr. Élisée-Louis Fatiguet, C.M., served as its architect; and second, the granite church would be 177 feet in length, 49 feet wide at its center point,

Such descriptions customarily referred to the pointed arches over doors and windows as well as (faux) ribbed interior ceilings, even though the buildings lacked the distinctive high thick walls, flying buttresses, and other features of those in Europe.[100] In general usage, Gothic seems to have meant (and still does) simply and vaguely "(old) European style."[101]

Semantics aside, the churches Vincentians built had few if any Chinese architectural features. On the other hand, their chapels were usually in the style of Chinese residential houses because occupation of an existing building constituted the quickest and most economical way to establish a place of worship. Regarding the typical rural chapel, the bishop of the Vicariate of Jiangxi North remarked in the early 1910s that "if the exterior form of the little structure is considered, nothing will be found to distinguish it from the secular house of the country."[102] As circumstance permitted, priests did construct chapels using locally available materials and workers to save time and money. The laborers they hired tended to know only what they always built, that is, the residential style of their home area and the construction techniques to that end. Priests went along because they always hoped for the congregation to grow and need a large, formal place of worship, for which their bishop would find the funds.

<hr />

with two front towers 75 feet high. Bray letter, 2 December 1895, *Annals CM-E* 3 (1896): 197–198.

100 Other factors limited the construction of tall Gothic-like churches, one being the lack of or, when available, the expense of quarried stone; another being the on-site priest's architectural expertise; a third, the skill level of the local labor force. One Jesuit priest stationed in southeastern Zhili commented that Chinese workers "have no conception of European architecture" and required constant supervision. Missionaries by necessity became "at the same time architect, builder, and mason." "China," *Annals PF* 28 (1867): 327–328. As such, they naturally tended to replicate the style of their particular home countries, now called Gothic Revival and Neo-Gothic. César Guillén-Nuñez, "Rising from the Ashes: The Gothic Revival and the Architecture of the 'New' Society of Jesus in Macao and China" in *Jesuit Survival and Restoration: A Global History, 1773–1900*, ed. Robert A. Maryks and Jonathan Wright (Leiden: Brill, 2015), 278–298.

101 Yang Qingyun discusses European architectural styles and posits that many churches in China show Gothic influence. By that she means one with a tower, steep spires, tall and thin pointed windows of stained glass, and columns. *Beijing Tianzhujiao shi* (Beijing: Zongjiao wenhua chubanshe, 2009), 126–134. A French observer comments that the style of restored churches in modern-day China is often "*pseudo-gothique*," and that this does not bother the government authorities who look at them as historical monuments and tourist sites. Joseph Bierchane, "Urbanisme et églises chinoises." *Églises d'Asie* 5 (November 2008): 70–71. That is to say, we may be concerned with the buildings themselves or "with opinions about the buildings." Elucidation between statement and opinion is necessary. Paul Frankl, *Gothic Architecture*, revised by Paul Crossley (New Haven: Yale University Press, 2000), 31.

102 "In the Country of Blessed Clet," *Annals PF* 76 (1913): 146.

A 1927 issue of *Catholic Missions and Annals of the Propagation of the Faith* stressed three important reasons, applicable worldwide, for building chapels for small congregations. First, they provided an appropriate place for the worship of God; second, they constituted "a means of increasing the devotion of native converts, and, perhaps, of winning others over to the Faith;" and third, chapels represented evangelical progress in a particular mission district, progress that would ultimately lead to the creation of a parish and diocese. In terms of appearance, it followed the architectural style of the country in which it was built. Unfortunately, the author mistakenly wrote that "the chapel in China is constructed somewhat along the lines of a pagoda, although it is easily distinguished from a pagan temple."[103] The publication reflects the Church's renewed interest in strengthening an indigenous Faith in accordance with its location. Unknown or forgotten was the fact that a few mid-nineteenth century Vincentian missionaries in China had out of expediency used Buddhist temples (which they called pagodas) temporarily as chapels, a practice soon discontinued because residential-type chapels gave way to a European-style church as soon as possible.[104]

3.5   *Sites*

Vincentian missionaries sought converts wherever they went, adjusting their travel to the political environment that defined the legality of their residency and therefore their freedom of movement. During the long span of the Qing dynasty, Beijing attracted priests because of its high concentration of powerful figures and large population. Employment by the emperor, whether in the Directorate of Astronomy or as court painters and tutors, presented them with the opportunity to open churches. Missionaries hoped that their status in the capital would translate into tolerance by government officials stationed in the empire's provincial capitals, prefectural-level cities, and county seats. If they could build sacred structures in or near administrative centers, they reasoned they could freely proselytize in the surrounding countryside. Political tolerance for Christianity waxed and waned: the literal rise and fall of churches was the reality until the 1858–1860 Sino-Western treaties created a modus vivendi that gave missionaries the right to rent and buy property to serve as church sites in any burg or hamlet in the empire. Despite treaty-specified protection, through the end of the nineteenth century property site disputes remained a contentious issue between uncooperative government officials and demanding

---

103   "Be It Ever So Humble," *Cath-M Annals PF* 4, no. 12 (December 1927): 366–367, 378.
104   Anouilh letter, 16 January 1866, *Annals PF* 28 (1867): 371.

priests.[105] The former preferred not to have them located within walled administrative centers because officials wanted to avoid contact with missionaries, all of whom they often found troublesome, thinking that one church's existence would inevitably lead to its multiplication in surrounding areas. Missionaries' relentless pressure, supported by Western diplomats in Beijing, led officialdom by the early twentieth century to concede the matter of site selection, priests unimpededly acquiring property to build on from a willing seller.

Concomitant with the Qing government's loss of control over sites for churches (zoning, in modern parlance), officials exercised virtually no influence on the size, height, and style of those that went up. In short, there was no building code and no civil building department existed to exercise any inspection control over new buildings. The difference between those constructed by Western missionaries and buildings erected by local Chinese, especially those in rural settings, was that the former were the tallest, largest, and nicest ones around—churches' physical and visual impact could not have been greater. Moreover, in urban and rural locales, many were the central and eye-dominating feature of an active mission compound that typically occupied an acre or more of space—a big footprint, often the locale's biggest.

3.6   Orientation

When it came time to lay out a church's foundation—that is, to determine its physical orientation, its axis—missionaries typically did not concern themselves with how well its placement affected the people of the area's understanding of its geomancy and attendant energy (qi) channels and flows, all of which they deemed deeply rooted superstitions. Geomancy was in fact a double-edge sword: concessions to it or incorporation of it into plot plans implied abidance with an unacceptable practice, though ignoring *fengshui* might cause unintended complications. Lay Catholics had trouble discerning exactly how *fengshui* conflicted with their religious beliefs but knew that in a community setting their non-Christian neighbors would blame a misplaced church, and them, for any deleterious natural occurrence. If people saw a building as improperly located, they might attribute to this everything from bad weather to inadequate harvests. A bishop in Shanxi Province said that "our church is looked upon by [local people] as a threat of ruin, which keeps

---

105   Property acquisition procedures and ownership issues plagued the nineteenth century's last four decades. The 1865 agreement known as the Berthemy Convention clarified that property purchased by missionaries would be owned by the local Catholics. In 1895, the Gérard Convention clarified that sellers did not need to give local officials prior notification of the sale and that regular registration fees would apply. Sweeten, *Christianity in Rural China*, 102–107.

off ... the wind and water of prosperity."[106] Nineteenth-century Chinese government documents indeed disclose that local antagonism to churches based on geomancy occurred regularly.[107] Missionary sources seldom mention community opposition except to say that the issue of *fengshui* seemed too easily trumped up.

This bias aside, when one visits surviving old churches that have retained original security walls and gates one may observe that priests apparently tolerated some local practices and traditions even though they tried to reject all superstitious and geomantic beliefs.[108] Priests built sacred structures at the villages (*cun*) of Xiheying and Yongning on a north-south axis with the main gate of the surrounding wall to each not aligning directly with their south entrances, an obvious concession related to the proper location of buildings' doors and walls' gates and the flow of "energy" through them.[109] At the same time, tangential beliefs that local "spirits" could not move in straight paths led to the erection of offset entryways or obstacles such as brick screens in front of gates to block them. A diagram of the complex reveals that such screens existed at the South Church in the eighteenth century.

Missionaries adapted in another way to the Chinese tradition that important buildings be laid out on a north-south axis. From the imperial palace, where the three main outer halls lined up north to south (with the emperor's throne in each facing south), to government offices at all levels this alignment was a construction norm. The south was a propitious direction as was the east, with traditional preferences for each permeating Chinese culture.[110] More often than not, missionaries from the seventeenth to the twentieth century used a north-south alignment for churches with the chancel in the northern

---

106   Mocacagatta letter, [no day given] June 1873, *Annals PF* 35 (1874): 332.

107   Sweeten, *Christianity in Rural China*, 120–128.

108   Instructions on building sacred structures, published by Jesuits in Hebei in 1926, advises missionaries to pay "attention to rational reasons related to climate and hush up the Chinese traditional rules of space arrangement based on the flow of energy and the harmony with the environment (*fengshui*)." Thomas Coomans, "A pragmatic approach to church construction in Northern China at the time of Christian inculturation: the handbook 'Le missionnaire constructeur', 1926." *Frontiers of Architectural Research* 3 (2014): 94–95. Going another step, one scholar concludes that it "had been decidedly hostile toward [an] indigenous style," a situation remedied by a manual in 1941 that provided "the technical knowledge required for adapting the Chinese style to religious architecture." *Handbook of Christianity in China, Volume Two*, 735.

109   At the two places mentioned, the old gates have survived and are still used alongside newer ones.

110   In imperial times the east represented civil activities that were ranked above military matters associated with the west.

section and the main entrance in the southern part. This constituted a basic difference with the European Catholic penchant for building sacred edifices on an east-west axis.[111]

In the earliest Catholic churches in China, men and women did not attend services together and often had separate places of worship. Later, when they are allowed under the same roof for religious services, the matter of former practices and directional preferences was present. Worshippers segregated themselves with men on one side of the nave, women on the other.[112] According to a commonly-practiced traditional Chinese view, "the left [is for] men, the right [is for] women" (*zuonan younü*). In pre-1949 China, Catholic men sat together on the nave's left side, the culturally propitious east side: women sat opposite them.[113] (The seating arrangement may still be observed in rural areas.) Missionaries accepted the north-south and left-right traditions, which led them to consider related matters such as where to appropriately place, in relation to the main altar, side chapels to Mary, certain saints, and angels. In the case of the second South Church, we may observe how they did this in Chapter 3's section on that sacred structure. A detailed discussion of the religio-cultural significance of these matters will not be pursued here.

3.7   Numbers

Most enumerations of sacred structures in Beijing, Tianjin, and Zhili/Hebei indicate a slow steady growth with few fluctuations. The first half of the seventeenth century is the easiest to review because of the miniscule numbers involved. In 1611, only one church stood inside Beijing (and none outside of it). The 1643–1644 collapse of the Ming dynasty in North China meant a time of

---

111   "In [Europe of] the past, all church buildings faced east, and it is still the case for eastern Orthodox churches today. A person who enters the church goes from west to east, which symbolizes going from the evil of the present world to the glory of the New Jerusalem to come." "Architecture and Furnishings," http://www.kencollins.com/glossary/architecture .htm (accessed 15 October 2015).

112   In pre-modern China, Buddhist temples sometimes banned women from entering when men were present; more commonly women were allowed to enter and burn incense and worship separately, without the use of partitions to enforce separation from men. All through the nineteenth century, Protestant missionaries grappled with the issue of mixed gender worship with some denominations installing screens or partitions to ensure that men and women sat apart. One study concludes that "segregation of the sexes in [Protestant] church life affected women's participation and leadership in the Christian community as a whole." Partitions, when present, "reestablished the gender distinction in society." Pui-lan Kwok, *Chinese Women and Christianity, 1860–1927* (Atlanta: Scholars Press, 1992), 70–74, 94 n. 21, 95 n. 29. How Catholic women were affected awaits exploration.

113   This assumes a south-facing perspective with the left corresponding to the east.

FIGURE 2.13   Women sitting on pews on the west side, Baoding cathedral. From the chancel
facing the entrance, this is the right.
SOURCE: PHOTO BY AUTHOR, 2016

FIGURE 2.14   Same seating preference, Xiwanzi church
SOURCE: PHOTO BY FRIEND OF AUTHOR, 2018

sociopolitical instability that limited the establishment of places of worship. As the Qing consolidated power, Catholicism expanded. One listing for 1663, places three in Beijing and one in Zhili out of thirty-two for the entire empire.[114] Many places of worship were small, temporary chapels or oratories—and not formally tabulated. About a half-century later in the 1720s, there were four in Beijing and three in Zhili's countryside (out of about 130 empire-wide). During the long period of proscription, maintenance proved extremely difficult and it became very hard to establish new ones.[115] A nadir was reached in the late 1830s when Beijing's Western missionary presence shrank to one, as did the number of its churches. Outside the city, as already mentioned, one stood at Xiwanzi. It served as a mission center, a place of refuge for the handful of missionaries and Chinese priests still in North China. Another stood at Anjia Village because of its sizeable congregation. The locations of a few other chapels and oratories are currently unknown. With the mid-1840s edicts of toleration Catholic missionaries succeeded in constructing churches and chapels, only to have most of them destroyed due to the turmoil generated by the large-scale rebellions of the 1850s.[116]

After 1860 churches became so numerous and geographically widespread that it is almost startling. Quantification is difficult due to ongoing domestic

114   Ferreux, *Histoire de la Congrégation*, 76. Statistics for the seventeenth and eighteenth centuries do not always distinguish between churches and chapels.
115   The bishop reported that for all of Jiangxi in 1840, there were only eighteen chapels. Rameaux letter, 25 March 1840, *Annales CM-F* 6 (1840): 353. Two of the eighteen may have been churches, as he seems to conflate the terms.
116   One source puts the number of "churches and chapels" for China in 1848 at 326 (most of which were chapels not evenly distributed and not easily counted). "Missions of China in the XIXth Century," *Annals PF* 10 (1849): 19–20. In Zhejiang Province, the Vincentian bishop's "state of the mission" summary for 1848 notes that only four chapels had been built from 1847 to 1848. He knew the location of Ningbo's former church, and that it dated to the Kangxi emperor's reign, but did not have funds for construction of it or even a small chapel. Lavaissière letters, 27 July 1847 and 6 October 1848, *Annales CM-F* 14 (1849): 236–260, 543–565. In 1854, Bishop François-Xavier Danicourt, C.M., wrote that there were only "twenty-six congregations, and five humble chapels" in the province. Buddhist monks had control of a "splendid church [site], with numerous dwellings and a spacious garden" that Jesuit priests had built many years earlier. Catholics in Ningbo, a treaty port since 1842, still used "two old Chinese houses, of unequal sizes, and connected together" as a chapel. Danicourt letter, 8 May 1854, *Annals PF* 15 (1854): 316–317. Without doubt, the Taiping situation delayed church construction in many places, including Ningbo. A visiting priest wrote in 1860 of "the little chapel for the Europeans" and that a "large and beautiful church [was] shortly to be built" at the site. Guillemin letter, 10 September 1860, *Annals PF* 12 (1861): 94. Regarding the Taiping's impact on Jiangxi, see Anot letter, 15 July 1859, *Annales CM-F* 25 (1860): 183–196 and extracts from it in *Annals PF* 21 (1860): 249–256.

turmoil and inconsistent reporting methods (new terminology and categories) between religious societies as well as between individual priests and bishops. One bishop provides a number for "churches, properly defined," chapels, and oratories, while another combines "churches and chapels" together. Lists frequently changed as thousands of places of worship across China vanished during the Boxer Uprising (1899–1900), Sino-Japanese War (1937–1945), Civil War (1945–1949), and Cultural Revolution (1966–1976). Beginning in the early 1980s, and particularly from the late 1990s onward due to a robust economy with rising per capita income, Catholics have enthusiastically restored many "lost" churches and constructed numerous brand-new ones. C.P.A.'s three-year project (2000–2003) to assemble a photographic collection of churches across China, counted five thousand six hundred official or registered sacred structures and a 2010 study found almost six thousand.[117] A surge of construction over the last decade makes the current number much larger. Any attempt to tally the sacred structures of the "unofficial Church" is fraught with difficulties and virtually impossible.

3.8   Chronological Categories

Churches for Beijing, Tianjin, and Zhili/Hebei may be chronologically categorized as follows: 1) pre-1900 ones, of which only a very limited number escaped the Boxer conflagration and still stand—individual congregations are proud of the senior status of these churches but are often unaware of similarly old sacred structures in other dioceses;[118] 2) post-1900 replacements that local Catholics built relatively soon after the Boxer Uprising at the same sites as their predecessors and which are often of the same architectural style as those burned; and 3) 1901–1949 era churches, that is, those constructed during this period. Those of these three categories all suffered heavy damage during the Cultural Revolution and those that survived have been extensively renovated or rebuilt to resemble their former appearance. 4) post-1979 ones entirely of

117   *Shengdian xinmao*, 3 vols. (Beijing: Zhongguo qingnian chubanshe, 2003), 1: foreword, 165. The Chinese Academy of Social Sciences reported a total of "5,967 churches or prayer centres." The latter are not defined. Anthony Lam Sui-ky, "The Decline of China's Catholic Population and its Impact on the Church," http://www.asianews.it/news-en/The-declin e-of-China%E2%80%99s-Catholic-population-and-its-impact-on-the-Church-38373 .html (accessed 16 February 2018).
118   I base this on numerous conversations with Catholics in rural Hebei over the last two decades.

recent construction are mostly at locations in the countryside. These rural congregations tend to be self-contained with only occasional contact with other
parishes.[119]

• • •

Missionaries like Mouly saw the Catholic Church's situation change from proscription to that of the treaty era, when Vincentian confreres went where they
pleased, caring for Catholics, baptizing new ones, and opening sacred structures as needed at rustic sites. Vicariates, like biological cells, divided and then
divided again, each generation more vibrant than the previous. Churches in
villages became more common than before with many laid out on a north-
south axis—without consultation with geomancers or locals. The narrative
above has provided the general background and socio-cultural factors that are
helpful to an in-depth investigation of specific old churches dealt with in the
chapters that follow.

---

119   A priest told me that he ignored diocesan matters that did not involve him, including
      those of neighboring parishes. He did not want others to see him as overstepping his
      authority or as being mettlesome. Author's field notes, 28 September 2011.

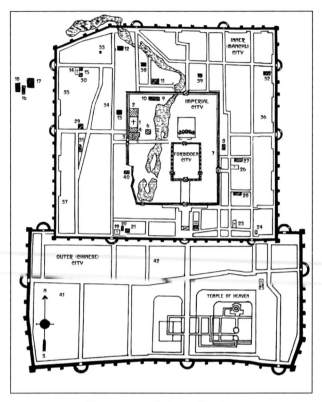

MAP 3.1   "Etablissements Catholiques de Pékin, 1950."

With minor adjustments to the original, the locations of Catholic-owned proper-ties are indicated. Due to the scale, nothing can be revealed about lot sizes and number of buildings, which ranged from a small chapel on a tiny lot to the North Church's huge footprint. Collectively, the Catholic Church owned more property and buildings, by square footage and with a higher value, than any other transna-tional entity in Beijing.

SOURCE: ARCHIVES CM, PARIS

1. North Church, Minor Seminary, Lazarist Press (Vincentians—V); 2. Orphanage (Daughters of Charity—DC); 3. St. Vincent Hospital (DC); 4. Sisters of St. Joseph (S S-J); 5. Girls Normal School (S S-J); 6. Sacred Heart Secondary School (Marist Brothers—MB); 7. Apostolic Delegation; 8. Synodal Commission; 9. Normal School (MB); 10. Girls Secondary School (DC); 11. Furen Catholic University (original site); 12. Girls Secondary School (Sisters of the Holy Spirit); 13. House of Studies (Scheutists); **14. West Church (V)**; 15. Girls School (S S-J); 16. Zhalan Church (V); 17. Regional Major Seminary (V); 18. MB Institute; **19. South Church (V)**; 20. Girls School (S S-J); 21. Secondary School (MB); 22. St. Michael's Hospital (DC); **23. St. Michael's Church (V)**; 24. Secondary School (MB); **25. Nangangzi Church (V); 26. East Church (V)**; 27. Old Folks Home (DC); 28. Sacred Heart School (Franciscan Sisters of Mary); 29. City Hospital (DC's until 1943); 30. Young Girls School (S S-J); 31. Chapel (V); 32. Trappists; 33. Boys School (Salesians); 34.–37. Chapels (V); 38. Jesuits; 39. Chapel (Franciscans); 40. Passionists; 41.–42. Chapels (V).

CHAPTER 3

The Historic Churches of Central Beijing

The Ming dynasty's Yongle emperor made Beijing his capital in the early fifteenth century, a decision that led to the construction of an enormous wall-enclosed palace complex (the Forbidden City), which was at the center of another walled area (the Imperial City) filled with government offices, important temples, and high officials' residences as well as parks and lakes.[1] A third set of formidably high walls surrounded both and protected additional residential space; later it would be termed the Inner City because in the sixteenth century a section that adjoined the city to the south, secured by extending the outer wall, became the Outer City. When the Manchus, a Northeast Asian people, militarily expanded southward into China in 1643, they took control of the Forbidden City, with their emperor occupying its throne the next year.[2] High-ranking Manchus followed suit as they relocated to the Imperial City, enjoying its conveniences and appreciating the security that came with bannermen's (i.e., soldiers' and their families') exclusive occupation of the Inner City, a situation made possible by the expulsion of its Han residents to the Outer City.[3] Segregation included exceptions, notably that of Catholic missionaries who built their most important sacred structures in different parts of the capital: one in the Imperial City, four in the Inner City, and one in the Outer City. These areas are treated as central Beijing.[4]

---

1 The emperor, his family, and concubines lived in the Forbidden City's opulent residences surrounded by beautiful courtyard gardens. Three huge halls were nearby for ceremonial functions and hundreds of other buildings for use by support staff. Situated to the palace's south, just outside the Imperial City (the area is now part of Tiananmen Square), were the central government's six main administrative ministries or boards.

2 Later Qing emperors preferred to live at and govern from the Summer Palace (the Yuanmingyuan, and, later, the Yiheyuan) and the more distant Mountain Villa in Rehe (Chengde). Some spent time in the traveling palaces that accompanied them when they went to the homeland's capital at Shenyang (Mukden) or on grand tours of the empire.

3 I use the terms Inner and Outer Cities for both the Ming and Qing periods. During the former era, people knew them as the Northern and Southern Cities, respectively. During the Qing, they were also known as the Manchu and Chinese Cities according to their primary occupants. Nanquin, *Peking*, 128–136, 290–292.

4 In other words, the area that is within the Second Ring Road. The modern city can be roughly divided into the "Central Urban Area" (everything inside the Sixth Ring Road) and the "Outer Suburbs [and] Count[ies]." *Beijing chengshi dituji* (Beijing: Dizhi chubanshe, 2008), inside cover and iii–iv.

© KONINKLIJKE BRILL NV, LEIDEN, 2020 | DOI:10.1163/9789004416185_004

After the abdication of the young Xuantong emperor (reigned from late 1908 to early 1912), Beijing's political position temporarily declined as militarists ruled China in fragmented fashion for over two decades. General Jiang Jieshi (Chiang Kai-shek) emerged as a unifying force in 1927 and formed a Nationalist government in Nanjing. Just ten years later Japan invaded, and a terrible war ensued until 1945. During these years and the four-year civil war that followed, Beijing escaped mostly unscathed. With Mao Zedong's announcement of the People's Republic of China's birth on 1 October 1949 Beijing resumed its place as the nation's capital. Soon to be a national-level municipality administered directly by the central government, the city's transformation began with projects that affected forever its landmarks.[5] In the 1960s, city planners ordered the Imperial, Inner, and Outer Cities' walls dismantled to create space for broad avenues, leaving behind only several large gate-towers as historical monuments. Although in post-revolutionary Beijing the Forbidden City continued to serve as China's iconic landmark, the removal of numerous buildings to its south opened up a huge area known as Tiananmen Square.[6] Elsewhere in the city, multi-storied apartment buildings replaced courtyard houses and neighborhoods changed. Beijing has slowly morphed into a modern city of high-rises with six historic churches in their shadows.

These sacred structures, the oldest surviving in Beijing and among the oldest in all of China, are the subject of this chapter. Individually, they have interesting historical and visual stories to share. Collectively, they provide a way to understand Christianity's presence, development, and role during times of dynastic change as well as war and revolution. Information available for each tends to be uneven, coming from a variety of sources and periods, their narratives varying accordingly in depth and length. All them are open to the public and this study has greatly benefited from my repeated visits to take photographs and appreciate their ambience. Below, the discussion is divided into two sections; the first deals with Beijing's original four sites and the second covers two churches that date to the early twentieth century.

---

5   The change in status came in 1954. Its geographic area of sixty-nine hundred square miles includes rural areas once under the jurisdiction of Hebei.
6   In 1925, officials opened parts of the Forbidden City to the public as the Palace Museum (Gugong). For insights into Beijing and what it represents spatially, see Hung Wu, *Remaking Beijing: Tiananmen Square and the Creation of a Political Space* (Chicago: University of Chicago Press, 2005).

1 The Original Four

The churches appear here based on the chronology of each one's first itera-tion. The South Church is the earliest, dating to the seventeenth century's first decade, followed by the East, North, and West Churches.[7] None of the sacred structures stand as initially built. Currently, the oldest structure dates to 1888 and the others to 1904, 1905, 1913, and 1923. Since they are reconstructions and renovations, one objective is to outline their respective histories with atten-tion to architectural details. Another goal is to determine how they changed over time and how to interpret the changes. At one time each site included additional support structures such as lodging, kitchens, schools, and foundling homes, most of which are no longer present or have been completely rebuilt. Church infrastructure, though necessary and important to proselytization, is not investigated. Prior to 1949, some churches had property at detached loca-tions, for example, chapels and cemeteries at Zhalan and Zhengfu si. Likewise, there were chapels for the Daughters of Charity of St. Vincent de Paul and other religious groups. These and buildings associated with them, most now gone, are treated only in passing.

1.1 The South Church (Nantang)

Encountering countless difficulties as he traveled overland from south China, Fr. Matteo Ricci, S.J., arrived at Beijing in 1601, four years later purchasing prop-erty near Xuanwu, the gate in the southwestern sector that allowed passage between the Inner and Outer Cities. He established a residence that included a small oratory; then, when baptisms increased to several hundred, opened two public chapels, one for men and dedicated to the Holy Savior and the other for women and devoted to Our Lady—Chinese custom at Buddhist temples pre-cluded gender mixing and this carried over to Catholic worship.[8] The chapels

---

7   The first South Church is the earliest of the Ming-Qing era, pre-dated by one built in 1299 by a Franciscan (John of Montecorvino) at the Yuan dynasty capital of Khanbaliq situated near modern-day Beijing. Little is known about it except that there was a tower whose three bells rang out at canonical hours. Paul Stanislaus Hsiang, *The Catholic Missions in China during the Middle Ages (1294–1368)* (1949; reprint, Cleveland: John T. Zubal, 1984), 2, 4–5, 9 n. 38, 14.

8   This continued to be the case during the early nineteenth century. Joseph-Martial Mouly remarked in 1836 that men and women worshipped separately and that it was "strictly observed at Pekin, where [women] had their private oratories or chapels." Mouly letter, 6 November 1836, *Annals PF*, old series (1838): 404. To Chinese opposed to Christianity in the late nineteenth century, and in the inflammatory publications they used to promote action against missionaries, men and women worshipping together constituted a taboo. A print that depicts this is in *The Cause of the Riots in the Yangtse Valley. A "Complete Picture Gallery"* (Hankow: n.p., 1891), "Picture III".

probably took over existing residential buildings due to availability and finances. Ricci, fluent in Chinese and talented in so many ways, worked with a few other priests and together they attracted more people to Catholicism.

The First South Church (1611–1651).[9] In 1610, Ricci started construction on a sacred edifice but death prevented him from seeing its completion the next year.[10] According to his confrere, Fr. Sabatino De Ursis, S.J., Ricci had planned to build a temple-like structure in Chinese style but changed his mind and modified its design to resemble a small version of the churches found in Europe. One scholar suggests that Ricci thought Chinese Christians and non-followers alike needed a taste of European-church style and did not want it confused with Buddhist places of worship.[11] The church was surely a modest structure because the Jesuits did not have any special status, nor the funds for something grandiose that imperial authorities certainly would have prohibited. In any case, Jesuits preferred simple and elegant, some would say "utilitarian," architecture, as exhibited in their mother-church (Chiesa del Gesù) completed in 1584 in Rome,[12] Not just by European style alone did Beijing's first church distinguish itself from Beijing's Buddhist temples, it also received the newly conferred name, tianzhutang, Chinese for Christian church or, simply, church.

Little is known about its construction, completed by hired labor, nor its cost. Following Ricci's vision, De Ursis supervised the erection of a building that measured fifty feet long by twenty-five wide.[13] Its height is unknown, though it must have been a low-profile building comparable to those within the Inner City, because anything tall would have altered Beijing's unexceptional skyline and been noted by either residents or visitors. Neither a lack of size nor verticality meant the church was devoid of features. Its façade had arched doors and windows, and "large cornices and classical attics or ornamental finishes that Chinese workers found difficult to construct."[14] In the end, de Uris prevailed with a distinctive European style that had the correct profile for Beijing.

---

9   I refer to it as the South Church for this period even though the name did not become current until 1702.

10   For it and others, I use the year of completion, typically the same year it was dedicated, as its start date.

11   César Guillén-Nuñez, "Matteo Ricci, the Nantang, and the Introduction of Roman Catholic Church Architecture to Beijing," in Portrait of a Jesuit: Matteo Ricci, 1552–1610 (Macau: Macau Ricci Institute, 2010), 105.

12   Ibid.

13   Guillén, "Matteo Ricci," 105. Another source provides slightly smaller dimensions of forty-five feet by twenty-four. Gail King, "Note on a Late Ming Dynasty Chinese Description of 'Ricci's Church' in Beijing," Sino-Western Cultural Relations Journal 20 (1998): 50.

14   Guillén, "Matteo Ricci," 105–106.

Significantly, he and his confreres had successfully established Christianity in the capital in the form of a public place of worship.

The Second South Church (1651–1775). In the Ming dynasty's last year (1643) at Beijing, Li Zicheng's rebel forces rampaged through the city somehow missing the church.[15] That same year Manchus expelled them, restored order, and continued expansion of their empire. With enthronement in the Forbidden City of a young Fulin (who reigned as the Shunzhi emperor, 1644–1661), regents began assembling the personnel needed to operate a hybrid Manchu-Chinese Confucian government. Fr. Johann Adam Schall von Bell, S.J., in Beijing since 1623 and previously an official of the Ming court, made his various skills in cannon making, mathematics, and astronomy known to the Manchus, who found him eminently qualified to supervise the compilation of the state calendar they deemed crucial for the timely performance of official rites integral to the administration of a harmonious empire. Schall's fine work at the Directorate of Astronomy, which he eventually supervised, and his deep knowledge of other subjects created a reputation that led to meetings with a curious and quickly maturing emperor. A relationship developed and in it Schall perceived an opportunity to replace one of the chapels that dated to Ricci's era. He sought and received an imperial donation of nearby property for the construction of a larger replacement that took form during 1650–1651.[16] The unknown amount of funds used to build it had come from either the emperor or high officials with nothing donated by local people.[17]

From a contemporaneous description of the church, its size and style indicate the start of a new period in construction. Schall had designed one bigger than Ricci's, approximately eighty-five feet in length by forty-eight feet wide with an estimated height ranging from forty-nine to sixty-five feet.[18] A cross on the roof's anterior pitch added further to the church's vertical stature and its stone face included Baroque-style ornamentation. A visiting priest saw it in 1652 and commented that "in the church's façade, new and quite beautiful, there are three large stone niches that explain in inscribed Chinese characters the three stages of divine law: natural law, codified law, and the law of grace."[19]

15   Bornet, "Les anciennes églises … Nant'ang [part 1]," 493.
16   Ibid., 492–494. What became of the 1611 building is unknown.
17   Guillén, "Matteo Ricci," 107.
18   Bornet, "Les anciennes églises … Nant'ang [part 1]," 494. Guillén's measurements are similar (eighty feet by forty-five); height is not mentioned. "Portrait of a Jesuit," 107. Bornet does not explain the height range, moreover, sixty-five feet tall seems quite high given Beijing's one or two-story norm.
19   Paul Bornet, "Les anciennes églises de Pékin: supplément," *Bulletin catholique de Pékin* 32 (1945): 246.

Windows adorned the front and sides, giving the interior natural light. Two rows of columns supported the roof while dividing the interior into a central nave and two side aisles. Over the sanctuary was a dome-like ceiling.[20] The sacred structure sat behind a walled enclosure just like government offices, temples, and the homes of the wealthy. Walls, of course, required gates, usually situated at points of the compass. Following tradition, an arched entranceway intersected the south wall and immediately within it was a large courtyard, about one hundred feet to each side, adjoining the front of the church.

In pre-modern Europe, a Catholic church's chancel was usually in the eastern part of the building and its entrance in the western section.[21] Schall laid out his on a north-south axis because he understood that Chinese cultural convention called for important buildings to have such an alignment. This situated the chancel in the structure's northern part and the principal entrance in the southern section.[22] The axis used had an impact on the location of the side chapels and altars.[23] In Schall's Church of the Holy Savior, the chapel for St. Ignatius of Loyola was located on the east side and St. Francis Xavier's was on the west. To the Jesuits on hand, this seemed "an unusual placement," but Schall knew that it properly conveyed to Chinese, who considered east above west, the relatively higher status of Ignatius.[24] An eighteenth-century drawing

---

20   Bornet, "Les anciennes églises ... Nantang [part 1]," 494; and Guillén, "Matteo Ricci," 107.

21   An east-west axis has a bearing on the location for readings from the Bible. "The Epistle is the last lesson before the Gospel, the first when there are only two lessons.... It was read from an *ambo*, the reader or *subdeacon* turning towards the people.... The common arrangement was that of an *ambo* on either side of the church, between the choir and the *nave*, as may still be seen in many old *basilicas*.... In this case the *ambo* on the north side was reserved for the Gospel, from which the deacon faced the south, where the men stood.... The north is also the right, and therefore the more honourable, side of the altar. The *ambo* on the south was used for the Epistle, and for other lessons.... This arrangement still subsists, in as much as the Epistle is always read on the south side (supposing the church to be orientated)." (Italics in original.) "New Advent, Catholic Encyclopedia," http://www.newadvent.org/cathen/09193a.htm (accessed 15 October 2015).

22   Per the note above, the axis change meant, if the Gospel was read from the west side facing east, men would stand on the eastern side. When churches were opened to joint worship this fit in with placement of women on the western part.

23   In regard to the placement of the altars, Bornet parenthetically notes that to the Chinese, the right side is "less honorable." "Les anciennes églises ... Nant'ang [part 1]," 495.

24   Ignatius founded the Society of Jesus and served as its first superior general. Some consider Xavier as a cofounder; both were canonized in 1622. At the Jesuits' Church of the Gesù in Rome, laid out on the east-west axis already described, the chapel for Ignatius is located on the north ("more honorable" Gospel) side and is viewed as the masterpiece. Xavier's chapel is opposite it on the south. (At present, there are another eight chapels; they are located on either the north or south and thus implicitly ranked.) "Church of the Gesù," https://en.wikipedia.org/wiki/Church_of_the_Ges%C3%B9 (accessed 9 May 2017).

of its interior shows the location of chapels at a later time (the Annunciation of Mary and St. Michael were on the east and St. Joseph and a Guardian Angel on the west).[25]

Although Jesuits were aware of certain changes in the layout, Chinese Catholics would not have been concerned with them in the same way. In China, traditions flowed through deep societal channels, making the trope *zuonan younü* more than just a saying—it was part of everyday life.[26] Therefore, when priests eventually allowed men and women inside churches at the same time for mass, women sat in the nave on the west (or right) side.[27] Over time, Mary's chapel often shifted from east of the main altar to the west—and gained proximity to them.[28]

During the 1650s, when the Shunzhi emperor went on hunting expeditions to Nanyuan, south of the capital, he passed through the Inner City, exiting at the Xuanwu Gate. He sometimes stopped to talk with Schall about a variety of subjects, including religious matters. His large imperial entourage made the visits impossible for the area's residents to miss. To Schall, every such occasion reflected positively on the church in that it was an unusual imperial gesture and implied respect.[29] The relationship gradually deepened with the emperor

---

Guillén, "Matteo Ricci," 107–108, uses the phrase "an unusual placement" and mentions the arrangement of chapels in Schall's sacred structure.

25 It is unknown when the various altars became part of it, the earliest documentation for their arrangement dates to the eighteenth century. Wang Lianming and Francesco Maglioccola [Ma Fangji, pseud.]. "The Architectural Drawings of an Eighteenth Century Jesuit Church (Nantang) in Beijing: Analysis and Reconstruction," in *Le Vie dei Mercanti. S.A.V.E. Heritage: Safeguard of Architectural, Visual and Environmental Heritage*, ed. Carmine Gambardella (Naples: La scuola di Pitagola editrice, 2011).

26 Schall and his confreres would have known *zuonan younü*, "the left (that is, east is for) men, the right (west is for) women." See the Chapter 2 sub-section that discusses orientation.

27 After 1692, missionaries began building separate worship places for the exclusive use of women. Bornet, "Les anciennes églises ... supplément," 247–248. Guillén notes the existence of a chapel for women's use in "Matteo Ricci," 107. Later, when priests permit the two genders to worship together, physical barriers separated them with women sitting on the western side and men on the eastern side.

28 Over time in sacred structures where the main altar was not dedicated to Mary, side chapels and altars to her appeared on the western side. I have observed this in many churches. Author's field notes, 1994 to 2018.

29 A diocesan publication states that the Shunzhi emperor went twenty-four times "in plain clothes" to see the priest. *Beijing Tianzhu jiaohui*, comp. Beijing Tianzhu jiaohui bianjihui (Beijing: Zhongguo minzu sheying yishu chubanshe, 2004), item entitled "Beijing jiaoqu Xuanwu men Nantang." (This is a boxed set of thirty-three items printed to commemorate the twentieth-fifth anniversary of Fu Tieshan's bishopric.) Nanquin mentions the same number of imperial visits in *Peking*, 304–305.

calling the priest *"mafa,"* a term of address in the Manchu language reserved for one's grandfather or elder.[30] In 1653, the emperor formally bestowed on Schall a literary title (*hao*), the "Religious Master Who Comprehends the Mysterious" (Tong wei jiao shi).[31] The emperor surpassed the gesture four years later with the gift of a stone stele replete with tortoise base and inscriptions in Manchu and Chinese for erection at the church. Truly, it constituted a high honor, but measuring from the ground to top at about eight or nine feet it was not impressive in terms of height. Cost may have been a factor—and the dynasty did face financial exigencies during the 1650s. Still, it was an imperially commissioned stele, and stylistically similar to (albeit smaller than) those bestowed during the early Qing dynasty to commemorate the military exploits of deceased Manchu warriors. Due to their placement at restricted-access gravesites, heroes' stelae were very private monuments.

The church's stele, on the other hand, was erected at a site publicly accessible to worshippers and a few scholar-officials, the latter occasionally going to the South Church. Covered by a small pavilion with imperial yellow roof tiles it stood in the courtyard on the eastern (superior) side of the church's entrance. Its inscription is significant because of its author and content.[32] In its first half, the emperor recounts the historical importance of accurate calendars for China's earliest rulers and the difficulty that various dynasties had in maintaining them. Emperors needed to mark precisely the seasons in that this led to a flourishing agricultural life, the basis of societal prosperity and harmony (Confucian influenced themes). Familiarly referring to him by his Chinese given name, the Shunzhi emperor pointed out Schall's role in eliminating astronomical errors and shaping an exact calendar for the dynasty. The

---

30   "Missions of China in the XVIIth and XVIIIth Centuries," *Annals PF* 9 (1848): 298; *Eminent Chinese of the Ch'ing Period*, ed. Arthur W. Hummel, 2 vols. (1943; reprint, 2 vols. in 1, Taipei: Ch'eng-wen Publishing, 1970), 256.

31   Huang Bolu, comp., *Zheng jiao feng bao* (Shanghai: Cimu tang, 1894), 25b. Initially, the name was "Tong xuan jiao shi." The second character was part of the Kangxi emperor's personal name, Xuanye, and prohibited for others to use. A slightly different translation is the "Religious Master who Penetrates the Mysteries." There is a pre-Tang dynasty Daoist work having to do with sexual techniques entitled "Dong xuan zi," translated by one scholar as the "Book of the Mystery-Penetrating Master." Joseph Needham, *History of Scientific Thought*, vol. 2 of *Science and Civilisation in China* (Cambridge: University Press, 1956), 147–148. The book, its content obviously not relevant here, may have been known to the emperor, or his advisors, who saw Schall's deep knowledge of another field as analogous.

32   One study of the stele suggests that it may be read from three vantage points: neutral, the emperor; pro-Catholic, Schall; and anti-Catholic, Yang Guangxian. Zhu Pingyi, "Jinshimeng—'Yuzhi tianzhutang beiji' yu Qingchu de tianzhujiao," *Lishi yuyan yanjiu suo jikan* 75, no. 2 (June 2004), 396–401.

emperor then transitioned to the inscription's second half in which he lauded Schall's fine character traits, noted his deep devotion to his religion, and observed the church's non-Chinese style. Following the meaning embedded in the literary name he had given Schall, the emperor wrote that this was "a beautiful place for comprehending the mysteries" (*tong wei jia jing*). Further imperial praise singled out Schall for his diligence, respectfulness, sincerity, and goodness; in short, for being a model religious man and servant.[33] A closing, epigraphic statement seems more appropriate for Schall's tombstone, though nine years premature.[34] The emperor's personalized testament reads, in fact, like that written for the heroes who had contributed to the dynasty's founding. Whatever personal interest the Shunzhi emperor may have had in Catholicism was not expressed, because he deemed it inappropriate or irrelevant to the point of the inscription. Schall, on his part, felt grateful and recognized that such an imperial gift helped him in his mission work.

After the Shunzhi emperor's unexpected death in 1661 at the age of twenty-eight, regents ruled in the name of his seven-year old son and successor, the Kangxi emperor. The regents jealously guarded their power, saw the Jesuits as potential threats, and in late 1664 closed as well as defaced the church. As the emperor matured, he moved to assert himself in governing the empire and used missionaries as a counterweight against the entrenched regents. In 1669, Fr. Ferdinand Verbiest, S.J., headed the Directorate of Astronomy, a high position that brought him into contact with supportive officials, which undoubtedly played some part in the church's reopening.[35]

Fr. Tomás Pereira, S.J., arrived in Beijing in early January 1673, soon concluding that through expansion of the sacred structure Jesuits could exploit Chinese curiosity about it to advance their mission work.[36] With Verbiest's

---

33 This phrase had to be revised for the same reason given in note 31. For the stele's Chinese inscription, see Huang Bolu, *Zheng jiao feng bao*, 27b–29b. A loose translation of it into French is in Willem A. Grootaers, "Les anciennes églises de Pékin: Nant'ang, texte et traduction des steles Nan-t'ang," *Bulletin catholique de Pékin* 31 (1944): 586–593. Appendix 4 provides the Chinese version and my thoroughly revised translation of it.

34 Schall died in 1666. The Kangxi emperor allocated 524 taels for his tomb, a larger amount by two to three times than that given later for other missionaries who served the dynasty. Most of the large sum went towards erecting an inscribed stone tablet, the content of which was mainly his name, date, and religious affiliation. Huang Bolu, *Zheng jiao feng bao*, 62. Details on Schall's tablet are in Edward J. Malatesta and Gao Zhiyu, eds., *Departed, Yet Present: Zhalan, the Oldest Christian Cemetery in Beijing* (Macau and San Francisco: Instituto Cultural de Macau and Ricci Institute, University of San Francisco, 1995), 132–135.

35 Bornet, "Les anciennes églises ... Nan'tang [part 1]," 498.

36 Bornet dates his arrival to 1672. "Les anciennes églises ... Nant'ang [part 1]," 499. Per Guillén, he arrived in January's first week, 1673. "Matteo Ricci," 107.

agreement and occurring sometime before 1681, he merged into each side of the façade two towers of undetermined height—both in European style. In one tower, he placed a large clock along with a carillon, featuring two bells, with one announcing in a harmonious way the arrival of each hour and the other sounding the hour as well as quarter hour. The second tower housed a small organ for the playing of music.[37] In a city devoid of tall structures except for those within the Forbidden City, a few special pagodas, and the multi-storied Drum and Bell Towers that announced the time for the opening and closing of the city's gates, the church's towers had a visual and aural impact that undoubtedly attracted curious non-Christians. Verbiest consented to other, smaller scale improvements during the 1680s. His emotional not to mention financial investment in the South Church led him to call it "the mother of Peking churches and of all China," a testimony that referred not only to its position as the first one in the capital but also its prominent European-like architectural stature.[38]

During the time Verbiest and Pereira considered how to re-work the church, the Kangxi emperor had become fully confident in his monarchial position. In July 1675, he visited them and took brush in hand to write "reverence heaven" (*jing tian*), meaning "respect [or honor] God," the understanding of which has shifted over time.[39] This famous calligraphy, as much appreciation for the Jesuits' imperial service as anything else, was interpreted by missionaries as the emperor's recognition of Christianity's God. Verbiest wrote in 1681 that he had added the characters (copied and inscribed in stone) to the façade as a plaque and sent paper copies of it to churches in the provinces to display as proof that the emperor favored them.[40] This contributed to its fame, as did

---

37   Bornet, "Les anciennes églises ... Nan'tang [part 1]," 499–500; and Guillén, "Matteo Ricci," 111.

38   Ibid., 491.

39   Huang Bolu marks the year of the gift as 1671. He mentions that in 1700 a different interpretation appeared, that is, respect teachers and elders. *Zheng jiao feng bao*, 69–69b, 121. As used later by the Qianlong emperor, *jing tian* was part of an ideological guide to good government and a harmonious society. In this context, it is translated as "reverence heaven." Jeffrey F Meyer, *The Dragons of Tiananmen: Beijing as a Sacred City* (Columbia, S.C.: University of South Carolina Press, 1991), 167.

40   Bornet, "Les anciennes églises ... Nant'ang [part 1]," 498. The emperor's calligraphy, written on silk or paper, would have been mounted scroll-like and thus inappropriate for use on a church's exterior because of its delicate materials. More likely, as was the case with other imperial inscriptions, the calligraphy was traced on to stone for engraving. It is not clear if the characters *tianzhutang* were present on the façade and the exterior wall's entry gate or on both. It is also unclear if those characters prefaced by *chijian*, "built by (with) imperial order (permission)," were present. Bornet writes that they were added later. Another study agrees. Noel Golvers, *The Astronomia Europaea of Ferdinand Verbiest, S.J. (Dilligen, 1687): Text, Translation, Notes and Commentaries* (Nettetal: Steyler Verlag, 1993), 12.

the erection in 1692 of a second stone stele in the courtyard to the west of the church's entrance, opposite the one from the Shunzhi emperor. Inscribed on it was a memorial written by high officials who described various missionaries' contributions to the Qing empire, such as those by Schall and Verbiest, and a recommendation that Catholicism be left alone. With the Kangxi emperor's endorsement, it became an edict and, as such, an expression of imperial toleration for Christianity in China that lasted for several decades.[41]

Bishop Della Chiesa stayed at the South Church on his occasional visits to Beijing and made it his nominal cathedral. Missionaries took pride in this and appreciated the various imperial favors bestowed on them. Indeed, they enjoyed an enhanced position in Beijing and even an early Chinese "guidebook" noted it as a place for educated travelers to visit.[42] Word spread, as priests had earlier hoped, leading some civil service candidates, in Beijing once every three years for the metropolitan examination (the highest of the tri-level civil service examination system), to catch a glimpse of it, maybe even visit it, before departing for home. According to the Jesuits' convert-the-elite-first strategy, these future officials would through the experience of seeing the church, learning something about the religion practiced there, and becoming aware of the imperial favors given, form a positive impression and take it back to their hometowns.[43] Ever-optimistic Jesuits thought their status in Beijing would aid them in constructing places of worship in other locales.

From about 1704 until his death in 1708, Pereira devoted himself to a renovation of the façade with the help of Bro. Charles de Belleville, S.J. One new feature included the addition of a large iron cross that measured about thirteen feet in height by six and one half wide. Workers anchored it firmly in

41   Grootaers, "Les anciennes églises de Pékin," 593–599. For an analysis of the edict, see Nicolas Standaert, "The 'Edict of Tolerance' (1692): A Textual History and Reading," in *In the Light and Shadow of an Emperor: Tomás Pereira, SJ (1645–1708), the Kangxi Emperor and the Jesuit Mission in China*, eds. Artur K. Wardega and António Vasconcelos de Saldanha (Newcastle upon Tyne: Cambridge Scholars Publishing, 2012), 308–358.

42   In the late Ming, published information existed about sites to see in Beijing which included the church as well as its furnishings and religious tenets. Craig Clunas, *Pictures and Visuality in Early Modern China* (London: Reaktion Books, 1997), 173. One such book dates to 1635 with several reprints, two during the early Qing. King, "Note on … 'Ricci's Church,'" 50; and Elisabetta Corsi, "Pozzo's Treatise as a Workshop for the Construction of a Sacred Catholic Space in Beijing," in *Artifizi della metafora: saggi su Andrea Pozzo*, ed. Richard Bösel et al (Roma: Artemide, 2011), 240.

43   Bornet, "Les anciennes églises … Nant'ang [part 1]," 497. One scholar concludes that Jesuits working for the imperial court saw their various artistic, technical, and other skills "as a means to bring home their spiritual message." Harrie Vanderstappen, "Chinese Art and the Jesuits in Peking" in *East Meets West: The Jesuits in China, 1582–1773*, ed. Charles E. Ronan and Bonnie B.C. Oh (Chicago: Loyola University Press, 1988), 122.

masonry at the façade's peak.[44] As noted in Chapter 2, the Kangxi emperor
had donated ten thousand ounces of silver to the project in 1705, funds that
unquestionably helped the entire mission complex. Workers completed the
South Church in 1711.[45] That same year, the Kangxi emperor gave priests a set
of three scrolls written on fine silk brocade.[46] One inscription that became
famously important to Catholics consisted of four characters, *wan you zhen
yuan* ("the true principle of all things").[47] It served nicely on a horizontal scroll
(or plaque *biane*) flanked by the two scrolls, that is, a couplet (*duilian*), each of
eleven characters for vertical display—together they constituted a traditional
Chinese presentation. The characters on the scroll that read *wu shi wu zhong
xian zuo xing sheng zhen zhu zai* were read first with missionaries interpreting
them and their counterpart in a Christian context: "there is no beginning and
there will be no end; from the start [He] has made all things; these [He] gov-
erns and in which [He] is the true master." Those on the other one, *xuan ren
xuan yi yu zhao zheng ji da quan heng*, translate as: "[He] is infinitely good and
righteous; [He] enlightens, illustrates, and rules all with supreme authority and
sovereign justice."[48]

---

44   Bornet, Paul. "Les anciennes églises de Pékin: Nant'ang [part 3]," *Bulletin catholique de
       Pékin* 32 (1945): 26.

45   Guillén, "Matteo Ricci," 113.

46   Huang Bolu, *Zheng jiao feng bao*, 127b–128.

47   *Wan you zhen yuan* has been translated into French as "*le vrai principe de toutes choses.*"
       Bornet, "Les anciennes églises ... Nant'ang [part 1]," 501; and Bishop Alphonse Favier
       writes "*au vrai principe de toutes choses.*" Refer to his *Péking: histoire et description* (Péking
       [Beijing]: Imprimerie des Lazaristes au Pé-t'ang, 1897), 190–191. It uses photographs,
       whereas the "2nd edition" (1900) and "nouvelle edition" (1902) provide engravings of
       them. Future references to it will distinguish by providing the publication year in paren-
       thesis. See the bibliography for details.
          According to a Qing specialist on the culturally influential *Yijing* (*Book of Changes*),
       wan you zhen yuan reflects its ideas, with which the Kangxi emperor was very familiar.
       "I would say with something close to certainty he had the *Yijing* in mind when he wrote
       that inscription." Professor Richard J. Smith, email to author, 29 December 2016. That
       said, Catholics of that day read it differently, seeing it as imperial support for Christianity.
       Today, a bilingual display at the church renders the expression as "the true source of the
       universe." "Nantang jianjie" (church courtyard display, 2009); and Author's field notes,
       27 September 2009. Usually displayed horizontally, *wan you zhen yuan* is now a commonly
       found addition to façades. I believe Catholics are emphasizing a Christian message, that
       is, "the true source of everything [is found in God]."

48   Bornet, "Les anciennes églises ... Nant'ang [part 1]," 501; and Favier, *Péking* (1897), 190–191.
       The three were displayed behind the North Church's main altar until the interior renova-
       tions of 2016–2018 led to removal of the couplet. Author's field notes, 12 May 2010 and 23
       August 2018.

Priests used them to enhance further their status in Beijing in two ways. First, they displayed the items on the wall of a reception room used to receive dignitaries.[49] This was the proper place to hang the scrolls and the means by which to impress visitors. Second, and this is not entirely clear from extant records, priests may have had the emperor's words copied for inscription onto the façade's stone facing or painted on wood (in scroll-like form) for hanging on the church's exterior or in some similar fashion made part of the ornamental outer gate.[50] Missionaries called the gate a "triumphal arch" (*arc de triomphe*), and it was stylistically similar to commemorative archways (*paifang*) erected at special sites to honor specific people for virtuous behavior.[51] By openly commending virtue, they presumably enhanced public morality. If priests used the archway to display the scrolls' message, its location provided excellent exposure to the large number of people using the lane in front of the church.

Towards the end of the Kangxi emperor's long reign, an earthquake jolted Beijing in 1720. Verbiest and Pereira's solidly rebuilt South Church suffered considerable damage that took many years to repair. Restoration was also affected by the negative political climate that came with enthronement of Yinzhen (reigned as the Yongzheng emperor, 1723–1735), who proscribed Christianity—a ban lightly enforced at Beijing due to priests' continuing role at the Directorate of Astronomy. Another earthquake occurred in 1730, prompting an imperial donation of one thousand taels for repairs that allowed priests to keep it open.[52] A handful of missionaries in the capital worshipped there, but elsewhere in the empire they remained isolated and vulnerable, most hiding in out-of-the-way locations.

An anonymous and undated ink drawing of the South Church, probably from 1729, provides a rare contemporaneous visual image of it.[53] The drawing provides a distant view of a structure slightly higher than two stories,

---

49   Bornet, "Les anciennes églises ... Nant'ang [part 1]," 504.
50   In letters of 1769 and 1775 a missionary commented on the South Church's "three grand and magnificent inscriptions." Ibid.
51   *Paifang* and *pailou* are not used interchangeably, the former having a commemorative function (as in those erected for chaste widows) and the latter as an archway to or from a certain district. *Mathews' Chinese-English Dictionary* (Rev. American ed., 1943; reprint, Taipei: n.p., 1963), 674, cites each as "an honorific arch or portal."
52   Huang Bolu, *Zheng jiao feng bao*, 135b.
53   Corsi, "Pozzo's Treatise as a Workshop," 240–241. Another study provides the drawing and a caption that reads "Nantang or Southern Church, Peking. Depiction of the church at the College of Peking completed in 1711." Liam Matthew Brockey, *Journey to the East: The Jesuit Mission to China, 1579–1724* (Cambridge, Mass.: Belknap Press of Harvard University Press, 2007), 196. It is possible the drawing dates to the 1770s and represents the next

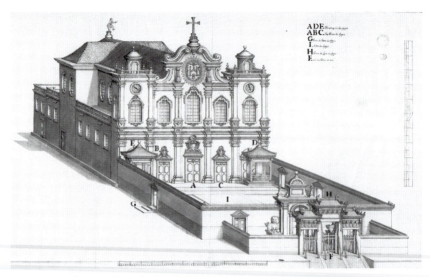

FIGURE 3.1   The second South Church, ink drawing, early eighteenth century
SOURCE: COURTESY ARQUIVO HISTÓRICO ULTRAMARINO, LISBON

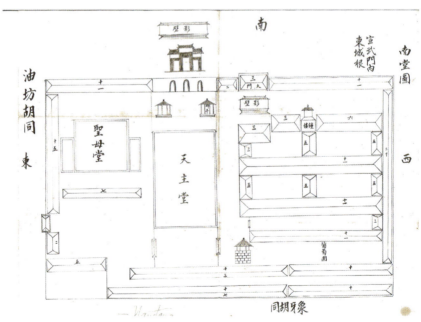

FIGURE 3.2   Undated plot plan of the South Church's grounds prior to 1785. These main
features are noted: top center (south to north), traditional spirit screen (*yingbi*),
memorial archway (*paifang*), three portal entryway, stelae pavilions, and the
church (*tianzhutang*). To the church's left (east) is "Our Lady's Chapel"
(Sheng Mu tang).
SOURCE: ARCHIVES CM, PARIS

laid out in a cruciform design with a simply styled façade and hip roof. The front is symmetrical, divided into two sections. In the lower section are six pilasters each topped with simple scroll type ornamentation often present on Ionic columns. There are three doorways with the area immediately above the central door empty (probably the location of Portugal's coat of arms). The upper section originally had four pilasters to match those below; with the addition of the towers there were six interspersed with five windows, probably of stained glass. Neither tower exceeded the façade's masonry apex that included a prominent cross. Above the slightly larger central window, the artist provided a circular design that contained the commonly used IHS monogram for Jesus Christ, which also served as the Jesuits' emblem. Above the upper section on the façade's central and highest section can be seen its most distinctive feature, softly curving decorative scrolls, a Rococo-style influence. The drawing confirms the ground-level existence on opposite sides of the portico of the 1657 and 1692 imperial stelae, each under a small open pavilion. The wall that protected the front courtyard merged into the church's sidewalls, not the surrounding structure. The courtyard had side entrances, opposite each other, as well as a decorative entry gate. Anterior to it was the aforementioned *paifang*. Surrounding it was a shorter wall that joined the main enclosure at a right angle and within this enclosed space were two guardian lions. An undated plot map of the grounds as it looked prior to 1785 gives another view and more details, most notably showing Our Lady's Chapel (Sheng Mu tang) used by women worshippers.[54] Although secured by a wall, a Korean visitor to Beijing in 1766 observed that guards with weapons stood at the gate.[55] It is unclear if they were there for security or to curtail worship.

The Third South Church (1776–1900). In the late eighteenth century, Jesuits in China felt the blow of two events: in 1773, the pope suppressed their society, and two years later, a fire destroyed the South Church.[56] Stunned Portuguese Jesuits used the façade, the only part to survive, to serve as the front of an edifice finished a year later with the generous help of the Qianlong emperor, who donated ten thousand Chinese ounces of silver (roughly, $12,500).[57] Priests dedicated it to the Immaculate Conception. Inside and behind the altar they displayed "*un grand tableau*" (that is, a large wooden retable with recesses and

iteration. Wang Lianming and Francesco Maglioccola [Ma Fangji, pseud.], "Architectural Drawings," 3; and Guillén, "Matteo Ricci," 109, 113–114.

54   Archives CM, Paris, Carton 1, "Mission Française de Pékin, 1783."
55   Lin Jizhong, comp. *Yan xing lu quanji* (Hancheng: Dongguo daxue chubanbu, 2001), 241–241b.
56   Paul Bornet, "Les anciennes églises de Pékin: notes et histoire, Nant'ang [part 2]," *Bulletin catholique de Pékin* 31 (November 1944): 527.
57   Available records do not indicate the total cost to rebuild.

shelves to hold the altar cross and other items) custom made by Bro. Panzi.[58] Three Vincentians arrived in Beijing in 1785 to assume control of Jesuits' properties and administer their ecclesiastical realms. At that time, the city had seven hundred Christians and four sacred structures.[59] Interestingly, Lord George Macartney, in Beijing in 1793 as head of a British diplomatic mission to open China to trade, made no comment about seeing them, in spite of observing that the city's buildings lacked height.[60] Vincentians not only kept a low profile as they worked in a closed country but also had to face two further Qing restrictions of Christianity that came in the early nineteenth century, the accumulative effect making it even harder for those still clandestinely in China.[61]

During these stressful years neither resident nor visiting priests said much about the South Church that had by the late 1820s started to deteriorate due to a dearth of funds and manpower to keep it up. Fr. Cayetano Pires held on tenuously, living within the church's walled enclosure as the last Western priest of this era to serve at the Directorate of Astronomy and reside in Beijing. In fact, the aged and failing priest had asked Russian Orthodox priests in 1829 to care for the sacred structure should he die. By the early 1830s, Pires's flock had shrunk to about 350.[62] Far from the capital, work continued under Chinese Vincentians joined by missionaries such as Joseph-Martial Mouly, who passed by Beijing on his way to Xiwanzi Village in 1835. Pires, worried that Mouly's presence might bring unfavorable attention to his congregation, decided he should not enter the city. Instead, they met at a dilapidated house near the Catholic cemetery outside the Inner City's western wall.[63]

Two years passed before Mouly dared return to discuss mission work with the frail bishop, hearing that his health had deteriorated.[64] In a letter from

---

58   Bornet, "Les anciennes églises ... Nant'ang [part 2]," 527.

59   Mouly letter, 6 November 1836, *Annals PF*, old series (1838): 398.

60   A member of the mission also noted that Beijing's houses were seldom more than one story high, again not mentioning any exceptions. Aeneas Anderson, *A Narrative of the British Embassy to China, in the years 1792, 1793, and 1794* (London: J. Debrett, 1795), 156, 160. The city's lack of a skyline impressed missionaries. In 1841, a Vincentian wrote: "the houses are low ... nothing rises to the heights of the ramparts." Huc letter, 15 September 1841, *Annals PF* 4 (1843): 54–55. Seventy years later another priest remarked similarly. "Pekin," *Annales CM-F* 76 (1911): 360. They took it for granted that this made their tall churches special.

61   See Chapter 1, note 9.

62   Mouly letter, 6 November 1836, *Annals PF*, old series (1838): 398. *The Vincentians*, vol. 3, *Revolution and Restoration (1789–1843)*, 687.

63   "Missions of China, in the XVIIth and XVIIIth Centuries," *Annals PF* 9 (1848): 310–312.

64   Alphonse Hubrecht, *La mission de Péking et les Lazaristes* (Péking [Beijing]: Imprimerie des Lazaristes, 1939), 210.

Beijing dated 26 February 1838 Mouly wrote briefly about the church, his perspective naturally colored by exposure to urban Beijing and by his recent construction of one in bucolic Xiwanzi. To him, "the cathedral, though small, would be regarded as very beautiful in Europe.... [I]t dominates without being very high" because "to elevate it more" would make the city's high officials, even the emperor, jealous. He noted that only the imperial palace contained tall buildings, and no one could build higher than those or the city's temples. Most people lived in low-level dwellings, though some wealthy individuals had homes with a "small second floor."[65] A rumor circulated that upon Pires's death the emperor intended to give the South Church to a prince who would pre- serve the building as a European relic.[66] Pires died in November and Chinese authorities did not permit his replacement, effectively closing the church— perhaps even officially sealing the gate. Russian Orthodox priests in Beijing acted as passive caretakers since they had neither the money nor motivation to maintain it properly.

With people scavenging bricks and other materials from the site and weath- er taking its toll, only a shell of a building remained in the 1840s. We may recall that Huc's long 1841 journey to Xiwanzi brought him near Beijing.[67] Later he journeyed widely and wrote popular books filled with facts, figures, and ob- servations about the Qing empire.[68] Although it is unclear if he actually vis- ited the South Church or not, he acquired information about the structure. Without mentioning its condition, he observed that outside the main entrance there was a "triumphal arch of white marble in form of a porch with sculpture representing various allegorical subjects built opposite the church." On either

---

65   Mouly letter, 26 February 1838, *Annales CM-F* 5 (1839): 368–370. By "small," it is unclear whether the priest meant compared to European churches or to his at Xiwanzi, which measured seventy-six feet long by thirty-eight wide. In 1836, he considered it "the largest of the kind in China." The reader will recall that Schall's was actually a little larger. For the one at Xiwanzi, see Mouly letter, 6 November 1836, *Annals PF*, old series (1838): 401. Also, the Xiwanzi section in Chapter 6.

66   Bornet, "Les anciennes églises ... Nant'ang [part 2]," 535; *The Vincentians*, vol. 3, *Revolution and Restoration (1789–1843)*, 695.

67   Huc letter, 15 September 1841, *Annals PF* 4 (1843): 51–56. In this letter, he provides a gen- eral description of Beijing and implies he visited the city (without mentioning the South Church).

68   Translators quickly made his books available in English with publishers producing vari- ous and different editions over the years. For example, Huc and Gabet, *Travels in Tartary, Thibet and China 1844–1846*; Évariste-Régis Huc, *The Chinese Empire*, trans. Mrs. Percy Sinnett (1854; reprint, New York: P. J. Kenedy, 1897); and Évariste-Régis Huc, *Christianity in China, Tartary, and Thibet*, 3 vols. (London: Longman, Brown, Green, Longmans, & Roberts, 1857–1858).

side of the arch were inscriptions including four large ones by the emperor.[69] Perhaps these are the same ones mentioned above that date to 1711. From the 1848 comments of another priest, Fr. Emmanuel Verolles, M.E.P., come more details about how it looked.[70] He found a structure in ruins, with broken windows and bricked up doors. Atop was a cross, some sixty feet off the ground—it dominated the façade's pediment and was easily visible in the neighborhood. Designed in the shape of a Latin cross, to Verolles it belonged to no architectural genre except that of "Portuguese churches." However, the portico appeared quite elegant to him, ornate from its decorations and the support ribbing in relief—all composed of plaster and nicely executed. He thought the capacity to be from twelve to fifteen hundred people, surely a standing-room-only estimate given its size.[71]

The author of a book devoted to Beijing's sacred structures writes that a Catholic bishop, who he does not name, wore Chinese garb as a disguise to clandestinely enter the capital in 1850 and seek out the South Church. From a distance, he spotted its rooftop cross and, upon drawing near, found a dilapidated building.[72] The cross was the famously tall one made of iron. It came down in 1853, the order given by one of the Qing's leading generals and supporters in its suppression of the Taipings, followers of a sinicized form of Christianity already occupying large chunks of the China proper. General Senggelinqin, a Mongol prince serving the Qing, anticipated that Taipings would be attracted to the church should they scout the capital in preparation for an attack.

Rather than Taipings, Westerners would next threaten Beijing. As noted in the previous chapter, in 1858 and 1860 China suffered humiliating defeats at the hands of Anglo-French forces whose ships and marines occupied strategic positions at Tianjin. The second round of fighting entailed a successful attack on Beijing that led to the looting and burning of the Summer Palace followed by occupation of the Forbidden City. Furious over what they saw as Qing deceptions, delays, and mistreatment of prisoners of war, the British contemplated destroying the Forbidden City in retaliation. In the end, they realized that such a humiliation might topple the dynasty and that another regime might renege

---

69 Huc, *Christianity in China, Tartary, and Thibet*, 2:384–386.
70 Sometimes written Verrolles, he served as bishop of the Vicariate of Liaodong and Manchuria, formed in 1839. He made his way there in 1841, traveling through North China and the frontier area without stopping in Beijing. Verolles letter, 12 March 1841, *Annals PF* 3 (1842): 233–237.
71 Bornet, quoting an 1848 letter from Verolles. "Les anciennes églises ... Nant'ang [part 2]," 541.
72 The author is referring to Verolles's visit. W. Devine, *The Four Churches of Peking* (London: Burns, Oates & Washbourne, 1930), 99.

on the commercial treaties in place and the recently signed Conventions of Beijing. French opinions ran equally strong, but they wanted peace, in good part to consolidate their nascent religious protectorate, one in which Catholic missionaries had certain treaty rights such as those spelled out in Article VI of France's Convention—that is, the return of all Church property, whether appropriated by the dynasty or occupied by private parties, and the acquisition of new sites.

Accordingly, in mid-October 1860 the French demanded return of all confiscated Catholic property. Two weeks later, with no reply in hand, the general commanding French troops ordered soldiers to take preemptive possession of the South Church, citing the pressing need to conduct funeral rites for soldiers lost in the war. The conjunction of French military cum national and religious needs justified a timetable running faster than diplomatic channels permitted. In early November, high Qing officials forwarded a document (certificate) dated 5 November 1860 to French diplomats for conveyance to Bishop Mouly. Tantamount to a deed (minus parcel boundaries and specifics about buildings or property improvements), the bishop now had formal control and legal ownership.[73] Over the next two months, the government issued deeds for three other former Catholic sites.

In November with his memory still fresh regarding the events, Fr. Louis-Charles Delamarre, M.E.P., an official interpreter for the French, described what he saw in the final days of October.[74]

The [French] general [Charles Montauban] decided that the burial [at the church's old cemetery outside the Inner city's wall] should take place on the 28th, and the service at the church on the following day.[75] This

---

73 *JWJAD*, Series I, volume 1, documents 187 and 188, p. 157. Following citations will use this format: series number/volume number/document number, then a comma and page number(s). Later, France and China exchanged numerous communications regarding Chinese official investigations into and clarification of property boundaries and improvements. There is an entire subsection devoted to the subject. *JWJAD* 1/1/187–235. For an English and Chinese chronology, primarily 1860–1866, 1/3/no document number, 1–40. Also, CM Archives, "Archives des Lazaristes de Pékin de Centre des Archives Diplomatiques de Nantes," Carton 9, "Petang 1860 Restitution."

74 Delamarre inserted an additional sentence into the Chinese text of the French Convention that gave missionaries property benefits not mentioned in the supposedly authoritative French text. Planchet [A. Thomas, pseud.], *Histoire de la mission de Pékin*, 2:389–391.

75 "Divers Missions," *Annals PF* 22 (1861): 103. Reference is to the Zhalan cemetery that was associated with the South Church. Known to some as the "Portuguese cemetery," most Jesuit missionaries were interred there. It remained in relatively good condition thanks to Russian caretakers.

FIGURE 3.3 The iron cross that stood on top of the South
Church until 1900. It was not reinstalled on the
rebuilt church and is shown leaning against a
wall, ca the 1930s.
SOURCE: ARCHIVES CM, PHILADELPHIA

arrangement allowed us three days to get the church ready, and it was
not too much. We hastened to go and examine that old ruin of by-gone
days, which is situated opposite and near to the Suen-oo-gate [Xuanwu
men]. Good Heavens! In what a dilapidation we found it! The wall of enclosure is almost entirely in ruins. Of the houses that were once inhabited
by bishops, and so many illustrious missionaries, the Schalls, Verbiests,
&c., there remains not a stone upon stone. The porch of the church, in

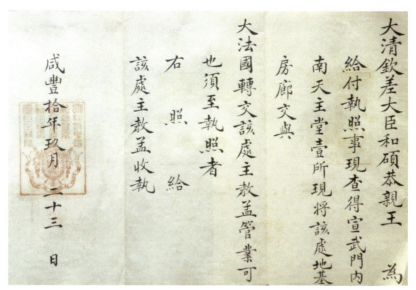

FIGURE 3.4 Certificate of ownership ("deed") for South Church, 1860. The content is
summarized as follows: the Great Qing's Imperial Commissioner Prince Gong
has investigated the South Church property located inside the Xuanwu Gate
and now transfers ownership of it to the French minister for conveyance to
Bishop Mouly and his control. Dated the Xianfeng reign's tenth year, ninth
month, twenty-third day, and stamped with the French Legation's seal.
SOURCE: ARCHIVES CM, PARIS

which are still to be seen two colossal marble tortoises, supporting a slab
bearing an inscription in Chinese and Mantchoo, is covered with briars,
thorns and bushes, forming a dense coppice. The doors have been carried
away, and their place blocked up with rubbish; the windows are broken,
the mosaic flooring disarranged: the whole place presenting a scene of
wreck and ruin. The church is composed of a single nave, with six lateral
chapels forming the wings. The high altar, as well as those of the chapels,
have been demolished; the ornaments with which they have been decorated are lying on the ground. The vault has been broken by a large hole,
and this is the most serious part of the damage. The frescoes of the vault
and nave are alone intact, and in a tolerably good state of preservation.
Such is the deplorable state in which we found this church, closed for
upwards of twenty years after the death of Mgr. Pirés, bishop of Nankin,
and administrator of Peking.... [A large sum] would be required for its
restoration. Pending this so desirable an undertaking, the general sent
two companies of engineers to clear it. The brambles were cut away, the
rubbish removed, and an altar set up again. The cross that surmounted

the front had been taken down in 1853 by Sen-Kolin-Sin, on his march against the rebels, who set up a false Christianity. General Montauban required that it should be delivered up to him and had it set up again on the top of the edifice. The church was hung with black, and adorned with the national colours; the floor was covered with felt and red carpets. A large tomb of state was placed, and surrounded with numerous lights. Our brave soldiers of the engineer corps managed, out of pure good nature, to conceal the desolation of this sanctuary.[76] (All alternative or unusual spellings in the original.)

Additional information comes from Favier, who had arrived at Beijing in July 1862. Five years later, he wrote about the historic South Church's condition based on information from his Vincentian confreres who had seen it: "it had the appearance of a poor, dismantled ship—no doors, no windows, no longer an altar; in fact nothing remained but some old picture-frames, the paintings having been torn away altogether or worm-eaten." Sadly, weather and time had taken a heavy toll on the outside walls and a large whole in the roof had allowed rain and snow to enter and leave "the mural paintings of the interior so injured as to be scarcely discernible."[77]

Repairs to the exterior and interior soon began, more reconstruction than restoration. Work included the addition of two wings to the church, one designated as housing for missionaries, the other for the reestablishment of schools. To summon worshippers residing in the vicinity, workers installed in one of the towers "three small bells" imported from Europe. It reopened for public services on Christmas night 1861, with additional work on it and other structures continuing over the next two years.[78]

An informed visitor, Bro. Joseph Guillon, S.J., who arrived at the Jesuit mission in 1861 and later built (and probably designed) the Xian County cathedral for the Jesuits' Vicariate of Zhili Southeast, saw the restored church. He approved of the completed work, stating that it preserved the architectural lines of what had been finished in 1776. Compared to other buildings in Beijing, he thought that its height of forty-six feet or slightly more made it exceptionally prominent. Architectural features included a central arched entrance composed of pilasters, cornices, and other ornamentations that occupied the

---

76   Delamare [Delamarre] letter, 18 November 1860, *Annals PF* 22 (1861): 133–134; Bornet, "Les anciennes églises ... notes et histoire," 541–543.

77   "China," *Annals PF* 28 (1867): 360–362; and Bornet, "Les anciennes églises ... Nant'ang [part 2]," 543–544.

78   "China," *Annals PF* 28 (1867): 360–361.

façade's center. The main entry led to the nave and two other doors gave access to the side aisles. The façade included the French royal crest, a replacement for Portugal's. Higher up was IHS, grandly styled as part of a cloud motif. Overall, Guillon thought the façade's various features well presented. He compared it stylistically to a Jesuit church in Paris, l'église Saint-Paul-Saint-Louis, and saw similarities with French Catholic churches of the era.[79]

The design aspects Guillon mentioned are visible in a unique color sketch of the South Church. Although the presentation is undated and the artist unknown, it was probably completed in the 1860s because, as indicated above, the cross had been added but not the east and west wings.[80] Its nicely drawn perspective conveys a sense of how the building and grounds looked before full restoration. The site's protective wall hardly exists except for a few bricks that indicate its boundary, an absence that does allow an unobstructed view of its south-facing front and eastern side. The third or top section of the building, of course, includes the façade's distinctive architectural scrolls. It is shown topped with a thin, almost skeletal cross suggesting it is of iron not stone. Its two towers and five windows in the façade (directly above three entryways) are clearly visible. A sidewall blocks the view of the church's front bottom half. Peeking over, it is possible to glimpse the top of one of the two pavilions that sheltered an imperial stele. An ornamental gate with three doorways, topped with an "orb," is part of the wall's south side. Between it and a busy lane is a traditional-style archway (*paifang*) with Chinese type roof tiles and slightly upturned end-ridges. Directly across from it sits the Inner City's wall and the Xuanwu Gate's tower, which the artist made look much larger and taller than the church; the low-level buildings to the west fade away nicely toward the horizon.

Almost contemporaneous to the sketch is a photograph taken in the early 1870s.[81] It shows the South Church as it looked straight on from atop the near-

---

79 Bornet, "Les anciennes églises … Nant'ang [part 2]," 531–532.
80 This is part of a large collection the Library of Congress purchased in 1906 from Vasil'evich Yudin, a Russian art and book collector who acquired the items between 1860 and 1900. Although the sketch is undated, if drawn as a retrospective presentation of the recently returned site, the artist would have needed to know to exclude the two wings that priests added in 1862. "Church in Peking," Yudin Collection, Library of Congress, https://www.loc .gov/item/2002715463/ (accessed 28 March 2016).
81 For an online copy of a photograph, cited as taken by Thomas Child in 1873, see "Lao zhaopian," http://www.360doc.com/content/13/0204/17/2280746_264220367.shtml (accessed 11 November 2015). This site posts a second photograph, dating it one year later and crediting it to Child. The 1874 photograph (in my opinion it is somewhat later) may also be found in an uncatalogued album in Archives CM, Paris. I believe someone other than Child took the shot because during his tenure with the Imperial Maritime Customs

FIGURE 3.5 Drawing of the third South Church. An undated, unsigned presentation of the
          South Church as it probably looked when Vincentian missionaries regained
          possession in 1860. Over the preceding two decades, the church had been closed,
          vacant, and poorly maintained, thus the outline of a dismantled perimeter wall.
          A narrow but active street stretching into the distance adds perspective and
          vibrancy while separating the church from the busy Xuanwu Gate (its tower on
          left) that was part of the Inner City's southern wall. In front of the church is a
          memorial archway (*paifang*) and one of the two stone guardian lions that sat to
          either side of a gated enclosure, which led to a courtyard (here, compressed) and
          the church's main entrance. Barely visible within the courtyard is the imperial
          yellow roof of a pavilion that provided cover for a stele donated to the church by
          the Shunzhi emperor in 1657.
          SOURCE: COURTESY LIBRARY OF CONGRESS

by Inner City's wall. From it we may confirm most everything known, hinting
I would venture that the French royal crest was located above the central entrance. In addition to the church, the photo shows the buildings surrounding
it and recently planted trees. In the Vincentians' Parisian archives is another

---

in Beijing from 1870 to 1889 he took over two hundred photographs, with no duplicates of
the same subject as far as I know.

photograph, taken by an unidentified person sometime in the 1870s–1880s. This one provides an excellent view of the church, again as seen from a position on top of the nearby city wall directly across from its southern entrance.[82] It provides valuable visual information regarding the sacred structure, confirming that, in general appearance, it had similar lines to the remodeled ones of 1651–1775 and 1776–1900. The photo shows IHS on the façade and at its apex a tall iron cross—and like the sketch, we have five front-facing windows at the second level, directly over three entry doors. Visible to each side of the main entrance are the tops of the pavilions that housed the two imperial stelae. Also readable are the characters *chijian tianzhutang*, built with imperial permission, over the main gate. In front of it is a Chinese-style archway with a bilingual inscription. According to Favier, it conveyed the same sentiment in Chinese and Manchu, "imperially bestowed, a fine place from which one enters Heaven" (*chi ci tong wei jia jing*).[83] When the two inscriptions first appeared this way is not clear; certainly, missionaries wanted the South Church's imperial connections quickly put on full display.

From the circa 1860 sketch and the 1870s–1880s era photograph, it is evident that priests had successfully restored the South Church while filling the grounds with additional buildings. By the start of the twentieth century, the walled compound included a large dwelling for themselves, schools, a hospital, the Marist Brothers' Franco-Chinese College, and the motherhouse of the Sisters of St. Joseph, a Chinese women's religious association.[84] In a busy district of the Inner City, virtually everyone knew of its religious activities or was aware of its physical presence in terms of a structure that soared above neighboring houses and businesses. To be sure, the South Church had incorporated some Chinese elements such as its imperially inscribed prominent ornamental archway and stelae yet it was its Baroque-like design that made it architecturally exceptional among Beijing's four historic sacred structures.

European features and connection to a foreign religion made it an obvious target during the spring and summer of 1900, when anti-Christian Boxers "swarmed like bees," as people described it, into the area surrounding the capital. Rural Catholics fled to churches in nearby towns and when those came under attack, they tried to find haven at Beijing's, hoping that Boxers

---

82   Archives CM, Paris, uncatalogued album. This photograph served as the model for gravures used in several books of different eras. J.-M. Planchet, *Le cimetière et les oeuvres Catholiques de Chala, 1610–1927* (Pékin [Beijing]: Imprimerie des Lazaristes, 1928); and Malatesta and Gao, *Departed, Yet Present*, 45, plate 37.

83   Favier, *Péking* (1900), 147. It may be loosely translated "the way to Paradise."

84   "China—Pekin," *Annals CM-E* 8 (1901): 64; Cholat letter, 15 November 1900, *Annals CM-E* 8 (1901): 215; and De Vienne letter, 19 April 1901, *Annals CM-E* 8 (1901): 508.

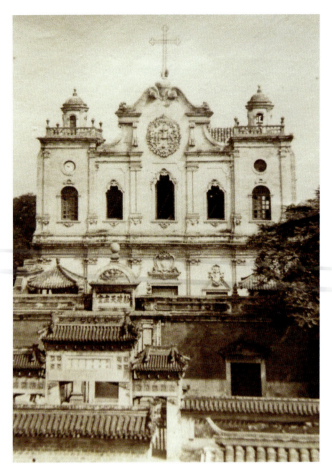

FIGURE 3.6 The third South Church, ca 1870s–1880s
SOURCE: ARCHIVES CM, PARIS

would dare not follow them there. Boxers fearlessly poured into the capital by the thousands, patrolled the streets, and harassed residents with impunity. Authorities did not stop them, often condoning their actions. Beijing's Catholics and recently arrived refugees found life increasingly dangerous and difficult. The South Church took in many, its size a limiting factor. Bishop Favier realized that should the conflict escalate he would not be able to defend it because of its location near a city gate the Boxers would use as an entry point into the Inner City. The church would also be vulnerable to gunfire from atop the nearby city wall. When the bishop decided to concentrate all defensive measures at the North Church, Catholic women and children began moving to it from the South Church. Unprotected, Boxers torched it on 14 June 1900

FIGURE 3.7   Details of South Church's *paifang* and gate
SOURCE: ARCHIVES CM, PARIS

with the remaining Catholics fleeing for their lives into surrounding neighborhoods or the Legation Quarter.[85] One Chinese priest searched the streets for
stragglers only to be captured by Boxers. His unfortunate fate included torture,
decapitation, and the hacking of his body into many pieces. Many others died
at this time.[86]

The Fourth South Church (1904–Present). Only part of the façade survived
the conflagration and workers had to raze it to prepare a foundation for the
construction that followed. The Congregation of the Mission received compensation from the Qing dynasty, conveyed through the French government,
for its extensive loss of life and property. Using an unknown amount of money,
Favier provided the general design, and rebuilt it in two years, 1903–1904 (the

---

85   "China—Pekin," *Annals CM-E* 8 (1901): 80.
86   An account of the priest's murder is in *Quanshi Beijing jiaoyou zhiming* (Beijing: Jiushi
      tang, 1920–1931), *juan* 1(Nantang, Beitang), 25a–25b. Once Allied forces suppressed the
      Boxers, Vincentians began collecting information from missionaries, Chinese priests, and
      Catholics concerning heroic tales of resistance and stories of lives lost. Over the years
      1920–1931, the Lazarist Press published in Chinese the aforementioned title, part of a
      multi-volume hagiography. Their collective testimony was meant to bolster the spirits of
      the faithful who had survived.

FIGURE 3.8 Ruins of the South Church and the low Beijing skyline, 1901
SOURCE: COURTESY LIBRARY OF CONGRESS

FIGURE 3.9 The fourth South Church, ca 1920s–1930s
SOURCE: ARCHIVES CM, PHILADELPHIA

destroyed *paifang* and gate were not replaced). Its style, as revealed by early twentieth century photographs, remained stylistically similar to earlier versions with only changes to the façade. Favier did not have the towers rebuilt, making it narrower than its predecessor. At ground level there were still three entryways; above them the number of windows had shrunk from five to three. At the façade's third level, directly above the windows was an addition, an oblong curving design, that helped accent the scroll-like design features directly above it. Added above the central window was a novel decoration, the coat of arms of Pope Pius X, elected in 1903. Its top part references his prior role as patriarch of Venice (St. Mark died there and is the city's patron). The lower part is the lion of St. Mark with his foot resting on a book. Below the lion is an anchor and sea waves, expressing the idea that hope will steady the soul in stormy times. Among those in Beijing, it is the only one with this feature. Above the papal emblem, Mary's monogram replaced IHS. The bishop rededicated the church to the Immaculate Conception.

The South Church, which survived Chinese warlords and the Japanese imperial army, did not fare well afterwards. Beginning in 1949, the government moved to expel Western missionaries and put places of worship under direct government control. The recently formed Religious Affairs Bureau had the C.P.A. order all places of worship to abide by new administrative regulations, which allowed them to remain open into 1965 as Chinese priests continued to say mass and perform their various religious duties. When the Cultural Revolution began in 1966, Mao Zedong pushed the capital—indeed the whole country—into sociopolitical turmoil as ultra-leftists directed movements to rid China of whatever remnants of the old society they perceived to exist. During this increasingly unstable period, Red Guards closed the South Church's doors, stripped the façade of all its religious symbols, emptied the interior of its altars and pews, and turned the building into a factory for refinishing toys.[87] The affiliated cemetery (at Zhalan) and its chapel were destroyed.[88] After the destruction and violence ebbed somewhat in 1971, authorities permitted a priest

---

87   Red Guards found alternative uses for some churches because well-made buildings had utilitarian value. One might argue that prior to 1980 "virtually all space became enfolded with the single space of the state, a space devoted to production, ideological inculcation, and surveillance." Post-1980 government provisions allowed for the return of Catholic-owned properties, with state "regulatory power" controlling and defining their use. Yang, "Spatial Struggles," 726, 738–739.

88   Malatesta and Gao, *Departed, Yet Present*, 97–98. The fate of Beijing's sacred buildings during the Cultural Revolution is discussed by Ming Xiaoyan and Jean-Paul Wiest [Wei Yangbo, pseud]. *Lishi yizong—Zhengfu si tianzhujiao fendi* (Beijing: Wenwu chubanshe, 2007), 52–53.

FIGURE 3.10   South Church, today. Video monitors were added
                in 2010 for use when the church is unable to
                accommodate all worshippers.
                SOURCE: PHOTO BY AUTHOR, 2018

to resume services for the small community of Westerners, mostly diplomats
and their families living in Beijing. By the mid-1970s, the Cultural Revolution
had effectively ended, and people regained a semblance of normalcy in their
everyday lives. In 1978, the government allowed the South Church to reopen,
the first one following the prior turmoil. People began returning for services.
Twenty years later, Beijing authorities granted it *Renminbi* (RMB) 1.3 million
yuan ($158,500) for renovations.[89]

89   "Nantang jianjie" (church courtyard display, 2009); and Author's field notes, 27 September
        2009.

FIGURE 3.11   Pope Pius x's coat of arms, South Church's façade
SOURCE: PHOTO BY AUTHOR, 2018

The South Church is a beautiful sacred edifice occupying a historical site that dates to Ricci's and Schall's days in Beijing during the seventeenth century. Although the grand exterior with its ornate *paifang* no longer exists, and entry (except for Sundays) is via a side entrance for security reasons, the South Church remains a distinctive part of a busy urban neighborhood. As a reminder of its long history, the imperial stone stelae of 1657 and 1692, minus their tops and bases, are preserved in walls to each side of the church's main entrance. Unfortunately, time and weather have effaced the inscriptions to the point that they are no longer readable. Catholics have restored the façade mirroring the style as it looked in 1904. In the front courtyard, tall trees provide shade for benches from which one may gaze at the sacred structure and be reminded of its uniqueness. It and the grounds, insulated from the hectic life of modern Beijing, provide a sense of serenity to worshippers and visitors alike.

1.2   The East Church (Dongtang)

Beijing's second oldest Catholic worship site can be traced to the Jesuits' early years in the capital. Like the South Church it has been rebuilt several times, each version with different details. It is well-known because it is near the popular Wangfujing shopping area's pricey stores and souvenir shops that line each side of a wide pedestrian-only boulevard. Most people refer to it as the Wangfujing church rather than the East Church. It is the only one of the six without security walls, leaving the grounds open to the public. A pavilion dedicated to St. Joseph sits to one side of a lovely front courtyard, paved and attractively landscaped, that jointly serves it and neighborhood as a pleasant, mini urban park. Despite advertising billboards and materialism infringing from every direction, people call the courtyard a Church Culture Square (jiaotang wenhua guangchang). Its superb location, famous history, and beautiful architecture naturally attracts more domestic and foreign visitors than any other church in Beijing.

   The First East Church (1655?–1691?). The Shunzhi emperor not only encouraged Schall to construct the South Church but also donated property in 1655 to two Jesuits, the Portuguese Gabriel de Magalhães and Italian Lodovico Buglio, for use as a residence and place of worship. Although when they completed the latter is unclear, by either 1655 or 1659, or even 1662, a modest church of European design stood at the site.[90] Priests dedicated it to the Holy Savior. Christians called it the East Church due to its location relative to the Forbidden City and the sacred structure at Xuanwu Gate. Priests liked the site because it projected a preferred status due to its position just outside the Imperial City's wall and not far from the Forbidden City's main eastside entrance, the Donghua Gate. Not much can be said about the building except that it was small with a gable roof topped by a stone cross at its anterior apex.[91] Two sculptures of kneeling angels, probably bas-reliefs, were part of the façade's tympanum. Over the main entrance hung a horizontal plaque with gold-colored characters stating the church, really the property, was a "Gift of the Emperor." The priests considered it an architectural triumph, evidence of Christianity's place and progress in Beijing. They hoped that it would give priests in the provinces confidence to build more European-style places of worship.[92]

   The church's status following the Shunzhi emperor's death in 1661 is unclear. Based on partial information on the subject, in 1665, during the regency period of the Kangxi emperor, a high-level opponent of Christianity named Yang Guangxian succeeded in razing the structure and expelling priests from

---

90   Brockey, *Journey to the East*, 326, implies that it dates to 1655. A diocesan publication agrees. *Beijing Tianzhu jiaohui*, item entitled "Wangfujing Sheng Ruose tang." Perhaps a chapel existed in 1655 when priests acquired the property; it seems unlikely they quickly erected a church. Paul Bornet, "Les anciennes églises de Pékin: notes d'histoire, Tongt'ang," *Bulletin catholique de Pékin* 32 (1945): 66, marks the year as 1659. Golvers, *Astronomia Europaea*, 158 n. 31, believes 1662 was the year of construction.

91   The cross may have been wooden. Bornet, "Les anciennes églises … supplément," 249.

92   Characters are not given for the quote. Brockey, *Journey to the East*, 116–117, 327.

the site. One scholar writes that the government demolished it in 1669 with priests rebuilding it in the 1670s. During this period, as at the South Church, the Kangxi emperor permitted a few priests to live at the site in modest housing. We do not know if they said mass in a rebuilt church or a small chapel. A third possibility, as pointed out by the author of a detailed book on the Jesuits in China, is that the East Church remained standing from the 1660s to the 1690s albeit with doors closed to the public. Such variance regarding the details of these early years simply reflects the limited number of primary sources that throw light on the church's appearance and life at it.[93]

The Second East Church (1692–1720). The situation at the end of the seventeenth century is a bit clearer in that with certainty, workers had finished construction of this East Church in 1692, the same year the Kangxi emperor confirmed by edict that churches and worship in them were to be tolerated.[94] The second iteration was a graceful structure no more than eighty-two feet in length, close in size to Schall's of 1655 and, like it, for men's use only.[95] Following what had become Jesuit tradition in China, the church was of European style, probably including Ionic pilasters or columns as part of its façade.[96] The walled enclosure included housing for priests and a chapel for women. In addition, priests had opened in 1695 an affiliated cemetery located outside the Inner City's wall near the Zhengfu si (temple). Five years later, when a French Jesuit became the superior of the Beijing missions, he and his religious compatriots resided at the East Church and controlled its associated properties. Consequently, clerics sometimes added national prefixes to distinguish the new French (East) Church and its Zhengfu si cemetery from the old Portuguese (South) Church and its Zhalan cemetery.

The Third East Church (1728–1811). An earthquake soundly shook Beijing in 1720 with tremors destroying many buildings, including the East Church. Two Jesuits in Beijing to serve the Kangxi emperor, Fathers Ferdinando Bonaventura Moggi and Xaver-Ernbert Fridelli, used funds from Europe for construction of a replacement that started the following year and continued until 1728.[97] One scholar writes that workers followed Moggi's design and built it in

---

93   Brockey, *Journey to the East*, 385; Guillén, "Portrait of a Jesuit," 113; and Paul Bornet, "Les anciennes églises de Pékin: notes d'histoire, Tongt'ang," *Bulletin catholique de Pékin* 32 (1945): 67.

94   Bornet, "Les anciennes églises ... Tongt'ang," 71.

95   This is the only measurement provided. Ibid., 70.

96   Bornet uses a source that describes it as "*de style ionique*" in his "Les anciennes églises ... Tongt'ang," 72; and Divine, *The Four Churches*, 37.

97   Given the slow pace of construction, it is unclear when missionaries considered it complete enough to resume religious services.

"a splendid Rococo style." Priests dedicated it to St. Joseph, the patron saint of China.[98] For Beijing, the church had a unique architectural feature: a domed section built into the rear roof, its circular lines visible from a distance. The missionaries used this change to make it even more distinctive in its Chinese environment and, as priests before them had attempted, attract additional people to Christianity.[99] A priest saw it and two others in Beijing in 1743, observing that they were "European-style, beautiful, large, well ornamented and nicely painted [structures that] would do honor to the largest cities of Europe."[100] Actually, some would have considered the East Church a bit small at seventy feet in length. Observers of it, unfortunately, do not give architectural details. Remnants of column bases, friezes, cornices, and two red marble columns that served as part of the church's main portal, found at the site a century later by Vincentians, hint that the façade exceeded anything that Beijing had previously seen.[101]

The political tides once favorable to Christianity receded during the remainder of the eighteenth century, sweeping away the incremental progress missionaries had made in Beijing and curtailing the activities of the Vincentians who had taken charge of the church in 1785. Over the next several decades they stayed low, hoping to go unnoticed by government officials in the face of another imperial decree against Christianity. In 1807, priests accidentally caused a fire in the East Church's library that led high Qing officials to gaze in their direction. Instead of allowing the priests to repair the damage, the emperor sent them to reside at the South Church and ordered the eastern one demolished in 1811. Afterwards, a few dilapidated buildings, an exterior gate, and stone debris were all that remained at the site. A tenacious catechist successfully turned one of the run-down structures into a temporary chapel and an accommodating Vincentian came periodically from the North Church (see below) to say mass.[102]

The Fourth East Church (1867–1884). When the fighting stopped in 1860, French diplomats pressured the Qing government to provide ownership documents for Beijing's four church sites. After the high officials issued a certificate for the East Church on 17 December 1860 Bishop Mouly, short on financial reserves, could only afford to have workers clean the grounds of rubble in

---

98   Giuseppe Castiglione, S.J., the famous Qing court painter, provided the interior décor. Guillén, "Matteo Ricci," 113. In 1668, missionaries in Guangzhou had made St. Joseph the patron saint of China.

99   Bornet, "Les anciennes églises ... Tongt'ang," 71.

100   Ibid., 72.

101   Bornet, "Les anciennes églises ... Tongt'ang," 72; and Favier, *Péking* (1902), 200.

102   Bornet, "Les anciennes églises ... Tongt'ang," 73.

preparation for later construction. One account of the era described it as "a large church" dedicated to St. Joseph for the use of the many followers living nearby.[103] Neither a large nor a formal place of worship, it was something else, a kind of aberration to missionaries. During the mid-1830s, Mouly had built a sacred structure at Xiwanzi with two separate sections, one in front of the altar for men and the other behind it for women (discussed in Chapter 6's section on this village.) Now thirty odd years later he did something different, ordering workers to construct two single-story buildings joined at an angle in a style known for looking like "人 ren" (that is, the character for person, renzi), in that it illustrated the floor plan.[104] Both configurations allowed members of each gender to enter from separate doors, sit apart, and nonetheless see the priest during mass.[105] Earlier in Beijing, the Chinese custom of segregated worship for men and women had meant the former used the main church and the latter a separate chapel. Mouly's present design allowed men and women to attend the same mass without physical contact, men segregated on the left and women on the right, if looking at the pews from the main altar. Accordingly, priests said just one mass.

Louis-Gabriel Delaplace, C.M., bishop of the Vicariate of Beijing and Zhili North from 1870 to 1884, said the building was "a miserable Chinese chapel, eaten away by humidity, with difficulty seating the fifteen hundred people who compose this beautiful parish." He wanted "a suitable church ... built à l'européenne."[106] The bishop's opinion, as well as its shape—different from any previous one in the capital—unsurprisingly leads one scholar of Beijing's old

---

103   "China," Annals PF 8 (1867): 361–362. The source does not provide dimensions. In regard to the lot size, Qing officials had difficulty determining the boundaries of Beijing's four church sites. Documents on the return of Catholic property in Beijing is in the subsection that editors devote to the topic: JWJAD, 1/1/187–235. East and West Church materials start at JWJAD, 1/1/193–195.

104   Some Chinese Catholics described this kind as a "renzi tang;" missionaries thought they looked like trouser legs. Thus, it was a "pants church." Handbook of Christianity in China, Volume Two, 736.

105   The bishop of the Vicariate of Jiangxi North writes of this custom and of a chapel at the village (cun) of Lingjia that had two sections, one for the men directly in front of the sanctuary, the other for women "who occupy another nave or, rather, another chapel to the right of the altar [that is, if facing the congregation]." An earlier prelate, Géraud Bray, having served in North China and Mongolia, brought the style to Jiangxi, but it was not popular among locals, nor among the next generation of missionaries. "In the Country of Blessed Clet," Annals PF 76 (1913): 146–147. Another floor plan with a sitting area (for women) at a right angle to the nave resembled "丁 ding" (that is, dingzi, the term for man as a tax unit).

106   Octave Chambon, ed., Vie et Apostolat de Monseigneur Louis-Gabriel Delaplace (Auxerre: Octave Chambon, Imprimeur, 1892), 250.

places of worship to give it only passing attention. He rejects it as an iteration of the East Church (as do Catholics today).[107] A well-studied Vincentian
historian chose to refer to it as a "temporary chapel."[108] Used for almost two
decades, workers removed it in 1884; the chapel had been just a passing ex-
periment in architectural design—at least for Beijing. Vestiges of gender segregation in churches located in North China continued well into the twentieth
century with separate entrances and seating patterns, men using pews on the
left and women on the right, if viewed from the chancel.[109]

   The Fifth East Church (1884–1900). Delaplace, under the advisement of his
confreres, decided to build a formal church to replace the chapel in the spring
of 1879. Favier took the lead and drew up plans inspired by the Holy Trinity
Church in Paris.[110] Workers began construction in July 1879 within the walled
compound, finishing it five years later.[111] Off a busy street, the compound's
main gate in the west led to a front courtyard that measured about 115 feet
square. This iteration rested on a raised rectangular stone foundation that
measured a large 230 feet long by 66 wide. Tall walls were composed of large,
high-quality bricks weighing fifty-five pounds each, custom ordered from imperial kilns. The tallest of three domed towers stood ninety-eight feet high (at
one-half mile from the Forbidden City, Qing officials wanted them lowered).[112]
Inside, the east-west oriented church, the chancel was situated in the eastern

---

107   Bornet, "Les anciennes églises ... Tongt'ang," 73. A billboard located outside the church
      (now removed) provided a brief history and mentioned that in 1860 priests built a simple
      one-story structure for use as a chapel, not counting it as anything else. Author's field
      notes, 27 October 2011.
108   Hubrecht, *La mission de Péking*, 317.
109   The cathedral at Yongping (Vicariate of Zhili East), built in 1910, had lateral doors, the
      one on the east side for use by men and the one on the west side for women. They then
      sat in opposite parts of the cathedral. "Tche-li-oriental: bénédiction de la cathédral de
      Young-ping-fou," *Annales CM-F* 75 (1910): 575. In the mid-1920s, a Franciscan missionary
      in central Henan wrote: "in China the churches are always built wide enough for a re-
      spectful distance between the sides set apart for the men and women and often a cloth
      or wooden screen divides the church or chapel into two halves." "The Chinese Woman,"
      Cath-M Annals PF 2, no. 4 (April 1925): 93. According to a priest born in 1926 at a village in
      Ji County, Hebei he remembered men and women sitting separately in church. Author's
      field notes, 26 September 2011. I committed the faux pas of sitting on the right side
      (if facing the pews) in a Catholic church at Nancheng, Jiangxi. An elder gently tapped me
      on the shoulder and quietly told me to move to the opposite side. I then observed that
      I had been sitting among women. Author's field notes, 20 July 1997. In Baoding, I observed
      a prayer group of about twenty women all sitting on the cathedral's west side with the east
      side completely empty. Author's field notes, 15 September 2016.
110   Favier, *Péking* (1902), 249; and Devine, *The Four Churches*, 168–169.
111   Chambon, *Vie et Apostolat*, 256–257.
112   *JWJAD*, IV/1/74–77.

section. Sixteen interior columns supported ornate beams upon which the roof rafters rested. The vaulted ceiling over the sanctuary rose to sixty-six feet in height.[113]

Visible in a photograph taken before 1900 are the main features of the façade, which had three large portals with semi-circular arches that formed an arcade in front of the doorways.[114] Each portal, framed by pilasters, had Chinese floral designs on the entablature. It is possible that Delaplace had masons sculpt it to match the remnants of the red marble columns found in the debris of the previous one. Just above the central door was a round and stylized "SJ" for St. Joseph. Directly over it were four large Chinese characters carved horizontally into stone as a plaque, a traditional Chinese presentation read from right to left. It stated: "confer kindness [or blessings] on my Orient" (*hui wo dong fang*). In two flat spaces between the central and the flanking doors were inscriptions of seven characters per side. The one on the right read: "protecting the people is a great virtue [of His] undertaken in China and abroad" (*bi min da de bao zhong wai*). The other read: "respecting father [or the Father] is a grand merit prominent in ancient and current times" (*shang fu hong xun guan gu jin*).[115] The couplet conveyed Christian sentiments with Confucian undertones.

On the façade's second level, two large windows occupied space directly over doors below them. In the center and encased in marble was a "wheel window" with four spokes. Above it was a third level consisting of the three short towers each topped with a cross. Part of the central one included an insert inscribed with Chinese characters that read vertically as follows: top center, "the great Qing [dynasty]" (Da Qing); then below from right to left in smaller size: "first built in [1711] the fiftieth year of the Kangxi emperor" (Kangxi *wushi nian chu chuang*) and "rebuilt in [1885] the eleventh year of the Guangxu emperor" (Guangxu *shiyi nian chongjian*).[116] From the wording of the plaque, I surmise that the Qing court presented it to the church for display.[117]

Its exterior, covered with architectural detail and fine features, makes it very different from the comparatively plain South Church. The various features of its symmetrical façade, absent massive walls, stylistically mimicked

113 Favier, *Péking* (1902), 248–249; Ferreux, *Histoire de la Congrégation*, 196–197; and Bornet, "Les anciennes églises ... Tongt'ang," 73.

114 Favier, *Péking* (1897), 304–305.

115 My translation was made in consultation with a priest assigned to the East Church. Author's field notes, 25 September 2012. To a Vincentian missionary whose time in China overlapped with Favier's, the inscription only had a religious message. Planchet [A. Thomas, pseud.], *Histoire de la mission de Pékin*, 2:597–598.

116 As described, I have seen no mention in any source of reconstruction in 1711.

117 The plaque read 1885, not the year of its completion and dedication.

FIGURE 3.12   The fifth East Church, late 1890s
                SOURCE: FAVIER, *PÉKING*, 1897

Romanesque ones in France and Italy. Building such a sacred structure was not cheap: recall that Bishop Delaplace had allocated over $80,000 for its construction and needed a sizable donation from Europe to finish it. The day the bishop chose for blessing it, 5 May, was the feast day of St. Joseph its patron. Many foreign legation dignitaries attended, as was the custom. This turned out to be Delaplace's final building project for he died three weeks after the dedication.[118]

In early 1900, the mission compound included the church and a room for catechism lessons as well as a girls' school and foundling home operated by the Sisters of St. Joseph.[119] A protective wall surrounded the comparatively few

---

118   Favier letter, 4 October 1899, *Annals CM-E* 7 (1900): 221; and Chambon, *Vie et Apostolat*, 256–257.

119   "China—Pekin," *Annals CM-E* 8 (1901): 64; and De Vienne letter, 19 April 1901, *Annals CM-E* 8 (1901): 509. Delaplace founded the Sisters of St. Joseph in 1872, their primary goals to be the education of Chinese girls and the training of female catechists. Chambon, *Vie et Apostolat*, 224. Initially, the Daughters of Charity helped them. Gradually, the

FIGURE 3.13   Ruins of the East Church, 1900
SOURCE: ARCHIVES CM, PARIS

buildings and small grounds, thus limiting its capacity to hold large numbers of people in normal times let alone shelter those in need during emergencies. As the Boxer turmoil enveloped Beijing, its locational circumstances, insufficient resources, and manpower led Bishop Favier to instruct Catholics to abandon it. Only sixteen years after construction, Boxers burned it to the ground on 14 June 1900.

The Sixth East Church (1905–Present). Favier gathered the resources needed and by 1905 had completed a place of worship, the second at this site by Vincentians.[120] The rebuilt version was virtually identical to its predecessor replete with the plaque and couplets mentioned above. One minor change to the façade came in the form of adding the year of construction to the top center

Sisters developed their own administration and spread throughout Zhili. *Handbook of Christianity in China, Volume Two*, 589.

120   A contemporaneous source gives its measurements in Chinese units that make it the same size as its predecessor. Alphonse Favier [Fan Guoliang, pseud.], *Yanjing kaijiao lüe* (Beijing: Jiushi tang, 1905), 58–59.

FIGURE 3.14   The sixth East Church, ca 1920s–1930s
SOURCE: ARCHIVES CM, PARIS

of the second section. A brief description of it, approved by priests at today's church, states that it is a "mixture of classic Western architecture and traditional Chinese detailing." Chinese designs, in the form of stylized flowers and vines, continued to be an East Church motif, features that distinguished it from others in the city. Some consider it Beijing's most attractive sacred structure— this is, of course, a matter of taste and debate.

After surviving the war years, the church remained open for almost a decade before government authorities closed its doors to religious services. An elementary school occupied some buildings and children used the compound's open space as a playground. In the 1960s, the Tiananmen Management Office had control of the property and used the main building for storage. The "owner" had a solid position and high-government connections that allowed the building to

FIGURE 3.15   Details of East Church's façade
               SOURCE: ARCHIVES CM, PARIS

survive the Cultural Revolution relatively unscathed. Still, authorities did not return the property to the C.P.A. until 1980, at which time Christians quickly restored it with an official reopening to the public on Christmas Eve, 1980.[121] To many, the exterior looked the same as it had in 1958 (and before that in 1905), something that gave them solace after many years of uncertainty.[122]

Perhaps the greatest and most unexpected change to the East Church began in the 1990s as China's economy boomed and the surrounding neighborhood buzzed with every manner of commercial activity. Due to its walking-distance proximity to Tiananmen Square and the Forbidden City, two of Beijing's most famous tourist sights, ever-increasing numbers came to Wangfujing Boulevard, which passes in front of the church. Countless shops and restaurants situated themselves along each side of the area's main north-south artery, all trying to divert customers from the flow of people passing by. Under these conditions the area's real estate value skyrocketed, hemming in the East Church and eliminating any chance of recovering more of its former grounds from their heavily invested occupants.

---

121   Author's field notes, 27 October 2011.
122   A comparison of photographs from different eras confirms this.

FIGURE 3.16   A recent view of the East Church
SOURCE: PHOTO BY AUTHOR, 2007

Towards the end of the decade, the Wangfujing area underwent an expensive makeover, with nicely appointed modern high-rise buildings popping up in every direction, many occupied by top-of-the-line stores carrying expensive international brands. A long portion of the boulevard banned through traffic and morphed into a wide pedestrian mall.[123] The East Church sat at the far north end of this urban renewal project, giving planners the opportunity to update it and the surrounding grounds. Workers cleaned and repaired the façade, removing what remained of the former security wall except for the front gate and about sixteen feet of wall to each side. A renovated all-white pavilion for St. Joseph occupied part of the repaved courtyard, with recessed lighting for nighttime enjoyment. Large flowerpots, bushes, and trees added to the site's inherent charm. Landscaping included low retaining walls for flowerbeds that also provided casual seating. Out of the courtyard setting workers created an

---

123   The project cost about RMB 80 million *yuan* or almost US $10 million. *Beijing Tianzhu jiaohui*, item entitled "Wangfujing Sheng Ruose tang."

urban park finished in September 2000. This lasted until 2016 when urban developers replaced the southern half of the park with a commercial building (economically, the plot's highest and best use).

Worshippers come daily for religious services and after morning mass the doors are left open so the beautiful interior may be appreciated by a never-ending stream of sightseers wandering in from nearby Wangfujing emporiums. It is an attraction for tourists, domestic and foreign alike. The courtyard and pavilion, with the church serving as an attractive backdrop, continues to beckon fully outfitted brides and grooms, only a few of whom are Catholic, for pre-wedding photographs. The courtyard has become a popular place for skateboarders practicing their techniques during daytime hours. In the evenings, portable speakers blare music as mostly middle-age women do dance exercises to a variety of musical tunes. Sometimes younger people also show up to express themselves via different tunes and practice break-dancing moves. For some, the East Church represents old times whereas the courtyard's mini-urban park has become a popular venue for twenty-somethings who care little about the past.

1.3   The North Church (Beitang)

The Kangxi emperor's long reign of sixty-one years might not have occurred save for the medical expertise of two French Jesuits, Fathers Jean de Fontaney and Claude de Visdelou. When the emperor became seriously ill in February 1693 and his Chinese doctors' treatments proved ineffective, the priests prescribed medicines that led to a full recovery. In July, grateful for their life-saving efforts, the emperor gave them a building to use located within the Imperial City to the west of Zhonghai, a lake not far from the palace complex's western gate. Such proximity to the Forbidden City constituted a special privilege. Seizing this unusual opportunity, they quickly established a home there the same month and a little later a chapel. The next year the appreciative emperor gave them an adjoining site three hundred feet long by two hundred wide on which he permitted them to erect a public worship place. With a small imperial donation in 1699 of two bolts of silk and fifty taels of silver along with some funds of their own, Jesuits began construction of another sacred structure in Beijing.[124]

The First North Church (1702–1827). De Belleville, mentioned for his work on the South Church, was more the building site supervisor than the architect, and as such made sure it took form quickly due to imperial interest. The Kangxi emperor ordered the imperial office of buildings to assist with the acquisition of labor and materials. This conveniently gave officials opportunity to report

---

124   Bornet, "Les anciennes églises ... Pei-t'ang [part 1]," 118–123.

on its size, height, and style or a direct way to verify that it conformed to building standards for the area. It passed all inspections and Fr. Claudio Grimaldi, S.J., dedicated it on 9 December 1702 to the Holy Savior.[125] Chinese Christians dubbed it the North Church because of its location relative to the first one near Xuanwu Gate.

Entry to it was from Canchikou Lane, which ran north-south, then via an even narrower east-west gated pathway to a doorway on the property's south side that led to a walled front courtyard approximately forty by fifty feet in size. On the courtyard's west side were rooms for receiving visitors with those on the east used for the instruction of catechumens.[126] In the reception rooms hung portraits of various royalty as well as art to enhance the missionaries' origins such as framed engravings from books showing the French court. Between these sets of rooms to the north a wide stairway, several feet in height, led to a formal archway that served as the entrance to a back courtyard.[127] One scholar describes it as a "Western-style three-door gate in the form of a triumphal arch."[128] Overhead and central on the *paifang* hung a horizontal plaque flanked vertically by a couplet consisting of nine characters per scroll. The plaque succinctly proclaimed: "a virtuous religion [exists] forever" (*de jiao chun cun*). From right to left, the long couplet stated: "[God] fixed the extent of the eight principles, purifying the world and achieving the truth" (*zhi ba jing zhi du lian chen cheng zhen*) and "[God] opened the way to the three constants, giving life and eliminating death" (*qi san chang zhi men kai sheng mie si*).[129]

The back courtyard, paved with stones and dressed up with potted greenery, was rectangular in shape, its measurements now unknown. The ceramic pots contained bonsai, identified by a visitor as cypresses and junipers.[130] On the east and west sides were long, roofed hallways open to the interior side. They provided some protection from rain and a bright sun when priests used the space to gather for special events such as feast day celebrations. In a painting that dates to the 1760s–1770s the artist shows a busy outdoor scene, probably the occasion of liturgical devotions to the Sacred Heart.[131]

---

125 Ibid., 125, 128.
126 In the 1770s, a priest noted that to the east there was a chapel (probably for use by Catholic women). Bornet, Les anciennes églises ... Pei-t'ang [part 1]," 128.
127 An early eighteenth-century visitor made these observations. Ibid., 123–124.
128 Lianming Wang, "Church, a 'Sacred Event' and the Visual Perspective of an 'Etic Viewer': An 18th Century Western-style Chinese Painting Held in the Bibliothèque nationale de France," in *Face to Face: The Transcendence of the Arts in China and Beyond*, vol. 1, *Historical Perspective*, ed. Rui Oliveira Lopes (Lisbon: Centro de Investigaçõe Estudos em Belas-Artes), 376.
129 Ibid. I have made some minor modifications to his translation.
130 Bornet, "Les anciennes églises ... Pei-t'ang [part 1]," 128.
131 Lianming Wang, "Church, a 'Sacred Event,'" 396.

FIGURE 3.17   Painting of the first North Church, ca 1760s–1770s
SOURCE: COURTESY BIBLIOTHÈQUE NATIONALE DE FRANCE, PARIS

At the north end of the courtyard, several steps led to an elevated foundation of a Baroque-style church built on a north-south axis that measured, according to a 1704 letter, seventy-five feet long by thirty-three wide with large
windows on its eastern and western sides.[132] Its height of thirty feet made
it roughly the equivalent of a two-story structure, tall given the low-profile
homes around it and their proximity to the Forbidden City's walls.[133] An open
porch, defined on three sides by an iron balustrade donated by the Louis XIV
of France, fronted the church.[134] The building's relatively simple façade consisted of two levels and a triangular pediment. On the first level, six column-
shaped, single-story high pilasters were spaced equally apart between three
doorways. Over the side doorways were niches filled with bas-reliefs of vases
with flowers. The higher central door's arch extended to an entablature. On the
second level, six flat pediments separated two recessed niches, again with bas-
relief vases filled with flowers, and a central rose window.[135] Another drawing of the church, perhaps made in the 1740s and differing a little from the
aforementioned one, adds scrolling effects to the upper edges of the pediment,
somewhat reminiscent of those adorning the South Church.[136] The horizontal
marble plaque mounted prominently on the pediment's lower side is most significant. Sometime around its completion, the Kangxi emperor had donated it
with the inscription: *chijian tianzhutang.*[137] This marks the first time a church
displayed the imperial endorsement, one that gave it ultimate prestige.

The solidly built sacred edifice withstood the 1720 earthquake—not as well,
the proscription of Christianity announced by the Yongzheng emperor four
years later. With increased risk to a shrinking number of priests in Beijing, the
daily celebration of mass and feast days became unusual occurrences. People
turned to catechists for help with rites or simply worshipped privately during

---

132   Bornet, "Les anciennes églises ... Pei-t'ang [part 1]," 124; and Hubrecht, *La mission de Péking*, 36.

133   The emperor overruled the officials who complained about its excessive height. Bornet, Les anciennes églises ... Pei-t'ang [part 1]," 125.

134   Jesuits do not mention how they transported these heavy iron railings from Macao to Beijing, surely a difficult and expensive task.

135   There were six windows on each side. Bornet, Les anciennes églises ... Pei-t'ang [part 1]," 124.

136   "Catholic Church with Walled Courtyard Garden in Beijing," Yudin Collection, Library of Congress, https://www.loc.gov/item/2011660670 (accessed 28 March 2016); and Wang Lianming, "Church, a 'Sacred Event,'" figure 1.

137   Paul Bornet, "Les anciennes églises de Pékin: notes d'histoire, le Pei-t'ang [part 2]," *Bulletin catholique de Pékin* 32 (1945): 173. When officials dismantled the building in 1827, they transported the plaque to the palace. Golvers writes that "the emperor gave the explicit order to build" it, thus the plaque. *Astronomia Europaea*, 12.

this time of extreme trial. The arrival of three Vincentians in 1785 hardly alleviated the clerical shortage.[138] In the late eighteenth century, court sensitivity to heterodox activities reached a climax due to a Buddhist White Lotus plot to attack the Forbidden City. Then, in 1805, Shandong officials detained a missionary for possession of a map of China demarked with ecclesiastical divisions. For officials, the map served to confirm their suspicions, in light of Beijing's heightened sense of security, concerning religious sects. Authorities posted guards outside the city's churches.[139]

The court worried about the loyalty of the few Western priests living at the North Church and continued to be concerned about its height. They responded by lowering the façade in an attempt to be less conspicuous and merge in with neighborhood structures. A missionary of a later era commented that "the edifice hardly rose higher than one of the respectable Chinese houses ... [that in this quarter] never exceed one story" and access to it came not from "the public road," rather from a narrow, gated private sub-lane.[140] With the gate closed most of the time, the North Church as a place of worship was secure, surviving more like a private chapel than a distinguished and public sacred place it had once been. By the 1820s, the last Vincentians had moved out and the few remaining worshippers, rarely visited by a Chinese priest, virtually abandoned the site.[141] In 1827, the Qing court confiscated the property and sold it to a high official. He cleared the property to erect a personal residence.[142]

The Second North Church (1867–1887). When Bishop Mouly returned in 1860, he found at the site only some dilapidated residential buildings erected thirty years earlier. "We sought for it [the North Church] earnestly, but, alas, even the very foundation stones had disappeared. All that remained to testify its having existed was a magnificent [iron] balustrade which was a gift of our kings," wrote another priest.[143] Regardless, it was Catholic property and Qing officials issued a certificate dated 28 November for conveyance to Mouly. He wasted no time in taking possession and assigning priests to occupy one of the habitable structures and modify another for use as a small, provisional chapel. They and some faithful from the immediate area celebrated the feast of Corpus Christi

138   *The Vincentians*, vol. 2, *The Eighteenth Century to 1789*, 547.
139   *The Vincentians*, vol. 3, *Revolution and Restoration (1789–1843)*, 668.
140   "China," *Annals PF* 28 (1867): 362.
141   *The Vincentians*, vol. 3, *Revolution and Restoration (1789–1843)*, 680. The French Revolution of 1789 led to the Congregation's disbandment until 1815. It dispatched no priests to China from 1800 to 1829. Hubrecht, *La mission de Péking*, 176–192, 283.
142   Bornet, "Les anciennes églises ... Pei-t'ang [part 2]," 182.
143   "China," *Annals PF* 28 (1867): 360.

there in 1861.[144] Three years later a fire destroyed these buildings—Mouly quickly had workers reconstruct them. One was a dwelling for himself and his confreres. Built in European style, it had a double veranda with archways that made it stand out in this area of Chinese-type buildings.[145]

Although Mouly initially had made the South Church his episcopal seat, he wanted a cathedral more centrally situated in the city, one that would radiate religious and national status. He chose the former site of the North Church over the other three options because, first, it alone had been the gift of a great emperor, and second, its proximity to the Forbidden City gave it high status.[146] Unlike the many missionary self-designed sacred edifices, including his own at Xiwanzi, the bishop wanted a professional to help and in late 1864 requested an architect in France to draw up plans.[147] Mouly approved the project plans and measurements, as did Zongli Yamen officials. The bishop put Bro. Paul-Joseph Marty, C.M., in charge of the construction, which entailed serving as the on-site design checker as well as master mason and carpenter because the Chinese laborers he employed had no experience with European-type buildings and had to be carefully supervised.[148]

On 1 May 1865 the bishop gathered dignitaries, representatives from the various legations and three high court officials, for the ceremonial laying of the first foundation stone. Workers then carefully laid a perimeter foundation of stone to a height of about five feet, on which they built walls of large bricks. Roof tiles and some other materials came from destroyed Buddhist temples in Beijing. The edifice stretched almost 161 feet in length and 99 in width at the transept.[149] Mouly had wanted a clock tower 150 feet in height though he realized this would be impossible given its close distance to the Forbidden City. So,

---

144   Thierry letter, 15 June 1861, *Annals PF* 23 (1862): 51–54.

145   Ferreux, *Histoire de la Congrégation*, 163, writes that it was a single-story building. Another source, writing in the late 1860s, says it had two stories. "China," *Annals PF* 8 (1867): 364.

146   The other options were the East and West Churches.

147   A layman with the family name Bourrière, then serving as architect for the department of Lot-et-Garonne in France, had the honor. Mouly letter, 10 December 1865, *Annales CM-F* 31 (1866): 645–649. Ferreux, *Histoire de la Congrégation*, 164. At about the same time, Bishop Zéphirin Guillemin, M.E.P., engaged a French architect (surnamed Hermite) to draw up plans for a Neo-Gothic style cathedral at Guangzhou with groundbreaking in 1867. His design copied the façade of the Basilica of St. Clotilde in Paris. Wiest, "The Building," 239–240.

148   Mouly letter, 10 December 1865, *Annals CM-F* 31 (1866): 645–649.

149   "China," *Annals PF* 28 (1867): 363–364. For comparison, in 1865, construction began on a cathedral in Wuchang, Hubei, that measured 197 feet long by 33 feet wide. "China," *Annals PF* 28 (1867): 78. The Guangzhou cathedral's outside measurements were 319 feet long by 213 wide with twin spires rising to 192 feet in height. Wiest, "The Building," 240–242, 250. In the early 1870s, Fr. Isaiah Spravalero, O.F.M., designed and built a sacred structure

he approved two shorter, square clock towers with small pinnacles that stood ninety feet high.[150] Their height attracted the attention of officials who after measuring them found no discrepancies with the plans they had approved earlier. Zongli Yamen officials advised the French minister that the towers rose skyward to ninety-eight feet and must not be any higher; the minister informed the bishop.[151]

Vincentians had chosen "the pointed style of the fourteenth century," imitating the Gothic look of those in France, without their thick walls, flying buttresses, and other typical features. Its façade had three entryways; over the central one an engraved marble tablet bore the Latin words *"Fiet unum ovile et unus pastor*—There shall be one fold and one shepherd."[152] Three small statues stood above it along with bas-relief spires. A rose window dominated the central section of the second level and on each side of it narrow windows that contained wood slats, later replaced with painted glass (not the more expensive stained glass). Between the towers, lower than their top sections, was a triangular pediment that included a recessed area with a statue of Jesus. Higher up was a white cross.

Blessing of the Church of the Holy Savior occurred on 1 January 1867 with priests and various legation dignitaries attending. Three altars dominated the interior, the center one dedicated to Jesus, and, if facing the main entrance, on the right side an altar to Mary and on the left one to Joseph.[153] One historian, influenced it would appear by reading Mouly's letters, comments that "of all the churches that have ever been built in the [Qing] empire, it was incontestably the largest and most beautiful."[154] As the bishop's seat, the North Cathedral had become the most important sacred structure in Beijing and at that site Catholics built residential and support buildings for use by the bishop, priests, and seminarians (the latter from Anjia Village).[155] In addition, Daughters of Charity operated a foundling home on the grounds.[156]

---

in Taiyuan, Shanxi that measured 130 feet long by 39 wide; its steeple's height is not provided. Moccagatta letter, June 1873, *Annals PF* 35 (1874): 331–332.

150   Mouly letter, 12 January 1867, *Annales CM-F* 32 (1867): 407. The height is given by Hubrecht, *La mission de Péking*, 312.

151   *JWJAD*, I/1/215, 163.

152   "China," *Annals PF* 28 (1867): 363–364.

153   Ferreux, *Histoire de la Congrégation*, 164–165. From others, I deduce the right and left placement of altars.

154   Bornet, "Les anciennes églises ... Pei-t'ang [part 2]," 183.

155   Ferreux, *Histoire de la Congrégation*, 163–164.

156   Favier did not think highly of the "large church" and other facilities there, the site probably too small and limiting for his nascent plans of expansion. "China," *Annals CM-E* 7 (1900): 516.

FIGURE 3.18   The second North Church, ca 1880s
SOURCE: ARCHIVES CM, PARIS

Neither the Empress Dowager Cixi, in control of court affairs for her young son (the Tongzhi emperor, r. 1862–1874), nor her conservative supporters appreciated having a tall church nearby. Even though agreed to earlier, the clock tower's height remained an issue that officials tried to resolve from 1867 to 1869. They asked that missionaries dismantle the tower, and, failing that, lower it because height and proximity to the Forbidden City made it, as a matter of general principle, a visual infringement.[157] Simply put, it could be seen from within the Forbidden City. The "Tianjin Massacre" of 1870 pushed the matter into the background for a couple of years. After 1872, officials wanted the church's complete removal from the site in order for the Empress Dowager to erect housing to live in when she "retired" from administrative matters.[158] The emperor's death in early 1875 kept Cixi active at court and she continued to live within the Forbidden City. The matter of the church remained an issue albeit not an urgent one.

The Third North Church (*1888–Present*). With the ascension of another boy ruler (the Guangxu emperor, r. 1875–1908), the Empress Dowager Cixi continued to dominante court politics. Under her self-centered control, supported by conservative-minded officials, the dynasty's programs to strengthen the empire slowed as they diverted funds to projects such as the construction of a sprawling and exorbitantly expensive Summer Palace (Yiheyuan).[159] Thinking that her role would shrink when the emperor came of age in 1887, she wanted to remain close to the palace and, if need be, monitor his policies. Moving to the Imperial City's northern sector, as she had hoped fifteen years earlier, continued to be blocked by the North Church's existence. High officials now claimed its towers would overlook an area available for housing and gardens. Using trees, walls, and screens to block sight lines carried little appeal because she (and court conservatives) in fact deeply resented Western Christians, really all Westerners, because of their prominent presence in Beijing. Removal of the church would restore a modicum of Qing dignity while bolstering her influence among certain factions at court. To some it meant that, similarly, they might one day remove Catholicism from China. On the vicariate's side, its leaders, from Mouly's time onward, appreciated its long history in an exclusive

---

157   *JWJAD*, 11/1/76, 69. Officials soon added the argument that from atop the towers one could gaze into the Forbidden City. 11/1/126, 115.

158   Cixi anticipated that after the Tongzhi emperor came of age and took the government's reins, she would need a mansion within the Imperial City and close to the palace to monitor imperial activities. Ferreux, *Histoire de la Congrégation*, 199–203. Residential space became the court's central reason for its removal. For personal reasons, the emperor liked the same area. Jung Chang, *Empress Dowager Cixi: The Concubine Who Launched Modern China* (New York: Anchor Books, 2014), 106. In the early 1870s, workers started clearing dwellings from a favored place but then stopped because of the emperor's death. The Guangxu emperor's assumption of power, his majority coming in the mid-1880s, led Cixi to reconsider use of the area for her residence. Young, *Ecclesiastical Colony*, 56.

159   It replaced the Summer Palace destroyed by Anglo-French forces in 1860. Provincial officials struggled to keep tax revenues flowing to the capital to fund a court increasingly out of touch with fiscal reality.

neighborhood as well as one-time imperial support for Christianity. When high officials approached Bishop Delaplace in 1872 and again two years later, he reacted slowly and carefully because he understood the implications of retroceding the property. He realized that the current site offered little available space for physical expansion; as his cathedral grew so would Catholicism. Only with exceptional incentives, that is, the right replacement property and hefty financial subsidies, might an agreement happen.[160]

Talks dragged on then stopped due to Delaplace's death in May 1884. Then another delay occurred due to war between France and China over control of Tonkin (northern Vietnam) that started in August. Fighting ended in April 1885, with discussions about the church's transfer resuming a year later. Bishop François-Ferdinand Tagliabue, C.M., relied on Beijing's most experienced missionary and savviest negotiator, Favier, who agreed with his former prelate's position on how to proceed. Accordingly, he sought a suitably located and amply sized replacement site within the Imperial City plus monetary compensation for the other buildings that would have to be abandoned. Favier eventually found a spacious location at Xishiku, a former imperial warehouse area about four-tenths of a mile to the northwest, its nineteen acres offering ample room for future expansion.[161] (Due to its location, it became known as the Xishiku church.[162]) Zhili Governor-general Li Hongzhang, highly respected and experienced, represented the Qing side. He and Favier worked out an agreement that Tagliabue found quite acceptable.[163] The vicariate would receive $567,000 for reconstruction of the church, gardens, and other buildings in addition to the Sisters' various facilities. Favier in a show of gratitude to Li magnanimously reduced the total sum to $441,000. Li Hongzhang responded by agreeing to the continued use of the words *chijian* on the façade and the erection of two stelae,

---

160 Chambon, *Vie et Apostolat*, 236–239. A detailed account of the negotiations involved in the transfer of the North Church is provided by Cordier, *Histoire des relations*, 2:605–624.

161 The area was 1,148 feet (north-south) by 722 feet (east-west) minus a small plot for an existing temple. Favier, *Péking* (1902), 255. Another study writes that it doubled the area of the former site. Ferreux, *Histoire de la Congrégation*, 203.

162 Outside the principal gate, a metal plaque identifies it as "The Xishiku Church" in English and Chinese. Author's field notes, 1 October 2016.

163 In the early 1880s, Li Hongzhang indicated an interest in establishing direct diplomatic contact with the Holy See as a way to weaken French involvement in religious cases, a change that would have proved detrimental to France's religious protectorate and, probably, to active missionaries like Favier. Young, *Ecclesiastical Colony*, 55–59, discusses how this issue and the transfer of the North Church became entwined. Another scholar thinks that the establishment of direct relations may have been a gambit on the part of Li Hongzhong to help convince the Vincentians to proceed with the negotiations to move it. Professor R.G. Tiedemann, email to author, 7 October 2017.

one inscribed with the imperial decree approving the settlement.[164] Although not previously mentioned by either side, Favier unilaterally ordered the verso of each stele to provide, from a religious perspective, information about the North Church's history and details about the agreement to move to the site. The Vincentians could not have done better than this. A confrere later lauded Favier for trading a site with limitations for one with a sacred edifice that had been "re-established and reconstructed, on the most liberal scale, at the expense of the Chinese government."[165] Whatever Qing officials thought, they did not complain publicly and ordered workers to demolish the buildings as soon as missionaries had departed the Canchikou Lane site in December 1887.

Unlike Mouly who in 1867 had time to employ a French architect to design his cathedral, Qing negotiators pressed Favier to vacate, leading him to act as chief designer and site supervisor. Accordingly, he fast tracked the project. In his book, *Péking*, Favier modestly says little about his architectural role and nothing about the acquisition of materials and construction. What is known is that after laying the first foundation stone on 30 May 1887 Favier pushed the workers hard to finish quickly and, to achieve this, increased the force employed to fourteen hundred. On a granite foundation, they built a church that stretched in length to 276 feet, its nave measuring 66 feet across and its transept 108 feet.[166] Internal columns limited the height, per agreement, to about 55 feet, lower than the previous one. Its spires were seventy or eighty feet high.[167] The façade had a nice symmetry with three entrances, each with Gothic-like pointed arches. Above the central doorway hung a wooden plaque vertically inscribed in Chinese: Guangxu *shisan nian chijian tianzhutang* ("[in] the thirteenth year of the Guangxu emperor [1887] the Catholic church [is] built by imperial permission"). A large rose window dominated the next level with three narrow windows flanking it on each side. At the center of the top level, the ornate façade had at its centerpiece a white marble bas-relief of the Good Shepard and his fold. Four narrow columns defined three triangular pediments. The façade included four statues of saints, at that time the only one in Beijing to do so.[168] Architecturally different from all others in Beijing, it was the

---

164   Ferreux, *Histoire de la Congrégation*, 204; and Favier, *Péking* (1902): 253–255.

165   "Province of China [L. de la Briere's report]," *Annals CM-E* 2 (1895): 246–247.

166   Favier, *Péking* (1902): 256.

167   The measurements are from Ferreux, *Histoire de la Congrégation*, 204. Slightly smaller ones are given in "China," *Annals CM-E* 7 (1900): 516–517. The spires' height in 1888 are my estimate based on today's measurements. A metal plaque outside the gate puts the current height at 102 feet. Author's field notes, 1 October 2016.

168   My description comes from a photograph taken in the late 1890s. Favier, *Péking* (1897). For another photo of it, see Diana Preston, *The Boxer Rebellion: The Dramatic Story of*

FIGURE 3.19   The third North Church, late 1890s
               SOURCE: FAVIER, *PÉKING*, 1897

city's as well as China's largest.[169] Favier trumpeted that it had been "erected at
the expense of the Emperor and at the cost of 160,000 dollars," also making it
the most expensive.[170] Through concerted and coordinated effort, workers had
finished it in less than one year. Bishop Tagliabue raised his episcopal cross at
his grand sacred structure on 9 December 1888.[171]

The abundantly large and rectangularly shaped cathedral grounds swiftly
filled with many buildings.[172] As agreed, in front and to each side of the church
were two white marble stelae. They were inscribed in Chinese and Manchu
with an imperial decree that detailed religious activities in Beijing at the former

---

China's War on Foreigners that Shook the World in the Summer of 1900 (New York: Walker
& Company, 1899), 264.

169   Favier, *Péking* (1902): 256.

170   Favier letter, 4 October 1899, *Annals CM-E* 7 (1900): 221–222.

171   Favier, *Péking* (1902), 255–259; Ferreux, *Histoire de la Congrégation*, 204; and Planchet
       [A. Thomas, pseud.], *Histoire de la mission de Pékin*, 2:605–624.

172   After 1900, Sisters of St. Joseph established their motherhouse about fifty yards to the
       southeast. Their site included a chapel and several structures, some still standing.
       Ferreux, *Histoire de la Congrégation*, 277. After destruction by the Boxers, they rebuilt. An
       eighty-year-old religious sister who grew up nearby remembers their activities at the loca-
       tion. The buildings are currently in very poor condition. Author's field notes, 3 October
       2016. The vicariate owned a lot of property, including a large chapel and land at Zhalan.
       "China," *Annals CM-E* 7 (1900): 516–517. "China—Pekin," *Annals CM-E* 8 (1901): 61–63.

FIGURE 3.20   Aerial view of North Church and grounds, 1899
                SOURCE: ARCHIVES CM, PARIS

site as well as information regarding the transfer to the new location. Pavilions
with imperial yellow roof tiles protected the stelae and sat prominently to each
side of the façade, further spotlighting the church's "right" to be there.[173] (See
Appendix 5 for details on the stelae and translations.) Their presence reminds
us of the pair at the South Church, standing similarly as imperial symbols to
bolster Catholicism's status.[174]

   The ground's south half included a reception building, garden area, dwellings, and support facilities for priests, two seminaries, and miscellaneous buildings. In addition to these, two important structures were: 1) a library building
that housed the church's famous collection of books that then numbered about

---

173   Hubrecht, *La mission de Péking*, 318.
174   I do not believe that the use or placement of these pavilions and stelae represent Favier's
      attempt to sinicize architecturally the North Church, but there are some minor details
      that may give such an impression. Modern-day Chinese scholars focus on small design
      features in order to write of a blended Sino-Western church style—and come across as re-
      peating politically correct verbiage. Favier's erection of a stele at the Wanghailou church
      in Tianjin in 1897 was part of his passive-aggressive approach with Qing officials (see
      Chapter 5's section on the second Wanghailou church). Likewise, the stelae at the North
      Church were for religio-political purposes. Note that formal interest in adding Chinese
      elements to sacred buildings would not begin until the 1920s (see Chapter 8). Also, see
      Anthony E. Clark, "China Gothic: Indigenous' Church Design in Late-Imperial Beijing,"
      History Faculty Scholarship. Paper 10. Spokane, Wash.: Whitworth University, 2015.

twelve thousand volumes; and 2) the Lazarist Press, a busy printing office with
workshops, and storage rooms. An east-west lane split the grounds in half with
the north side occupied by the Daughters of Charity, who had their own chapel
and residential buildings as well as an orphanage, nursery, sewing room, and
"a [women's] catechumenate." With space to expand, they added a girls' school,
dispensary, embroidery workshop, and many miscellaneous structures. Some
referred to their facilities under the Chinese name Renci tang, often translated

FIGURE 3.21   Alphonse Favier, wearing his padded winter coat, late 1890s.
               He arrived at Beijing in 1862, first working with Bishop
               Mouly and then with others in northern Zhili until serving as
               bishop himself from 1899 to 1905. Active in the 1870 Tianjin
               settlement, the transfer of the North Church in 1887–1888,
               the reconstruction of the Wanghailou church in 1897, the
               Boxer siege of the North Church in 1900, and many other
               important matters, he is arguably the most notable
               Vincentian of the era.
               SOURCE: ARCHIVES CM, PARIS

as "House of Mercy."[175] At the end of the century, a photographer in a hot-air balloon captured an aerial view of Beijing's (and China's) largest mission compound, one that can only hint at the numerous activities there.

Although the bishop had not predicted the apocalyptic fin de siècle Boxers rampaging through North China killing Western missionaries and Chinese Christians as well as destroying churches, he still saw the need for security. Moreover, virtually every place of status, whether a government office, temple, or high-ranking person's mansion, were enclosed by walls. The expensive cathedral contained, as did its many support buildings, valuable mobile property. Favier ordered the site's perimeter secured by a tall, well-built brick wall that measured over seven-tenths of a mile in total length.[176] Its immediate security value is self-evident; who would have thought of it serving as a formidable defensive barrier against armed attackers?

Inside the protected grounds during the summer of 1900, Bishop Favier took responsibility for the lives of 71 Europeans and approximately 3,300 Chinese of whom more than 80 percent were Catholic refugees from inside and outside the city.[177] He and his confreres, with the crucial aid of a small contingent of soldiers, defended the compound against the Boxer siege that lasted for several months.[178] Determined Boxers fired at them with rifles, used cannons to shell the grounds indiscriminately, and tunneled under the walls in attempts to enter as even more resolute defenders rallied repeatedly to repel them. Catholics died and buildings took gunfire hits, though the cathedral went relatively unscathed. In mid-August, Allied (Western and Japanese) military forces stormed into Beijing, forcing Boxers to flee for their lives, and quickly relieving the Legation Quarter and North Church. A photograph of the time shows a grateful bishop standing on the church's front steps surrounded by French officers and soldiers who came to give thanks (singing "*Te Deum*") for victory over the Boxers. Afterwards, workers quickly completed minor repairs. Given the dynasty's weakened position vis-à-vis the Allied powers, Favier did not ask for the court's approval before ordering the façade's top sections increased in

---

175 "China," *Annals CM-E* 7 (1900): 517; De Vienne letter, 19 April 1901, *Annals CM-E* 8 (1901): 507–508; and Ferreux, *Histoire de la Congrégation*, 277.

176 "Mgr. Favier at Rome and in France," *Annals CM-E* 8 (1901): 225; and Ferreux, *Histoire de la Congrégation*, 244.

177 Within the Legation Quarter, a roughly defined line of defense consisting of walls and street barricades arose. There, more than four thousand people took refuge, over 75 percent of them Chinese Christians (Protestant and Catholics), some rescued from certain death when Boxers attacked Beijing, others fleeing there from the countryside. Preston, *Boxer Rebellion*, 66–86.

178 The bishop gives these numbers for 22 June in his account of three hard months of fighting. Favier, *Heart of Pekin*, 29–30.

height by about twenty or thirty feet (with the central portion left as before). This made it very close to the height of the former North Church. With the Empress Dowager Cixi still in Xi'an—she had fled there in 1900—the bishop simply ignored the 1887 agreement on the church's verticality, taking it for granted that he had the power to do what he wanted.[179] He diplomatically skipped mention of the change in letters and reports. Others did not comment on Favier's unilateral action—what was there to say? The only acknowledgment of it I have seen is a short sentence in a courtyard display that plainly says that after 1900 the church was repaired—and made higher, like it is today.[180]

Over the next three decades, priests saw a resurgence of interest in religion. From his cathedral, the bishop emphasized a two-prong strategy of making converts and building sacred structures for all the urban as well as rural districts. During the war years, 1937–1949, expansion could not be sustained, and efforts shifted to relief work. After 1949, activities directed out of the North Church steadily declined and with the death of its bishop in 1964 the diocese had no episcopal leader.[181] Two years later, when the Cultural Revolution buffeted Beijing, the situation worsened. Red Guards toppled the stelae and desecrated the building by stripping the façade of its icons and emptying the interior of everything religious. Size and height provided protection in a sense because political zealots did not have the means or will to destroy it. Eventually, a middle school occupied the grounds and used the many buildings for a variety of purposes. Most of the security wall came down and, on all sides, residential and commercial buildings impinged on Catholic property. By the time the Beijing government returned the property to the Catholic Patriotic Association, its footprint had been greatly diminished.

The diocese moved quickly in the 1980s to restore the North Church for religious services, with a formal opening on Christmas Eve 1985. Since then Catholics have expanded their activities, in the process remodeling old structures and constructing new ones. An exterior project initiated in 2016 and completed two years later left the façade looking virtually the same as it did in the early twentieth century, except perhaps for its color, a pastel blue. Over the main door hangs a tablet, a reproduction of the original one, Catholics still

---

179   Cixi did not return to Beijing until January 1902. Chang, *Empress Dowager Cixi*, 309. Important matters related to the aftermath of the Boxer Uprising awaited her and she ignored the church's change in height.

180   "Beitang jianjie" (church courtyard display, 2007); Author's field notes, 14 October 2007. A comparison of pre- and post-1900 photographs confirms the façade's alteration.

181   It would be 1979 before the Beijing Diocese had a bishop appointed. Dating back to 1307, he is counted as the thirty-first bishop. *Beijing Tianzhu jiaohui*, item entitled "Beijing jiaoqu Mi'e'er Fu Tieshan zhujiao jinmu ershiwu zhounian, 1979.12.21–2004.12.21."

FIGURE 3.22   The renovated third North Church, 1901–1902
SOURCE: ARCHIVES CM, PARIS

proudly proclaiming that they had built it with imperial permission. Likewise, reconstructed pavilions house reproductions of the imperial stelae mentioned above. The tops of the stelae, damaged during the Cultural Revolution, rest on the ground not far from the pavilions. In the church's far northern portion, behind the apse, a small chapel shelters Favier's tombstone.[182] Given his prominent role in building and protecting the North Church it seems fitting that his remains and marker are there, a personal testimony of sorts at Beijing's oldest extant sacred structure to the connection between the past and present.

This section cannot end without a brief comment on the extensive changes made to the interior and finished in 2018. In a turn toward a non-traditional look, the chancel has been spatially, visually, and conceptually opened up. Reflective and colorful mosaic tiles cover the pulpit and altar making them sparkle in the seemingly enlarged ritual space. Visible on the far back wall, written in traditional type Chinese characters, are the Kangxi emperor's well-known words, *wan you zhen yuan*. The accompanying couplet that once hung behind the altar has been removed. The interior columns are painted in blue and gold shades that coordinate attractively with the red and gold highlighting

---

182   Author's field notes, 12 May 2007. At Xuanhua (see Chapter 6's section for this place), two bishops are interred within the cathedral. It is the only other example I know of.

FIGURE 3.23   The present-day North Church. Note the Our Lady of China sacred grotto (far
right) and the two pavilions with replicas of late Qing stelae.
SOURCE: PHOTO BY AUTHOR, 2018

of the ceiling ribs. There are new, intricately designed stained-glass windows
in the nave and side chapels.[183] They tell Catholicism's story in China and
the world with certain aspects and figures given special attention. On the
nave's east side, the next to last window features a likeness of Favier holding
a Chinese copy of his book on Catholicism in Beijing. The church as it looked
before 1901–1902 is depicted above him. On the opposite side of the nave in a
side chapel area is a decorative window depicting Mary holding a young Jesus,
a popular rendition of Our Lady of China. The interior is beautifully twenty-
first century in appearance yet preserves and subtly emphasizes cultural and
religious features relevant to its century-long place as Beijing's cathedral.[184]

---

183   The stained glass is marked: "Sheng Lujia yishu SLucaart (*sic*) Beijing 2017."
184   Author's field notes, 23 and 26 August 2018.

1.4   The West Church (*Xitang*)

During Qing times, the Xitang's location was on a street in the northwestern corner of the Inner City about a mile from Xizhi Gate, where the emperor exited on his way to the Western Hills for their scenic beauty and cool temperatures. Based on its location relative to the other three sacred structures, it naturally became the West Church. Many people prefer to call it the Xizhimen church. It is the little sister of Beijing's historic ones, the smallest and last built, dating to the first quarter of the eighteenth century.

The First West Church (1723–1730). In late 1705, a papal legation headed by Carlo Tommaso Maillard de Tournon arrived in Beijing to promote Catholic activities and harmonize relations among the various missionary groups. His main duty was to inform the Jesuits that the pope did not agree with their toleration of Chinese Christians' practice of ancestral veneration. When word of the pope's formal order to discontinue the practice reached Tournon, he told the Jesuits to abide by the decision or face excommunication. The Kangxi emperor learned of the decision and objected on several grounds: the Rites Controversy had begun. Demonstrating his own authority, the emperor commanded the arrest of Tournon not knowing that he had already departed the capital and was safely in Macao. There, in 1710, he met Fr. Teodorico Pedrini, C.M., a member of the papal-directed legation who had arrived late in China after taking a separate, circuitous route. In spite of priests becoming persona non grata, Tournon knew of the emperor's interest in Western music and recommended that Pedrini use his talent in that field to gain access to the capital. He went the next year and became a highly regarded composer, performer, and music teacher at the Qing court. Confident that his position was long term, he requested imperial permission to purchase residential property for himself and the handful of non-Jesuit Italians residing in Beijing.

Pedrini found a site that included seventy rooms dispersed among a number of residential buildings and ten courtyards—there may have been an attached vacant parcel as well.[185] The priest spent nineteen hundred taels of silver to purchase the property, the money coming from mission funds, donations, and savings from his imperial salary. Since the emperor did not authorize construction of a formal sacred structure, Pedrini discretely made space within an existing structure for a small chapel. After the Kangxi emperor's death, Pedrini

---

185   The area is said to have been six and two-thirds acres (forty *mu*). Yang Qingyun, *Beijing Tianzhujiao shi*, 148. Paul Bornet gives the north-south measurement as roughly 317 feet, implying a two-acre parcel. See his "Les anciennes églises de Pékin: notes d'histoire— le Si-t'ang, *Bulletin catholique de Pékin*" 32 (1945): 297. Also, *The Vincentians*, vol. 2, *The Eighteenth Century to 1789*, 510.

served the Yongzheng emperor, and, in accordance with his position at court, friendly high officials gave him permission to enlarge his place of worship. In 1723, he dedicated it to Our Lady of Seven Dolors. Propaganda Fide exercised authority over it and mostly Italian priests used it. It was the first non-Jesuit built church in Beijing, and as such it is unfortunate that historical sources reveal nothing about its architecture. It may be deduced that funding and circumstances did not allow for a grandiose structure. Indeed, one scholar describes it as "very little."[186]

The Second West Church, 1730–1811. Although it did not survive the 1730 earthquake that flattened houses all over Beijing, Pedrini rebuilt quickly with high officials unconcerned about or unaware of a modest-sized church tucked away unobtrusively among many dwellings. The entire site had a security wall surrounding it, shielding it further. Unlike the other sacred structures, it had neither the imperial cachet of *chijian* nor the receipt of construction funds directly from the imperial treasury—only the tolerance of those that knew of the missionary's ties to the court.[187] Shortly after the enthronement of the Qianlong emperor in 1736 high officials ignored its existence, reporting that there were three not four churches in the capital.[188]

Whether it possessed private or public status, Pedrini made the West Church operational with mass and rites. "It is poor and small," Pedrini wrote, "but quite busy; I fulfill there all the functions that one has in the other churches."[189] From the street, entrance to the site was via a gate that led to a front courtyard and two adjoining rooms that were used for congregational activities and as shelter from bad weather. The sanctuary was far enough away from the priests' residential quarters that people could come and go without disturbing them. The church's main entrance was, if true to today's orientation, on the north side of the structure and close to the street. An activity unique to the location that Pedrini instituted in 1744 was the Confraternity of Our Lady of Seven Dolors— women helping other women. Pedrini built and lived at the site until his death on 10 December 1746 at the age of 76. Confreres interred Pedrini at the church's own cemetery, located not far away.

For the next sixty-five years of the church's existence (1746–1811) we have only a few hints of religious activities. In 1780, Giovanni Damasceno Salutti (an

---

186 *The Vincentians*, vol. 2, *The Eighteenth Century to 1789*, 516. The West Church had its own cemetery known as the "Italians' Cemetery," and the "Cemetery of Propaganda [Fide]," at a site facing the Zhalan cemetery. Bornet, "Les anciennes églises … Si-t'ang," 294.

187 Yang Qingyun writes, without citation, that the Yongzheng emperor donated one thousand taels of silver for its renovation. *Beijing Tianzhujiao shi*, 147. She may have confused it with the emperor's gift of the same sum for the South Church's repairs.

188 Bornet, "Les anciennes églises … Si-t'ang," 297.

189 Ibid.

Augustinian in China under Propaganda Fide) received consecration as Bishop of Beijing there. A few years later, several priests stayed at it while awaiting deportation to Macao. Given the dwindling number of missionaries still working in or visiting Beijing and the heavy weight of the imperial proscription of Christianity, a dearth of information is not surprising. Propaganda Fide eventually authorized its priests in Beijing to sell the site; since no buyer came forward high officials paid an undisclosed sum and had it razed in 1811.[190] Priests at the North Church did their best to shepherd the small flock living near the West Church. As previously noted, by the 1830s Beijing had just one church and one elderly missionary in poor health. During the next three decades, the Beijing neighborhood that surrounded the West Church site reabsorbed the property into its residential life.

The Third West Church (1867–1900). With the French Convention of 1860 stipulating the return of former Catholic-owned properties, the Xianfeng emperor ordered an official inquiry to determine details regarding the West Church's former location, size, and current occupancy. Officials found the site and measured it at 188 feet to each side, or about eight-tenths of an acre, much smaller than that indicated by Pedrini. Buildings included a house used as a rice-noodle shop, some low-level government offices, dwellings, and a vacant courtyard to the site's backside.[191] The report made no mention of ongoing religious activities. Bishop Joseph Mouly received an ownership certificate to the site on 10 January 1861. His priorities in the early 1860s were in this order: repair the South Church; rebuild the North Church and make it his episcopal seat; build a chapel at the East Church site; and, last, construct the West Church.

Guillon, a Jesuit interested and experienced in restoring places of worship, looked for the west-side one in 1863 only to find a few poorly constructed buildings that catechists utilized as a makeshift school and chapel.[192] What few Catholics still lived in the vicinity slowly and hesitatingly returned for mass. Mouly wrote in early 1867 that three rooms in an old building there had collapsed one night and, if there had been rain, "the apartments we use for a chapel would have also been in ruins." Despite his assignment of two Chinese priests to work there, the site remained grim with "neither the chapel nor the housing" suitable for sustained use.[193] That year from his limited financial reserves he found funds to commence construction of the sacred structure, with supervision of the project placed on Bro. Marty's shoulders since he

---

190   The Vincentians, vol. 3, Revolution and Restoration (1789–1843), 667.
191   The following quotes Zhouban yiwu shimo as one of its sources. "Xizhimen tianzhutang," http://baike.baidu.com/view/764328.htm?fromtitle=%E8%A5%BF%E5%A0%82&fromid=5814456&type=syn (accessed 21 October 2016).
192   Bornet, "Les anciennes églises … Si-t'ang," 298–299.
193   "China," Annals PF 28 (1867): 362.

FIGURE 3.24
The third West Church, late 1890s
SOURCE: FAVIER, *PÉKING*, 1897

had experience building the North Church. Its probable cost ranged between $10,000 and $20,000.[194] Later, dwellings and schools found space on the
grounds.[195] Needless to say, Boxers burned every building to the ground in June
1900.

---

194   Favier knew the construction expenses for Beijing's East and North Churches (see
      Chapter 2's section on costs) and stated that "the cost of the other large churches ranges
      from 10,000 to 20,000 dollars." Favier letter, 4 October 1899, *Annals CM-E* 7 (1900): 221. The
      only large ones were the West Church and those (usually called chapels) at Zhengfu si and
      Zhalan.
195   "China—Pekin," *Annals CM-E* 8 (1901): 64.

FIGURE 3.25   The West Church, today
SOURCE: PHOTO BY AUTHOR, 2018

The Fourth West Church (1913–Present). Worshippers had to use a provision-ary chapel for over ten years before Bishop Stanislas-François Jarlin, C.M., acquired construction funds, primarily from the generous donation of Sr. Rosalie Branssier of the Daughters of Charity. A Vincentian father, François Selinka, supervised the work. As at other churches, to ensure standardized size and high quality he ordered custom-made bricks. Visible on the building's west wall are bricks imprinted with Chinese that marked them for use here. Also preserved in an exterior wall is a rectangular masonry frame, within which is presented four roof tiles and four bricks bearing the marks "Pierre Engels,

Tchan[g]-sin-tien," the man contracted to monitor their manufacture at the village (*cun*) of Changxindian, a locale with a large congregation located south of Beijing.[196] (The West Church is unique in China for making former construction materials into a historical display.) From the bricks assembled, Selinka watched the erection of a simple, beautiful structure approximately 154 feet in length by 36 wide with a vaulted ceiling 34 feet above the floor.[197] The façade was not ornate, distinguished by a tall bell tower (several stories in height, my estimate is 104 feet high) with a steep hip roof topped by a cross that made it unique among the four historic ones of Beijing. The church's axis is north-south with the chancel on the south side far away from the nearby street and main entrance to the courtyard.

The bishop had Latin and Chinese inscribed in two black marble slabs placed opposite each other at eye level in the interior's entrance walls to inform all who entered something about the church's history. The translated Latin version reads as follows:

> To God, Best and Greatest.
>
> In 1723, Teodorico Pedrini, a priest of the Congregation of the Mission and tutor of the Kangxi emperor used his own money to purchase this site and on it dedicated a church to God under the auspices of the Seven Sorrows of the Blessed Virgin Mary.
>
> In the time of the persecution of the Jiaqing [emperor's] (1811) reign this church was totally destroyed. In 1867, Most Illustrious Bishop Mouly, C.M., built here a new sanctuary that on June 15, 1900 was burned by the Boxers while they cruelly killed Maurice Doré, C.M., the pastor of the church.
>
> Finally, in 1912 through the generosity of Rosalie Branssier of the Daughters of Charity a third church named Holy Mary of Mt. Carmel was built here. In memory of all this Most Illustrious Bishop Jarlin, C.M., Vicar Apostolic of Beijing, has erected this stone.[198]

---

196   In the mid-1930s, over sixteen hundred Catholics lived in the Changxindian area—they had a church and at least one chapel. Archives CM, Paris, Folder 163-I, "Vicariat Apostolique de Pékin. État de la Mission, du 1er Juillet 1936 au 30 Juin 1937," 202.

197   Using various means to check, these measurements seem accurate. Author's field notes, 4 September 2016.

198   Jiaqing reigned from 1796 to 1820. My thanks to Rev. John E. Rybolt and Professor Charles A. Litzinger for help with the translation. For the Latin text, see Appendix 6.

Fr. François-Xavier Desrumaux, C.M., dedicated it on 16 July 1913, the liturgical feast day of the patron, Our Lady of Mount Carmel.[199] The church survived
the founding of the Republic of China, the Sino-Japanese War, and the Cultural
Revolution, though not unscathed. In the 1960s, Red Guards demolished the
bell tower, stenciled slogans in large red characters on the façade (still faintly
visible today) and removed from the interior all religious icons and furniture.
During those tumultuous years, button, electric fan, and pharmaceutical factories variously used the large grounds with the church sometimes serving as
a warehouse. The users demolished some buildings and in time projects on
the east, west, and north sides impinged on the property, these multi-storied
buildings too valuable to be removed. In 1994, the West Church reopened for
religious services, the last of the early ones to do so. The congregation has
gradually restored the interior, replacing missing stained-glass windows with
recently designed ones that tell the history of the Catholicism in Beijing, and
rebuilding the bell tower. When more funds became available in 2008–2009,
the diocese refurbished it further with attention to the tower and courtyard
that features a small sacred grotto for Mary.[200] Various improvements continue with workers present in the summer of 2018 to replace uneven and broken
courtyard pavers.

2   Two Early Twentieth Century Sacred Structures

The churches discussed above are certainly Beijing's most celebrated. During
the early twentieth century two more joined the cityscape. The first, located
southeast of the central city's prominent Tiananmen Gate is St. Michael's.
When erected it was in the Legation Quarter, just inside the Inner City's southern wall, not far away from high-level Qing government boards and luxurious
mansions occupied by high officials. After 1860, Western countries established
diplomatic offices in this area. Surrounded by various security barriers it became the Legation Quarter. Narrow Dongjiaomin Lane ran through its center,
which foreigners expanded and renamed Legation Street. Today, off the eastern side of Tiananmen Square, is the easily missed entrance to the street. It
extends for about a mile past government offices, chic businesses, and dated

---

199 Our Lady of Mount Carmel is the title given to Blessed Virgin Mary in her role as pa-
      tron of the Carmelite Order. "Our Lady of Mount Carmel," https://en.wikipedia.org/wiki/
      Our_Lady_of_Mount_Carmel (accessed 13 April 2016).
200 "Xizhi men tianzhutang," http://baike.baidu.com/link?url=866ut-Z4lacbFogA14D5PhJb2
      EINaRl9cz95zEKxJFkBhxlLNSBNhP-etap63WOAOnTIFovOfPT1FIs4r5XFzA89ziAZd
      2PiO1aFoQGMepqz0s1l6eVjRupZXpFkZQwoh69i7nOie1HwPxsLHL5-xk (accessed
      13 April 2016).

buildings to the Church of St. Michael.[201] The second church, St. Thérèse's, arose at Nangangzi, a small area within the former Outer City. Situated inconspicuously in a neighborhood of meandering alleyways and longstanding courtyard houses, once common all over Beijing, not much has changed—the ambience hinting of days gone by. A local man jokingly told me that the area's residents are Beijing's "aborigines."[202] Unmarked on most maps, few domestic or international travelers visit the parish.

2.1   The Legation Street Church, St. Michael's (1904–Present)

When the French minister officially moved to Beijing in late 1860, he occupied a Qing nobleman's mansion located about one mile south and slightly east of the main entrance to the Forbidden City. In late Qing times, the area had great symbolic importance to the foreign powers because proximity to the emperor brought a semblance of the national respect they demanded and the equality in relations the Qing court pretended to concede. Great Britain soon joined France at this location, with the representatives of other countries arriving later.[203] Over the next four decades, the Legation Quarter area expanded as the number of diplomats assigned to Beijing grew. They built Western-style houses, offices, banks, post offices, hotels, and restaurants, and acquired additional property in a mixed area that included fewer and fewer Manchus and Chinese. For a time, only the South Church stood open to worshippers, but even with the reconstruction of three more places of worship, Catholics living in the Legation Quarter found it inconvenient to go to any of them for daily mass. To alleviate this, Vincentians first established a small chapel within the grounds of the French Legation. By the early 1880s, worshippers had outgrown the space. Favier, with financial assistance from the French minister, then constructed separate chapels for Chinese and Westerners as well as housing for the pastor: the total cost came to approximately $7,100.[204]

Boxers entering Beijing in 1900 made Christians and Westerners their primary targets. Following the traumatic effects of seeing Boxers burning, looting, and almost breaching the walls of the North Church and the Legation Quarter, the French took measures to secure their future place in the capital. One was to increase the number of diplomatic and military personnel stationed in the capital, personnel that would need a large Chinese support staff. Westerners

---

201   A bronze plate with historical information is mounted on a wall across the street from the main entry. Author's field notes, 21 October 2011.

202   Author's field notes, 24 September 2016.

203   The Legation Quarter served as the diplomatic headquarters for various countries until 1959, when they were moved to another area.

204   Planchet [A. Thomas, pseud.], Histoire de la mission de Pékin, 2:591–593 (for more on the legation, see his vol. 2, chapter 5, section 4).

considered local Catholics to be the most trustworthy workers and hired as many as they could. The chapel inside the French Legation's walled grounds soon became too small for them and its location involved security issues. Consequently, Favier decided the time had come to construct another sacred structure. In 1901, he signed a ninety-nine-year lease agreement for $2,630 with the French minister, who specified that this part of the legation's property was to be under the sole control of "Lazaristes français."[205] Favier proceeded to design the church himself.[206] Preoccupied with many matters, he put a Vincentian in day-to-day charge of a project that extended over three years.[207]

Off Legation Street, workers built it of grey bricks; its size, about ninety-eight feet in length by thirty-three wide, gave it a smaller footprint than any of the other churches already examined. Favier ordered that it follow the traditional Chinese directional layout for buildings, which put the chancel in the north and the entrance in the south. This version's size proved inadequate and within a few years it was enlarged to its current size—I estimate it to be about 165 feet long by 48 in width. Its seating capacity rose to about one thousand people.[208] Parishioners think it is a "small and exquisite" Gothic-style church that combines some of the best features of Beijing's other sacred structures. From an examination of the sole old photograph of it, the current façade reproduces accurately the original.[209] Then and now it comes across as a unique design, especially since it has prominently displayed on its exterior a statue of St. Michael and two other saints. The narrow façade consists of three horizontal sections: the lower central one recessed and consisting of two tall doors with a triangular window and pointed arches above. On the second level is a white sculpture of a winged St. Michael, sword in hand, on a pedestal that extends outward from the façade. This presentation gives it additional prominence. The highest level of the middle portion is a triangular pediment topped by a cross. On either side of the entryways are square towers that at the first level include niches for two white sculptures: the one on the east is of St. Paul and the west side one is of St. Peter. Replicated over each at the next level are narrow windows filled with wooden slats. The third tower level is octagonal

---

205 The money was probably not paid, the lease's sole purpose to convey legally the property "ownership" rights. Archives CM, Paris, Box "Soeurs Josephines."

206 Proactive Favier would have deferred to no one in designing it.

207 Chinese materials identify Gao Jiali as the priest who supervised the construction. *Beijing Tianzhu jiaohui*, item entitled "Dongjiaominxiang tianzhutang;" and Author's field notes, 21 October 2011. Fr. Jean Capy, C.M., was probably the priest; he went by the Chinese name Gao Rohan. Van den Brandt, *Les Lazaristes*, 115–116.

208 *Beijing Tianzhu jiaohui*, item entitled "Dongjiaominxiang tianzhutang;" and Author's field notes, 21 October 2011.

209 *Beijing Tianzhu jiaohui*, item entitled "Dongjiaominxiang tianzhutang;" and Author's field notes, 21 October 2011.

FIGURE 3.26   Beijing's St. Michael's Church (completed, 1905) as seen in 1948
SOURCE: ARCHIVES CM, PARIS

shaped and topped with sharply angled spires rising high above the central section's cross. The building's narrowness gives emphasis to verticality, the architectural sum effect making it resemble, if any, the North Church.

In 1904, Bishop Favier dedicated it to St. Michael, the guardian archangel who in Heaven had led righteous spiritual forces to victory over those of evil, perhaps a not-so-subtle way of referencing recent events. Coincidentally, he was the bishop's own patron saint.[210] On grounds of about one acre, workers

---

210   St. Michael represents a sort of spiritual warrior fighting against evil on personal and societal levels. "Saint Michael in the Catholic Church," https://en.wikipedia.org/wiki/Saint_Michael_in_the_Catholic_Church (accessed 6 April 2106). A Chinese author writes that

FIGURE 3.27   St. Michael's Church, a popular venue for pre-wedding
               picture staging
               SOURCE: PHOTO BY AUTHOR, 2011

added a house, catechumenate, and school. A Vincentian, Jean Capy, served as
the first pastor of a fast-growing congregation.[211]

Its location in the diplomats' area helped St. Michael's survive the various
conflicts consuming China from the 1920s to the 1940s. Undamaged and open
in 1949, priests continued to say mass until 1958 when government authorities
closed it. During the Cultural Revolution, Red Guards stripped the grounds of
all religious iconography and allowed a neighborhood elementary school to

---

Michael the archangel protects Catholics, and they all revere and love him. Yang Qingyun,
Beijing Tianzhujiao, 148; and Ferreux, *Histoire de la Congrégation*, 276.

211   Ferreux, *Histoire de la Congrégation*, 276.

FIGURE 3.28   Present-day St. Michael's
SOURCE: PHOTO BY AUTHOR, 2016

occupy several buildings, with children using the sanctuary as an auditorium
and the courtyard as a playground. At one time a restaurant operated out of
a structure on the premises. After its return to diocesan control in 1986, the
school and restaurant had to vacate the site and funds were raised for restoration. It formally reopened for worship on 23 December 1989. In 2000–2001,
additional funds became available for further renovation of the exterior and
interior. Since then it has been an active parish church and in the last decade
has become popular among brides, most not baptized, for use as a backdrop for
wedding pictures. This provides the church with a steady source of income.[212]
There is a metal plaque on the gate that indicates it is St. Michael's Church
(Sheng Mi'e'er tianzhutang)—but most people know it by the locational name,
the Dongjiaominxiang tang.

---

212   *Beijing Tianzhu jiaohui*, item entitled "Dongjiaominxiang tianzhutang;" and Author's field
       notes, 21 October 2011.

2.2   The Nangangzi Church, St. Thérèse's

Of Beijing's notable places of worship, this is the only one not within either the Imperial or Inner Cities. The vicariate had it built after the Boxer Uprising in the Outer City, northeast of the Temple of Heaven in an area called Nangangzi. Its location is on a narrow lane that is part of a heavily populated urban district. Not well known to many Beijing residents, the church is semi-hidden among twisting alleys, its steeple not visible from a distance. Only the most knowledgeable of taxi drivers can bring you to it without resorting to GPS-aided directions. Both the original and second iteration were small with a low-profile. Size should not diminish our interest in their unique background, distinctive architecture, and special place among the capital's old sacred structures.

The First Nangangzi Church (1910–1923). In the aftermath of the Boxer destruction, Beijing's Catholics quickly reconstructed their landmark churches, at the same time realizing that there was an increased interest on the part of women in religious service. The bishop approved the construction of a sacred structure with an adjoining convent, if Catholics could arrange finances for a suitable location with proper privacy. Monetary assistance came from a Western priest assigned to St. Michael's, a Sister affiliated with the Daughters of Charity, another with the Sisters of St. Joseph, and other people. One particularly devoted and generous Catholic, Zhang Yuanlin, donated three vacant lots.[213] At property located off East Yuqingguan Street, a school, kindergarten, and small building known as the Universal Charity Church (Pu'ai jiaotang) were built. With twin towers only two stories in height, it was a small, modest, low-cost structure. On a second lot in front of a neighborhood temple two more buildings were erected, one for use as a pharmacy, the other as classrooms for girls use as well as residential quarters for the Sisters. Finally, near the temple was another lot with a large, new building used for teaching abandoned girls how to embroider and sometimes for lectures.[214]

The Second Nangangzi Church (1923–Present). In 1923, the Daughters of Charity funded additional expansion by donating $20,000.[215] At a place called Fangshengchi (near today's Yongsheng Lane) they purchased about seven acres of vacant land and constructed on it two large, multi-storied structures. The one on the east side contained thirty-seven rooms shared by elderly and

---

213   "Nangangzi Tianzhu jiaotang jianjie" (church courtyard display, 2008); and Author's field notes, 8 October 2008.

214   Yang Qingyun, *Beijing Tianzhujiao shi*, 149–150; and "Nangangzi tianzhujiao tang," http://baike.baidu.com/view/1434159.htm (accessed 28 February 2012).

215   "Nangangzi Tianzhu jiaotang jianjie."

FIGURE 3.29   The second Nangangzi church, ca 1930s
SOURCE: ARCHIVES CM, PARIS

FIGURE 3.30   The current Nangangzi church
SOURCE: PHOTO BY AUTHOR, 2008

infirm Sisters; there were also single-floor buildings used as a clinic, dormitory, and for sheltering milk cows. On the west side, they built a house for the pastor, a kitchen, other facilities, and a separate school building. The most important structure was a church that measured about 107 feet in length by 45 feet wide with a bell tower 49 feet tall.[216] The façade's appearance is presumably similar to the current version, though no old photographs of it have been found to confirm this. The bishop, honoring the prior work of women, dedicated it in 1925 to St. Thérèse of Lisieux, famous in France and known as a patron of missions.[217] Formally, it was the Church of St. Thérèse (Shengnü Xiaodelan

---

216   Yang Qingyun, *Beijing Tianzhujiao shi*, 150.
217   The Vatican beatified Thérèse of Lisieux on 29 April 1923 and Pope Pius XI canonized her on 17 May 1925. Her feast day, added to the Church's calendar of saints in 1927, is now celebrated on 1 October. "Thérèse of Lisieux," https://en.wikipedia.org/wiki/Th%C3%A9r%C3%A8se_of_Lisieux (accessed 1 April 2016).

tang and Xiaodelan shengtang). People usually referred to it based on location, that is, as the Nangangzi church.

In 1952, the Sisters' residential quarters became a foundling home. Six years later the government stopped religious services, allowing the Chongwen District's education office use of the building as an elementary school. The school could neither maintain nor protect the grounds. In the 1960s, Red Guards removed the bell tower, heavily damaging the façade. After the school closed, various government units used the buildings for miscellaneous storage. Government officials returned the building to the Beijing Diocese's control in February 1986, and over the next seven months it underwent restoration before formally reopening for religious services on 1 September. At the same location in the same year, the Novitiate of St. Joseph (Sheng Ruose xiunühui chuxueyuan) opened and instruction began.[218] In 1988, Chongwen District authorities added it to a list of protected architectural sites. The status and condition of the church led to a second restoration in 2005–2006 that cost about $36,600, funds coming from government and private sources.[219]

Inside the property's security wall is a small courtyard, barely large enough to accommodate a small sacred grotto devoted to Mary, the pastor's car, and a hundred worshippers. Built on a raised foundation and on a north-south axis, the chancel is in the south and the entrance in the north. Such a nontraditional alignment cannot be explained by available space.[220] The front is pierced by three entranceways, each defined by a rounded brick arch over which is a pointed one. The façade consists of three levels, the first directly over the main and central entrance, outlined by twin pilaster-like brick columns to each side. A rose window defines the next level while the narrow top section stands alone without distinctive architectural features. Brick columns accentuate the church's tower, at the apex of which is a small cross. The parish describes it as being of the classic European Gothic style used for small sacred buildings.[221] It is a busy worship place with mass times and scheduled activities posted on the gate.

---

218   Yang Qingyun, *Beijing Tianzhujiao shi*, 150. "Nangangzi tianzhujiao tang jianjie,"
       http://2008.people.com.cn/GB/22192/116781/118467/118479/7008345.html (accessed
       28 February 2012).
219   RMB 300,000 *yuan*. Yang Qingyun, *Beijing Tianzhujiao shi*, 150.
220   An older Catholic man thinks that surrounding buildings gave workers no other choice.
       Author's field notes, 25 September 2016.
221   "Nangangzi tianzhu jiaotang jianjie."

FIGURE 3.31   "The Catholic Nangangzi Church's Schedule of Important Activities."
                In addition to mass times and various church functions, item five
                mentions that the church undertakes wedding celebrations for
                Catholics and non-Catholics.
                SOURCE: PHOTO BY AUTHOR, 2016

• • •

Catholic churches in Beijing have a long history: the first of the distinctively
European-style ones dating to 1611 and the last, a more modest one (like those
found in outlying areas), built in 1923. At one time or another, all have been
reconstructed or restored—a common story to be sure given how hard it has
been to maintain a presence in China's political center. Times have changed
and at present each is the spiritual center of an active parish—several attract-
ing people interested in their background and unique architecture. Whether
for Catholics attending mass or for domestic tourists on holiday or couples
using them as a backdrop for pre-wedding photographs, old sacred structures
have a certain physicality that people appreciate.

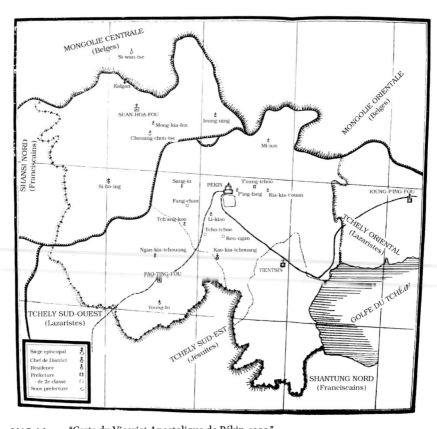

MAP 4.1   "Carte du Vicariat Apostolique de Pékin, 1900."
The map is slightly modified to show select churches of the greater Beijing area.
Some places and church sites included on the original map are retained for general
reference.

SOURCE: ARCHIVES CM, PARIS

Chouang-chou-tse (Shuangshuzi); Fang-chan (Fangshan); Ioung-ning (Yongning);
Ioung-ping-fou (Yongping fu); Kao-kia-tchouang (Gaojia zhuang); Kalgan
(Zhangjiakou); **Kia-kia-t'ouan (Jiajiatuan)**; Kou-ngan (Gu'an); **Likiao (Lijiao)**;
Mi-iun (Miyun); Mong-kia-fen (Mengjiafen); Ngan-kia-tchouang (Anjia zhuang);
Pao-ting-fou (Baodingfu); Pékin (Beijing); **P'ing-fang (Pingfang); Sang-iu
(Sangyu)**; Si-he-ing (Xiheying); Si-wan-tse (Xiwanzi); Suan-hoa-fou (Xuanhuafu);
Tch'ang-koo (Changgou); Tcho-tchoo (Zhuozhou); Tientsin (Tianjin); Toung-lu
(Donglü); Toung-tchoo (Tongzhou).

Greater Beijing's Old Church Sites and Churches

The sacred structures featured in this chapter are all located in what may be termed greater Beijing, the various districts and counties that encircle today's capital city's central area and stretch the municipality's perimeter boundaries far outward and its total area to over sixty-three hundred square miles.[1] To be sure, subway lines and a network of roads now conveniently connect the center to the densely packed residential neighborhoods that have intruded far into the area's former agricultural zone. To reach the farthest outlying places, a distance of over one hundred miles, may take longer than expected depending on the route, mode of transportation, time of day, and traffic. For example, from the central city to Housangyu is about thirty-four miles as the crow flies, with the actual route by car or long-distance bus through a variety of locales taking several hours. On the other hand, Pingfang is ten miles away from central Beijing, less than an hour by crowded public bus through concrete valleys of apartment buildings.

Two of the sacred structures presented in this chapter, the ones at Housangyu and Jiahoutuan, are not original, and although their parishioners do not claim they are old sacred structures, they still clearly consider the sites themselves to be historically significant. I agree and provide information about them for comparative value and to give a glimpse of how contemporary ones look and have fared. Those at the other four sites all date to the twentieth century and have survived the damage brought by the political turmoil of that century, each having undergone restoration and some reconstruction. For all these churches, scarce and scattered primary sources (including a few old photographs) provide narratives regarding the role they played in their early years as well as how they lasted in one form or the other to this day. They deserve our attention.

1 Housangyu (Sangyu) Village

Among Catholic circles one well-known rural congregation is located at the village (*cun*) of Housangyu, west of central Beijing in a mountainous area of

---

1 "Beijing," https://en.wikipedia.org/wiki/Beijing (accessed 14 May 2017).

Mengoutou District.[2] Missionaries built a small church for the area's one hundred believers in 1334 during the Yuan dynasty but it disappeared long ago, and nothing is known about its size or style. Over the next two centuries, no foreign priests served in China and people struggled to maintain their faith. Those at Sangyu Village demonstrated their ongoing commitment to Christianity by constructing a place of worship in 1543, the Ming's Jiaqing emperor then on the throne. It measured fifty-four feet long by thirty-three wide and could accommodate two hundred people. Per local tradition, in the same year as its construction the emperor wrote the Chinese characters *wan you zhen yuan*, which they proudly displayed on a large horizontal plaque that hung on the outside of the church.[3] The assertion does not explain why a Ming ruler would be interested in a small, rural congregation, let alone why he would bestow such an honor on it. Likewise, no mention is made about the Kangxi emperor's eighteenth-century dictation of the same words for the South Church. Not to make more of this discrepancy than is warranted: people are simply emphasizing the village's long association with Christianity.

As already noted, Jesuits did not reside in Beijing until the early 1600s, after which time they began to seek information about former congregations, praying that some might be revived. The fulfillment of these prayers came very slowly and in the case of Sangyu its name begins to appear in letters written by Jesuits in Beijing during the 1740s, when they occasionally went to the village to minister to the area's Catholics. Imperial proscription further curtailed religious development, with the arrest, imprisonment, and even exile of some missionaries. After 1844, the situation gradually improved and by 1873 villagers themselves had raised the funds to build a church.[4] A gazetteer states that in the 1880s–1890s more than three hundred Catholics lived in Sangyu, plus another two hundred or more distributed among ten nearby villages.[5] Such numbers warranted expansion of their sacred structure in 1896, that version measuring ninety-eight feet long and thirty-three wide.[6]

---

2 By the early twentieth century, Sangyu Village had grown, with its back section known as Housangyu. This is the church's location. I refer to it by both names, according to the period.
3 *Beijing Tianzhu jiaohui*, item entitled "Mentougou Housangyu tang;" and "Sangyu jiaotang jianjie" (Housangyu: n.p., n.d. [ca 2009]), Church internal circulation material, pamphlet.
4 J.-M. Planchet, *Documents sur les martyrs de Pékin pendant la persécution des Boxeurs* (Pékin [Beijing]: Imprimerie des Lazaristes, 1923), 2; and *Quanshi Beijing jiaoyou zhiming, juan* 6 (*Sangyu*).
5 *Beijing shi Mentougou quzhi* (Beijing: Beijing chubanshe, 2006), 671–672.
6 "Sangyu jiaotang jianjie;" and "Tianzhujiao Beijing zong jiaoqu," http://blog.sina.com.cn/s/blog_87ca2ce40101pjcj.html (accessed 23 January 2017).

In the spring of 1900, the Boxer movement raged into northwestern Zhili and Bishop Favier warned the pastor to prepare for the trouble headed his way. With donations from several Catholics, they bought thirty rifles, cases of bullets, and one hundred pounds of gunpowder. By June, Boxers controlled the area and began murdering people who lived in outlying, vulnerable congregations. Communication with the bishop at Beijing's North Church became dangerous as couriers found the roads controlled by Boxers. A sixty-year old farmer named Yang Yuxiu, a resident of Sangyu and for twenty years a Catholic, volunteered to carry a letter to the capital. En route Boxers stopped him, demanding to know his home village, what he was doing, and if he believed in Catholicism. Men like Yang did not lie and, upon hearing his answers, a Boxer slashed his head with a sword. He fell to the ground still alive as Boxers dragged him away. They found a spot with some brush and covered him with it. Someone ignited it and he burned to death.[7]

Boxers treated all Christians cruelly, not caring about how death and destruction affected people—poor, common people—no better off than themselves. Catholics from remote rural areas fled for their lives to Sangyu. There they found the Chinese pastor and lay leaders putting together a defensive plan that consisted of digging a wide trench on three sides of the church. To its rear was a hill and on it they built a protective wall. Behind these hastily erected barriers from 15 to 20 August, armed with spears, swords, and guns, they somehow held back a large force of Boxers, perhaps numbering as many as two thousand. The defenders' valiant efforts saved many lives.[8] When the Boxers fled the area, they looked back and saw the village church still standing.

After 1900, daily life for Catholics slowly resumed, with some religious activities taking on special meaning. Many believed that Mary had intervened to save their village from the Boxers, a sentiment the pastor took to heart in 1902 when he organized the construction of a grotto-like sacred shrine to her on top of a nearby hill. A foundling home and school soon arose nearby while two villages in the vicinity saw the construction of places of worship for growing congregations.[9] Statistics for 1904–1905 indicate that 432 Catholics lived in Sangyu (including 18 recent baptisms) with another 184 (24 were new converts) in six nearby congregations that included one public and two private oratories.[10]

---

7   *Quanshi Beijing jiaoyou zhiming, juan 6 (Sangyu)*, 21b–22b.
8   *Beijing shi Mentougou quzhi*, 671.
9   Ibid., 672.
10   Archives CM, Paris, Folder 163-I, "Vicariatus Apostolicus Pekini et Tche-ly Septentrionalis. Status Missionis, 1904–1905," 14; and Folder 164-I-b, "Fructus Spirituales, a die 15 Augusti 1904 ad diem 30 Junii 1905."

FIGURE 4.1 Housangyu church and village, late 1910s–early 1920s
SOURCE: PLANCHET, *DOCUMENTS SUR LES MARTYRS DE PÉKIN*

Over the next thirty years, religious activities increased, and numbers went skyward. A report for 1936–1937 notes that the Sangyu area (identified as a mission "residence") had seventeen congregations with a total of 1,398 Catholics (11 were new baptisms), of whom 418 (with 8 just baptized) lived at Sangyu Village.[11] Most people worshipped at the church there because elsewhere there were only two public oratories (perhaps chapels) and one private one. The report includes a photograph of the church that shows a plaque with the four-character imperial quote mentioned earlier.[12] The Japanese military occupied Hebei in 1937 and people at Sangyu supported the Eighth Route Army's efforts against them. Several young Catholic men enlisted and later received promotion to officer rank. In 1939, Japanese soldiers searched the church and found materials critical of them, which gave them cause to torch it.[13] Local people

---

11 Recent or new converts and baptisms means within the period of the report, which does not specify adults or children. I surmise that it refers only to the former. "Residence" here refers to an area; it can also refer to a specific mission center.

12 Archives CM, Paris, Folder 163-I, "Vicariat Apostolique de Pékin. État de la Mission, du 1er Juillet 1936 au 30 Juin 1937," 53–54, 202.

13 *Beijing shi Mentougou quzhi*, 672.

still honor Catholics of this era as prime examples of religious faithful who acted as patriots.[14]

Catholics did not rebuild prior to 1949, as worshippers made do with home-based oratories that Red Guards later closed during the Cultural Revolution. Fifty years after the church fell to flames, the parish finished construction of one dedicated to the Sacred Heart of Jesus (Yesu sheng xin) in August 1989. The structure was laid out on an east (chancel) to west (entrance) axis and tightly nestled among dwellings. With limited ground space, workers erected a modest structure composed of bricks faced with concrete stucco and ceramic tiles, the same sort of basic construction seen all over China in the 1980s.[15] In 1997, parishioners renovated it, adding a sixty-nine-foot-high bell tower.[16] A diocesan pamphlet says it is Gothic without mentioning any stylistic features to support the claim. Its façade has one portal and two large windows at the same level, over which stands a cross-topped tower. The Chinese words meaning "the true principle of all things" again adorn the front of the church. The interior is equally simple with a maximum seating capacity of four hundred people. In addition to the sacred structure there is a small religious library and medical clinic, operated by Sisters of St. Joseph.[17]

In 1993, the Beijing bishop assigned a full-time priest to the parish, who worked hard to reestablish regular parish activities. He soon realized the importance of restoring the post-Boxer era shrine built for Mary atop a hill behind the church (see fig. 1.2). Besides being used by worshippers (mostly women) for daily devotional prayer, the shrine has become a famous pilgrimage site and Catholics from other areas visit every May to pray to Mary, usually referred to as "Our Lady of China" (Zhonghua Sheng Mu).[18] At other times of the year, various congregations promote and assist visitors because it is a way to build faith and connections between parishes.[19]

---

14 *Beijing Tianzhu jiaohui*, item entitled "Mentougou Housangyu tang." Internet accounts support this view, e.g., "Tianzhujiao Beijing zong jiaoqu."

15 Author's field notes, 25 September 2009.

16 "Tianzhujiao Beijing zong jiaoqu."

17 *Beijing Tianzhu jiaohui*, item entitled "Mentougou Housangyu tang."

18 "Beijing de jiaotang: Housangyu cun tianzhujiao tang," http://blog.sina.com.cn/s/blog_494d86ef01019p73.html (accessed 23 January 2017).

19 At the South Church I saw a signup sheet for a group visit to the Marian shrine at Housangyu. Author's field notes, 26 September 2011. Unlike the pilgrims to the village (*cun*) of Donglü, near Baoding (see Chapter 6's section on that city), officials have not created obstacles for visitors.

FIGURE 4.2 Today's Housangyu church
            SOURCE: PHOTO BY AUTHOR, 2009

2   **Yongning Village**

During the nineteenth century, Western missionaries in Beijing fanned out in all directions seeking to make converts. Some went about forty-five miles to the northwest to the village (*cun*, now a *zhen* or town) of Yongning, located about ten miles east of the Yanqing Department Seat that was then an administrative component of Xuanhua Prefecture. Currently, Yanqing is neither part of Xuanhua nor the province; instead, it is classified as one of Beijing Municipality's districts. From the capital via a divided highway in moderate traffic it takes about three hours to get there and only a few minutes more to find its "old town," a small district with several historical sites (the Catholic church included) intended to attract domestic tourists.

Vincentian personnel records indicate the assignment of a priest to the village occurred as early as 1862.[20] By 1873, Catholic numbers necessitated construction of the area's first sacred structure, which people simply called "the church," though its formal name was the Sacred Heart of Jesus Church (Yesu sheng xin tang).[21] Unfortunately, no information about its architectural style or old photographs have been found. Nineteenth century missionaries worked determinedly, and their efforts proved successful among the poor farmers, who planted sorghum in the summer and barley in the winter season. Convert numbers increased annually and Yongning grew into a mission center with a foundling home and other buildings.[22] On the eve of the twentieth century, about seventeen hundred Catholics lived in rural communities scattered around Yanqing Department and two other administrative areas.[23] The church brought everyone together for mass and religious festivals.

When the Boxers moved into Zhili's northwest in the spring of 1900, Yongning became the first important locale targeted due to its proximity to the capital and the congregations there. Boxer organizers found the local people receptive to their antiforeign, anti-Christian slogans, as were many Yanqing government officials, a volatile situation that raised the threat level for Catholics. Yongning's, Chu Deming, C.M., a young, inexperienced priest ordained just two years earlier, hailed from nearby Xuanhua County. He quickly developed a good relationship with the locals.[24] Like many others he had no idea what the Boxer movement would bring or how it would affect his congregation, therefore he took no measures to fortify the mission compound. As Boxers harassed his satellite congregations and refugees began appearing at his church, the priest made the decision to abandon Yongning for the nearby village (*cun*) of Konghuaying, reasoning that they might have a better chance there to prepare barricades and defend themselves. On 21 June, a market day, Boxers arrived and began putting torches to the abandoned church and nearby houses owned by Catholics as well as killing two elderly residents who had not fled.[25]

The next day the Boxers attacked Konghuaying, then pulled back after suffering some casualties. They quickly regrouped and, with soldiers from the Yanqing Department Seat, returned to overwhelm the poorly armed Catholics. Boxers and soldiers murdered about 380 men, women, and children, and would

---

20   Archives CM, Philadelphia, *Catalogue des maisons et du personnel de la Congrégation de la Mission* (Paris: Imprimerie Saint-Générosus, 1879), 40.
21   *Beijing Tianzhu jiaohui*, item entitled "Yongning tianzhutang."
22   Archives CM, Philadelphia, *Catalogue des maisons* (1879), 40.
23   Planchet, *Documents sur les martyrs*, 336.
24   In French romanization, Tch'ou Té-ming. Van den Brandt, *Les Lazaristes*, 191.
25   Planchet, *Documents sur les martyrs*, 336–362.

have killed more had the priest not led them into the mountains and the temporary shelter of shallow caves. Boxers later flushed them out and killed another eighty people. Fr. Chu Deming and remnants of his congregation escaped, eventually making it to Xiwanzi Village, their home until peace returned. The pastor wrote in a letter of 31 August to Favier that approximately fourteen hundred Catholics at Yongning and nearby rural congregations had died. Except for those in one village, Boxers looted or burned the property of everyone else.[26]

From Boxer settlement funds received, the vicariate allocated ten thousand taels of silver ($7,400) for losses in the Yanqing Department, some of which went towards the construction of a sacred edifice that workers completed in early 1902 on the foundations of the 1873 Yongning structure.[27] It measured eighty-seven feet long by forty-four feet wide with its chancel in the north and the main entrance in the south.[28] Workers followed a design that led to the construction of a sacred structure of similar size to its predecessor, with a relatively simple façade and a few features borrowed from Beijing's North Church. On completion, Catholics erected a stone tablet that memorialized its reopening and honored those lost in 1900.[29] By 1905, the pastor had responsibility for 166 Catholics (70 were recent baptisms) as well as 575 others (73 newly baptized) scattered among fifteen villages, six of which had public oratories.[30] Ten years later, continued growth had necessitated the addition of more buildings to accommodate various religious activities. When Propaganda Fide approved the formation of the Vicariate of Xuanhua in 1926, Yongning came under its ecclesiastical jurisdiction, and with help from the bishop it weathered the wartime trials of the 1930s and 1940s.

After two decades of war, Chinese government leaders of the 1950s thought in terms of political movements to achieve national recovery and domestic reconstruction. The closure of churches, confiscation of property, and control of Christians (really, all people) were a means to an end. All over Hebei officials

---

26   Planchet, *Documents sur les martyrs*, 336–362. Presently, the number killed is estimated at eight hundred. *Beijing Tianzhu jiaohui*, item entitled "Tianning zhensuo."

27   Per the plaque located near the front entrance, it dates to 1902. Author's field notes, 8 October 2011. One source gives the year as 1904. *Beijing Tianzhu jiaohui*, item entitled "Yongning tianzhutang." Another source indicates that a French priest built it in 1905. "Guanyu luoshi Yongning tianzhujiao jiaohui fangchan yijian de baogao," comp. Yanqingxian minzhengju, 20 June 1985, Church internal circulation material, photocopy.

28   "Beijing Yongning tianzhujiao tang misa shijian," http://bj.bendibao.com/tour/20151123/208900_3.shtm (accessed 13 May 2016).

29   *Yanqing xianzhi*, (Beijing: Beijing chubanshe, 2006), 683–684; and Author's field notes, 8 October 2011.

30   "Vicariatus Apostolicus Pekini et Tche-ly Septentrionalis. Status Missionis, 1904–1905," 32.

FIGURE 4.3 Yongning church, late 1910s–early 1920s
          SOURCE: PLANCHET, *DOCUMENTS SUR LES MARTYRS DE*
          PÉKIN

reallocated Catholic resources for public use. Churches became meeting halls
or warehouses and ancillary structures became agricultural storage or housing. Red Guards later decided to strip them down further, removing façades'
decorative columns, dismantling bell towers, and emptying interiors of altars
and pews. The one at Yongning suffered the same fate. A government office for
grain management occupied the grounds from then until the mid-1980s. The
largest building was the church and it became a warehouse facility. Grain management staff and their families occupied some buildings, tore down others,
and removed the protective wall that encircled the property.

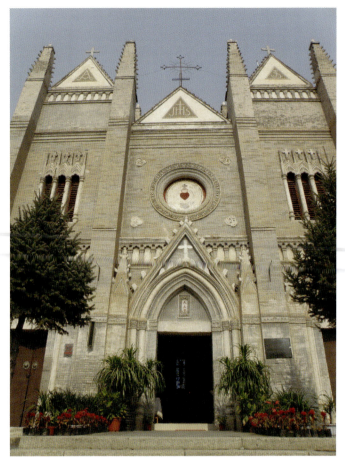

FIGURE 4.4 Yongning church, today
SOURCE: PHOTO BY AUTHOR, 2011

In 1985, authorities returned the property to the Beijing Diocese. After searching its records for information regarding the church, the extent of its properties, and how to compensate for its losses, officials first tallied up the various buildings' (both existing and those destroyed) aggregate size based on the number of rooms in order to calculate the amount of lost rent (since they had been occupied) over the years. Accordingly, they gave $3,770 as compensation to Catholics and agreed to help provide materials for the church's restoration.[31] With funds, materials, and most importantly the property under Catholic control, people quickly began cleanup of and repairs to the building,

31 *"Guanyu luoshi Yongning Tianzhujiao jiaohui fangchan yijian de baogao."*

its spacious surrounding grounds, and its garden.[32] Workers found the stone tablet from 1902 in a rubble pile, and though badly defaced it still had readable characters along the edge of its face. To this was added text in gold-colored calligraphy: "[Memorial] stone for the Catholic fatalities [of 1900 at Yongning]" (*zhuwei xinyou zhimingzhe zhi mu*). The congregation placed it a few feet to the east of the main entrance for maximum visibility and impact.[33] In May, a priest arrived from Beijing to offer mass.[34] After Bishop Fu Tieshan presided over rededication ceremonies on 9 November 1987, he regularly sent priests from Beijing to help revive religious activities. They brought the congregation to life, warranting in 1993 the assignment of a resident parish pastor.[35] In 2001, the Beijing Cultural Protection Bureau added the church to its list of historical sites and provided financial assistance for additional refurbishing.[36]

The Yongning sacred structure, now renovated and modernized, is said to re-semble one in Beijing; thus, its nickname "Small North Church" (Xiao Beitang). Using architectural features such as four narrow columns topped with spires to emphasize verticality, it is another self-described Gothic-style place of worship.[37] The façade's first level includes three entrances, each framed by pointed arches and the central one garnished by a stylized cross with four-petal flowers. Above the main doorway at the second level is a rose window; once of stained glass, it is filled in with concrete and painted with a red heart to evoke its formal name. A border of sculpted flowers attractively encircles the round window. Over the other two doorways are windows, each subdivided into three vertical sections by four short semi-circular columns. The top level has three triangular pediments outlined in white. The security wall has a gate directly in front of the church's main doorway, and down a narrow lane is the original exterior gate. It has old-style double wooden doors above which are stylized fleurs-de-lys and a blank horizontal plaque that once included the words *tianzhutang* in Chinese.[38]

---

32   The Beijing Diocese and the local government furnished funds. *Beijing Tianzhu jiaohui*, item entitled "Yongning tianzhutang."

33   Author's field notes, 8 October 2011.

34   *Yanqing xianzhi*, 683–684.

35   *Beijing Tianzhu jiaohui*, item entitled "Yongning tianzhutang."

36   Some information comes from a metal plaque on the side of the church. Author's field notes, 8 October 2011. Also, "Beijing Yongning tianzhujiao tang misa shijian."

37   The author of an online article calls it "Gothic Revival." "Beijing Yongning tianzhujiao tang misa shijian."

38   Author's field notes, 8 October 2011. See a personal view at "Yongning tianzhutang," http://baike.baidu.com/link?url=QU94hk3c_FNEpl8oQYra1Lhf7zDuAdOtSJSHOZoYc9 ClG8tWKKhcAliSdRnmoojdxhGiegYeOZXoHQKRNBQPbSHU4r_U1058hboS2WQNsOE 00XdIDhyTNm-sW6OSgRDr (accessed 24 January 2017).

FIGURE 4.5 Old entrance gate to the Yongning church
SOURCE: PHOTO BY AUTHOR, 2011

This is the only sacred structure of any size in Yanqing and its presence continues to have an impact on the area's Catholics because they are very cognizant of its historical place in the diocese. An enthusiastic parish pastor watches carefully over the congregation and, as funds become available, gradually makes improvements to the facilities and grounds. In the courtyard a sacred grotto for Our Lady is surrounded with greenery and flowers, symbolic of a budding Marian movement in the area. With a regular schedule of religious classes, a reading room filled with materials, and guest housing for students, education is a mainstay of the parish's present and future development.[39]

---

39   Author's field notes, 8 October 2011.

FIGURE 4.6 Memorial stone for the Catholic fatalities of 1900
            SOURCE: PHOTO BY AUTHOR, 2011

3   Jiahoutuan (Jiajiatuan) Village

During the Qing the village (*cun*) of Jiahoutuan, as it has been known since the
early twentieth century, could be found not far from the Bai River, which at this
location served as part of the Grand Canal. It was situated in Tong Department,
one part of the important Shuntian Prefecture, called the Metropolitan or
Imperial Prefecture because it encompassed the capital city. Tongzhou is
currently one of Beijing Municipality's several districts, each with a swelling
commuter population. Despite numerous high-rise apartment complexes,
considerable agricultural space remains and there are still many rural communities. One is Jiahoutuan, which has been home to generations of Catholics,

the earliest dating to the 1690s. They mostly carried the surname Jia and lived at the same location—thus its earlier name, Jia Family Village or Jiajiatuan. Catholicism's expansion began in the mid-nineteenth century and continues to this day. A diocesan pamphlet notes that more worshippers live there than any other rural locale in Beijing Diocese's eastern section.[40] In the early 2000s, the village's population was about two thousand with 95 percent of them Catholic. Its history and demographics warrant examination.

According to a local account, sometime in the late 1860s a villager named Jia Mou made his living in Beijing as a fortuneteller often working near Xuanwu, the busy city gate close to the South Church. Curious, he began listening to sermons, which led to studying the catechism and then to baptism. Upon returning home, he told his friends and relatives about his conversion, sharing details about his faith with them. To encourage further interest, Beijing's Bishop Mouly sent priests to Jiahoutuan to proselytize. Their success increased convert numbers to the point that by 1871 the village had its first resident priest.[41] Two years later the bishop sent another priest to establish its first sacred structure, known formally as the Church of the Annunciation (Sheng Mu lingbao tang).[42] Unfortunately, sources provide no details about it. Twenty-five years later the congregation replaced it with a solidly built structure. A diocesan brochure states that it was Romanesque in style with a seating capacity of about six hundred, which for a rural place at the time was quite large. The only old photograph of it shows a large building with a gable roof and simple design. A gazetteer tells us that its measurements were 131 feet long by 49 wide.[43] Built on an east-west axis, the façade consists of three levels and although the foundation cannot be seen in the photograph, it is possible to observe the tops of three covered entrances, each with a short overhang. Seven windows constitute the main feature of the second level, the largest one directly over the main entrance and each recessed with a slightly rounded arch over it. The windows were separated from each other by pilasters, six of them extending in staggered heights to the third level and topped by what appear to be decorative vases. The third level is the width of the central window and its two pilasters. This level is a modified tower that includes a window of the same size as the one below it. The tower exceeds the roof's peak but not by a large amount, even

---

40   "Jiahoutuan jiaotang xingshuai shi" (Jiahoutuan: n.p., n.d., ca 2009), Church internal circulation material, pamphlet.

41   *Quanshi Beijing jiaoyou zhiming, juan* 13 (Tongzhou), 1.

42   Archives CM, Philadelphia, *Catalogue des maisons et du personnel de la Congrégation de la Mission* (Paris: n.p., 1877), 40.

43   *Tongxian zhi* (Beijing: Beijing chubanshe, 2003), 602. This source gives the year of construction as 1898; local people say it was finished the previous year.

FIGURE 4.7   Built in 1897, the second Jiahoutuan church, ca 1930s
SOURCE: ARCHIVES CM, PARIS

with the cross that sits on top of it factored in. The façade is devoid of architectural details and conveys a style that seems heavy and massive.[44]

Over the next twenty-seven years a succession of Vincentians worked
tirelessly in the village converting enough people to make it predominately
Catholic. Missionaries considered it a "Christian village," which made it a target when Boxers spread from the Zhili-Shandong border area north towards
Beijing and Tianjin, destroying everything that epitomized the non-Chinese
world: telegraph lines, railroads, and foreign-style buildings. Boxers hated all
Chinese Christians, Catholic and Protestant alike, with the former constituting

44   A copy of a photograph is available in "Vicariat Apostolique de Pékin, État de la Mission,
      1936–1937," 92. The same photograph is reproduced in "Jiahoutuan jiaotang xingshuai shi."

FIGURE 4.8 The third Jiahoutuan church, completed in 1986
SOURCE: "JIAHOUTUAN JIAOTANG XINGSHUAI SHI"

the older, more established, and more numerous minority that Western priests
actively supported. Because many priests had full beards, Chinese had for a
long time derisively, generically, and sometimes jokingly referred to them
(in fact to all Westerner men) as "big hairy (furry) creatures" (*da maozi*). The
locals who followed Christianity became "little hairy creatures" (*er maozi*)—
that is, "wannabes," aspiring to be like the bigger, more powerful version.[45]
Dehumanizing names, of course, made it easier to take prejudices to the level

---

45   Literal translations, such as "Hairies" for foreigners and "Secondary Hairies" for Chinese
      Christians (Chang, *Empress Dowager Cixi*, 267), lose too much meaning. "Wannabe" is
      modern slang, used appropriately (albeit anachronistically) here.

of physical assault. In one recorded account that occurred in May 1900, the Boxers captured a man surnamed Li near the Tong Department Seat's south gate. One accusingly asked, "You're a 'wannabe,' aren't you?" Li bravely replied, "I'm not an *er maozi*, I'm a catechist from Jiajiatuan."[46] They then tied him to a tree before hacking him to death with swords.

At Jiahoutuan, Li's Catholic friends dug a trench and built barriers to protect their village from the Boxers they knew would come to attack them. When Boxers arrived and surrounded the village, they repeatedly failed to find a way to breach the defenses. Sometimes they even shouted that they had killed the catechist—and that the villagers were next. The Catholics ignored the taunts and fought back desperately because they realized that defeat meant certain death. The Boxers' siege lasted forty-eight days. In the end many died, including the Chinese pastor who had organized his followers to take defensive measures.[47] Later in the summer, when Allied forces passed through the area on their way to Beijing, Boxers broke off the siege and fled.

In the years following the Boxer Uprising, the congregation flourished as residents of small neighboring hamlets came to Jiahoutuan for catechism and baptism. In 1904–1905, 981 Catholics (including 22 new converts) lived in the village, which had become a principal mission center or "residence." Sometimes more than one priest ministered to the eleven surrounding congregations (with a total of 833 Catholics, counting 29 recent baptisms), eight of which had a public oratory.[48] By 1927 Catholicism had expanded to nine more villages.[49] A decade later, the bishop stationed three priests in the area, called a "quasi-parish" in a report that counted twenty-two congregations with a total of 3,526 Catholics (12 were recently baptized). The smallest congregation had only nine people from two or three families. The largest was at Jiahoutuan and numbered 1,447 (including 1 new convert). At the village (*tun*) of Niumu about ten miles away, an active congregation of almost two hundred wanted and got a church of their own.[50]

The Jiahoutuan congregation weathered the Sino-Japanese War and saw Communist forces arrive at their village in 1946 to take control. They expelled the priest but allowed his confreres to return on important religious dates to say

46   *Quanshi Beijing jiaoyou zhiming, juan* 13 (Tongzhou), 7b.
47   "Jiahoutuan jiaotang xingshuai shi;" and *Quanshi Beijing jiaoyou zhiming, juan* 13 (Tongzhou), 1b–2.
48   "Vicariatus Apostolicus Pekini et Tche-ly Septentrionalis. Status Missionis, 1904–1905," 5.
49   "Jiahoutuan jiaotang xingshuai shi."
50   "Vicariat Apostolique de Pékin, État de la Mission, 1936–1937," 92. "Quasi-pariosse" (quasi-parish) is used in this source and implies the bishop recognized that its nominal status (and the vicariate of which it was part) had evolved. (Also, Chapter 2, note 10).

mass, a practice that stopped in 1958 when the government closed the church to all activities. From then through the Cultural Revolution years, cadres used the building as an elementary school, auditorium, and warehouse, secular functions that allowed it to remain useful for most of the Cultural Revolution. In 1973, Red Guard extremists, in a final act of hatred for Christianity, brought the sacred structure's one hundred years of existence to a fiery end.[51]

In the late 1970s, revised national regulations emerged to govern religious activities, which led Catholics to receive back former Church-owned buildings and other real estate as well as compensation for damages suffered. Different areas negotiated different settlements. Jiahoutuan's congregation pressed officials to help in the construction of a sacred edifice and they did so to the tune of RMB 10,000 *yuan*. Beijing Diocese contributed 50,000 *yuan* and Catholics, together with other local sources, provided about 40,000 *yuan* (for a total of about $20,000).[52] Under the direction of a construction company, work began at the site of the original one on 18 April 1986 and finished less than eight months later on 7 December. The next day Bishop Fu Tieshan arrived from Beijing to dedicate it as the Church of the Immaculate Conception (Sheng Mu wuranyuanzui tang) and participate in a grand celebration attended by most of the area's Catholics.[53]

The sacred building, laid out on a north (chancel) to south (entrance) axis, resembled its predecessor neither in style nor in size. Notable features of its façade included three doorways with rounded arches. Two square windows on each side sat above the flanking doors and, above them, a semicircular pediment with religious monograms and crosses. In ascending order above the central entrance were two windows, a statue of Mary in a small niche, the Chinese characters *tianzhutang* and two more windows, and a semicircular pediment with a white cross. A light pink color covered most of the façade, which contrasted with the light blue pediments and dark blue doorways, projecting a pleasant image. In 2005, major structural problems necessitated its closure and destruction. Two years later workers completed a replacement for about $57,300. Made of steel-reinforced concrete and designed to last for generations, the beautiful church has a seating capacity equal to or more than that of the 1873 structure. Its tall, red steeple topped with a white cross is equivalent in height to a three or four-story building and is visible from everywhere in the

51   "Jiahoutuan jiaotang xingshuai shi."
52   *Tongxian zhi*, 602; and "Tianzhujiao Beijing zong jiaoqu."
53   "Jiahoutuan jiaotang xingshuai shi." This website shows a photograph of a church bulletin
      board display that summarizes its history. "Jiahoutuan tianzhutang," http://blog.sina.com.
      cn/s/blog_87ca2ce40102vkow.html (accessed 25 January 2017).

FIGURE 4.9 The fourth Jiahoutuan church, built in 2007. Our Lady of China sacred grotto is on
the left.
SOURCE: PHOTO BY AUTHOR, 2011

village. A pamphlet describes it as Romanesque—and as such, it represents
the village's past and present.[54]

Jiahoutuan remains famous as one of a handful of "Christian villages" that
successfully defended itself against the Boxers, a matter of which people are
still aware and proud. I visited the church there in 2011 and inquired if anyone
had written materials concerning the area's Catholic history. One man went
home to retrieve a small tattered tome, its pages yellow and crumbling, some
missing.[55] I held one part of a larger series entitled "Beijing Catholic fatalities during the Boxer period" (*Quanshi Beijing jiaoyou zhiming*) produced by
Chinese confreres under the guidance of a Vincentian priest and historian to
memorialize their experiences during the Boxer period. The Lazarist Press,
from 1920 to 1931, published a set of eighteen "books" (*juan*) using traditional
style Chinese binding.[56] Book number thirteen, published in 1926, is devoted
to the Tongzhou area's fight against the Boxers and serves as a hagiography of
those who died during the defense of Jiahoutuan. Since complete sets of the

---

54   In Chinese currency, the cost was RMB 470,000 *yuan*. "Jiahoutuan jiaotang xingshuai shi."
55   Author's field notes, 30 September 2011.
56   Intended for a Chinese audience, this publication is longer and more detailed than
      Planchet's *Documents sur les martyrs*, which appeared in 1923.

publication still exist, finding this one volume did not fill any historical lacuna. Rather its significance is that it had survived the turmoil of world war and civil conflict as well as the Cultural Revolution era, when Red Guards tried to destroy all such materials. That one family dared to preserve it is a testament to their memory of and pride in the area's religious history.

4   Pingfang Village

In the late nineteenth century, Vincentian missionaries began working at the village (*cun*) of Pingfang, the place considered at the time to be a fair distance from the capital city's walls. Today, it is more a neighborhood than a village in a not-so-well-known part of Beijing's Chaoyang District, just inside the Fifth Ring Road. Enveloped by urban sprawl in an area still developing and without identity, few know of the church. Given the sacred structure has taken hard blows, it is remarkable that it remains standing, and its congregation is alive and well with its own pastor. The congregation needs more aid from the diocese; however, resources are limited and dispensed sparingly to such small, slow growing parishes.

It took over twenty years of apostolic work before numbers justified the construction of a sacred structure at Pingfang, which a Chinese priest began in 1916. He laid it out on a north-south axis, parishioners entering from south side. Dedicated six years later to Jesus, the King (Yesu junwang), it stood as the centerpiece of a "quasi-parish" that by 1936–1937 included a total of thirty-five congregations and 3,108 Catholics (23 had been baptized recently). Pingfang had 304 worshippers, the second largest number of any congregation—the range going from 360 down to 18 with an average of 89 per location.[57] There were six public oratories scattered among the surrounding villages with the church serving as the centerpiece, the place where worshippers went to celebrate the important feast days.

A 1930s-era photograph shows a one-story gable roofed structure with a tall bell tower. Extending outward from the church's main plane, the tower provided not only the central and main entry, with a sharply angled archway but also the main architectural feature as it extended skyward for three full stories, topped by a spire and cross. Above the entryway was a rose window, followed at the next level by two narrow, vertical windows with a smaller round one above them, all recessed within an attractive rounded archway. The same feature was repeated at the third level. Architecturally, the tower conveyed size and presence, a religious statement of wealth and power.

---

57   "Vicariat Apostolique de Pékin, État de la Mission, 1936–1937," 99–100.

FIGURE 4.10   Pingfang church and pastors, ca 1930s
            SOURCE: ARCHIVES CM, PARIS

FIGURE 4.11
Today's Pingfang church
and Our Lady of China
pavilion
SOURCE: PHOTO BY
AUTHOR, 2010

Less than a decade after the establishment of the People's Republic, authorities closed the Pingfang church and revamped the building into a light bulb factory, with other buildings on the mission center grounds becoming housing for the elderly. During the mid-1960s, Red Guards found the bell tower too prominent and too religiously symbolic, good-enough excuses for them to demolish it to the ground level while, as elsewhere, the shell of the sacred structure continued to be used for other purposes. Devoid of its tower, the building looked stark.[58] In the late 1980s, the government returned the property and buildings to the c.p.a. and in turn to the diocese, which in 1991 reopened the church with a seminary located close by. In 1996, the parish rebuilt the tower, replicating as best it could the original. On a plaque located on the tower between the first and second sections is "1922," the year of its dedication.[59] Here, and in other locales, this was a time of rapid Catholic expansion.

At present, the church's angular lines and white color give it a distinctive appearance. Just in front of it is a Chinese-style pavilion featuring a statue of Mary. Whereas many sacred structures have a sacred grotto to honor her, the Pingfang congregation has a special building that adds a colorful, traditional touch. In 2004, there were about three hundred parishioners. Six years later, with numbers increasing, they wanted a complete renovation of the interior. The work took over a year to complete, during which time worshippers used a temporary metal structure for mass. The pastor told local worshippers the exterior's renovation will be next. In this way, Pingfang is catching up with other parishes in the Beijing Diocese.[60]

5   Lijiao Village

The village (*cun*) of Lijiao belonged during the Qing and Republican periods to Liangxiang County, a civil jurisdiction that no longer exists because it has been absorbed and reconfigured into the vastness of Beijing Municipality. The village is conveniently located just east of the Beijing-Shijiazhuang highway in the southwestern section of Beijing's large Fangshan District, next door to Hebei. It is part of Beijing Diocese. The distance to central Beijing is approximately twenty-five miles, with good roads and a rail line making for an easy

---

58   For a photograph of it taken in the late 1980s or early 1990s, see *Beijing Tianzhu jiaohui*, item entitled "Pingfang jiaotang."

59   *Beijing Tianzhu jiaohui*, item entitled "Pingfang jiaotang;" and Author's field notes, 5 May 2010.

60   Author's field notes, 5 May 2010.

journey. During the early twentieth century it was just one of many congregations belonging to the "Capital South" District's "Zhuozhou residence," that is, mission center (see Chapter 7's section on mission status).

During the late Ming dynasty, missionaries passed through the village on their way to Beijing. We know that the first converts carried the surname Shi, yet little can be said either about their lives or about those of subsequent Catholic generations.[61] During the next dynasty, the Shi lineage became the largest in the community. Among its members, those believing in a Christian God constituted only a small minority. In the late 1860s or early 1870s, missionaries returned on a regular basis to Lijiao Village.[62] Catholics lived peacefully among their neighbors, most of whom they knew well, and were involved in local affairs. In fact, at the end of the nineteenth century, a sixty-six-year-old Catholic farmer named Shi Guozhen (baptismal name, Peter) acted as one of his lineage's leaders. When kith and kin heard the news of an anti-Christian movement and that Boxers had arrived in the area, they urged him and others to leave. They all refused. "We are Christians, we are God's sons and daughters," Shi Guozhen proclaimed. "We pray fervently and depend on God's will. We cannot run away. When the Boxers arrive, we will not deny our faith. If they kill us, then we give our lives to God and go to Heaven together."[63]

One night towards the end of May 1900, Boxers surrounded Shi Guozhen's house before bursting through his gate into his courtyard. He confronted them and demanded, "What are you doing?" The Boxer leader replied, "We're exterminating Christians." Without hesitation he countered, "What bad things have Christians done? We raise our children and do our work; we plant and harvest, not breaking any laws. We Christians do not impede you Boxers and your affairs. Why do you come into our homes during the night, burning and killing?" They argued further and loudly. Tired of the opposition, the Boxers bound him with rope in order to drag him away then thought the better of it and murdered him on the spot. Faithful and defiant to the end, thirteen Catholics all surnamed Shi died—they ranged in age from ten to sixty-six. Survivors buried them in the church's small cemetery.[64] Many others in the vicinity perished as well.

After the Allied forces defeated the Boxers and restored peace, it took time for people to find normalcy, which meant rebuilding their homes, planting

---

61   *Quanshi Beijing jiaoyou zhiming, juan* 9 (Jing xi'nan), 18–22; and Planchet, *Documents sur les martyrs*, 62.
62   *Fangshan quzhi* (Beijing: Beijing chubanshe, 1999), 658.
63   *Quanshi Beijing jiaoyou zhiming, juan* 9 (Jing xi'nan), 18–22.
64   *Quanshi Beijing jiaoyou zhiming, juan* 9 (Jing xi'nan), 18–22; and Planchet, *Documents sur les martyrs*, 65.

crops, and pursuing life's various activities. A 1904–1905 mission-status report indicates that Lijiao's seventy-six Catholics constituted the area's second largest number—not enough to warrant a church or chapel.[65] Over the next decade, many people converted with the bishop deciding in 1916 to build a formal place of worship and assign a pastor to it. One source put the total at ten thousand Catholics—a very rough guess, it seems.[66] The brick structure, laid out on a north-south axis, had a gable roof with a two-story tall tower dominating the façade. The tower included a central entrance with two other doors flanking it, a rose window, and at the second level two narrow windows. Above them came the spire topped by a cross.

A diagram of the property drawn in 1928 shows that the mission "residence" had quickly expanded to include more than just the church, with the addition of a lodge for the priest, a building for the domestic staff, a small school and dormitory for boys, a stable, and a few other structures. A perimeter wall enclosed a rectangular plot that measured approximately 129 by 302 feet, that is, nine-tenths of an acre.[67] According to a modern-era gazetteer, in the mid-1930s the area counted 3,178 Catholics.[68] This number corroborates statistics for the same period that indicate the congregation at Lijiao had increased to 429 (with 8 recent converts) and the twenty-seven villages attached to it added another 2,695 (including 14 newly baptized). For formal worship, they only had Lijiao's church and two public oratories or chapels as worship places.[69] By this time, the bishop had created the Zhuo County District (discussed in Chapter 7) with a place of worship within the city walls of the Zhuo County Seat as its focal point and with Lijiao and seventeen other villages serving as the centers of "quasi-parishes."

Details on the area's fate during the Japanese occupation of Beijing and Hebei are hard to find. Its church survived the war years followed by the

---

65   The Zhuozhou city congregation was the largest with eighty people. "Vicariatus Apostolicus Pekini et Tche-ly Septentrionalis. Status Missionis, 1904–1905," 10. There is no breakdown on how many recent baptisms had been made per congregation.

66   Planchet reported the number, which came from a local informant (*Documents sur les martyrs*, 65). Chinese sometimes express large, estimated numbers this way. Based on later information, the meaning here is several thousands.

67   Archives CM, Paris, Box "Lazaristes [16]," "Projet de division du Vic. Ap. de Pekin et formation du Vic. Aps. de Chochow à confier au clergé séculier indigène, [1928–1931]. (All abbreviations used in the original.) Measurements are in *zhang* and *chi*. The former equates to 141 inches for tariff purposes. Ten *chi* make one *zhang*. The exact lengths of the two varied slightly from province to province. *Mathews' Chinese-English Dictionary*, 21, 144; and Endymion Wilkinson, *Chinese History: A Manual, Revised and Enlarged* (Cambridge, Mass.: Harvard University Asia Center, Harvard-Yenching Institute, 2000), 238.

68   *Fangshan quzhi* (Beijing: Beijing chubanshe, 1999), 659.

69   "Vicariat Apostolique de Pékin. État de la Mission, 1936–1937," 77–78.

FIGURE 4.12   Lijiao church and pastor, ca 1930s
                SOURCE: ARCHIVES CM, PARIS

Nationalist then Communist liberations of the capital. Land reform soon led local authorities to close all sacred structures and confiscate Catholic property for utilization in other ways. People used the sacred sanctuary mainly for the regular political meetings they had to attend. Complete secularization did not come until the Cultural Revolution, when Red Guards tore down all the way to foundation level the church's most prominent feature, its tower. Red Guards made the building their revolutionary headquarters, using it as an auditorium for political meetings. On the north wall, near where the altar had once been, zealots added a fresco of Chairman Mao Zedong, one of his poems, and political slogans. Outside, the flat, south-facing façade displayed an even larger painting of "Mao Zedong at Beidai he" and Cultural Revolution slogans, remnants of which were still visible thirty years later.[70] After 1976, some villagers used the building for storage. Later, when the economy improved, they found better sites. Desecrated, dilapidated, and filled with trash, the abandoned

---

70   "Lijiao cun li de tianzhutang," http://blog.sina.com.cn/s/blog_69cda1bf01017pmu.html
      and "Taihe zhuang tianzhutang," http://blog.sina.com.cn/s/blog_87ca2ce40102vkox.html
      (both accessed 26 January 2017).

FIGURE 4.13   The Lijiao church, renovated and reopened
                SOURCE: PHOTO BY AUTHOR, 2011

building could not have been in any worse condition. Nevertheless, Catholics wanted it back.

Local authorities returned the former mission grounds to the Beijing Diocese in 2009 and the bishop assigned a young priest to serve as the pastor. He and members of the congregation spent hours cleaning the premises of debris. Hired workers rebuilt the church's central tower, strengthened the walls, replaced the roof, and renovated the interior. They restored its appearance as much as possible to how it looked in the early 1930s, using an old photograph to guide the restoration. With no interior shots available, parishioners have appointed it simply. It reopened in 2010, dedicated to Our Lady of China.[71] The next year, the pastor had a white statue of Mary installed on a three-foot high pedestal outside the front entrance. The area to the west side is paved and open for parking or outside activities. On the northwest side, the pastor has on-site

---

71   An online source mistakenly writes that it is dedicated to Our Lady of Lourdes. "Taihe zhuang tianzhutang."

housing and several buildings for use by his staff or guests. A conference room has a big table with executive-type desk chairs and a large flat-screen television. The pastor says that he does not proselytize outside the compound's walls, and this partially explains why his congregation is small, with only about fifty people regularly attending daily mass.[72] Lijiao parish looks well enough on the outside and one day will grow.

6   Changgou Town (Taihe Village)

Another old sacred building stands about ten miles to the southwest of Lijiao at Changgou, administratively a town that belonged to Fangshan County during the Qing dynasty. It is presently located in greater Beijing Municipality's southwestern district of Fangshan. Records refer to the sacred structure as part of the town, though it actually was located in the adjoining village (*zhuang*) of Taihe, which locals continue to recognize as a separate community—one without noticeable boundaries or space around it. Transportation to it from Beijing is convenient and fast, no more than ninety minutes by public bus using the highway. Nonetheless, few domestic and foreign tourists make the trip because the area offers little in terms of sightseeing. Only a former church in ruined condition attracts an outlier, such as the author, curious to determine how it is faring.

Proselytization began around the turn of the twentieth century when a priest visited the area, but his conversion of only a few people to Catholicism did not warrant a formal place of worship. After the Boxer flood receded, priests returned to the town and neighboring locales to check on the survivors and seek new believers. The first mention of it comes in 1904–1905 records that list its place in the hierarchy as follows: Vicariate of Beijing and Zhili North; Capital South District; Zhuozhou residence; Changgou congregation—eighteen Catholics, no church or public oratory.[73] By 1914 there were enough Catholics to warrant a place of worship, and the building erected dominated neighboring farm houses in terms of size and height.[74] The only extant image available of it was taken about twenty years later, from which, along with on-site observations, a brief description may be composed. Solidly constructed of bricks on a north-south axis, the single-story structure had a gable roof with

---

72   Author's field notes, 28 September 2011.
73   "Vicariatus Apostolicus Pekini et Tche-ly Septentrionalis. Status Missionis, 1904–1905," 10.
74   A modern gazetteer (and, today, a sign near the main road) identifies it as Taihe. *Fangshan quzhi* (Beijing: Beijing chubanshe, 1999), 658.

slate tiles. Its simple south-facing façade displayed few architectural extras and had only one entranceway flanked by narrow windows. Over the entrance hung a plaque with the three Chinese characters, *tianzhutang*, above which were a rose window, a "footed" Christian cross (*croix pattée*), and at the pediment's peak another cross. Flanking the pediment were two narrow towers with spires each standing approximately forty feet high.[75] Above the gate was a plaque with writing that matched those on the façade. The church also had entrances on the west and east sides for the separate use of women and men, respectively.

A 1928 diagram of the mission compound reveals infrastructural improvements that represent for the most part the extent of religious activities. In addition to the sacred structure and a house, the vicariate had added quarters for the priest, two buildings for his domestic staff, a gatehouse, school, and one more structure. A protective wall with a gate as part of its southern side surrounded the premises of about three-fourths of an acre. Although initially quite small, Catholicism at Changgou Town had rapidly grown and made the place of some local importance. We learn from a gazetteer that in 1935–1936 the area had 4,128 Catholics, one church, and two chapels.[76] A vicariate statistical report dated one year later notes 665 Catholics (none were recent converts) residing in Changgou with another 3,249 (including 15 that were newly baptized) living in seventeen surrounding villages that were part of either Fangshan County or Zhuo County. Among these communities, only two had public oratories (chapels) and another two had private ones—therefore most everyone went to the church for mass.

War between China and Japan became official on 7 July 1937 when the latter's troops attacked Nationalist forces at the Marco Polo Bridge. Shortly thereafter Japanese army units began maneuvering to secure Beijing's southern flank in preparation to take control of the city. By September Japanese soldiers had moved into Fangshan County without any resistance from the Chinese army, which had already withdrawn; the occupying units certainly did not expect any trouble. Locals with scant weaponry began organizing themselves to harass the Japanese, with their "militia" force growing to three thousand. The Catholics among them had volunteered and readily allowed the Changgou church to be their headquarters. Captured Japanese scouts were taken there for interrogation. On 23 December the Japanese attacked, covering the village's main escape route with a machine gun. When the smoke cleared, seventy-eight Chinese lay dead and several homes had been burned, but not the church.

---

75   The height is my estimate. "Vicariat Apostolique de Pékin. État de la Mission, 1936–1937."
76   *Fangshan quzhi*, 659.

FIGURE 4.14   Changgou (Taihe) church and pastor, ca 1930s
SOURCE: ARCHIVES CM, PARIS

FIGURE 4.15   The former Changgou church building
SOURCE: PHOTO BY AUTHOR, 2011

Called the "Taihe Village Massacre" (Taihe zhuang can'an), it is still remembered by the area's residents.[77]

The role Catholics played in opposing Japan did not matter to the leaders of the revolution of the 1940s and the organizers of the political movements of the 1950s. Communists ran them over in the name of national consolidation and those who got up had Red Guards batter them again during the Cultural Revolution. Like all others, Changgou's sacred building closed, its pastor sent off for re-education by manual labor. Devoid of religious symbols, its towers demolished, the building proved useful for meetings with political slogans painted on its interior walls. Sometimes the commune utilized it for bulk storage.

No longer accessed via dusty dirt roads, paved lanes lead to an unusable, vacant building; only one of its former staff support buildings remains, it too rundown and uninhabitable. That no one cares is evident by its deplorable condition and the trash dumped inside. It sits in a neighborhood of one-story residential houses owned by farmers with nearby fields planted with corn during May and June. Three months later, in late summer or early fall, farmers take over the empty space around the church to sun dry shucked ears before storing them for later consumption or sale. This is common practice in North China and people utilize any available open space such as courtyards and roadways this way. The corn's bright yellow color contrasts with the church's gray patina and the red brick addition to its front. The existing building, which has had its windows and doorways bricked up, is no longer used for storage or anything else. Somehow, the façade's *croix pattée*, actually an imprint or shadow of it, remains visible and is practically all that still identifies it as a former church. As of autumn 2011, it remained under the ownership and control of the local government. Diocesan personnel have preliminarily raised the matter of its return with civil authorities.[78] Since few practicing Catholics live in the area, there is no pressing need for a decision.[79]

---

77   "Taihe zhuang tianzhutang."

78   Author's field notes, 28 September 2011.

79   I visited the village accompanied by a priest wearing lay attire. At one point, we chatted with a friendly middle-aged woman at her home directly across from the church. Seeing our interest in the building and its history, she casually said "I am a Catholic." The priest wanted to find out more about her beliefs and, indirectly, about others in the neighborhood. He inquired, "What is a Catholic?" "I don't know," was her reply. She is the descendant of Catholics and knows of no religious activity in the village. Author's field notes, 28 September 2011.

• • •

In the nineteenth century, missionaries built many sacred structures in small rural towns or large villages that were linked to Beijing by seasonally dusty or muddy roads. Travel took much time and energy, yet a handful of priests visited regularly to tend to the congregations, some eventually finding ways to stay with them whether in a room or house attached to a church. The area's Catholics were relatively few, isolated, and vulnerable to attack. Many congregations survived and grew. However, events like war with Japan, the Communist revolution, and mass movements revealed the fragility of rural religious life. At present, some congregations have renovated churches and show signs that a religious resurgence is possible—while others remain dormant.

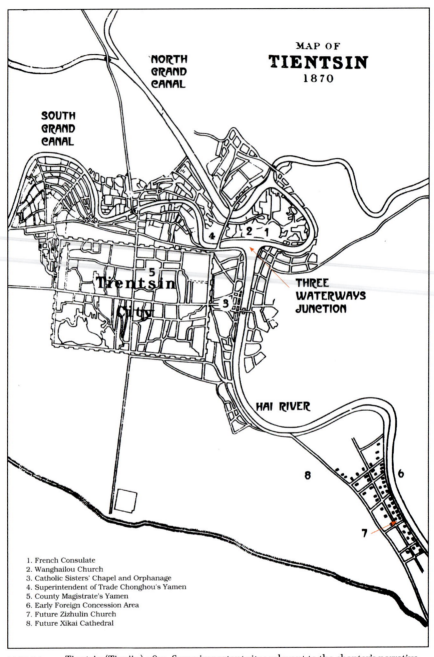

MAP OF
TIENTSIN
1870

NORTH
GRAND
CANAL

SOUTH
GRAND
CANAL

4 2 1

Tientsin
City

5

3

THREE
WATERWAYS
JUNCTION

HAI RIVER

8   6

7

1. French Consulate
2. Wanghailou Church
3. Catholic Sisters' Chapel and Orphanage
4. Superintendent of Trade Chonghou's Yamen
5. County Magistrate's Yamen
6. Early Foreign Concession Area
7. Future Zizhulin Church
8. Future Xikai Cathedral

MAP 5.1   Tientsin (Tianjin), 1870. Some important sites relevant to the chapter's narrative
are amended to the original map.

SOURCE: MORSE, *INTERNATIONAL RELATIONS*

CHAPTER 5

Tianjin's Old Sacred Structures

Although missionaries had been active in Beijing and North China from the early seventeenth century onward, they focused their work on the capital city and, when that was not possible, retreated to the countryside, usually to the southwest or northwest. Those of the next century ventured to the Tianjin area and learned of its importance as a large walled prefectural-level administrative center near the "Three Waterways Junction" (Sancha hekou). This was the strategic point at which barges coming from the south, heavily laden with Yangtze Valley rice to feed Beijing's droves of hungry bureaucrats and residents, navigated from one Grand Canal segment to another.[1] Residents of urban and rural Tianjin, however, did not welcome priests, who made few converts and had no reason to build any churches. Western interest in Tianjin increased during the mid-nineteenth century for political and military reasons. A brief narrative regarding the 1858 and 1860 Anglo-French attacks in North China and subsequent treaty agreements has already been presented. What will be added below is information on the profound impact that these events had on Tianjin physically and its residents psychologically. Twice Western military forces encamped near the junction at Wanghailou, a waterfront spot across from the city wall.[2] With peace re-established, the French stayed there since the city was a treaty port and France had the right to establish a concession area. And missionaries joined them since they had the right to acquire property.

---

1 Hosea Ballou Morse, *The International Relations of the Chinese Empire*, 3 vols. (1910–1918; reprint, 3 vols. in 2, Taipei, n.p., n.d.), 1:518, 2:240. At the junction the South Grand Canal merged with the Bai and Hai Rivers. The Bai flows from the Beijing area to Tianjin, a portion of it used as (and called) the North Grand Canal. From there, the Hai moves eastward to the Gulf of Zhili (Bohai Sea). For more on these waterways, see Bishop, *China's Imperial Way*, 29–54; and "Hai River," http://en.wikipedia.org/wiki/Hai_River (accessed 22 April 2015). In some old English-language accounts, the Bai River, written "Pei-Ho," was mistranslated as the North River. A few nineteenth century descriptions mention only the "Pei-Ho" and imply it flowed to the sea. "China" [report], *Annals PF* 28 (1867): 365.
2 The Treaties of Tianjin were negotiated there. "China," *Annals PF* 28 (1867): 365.

1   Wanghailou Tianzhutang, the [Tall] Catholic Church Overlooking
     the Hai River: Our Lady of Victories (1869–Present)

The process of obtaining real estate started in 1858 when Fr. Qiu Anyu, C.M.,
rented a building outside Tianjin's city walls to use as a small pharmacy. Working
incognito, he hoped the medicines he dispensed would open hearts and minds
to God.[3] Later he moved to be near the French military camp at Wanghailou.
His successor, Fr. Léon-Vincent Talmier, C.M., asked the acting French consul for help in finding a location for a church. With the help of Henri-Victor
Fontanier, interpreter of the French legation at Beijing, negotiations began.
Tianjin's highest-level official was a Manchu with Qing court connections
named Chonghou. He served as the first superintendent of trade for the three
northern (treaty) ports in early 1861. Since the matter involved a French diplomat and missionary, he decided in December to offer Talmier a two and one-
half acres site at Wanghailou. The priest quickly accepted and established his
home and a chapel there. The Chinese considered this arrangement temporary
since it was only a lease with annual payments to be paid by the consulate. The
missionary and consul saw it more like an addition to the French concession;
neither of them nor future parties mentioned lease payments.[4] Whatever the
case, Talmier had succeeded in acquiring property and felt a semblance of security by being near French troops and the consulate.

    The French had occupied a locale filled with shops and houses as well as
two old temples.[5] One particular place was famous for the multistoried buildings used by the Qianlong emperor as his travel or temporary palace (*xinggong*) when he visited, the very reason locals had dubbed it Wanghailou, the
"Tall Building[s] Overlooking the Hai [River]." By the mid-nineteenth century,
the imperial structures had vanished, but many still cherished the site's association with a great emperor and good times. Sentimental attachments aside,
property owners and business people had vested economic interests at stake.
The British did not care for these complications or the site's enlargement limitations and moved to the Black Bamboo Grove (Zizhulin) area, a marshy tract
about two miles downriver on the same side as the walled city. There they demarked a concession district—governed under their own laws, as permitted by
the treaties that China had signed. The French also staked out their concession

---

3   In French romanization, he was K'ieou Ngan-yu (baptized Joseph). Van den Brandt, *Les
     Lazaristes*, 43.
4   For details, Planchet [A. Thomas, pseud.], *Histoire de la mission de Pékin*, 2:417–420; and
     Planchet, *Documents sur les martyrs*, 243. For additional information, see "China," *Annals PF*
     28 (1867): 365; and Morse, *International Relations*, 1:518 and 2:240–241.
5   Their names were Chongxi guan and Wanghai si.

yet stayed at Wanghailou because they had already preemptively established a consulate there: its staff found the adjacent chapel convenient.

1.1 The First Wanghailou Church (1869–1870)

A book on Tianjin's churches explains Catholic interest in Wanghailou by quoting the Vicariate of Beijing and Zhili North's Bishop Mouly. "This place in Tianjin's suburbs is an excellent location," he remarked. "On the way to Beijing, Tianjin is the first gateway and Europeans will pass this way. [Therefore,] we must successfully open it up [with a church]."[6] On the bishop's return from Paris in July 1862, he transited Tianjin, instructing five of the fourteen Daughters of Charity with him—the first to serve in North China—to remain with Talmier. Their main tasks were rescue of abandoned or orphaned children and aid to the sick.[7] They opened a small foundling home (orphanage) called the House of Mercy (Renci tang) about one mile away from the chapel at a rented site located between the river and the city wall near its east gate. These "eastern suburbs" were a busy and crowded place suitable for their work; in terms of security, it was an exposed and unprotected location, but this did not worry them. Talmier died unexpectedly in the summer of 1862 and a replacement was sent. Financial help arrived in 1864–1865, when the Holy Childhood Society gave the Vicariate of Beijing and Zhili North $37,000, of which $13,320 went to the Sisters at Tianjin. For that year, the vicariate's priests and Sisters had baptized 8,422 dying children. Missionaries concomitantly took charge of 1,800 children, some going to hired wet nurses, many boarded at schools, and 162 cared for at two orphanages.[8] About 25 percent of the baptisms had taken

---

6   *Tianjin lao jiaotang*, comp. Tianjin shi dang'anguan, Yu Xueyun, and Liu Lin (Tianjin: Tianjin chubanshe, 2005), 3.

7   The clergy (and assistants) baptized weak, severely ill, and dying infants to give, according to doctrine, their innocent souls a salvational path to heaven. Background on the theological importance of this work with a China context is in Michelle T. King, *Between Birth and Death: Female Infanticide in Nineteenth-Century China* (Stanford: Stanford University Press, 2014), 114–118. Many non-Catholics could not comprehend why the death rates of abandoned infants under Catholic care were alarmingly high, or the purpose of baptism.

8   *Annales OSE* 17 (1865): 97, 109. Statistics are not available for every year and some appear to be rough estimates. Fr. Edmond-François Guierry, C.M., commented that an 1867 summary of mission work in China indicated more than four hundred thousand dying children had been baptized. This number included twenty thousand who had died at orphanages (out of forty thousand under Vincentian care). *Annales OSE* 20 (1868): 6. Guierry arrived in China in 1853, working in Zhili from 1865 to 1870 and then serving as bishop for a year after Mouly's death. A report for the Vicariate of Beijing and Zhili North made during the late 1870s mentions the baptism of 11,078 non-Catholic dying children. Archives CM, Paris, Folder 168-I, "Vicariatus Apostolicus Pekini et Tche-ly Septentrionalis. Fructus Spirituales, a die 15 Aug. 1878 ad diem 14 Aug. 1879." For another part of China, in the Vicariate of Northern Jiangxi,

place in the Tianjin area, with roughly half the children staying at the institution in Tianjin City.

Fr. Claude Chevrier, a Vincentian, was assigned to Tianjin in 1866 and before long began making plans for a large sacred structure to replace the chapel. When Mouly visited in July 1868, Chevrier suggested that they build in front of the current chapel and alongside the French consulate, since the properties adjoined one another.[9] About this time, the priest began gathering the funds (eight thousand taels, that is, $11,840) needed for construction—his main financial sources were the French government, his sister in Lyon, compatriots (such as Favier who donated a cross for exterior use), and the Vincentian procurator in Shanghai.[10] Chevrier had experienced the challenges of working in Tianjin and wanted a sacred structure that would be to him, figuratively if not literally, an "impregnable mansion," a veritable religious armory in the fight against satanic forces.[11] The bishop agreed, assigning Bro. Marty to help with the project because he had experience supervising construction of the North Church a few years earlier. Everyone liked the riverfront location and thought that it would make the church the landmark Mouly wanted. Before the bishop departed he blessed what would be the first stone laid when construction started on 16 May 1869 at the site of the Chongxi Temple.[12] Once work started, Marty supervised everything from the building of a quay for the delivery of materials to the laying of the foundation on a north-south axis (the chancel situated in the north and the entrance in the south) and the installation of roof tiles. As completion neared, neighborhood people naturally worried that its presence (and the existing French consulate's) would negatively affect their pocketbooks and lives. At the same time, they saw it as an affront to the memory of the Qianlong emperor and to the temple it had displaced. A visiting

---

1870–1886, Vincentians cared for about six thousand children of whom four thousand died. During this sixteen-year period, priests and Sisters baptized one hundred thousand dying children. Sweeten, *Christianity in Rural China*, 187.

9   Fr. Armand David, C.M., visited Tianjin in May 1868 and reported that the Chinese had "ceded" to France the property on which the consulate and "our small Chinese chapel" stood. Armand David, *Abbe David's Diary: Being an Account of the French Naturalist's Journeys and Observations in China in the Years 1866 to 1869*, trans. and ed. Helen M. Fox (Cambridge, Mass.: Harvard University Press, 1949), 151–152, 154.

10   Mouly letter, 28 October 1868, *Annales CM-F* 34 (1869): 283–285; and Archives CM, Paris, Carton 14, "Biens Temporels, Indemnités de 1870."

11   Maurice Collard, *Les Martyrs de Tien-Tsin* (Paris: Librairie-Éditions A. Giraudon, 1926), 51.

12   Mouly letter, 28 October 1868, *Annales CM-F* 34 (1869): 283–285. Planchet [A. Thomas, pseud.], *Histoire de la mission Pékin*, 2:516; and *Tianjin lao jiaotang*, 2. Whether the temple was in use or in ruins and what had to be removed to make room for the church is unclear.

priest commented that "the Chinese still suffer keenly at seeing *western devils* established in a residence of the *Son of Heaven*" (italics in original).[13]

In late 1869, Chevrier dedicated the church to Notre-Dame des Victoires, a name that suggested to him a solidly built place for worshippers to use as they prepared to battle for Mary.[14] The name connoted to religious and secular French at home their country's national reemergence in European affairs. In China, it nominally acknowledged French imperial power via an active religious protectorate for the Catholic presence.[15] Its Chinese name, Sheng Mu desheng tang, carried a specific meaning to locals who saw *desheng* ("victories") in light of France's recent battles in China since few had any knowledge of its name in a religious or European context.[16] Many Catholics in Tianjin avoided the potentially controversial formal name by attaching a locational association to the building, a pattern already noted. They called it the "Tall [Hai] River Church" ([Hai]helou jiaotang) and the "Tall Church Overlooking the Hai [River]" (Wanghailou jiaotang). The latter became the popular choice and is still commonly used.

Some have described it as Gothic, and this is true to a degree given several of its architectural features, yet the Wanghailou church was different in significant ways from those built in Beijing during the same period. The large and architecturally unique structure had embedded in its solidly built brick façade a white marble plaque inscribed with the words "N.D. DES VICTOIRES." The façade's most noticeable feature was its tall, rectangular-shaped, flat-topped bell tower with narrow windows on each side, a cross on its south side adding more height.[17] Flanking it were shorter, octagonal towers with similarly

---

13   David, *Abbe David's Diary*, 152.
14   Collard, *Les Martyrs*, 51. Song of Songs 4.4 reads: "Thy neck, is as the tower of David, which is built with bulwarks: a thousand bucklers hang upon it, all the armor of valiant men." Metaphorically open to interpretation, Chevrier uses the verse to reference the church.
15   In Shanghai in the late 1860s, the Jesuits established a shrine for Mary whose name they changed in 1871 from Our Lady of Victories to Our Lady, Help of Christians. Young, *Ecclesiastical Colony*, 3, 262 n. 3. Vincentians did not favor the name in their several vicariates and I know of only one other similarly dedicated, its location at Ji'an, Jiangxi. Boscat letter, 23 May 1884, *Annales CM-F* 49 (1884): 606–607; and "Vicariat du Kiang-si Méridional," *Annales CM-F* 56 (1891): 478–479.
16   Noted in *Huoshao Wanghailou—1870 Tianjin renmin fan yangjiao douzheng*, ed. Tianjin lishi yanjiusuo and Tianjin shihua bianxiezu (Tianjin: Tianjin renmin chubanshe, 1973), 9.
17   The one at Wanghailou does not resemble at all the current Basilique Notre-Dame des Victoires in Paris first completed in 1629 by Augustinians with financial help from Louis XIII, who recognized the Virgin's role in his successful battles to unify the kingdom. In 1836, the pastor consecrated his parish to the Immaculate Heart of Mary. "Basilica of Notre-Dame-des-Victoires, Paris," http://en.wikipedia.org/wiki/Basilica_of_Notre-Dame-des-Victoires,_Paris (accessed 12 January 2015). Vincentians in China had

shaped windows on every side and below them even smaller, narrower ones. Looking like watchtowers with gun slots, they gave the church a fortress-like profile. Workers laid a foundation measuring ninety-eight feet long by thirty-two wide with a central tower probably rising to a height of sixty-seventy feet, about the same as the city wall tower across the river.[18] Chinese of that era saw Tianjin's single largest, tallest freestanding structure.[19] It would not be surprising if some thought the French built it (and the adjoining consulate) to demonstrate control of river traffic and ensure future access to Beijing because it physically dominated the Three Waterways Junction. As events will show, this "strange" (*guguai*) structure stood as a visual reminder of the shameful routs of 1858–1860 and the postbellum presence of unwanted Westerners.[20]

To this, evangelical endeavors added another level of misunderstanding. As mentioned, the bishop knew of the hardships that Tianjin's poorest children faced, accordingly sending Talmier help in the form of religious sisters together with funds to establish a foundling home. They worked tirelessly to relieve the plight of those suffering from homelessness, malnourishment, and illness. Some received baptism followed by, when efforts to treat them failed, the rite of extreme unction, and proper burial in a Catholic cemetery. People in Tianjin and all over China found it hard to comprehend why missionaries focused inordinately on sick and fatally ill children, speculating that there had to be a nefarious link between the children's deaths and religious rites they did not understand. Vile rumors circulated, many of which were common in other parts of China, that priests and Sisters murdered the helpless young in their care to harvest body parts and organs for despicable religious purposes. Such crude stories spread with ever-increasing elaboration and speed, fed further by gossip about the kidnapping of children for the foundling home and

---

no direct connection to it. In 1899, after the Qing government issued decrees favoring Catholicism, Propaganda Fide celebrated a mass of thanksgiving at Our Lady of Victories in Paris. "China," *Annals CM-E* 6 (1899): 365–366.

18   The length and width are based on the second iteration, which used the original foundation to replicate the first structure. An online source reports the tower's height to have been thirty-three feet. "Tianjin Wanghailou jiaotang de jianjie," https:// zhidao.baidu.com/question/714426023923780045.html?qbl=relate_question_0& word=wanghailoujiaotangduoda (accessed 26 November 2016). The central tower of the third version was seventy-two feet high; a comparison of photographs of the three churches makes me skeptical that the first one's tower was as low as thirty odd feet.

19   *Tianjin lao jiaotang*, 3.

20   *Tianjin lao jiaotang*, 3–4. For background information concerning popular sentiments of an anti-foreign and anti-missionary nature in Tianjin and other parts of China, see John K. Fairbank, "Patterns Behind the Tientsin Massacre," *Harvard Journal of Asiatic Studies* 20, no. 3/4 (December 1957): 503–505.

anonymous accounts of locals finding disfigured bodies (which dogs had possibly disinterred and mangled) at the Wanghailou church's cemetery.[21]

With Tianjin's atmosphere fouled with volatile fumes, the Chinese-speaking Fontanier, who had become the French consul, quarreled with various officials over Chinese security measures, a final, fateful encounter occurring on 21 June 1870. After meeting Chonghou at his yamen to discuss what was being done about suppressing the wild rumors and preparing security for the church, a disgruntled Fontanier (accompanied by a French staff member) encountered the county magistrate on a nearby street. They argued loudly over the same issues and attracted a fast-growing collection of rowdy people curious about the spectacle. Angered beyond reason, perhaps even feeling threatened by the crowd that he wanted to withdraw, the consul apparently fired his pistol at the magistrate, the bullet hitting instead one of his attendants. Onlookers immediately reacted and killed the two Frenchmen. This specific event quickly turned into a violent rampage.[22] "Kill [all] the foreign devils [but] first kill the French devils" (*sha yang guizi xian sha Faguo guizi*) was a catchphrase that filled the air.[23]

That day local Chinese murdered every French national they could find; altogether twenty died, among them, Chevrier and ten Daughters of Charity.[24] During the turmoil, local Catholics, children under the Sisters' care, and a Chinese priest died, too.[25] Among the property destroyed was the Wanghailou

---

21   For example, Dong Conglin, *Yanzhao wenhua de jindai zhuanxing* (Shijiazhuang: Hebei jiaoyu chubanshe, 2000), 46–50.

22   These events are nicely recounted by Bickers, *The Scramble for China*, 231–236.

23   Zhang Li and Liu Jiantang, *Zhongguo jiao'an shi* (Chengdu: Sichuan sheng shehui kexue yuan chubanshe, 1987), 409.

24   The estimate of the number of murdered Westerners varies. A missionary in Shanghai provides the names and nationalities of seventeen victims, seven identified as French as well as ten religious sisters (six from France and four from three other countries). "China" (quoting Lemonnier letter, 6 July 1870), *Annals PF* 31 (1870): 334–336. The French chargé meanwhile counted nineteen (see note 37 below). Morse counts twenty-one dead (plus thirty to forty Chinese employed by the priests and Sisters), *International Relations*, 2:246. Ferreux puts the total at twenty-one, including one Chinese priest. *Histoire de la Congrégation*, 187. A recent, general history mentions nineteen. Spence, *Search for Modern China*, 205. And a Chinese book lists twenty "foreign devils" (*yang guizi*) by nationality, that is, thirteen French, three Russians, two Belgium, one British, and one Italian. *Huoshao Wanghailou*, 20. These are minor discrepancies, to be sure, but suggest that the violence (and aftermath) may benefit from a thorough review.

25   The exact number of Chinese killed, many of whom were Catholic and worked at the French consulate or for the Church, has not been determined. One priest estimated that "more than one hundred orphans" died. "China" (quoting Lemonnier letter, 6 July 1870), *Annals PF* 31 (1870): 334. Much later, another priest wrote that twelve children perished. Ferreux, *Histoire de la Congrégation*, 187.

church (its façade with parts of its walls left standing); a dwelling; the Sisters' foundling home, chapel, and miscellaneous buildings; and the French consulate as well as adjoining structures.[26] Locals also burned down several small Protestant churches, rented houses used as such.[27] Western accounts wrote of the horrible and tragic "Tianjin Massacre" while Qing officials preferred the less emotionally charged "Tianjin affray between [local] people and Christians" (Tianjin *minjiao zishi*) and the generic, commonly used "Tianjin [Christian] Religious Case" (Tianjin *jiao'an*). City residents simply called it "the burning of the Wanghailou [church]" (*huoshao* Wanghailou), which artists depicted via woodblock prints included in cheap books or crafted into hand-held colored fans that became popular mementoes.[28] Street musicians and other people sang about its destruction in folk ditties, some verses of which are still remembered today.[29]

Given the loss of Western lives and property, Chinese officials treated the matter with gravitas. Superintendent of Trade Chonghou reported to the throne on 23 June about the heated meeting at his yamen two days earlier with Fontanier.[30] Chonghou wrote that he had done everything he could to avoid trouble as residents became angry and uncontrollable. In his words, "the initial cause of this affair was in the [missionaries'] burying of children and [local people] spreading rumors about [missionaries] gouging out eyes and cutting out hearts." Moreover, "the bandit kidnappers who officials apprehended gave evidence against individuals affiliated with the church, such that the masses harbored doubts and piled up indignation. It was from this provocation that the affair occurred." Afterwards Chonghou had ordered arrests and brought

---

26   Western visitors in July reported that the side walls still stood. *Papers Relating to the Massacre of Europeans at Tien-tsin on the 21st June, 1870* (London: Harrison and Sons, 1871), 64. A photograph of it, mislabeled as having been taken in November 1869, shows the east wall still standing. *Tianjin lao jiaotang*, 2. The side walls collapsed within a year or two, leaving only the façade.

27   A few sources mention in passing other property losses. One notes that "patriots" destroyed Protestant churches, two of them American and four British. *Huoshao Wanghailou*, 20.

28   Fans depicted the conflagration with Westerners in front of it under attack. An American publisher obtained a fan, noting that one like it "was shown in an article which had been in our possession for some years, from the 'Every Sunday—An Illustrated Journal of Choice Reading,' published in Boston MA on 24 December 1870." "Les Martyrs de Tien-tsin," http://eventail.pagesperso-orange.fr/martyrs/martyrse.html (accessed 9 October 2015). For one version of the fan, see Bickers, *Scramble for China,* illustration 14. A section of a similar fan is reproduced in *Tianjin lao jiaotang*, 7. The paper portion of what was once a fan may be found in Archives CM, Paris, Folder 164-I-a.

29   *Tianjin lao jiaotang*, 7. *Huoshao Wanghailou*, 25, mentions the different media used to commemorate the event: poems, ballads, drawings, woodblock prints, even the clay figurines that Tianjin is famous for.

30   Cordier, *Histoire des relations*, 1:350.

FIGURE 5.1   The first Wanghailou church, after the arson of 21 June 1870
            SOURCE: MORSE, *INTERNATIONAL RELATIONS*

FIGURE 5.2   Woodblock print of the attack on Westerners and the church. Prints were folded
            and glued to bamboo strips that served as frames for hand-held fans. Similar
            versions were sold in the 1870s.
            SOURCE: ARCHIVES CM, PARIS

the situation under control. Still he wanted, in a typical Chinese bureaucrat-ic move aimed at absolving himself, an independent review. He specifically requested that the province's top-ranking official, "Governor-General, Zeng Guofan, come to Tianjin and make an accurate investigation so as to pacify the locality."[31] Zeng came with a well-deserved reputation for competence and loyalty, in good part due to his crucial military role in defeating the Taipings. He went to Tianjin and determined that the priests and Sisters bore responsi-bility for their work and the outbreak. To prevent future trouble, he called for restrictions.[32] The court accepted his findings and, as far as locals were con-cerned, put blame where blame was due.

The French legation in Bejing dispatched Chargé d'affaires Julien de Rochechouart, accompanied by Fathers Favier and Pascal d'Addosio, C.M., to Tianjin to investigate and meet with officials.[33] The French saw themselves as innocent victims and demanded punishment of the officials, who had not prevented the incident, and of the perpetrators. Of course, they expected reparations.[34] Prince Gong as head of the Zongli Yamen took charge of ne-gotiations for the Qing and mollified the French with an offer that included a Chonghou-led delegation to Paris to apologize directly to the French president (and nation), punishment of culpable officials and the culprits involved in the attacks, and compensation.[35] This satisfied Rochechouart, but how he and the vicariate's leaders handled the reparations illustrates both France's fixation on obtaining reimbursement for every incident involving injury, death, or prop-erty damage and the missionaries' increasingly passive-aggressive approach.

The chargé demanded two hundred ten thousand taels ($310,800) for all property losses, implicitly taking responsibility for deciding what portion to give the vicariate. He wanted another two hundred fifty thousand taels

---

31   See "Tianjin Massacre—Chonghou's Report," http://www9.georgetown.edu/faculty/
      spendelh/china/TJ700623.htm (accessed 4 February 2013) for a translation of Chonghou's
      report to the throne. In 1870, Governor-general Zeng moved his office from Baoding to
      Tianjin and served concurrently as superintendent of trade for the northern ports.
      Li Hongzhang replaced him later in that same year, retaining the appointment for most of
      three decades. Until his death in 1901, he would be involved in all manner of Sino-foreign
      negotiations. *Eminent Chinese*, 209, 466–470.

32   Charles A. Litzinger, "Patterns of Missionary Cases Following the Tientsin Massacre, 1870–
      1875," *Papers on China* 23 (July 1970), 87–108.

33   Planchet [A. Thomas, pseud.], *Histoire de la mission de Pékin*, 2:527.

34   Beginning with Britain's Treaty of Nanjing, Western countries demanded that China pay
      them for war-related expenses and losses. In the years that followed, France made sure
      that Catholic priests received compensation for incurred losses of property and personal
      items.

35   For information on Prince Gong, see *Eminent Chinese*, 209–211.

($370,000) as compensation for the deaths of French nationals (and the Sisters from other countries). Of that sum, the chargé allocated 48 percent ($177,600) for the diplomat and civilian lives lost and 52 percent ($192,400) for those associated with the vicariate.[36] Prince Gong agreed to pay the amount asked of him, neither quibbling nor seeking clarification on how Rochechouart had arrived at the large numbers, especially those for the lost lives.[37] They settled the matter by October, and sometime before the end of the year Qing officials paid the sums agreed upon, two hundred fifty thousand taels coming from custom duties collected from Western traders at Shanghai and Guangzhou and two hundred ten thousand from those at Tianjin.[38] Separately, the dynasty paid reparations to Russia, Britain, and the U.S. for property damage as well as five thousand taels ($7,400) for local Catholics' losses.[39] Missionaries never subsequently mentioned the funds earmarked for locals or their dispersal to them.

To complicate matters, the newly appointed bishop of the Vicariate of Beijing and Zhili North, Louis-Gabriel Delaplace, had been in Rome for meetings

36   As reported in Western newspapers and a summary published in a volume of the *Annals of the Propagation of the Faith*, it is clear that the French divided the funds as follows: one hundred twenty thousand taels for non-Catholic lives lost and one hundred thirty thousand for those connected to the Church. "Southern Pe-tche-li," *Annals PF* 32 (1871): 115–116; and Morse, *International Relations*, 2:258.

37   Rochechouart sought the following compensation for the lives lost: French consul (Fontanier), thirty thousand taels; chancellor/staff (Simon), twenty thousand; chancellor/staff (Thomassin and wife), fifty thousand; merchant (Challemaison and wife), twenty thousand; and Church personnel (thirteen people, some not French nationals), one hundred thirty thousand. Cordier, *Histoire des relations*, 1:385–386. Another source provides similar information with Mrs. Challemaison excluded by mistake. Planchet [A. Thomas, pseud.], *Histoire de la mission de Pékin*, 2:529. Following the Boxer Uprising, France asked for one hundred thousand taels as compensation for the loss of five Marist brothers, claiming the amount reasonable because of the reparation paid for Fontanier and Simon in 1870. Archives CM, Paris, Carton 14, "Biens Temporels, Indemnités … 5 Confrères Massacrés en 1900."

38   Cordier cites a letter of 18 October 1870 from Prince Gong to Rochechouart that the funds' source would be duties collected at Shanghai and Guangzhou. *Histoire des relations*, 1:385–386. The letter, translated into French and English, may be found in *Papers Relating to the Massacre of Europeans at Tien-tsin*, 238–239. Some missionaries believed the money had come from "the duties paid on merchandise imported or exported by foreign traders," not from the Tianjin government or levies on its residents. Some felt that the people of Tianjin should bear the financial burden as part of the punishment. "Southern Pe-tche-li," *Annals PF* 32 (1871): 116–117. Figures are mentioned in *JWJAD*, II/I/384, 331b and II/III, "Chronology of Major Events," 33. The *JWJAD* collection of Zongli Yamen communications does not include specifics about the indemnities.

39   Russia received 30,000 taels ($44,400); for four churches destroyed, Britain got 2,500 taels ($3,700); and the U.S., 4,785 taels ($7,082). Zhang Li and Liu Jiantang, *Zhongguo jiao'an shi*, 409, 412–413.

(Vatican 1), only arriving at Beijing on 1 November 1870. He had neither participated in the negotiations nor had an opportunity to provide input regarding the settlement.[40] In a January 1871 letter to Rochechouart, he expressed his opinion at how things had been resolved, in effect criticizing the chargé's decisions and indirectly challenging his authority.[41] As for the property settlement, the bishop added a qualification meant for conveyance to the Chinese. He wrote: "We shall accept this sum *provided that* the conditions, asked by us, as guarantee for the future have been fulfilled; if the mentioned conditions are not admitted, we do not accept anything. I say: *provided that the conditions which were pointed out by us have been fulfilled*" (italics in original).[42]

Before discussing what his caveat meant, note that the French legation had not estimated nor itemized values for the Wanghailou church, foundling home, French consulate, or any of the destroyed buildings. As mentioned, all that is known about these costs comes from a source that says that the church had been built for $11,840.[43] Given it was the most expensive building, could the total cost of all the structures have amounted to another $298,960? Clearly, the property settlement constituted a grossly inflated increase over original costs. The Chinese did not complain because it was better for them to pay up and conclude the negotiations than risk additional demands.[44] Vincentians received their share of the property reparations but left behind no records of how much or how they used it except that the bishop allocated some of the

---

40   Delaplace served as bishop of the Vicariate of Jiangxi (1852–1854) and the Vicariate of Zhejiang (1854–1870) before assignment to the Vicariate of Beijing and Zhili North on 21 January 1870, leading his confreres until his death on 24 May 1884. Van den Brandt, *Les Lazaristes*, 51–52.

41   The full letter is in Chambon, *Vie et Apostolat*, 208–212. Also, Cordier, *Histoire des relations*, 1:388–390. A Vincentian historian writes that Delaplace's refusal to accept compensation for the dead victims had "embarrassed" Rochechouart. Planchet [A. Thomas, pseud.], *Histoire de la mission de Pékin*, 2:532. If the chargé considered the negotiations successfully completed, the bishop's statement about refusing money and other conditions contradicted him, effectively voiding part or all of the chargé's settlement. In any case, Rochechouart did not re-open negotiations with the Chinese because he had accepted France's share of the reparations and the C.M.'s procurator in Shanghai, on behalf of the Vincentians, had accepted their portion. More information may be found in Planchet [A. Thomas, pseud.], *Histoire de la mission de Pékin*, 2:530–532.

42   Chambon, *Vie et Apostolat*, 208–212; and Ferreux with minor differences in wording, *Histoire de la Congrégation*, 190.

43   "Biens Temporels, Indemnités de 1870." The church's cost is not mentioned in the 1870 negotiations. A brief reference to it is in a report compiled by the French government in 1934 (per the citation given).

44   That is, as already specified, dismissing or punishing culpable officials, apprehending the principal culprits, and agreeing to send a diplomatic mission to France to apologize.

funds to build and equip the Church of St. Louis, finished in 1872, and, probably, to construct facilities for the Daughters of Charity.[45]

The bishop's "conditions" meant he would not rebuild until he felt the insult to Catholics had been rectified via a public apology from the Qing court, something that Tianjin residents would not be able to ignore. "I would like a monument erected, *by imperial decree*, along the river between the consulate of France and our ruined church," he wrote. It should be "a marble monument [with imperial] yellow tiles [for a roof covering it] and inscriptions that condemn the authors and perpetrators of the June slaughters and categorically contradict the calumnies that still weigh on our Missionaries and Daughters of Charity" (italics in original).[46] If the emperor did not order an inscribed stele, in effect a monument of shame, Delaplace thought the damaged façade still topped by a cross would substitute as a reminder, not of the damages paid nor of the punishments administered, but rather of the tragic memory of the death and destruction that had occurred. The vicariate's leaders in Beijing, as we shall see, never forgot his words.

Finally, Delaplace found it repugnant to take even one ounce of silver for the lost lives. "Regarding the moneys granted to compensate for human lives, we refuse them with disdain," he wrote emotionally. "It repulses us to accept this blood money (*prix du sang*), for the principal reason that when missionaries or Daughters of Charity give themselves for the missions, they do so to give their work, their sweat, their life: to give not sell them. Let them speak, our victims of Tianjin, and indignant they will exclaim, with us, that they never had the intention to put their blood on a scale against the weight of taels!"[47] The bishop hoped he could somehow undo Rochechouart's acceptance of France's portion and the Vincentian procurator's receipt of his congregation's share. Not surprisingly, the chargé did nothing and Delaplace's influence did not extend as far as he thought, the Shanghai-based procurator stating that he would not return the money to the Chinese unless the superior general of the Congregation of the Mission in Paris ordered him to do so.[48] The Qing had paid the Vincentians in full and neither Delaplace nor his successors ever claimed otherwise.

---

45   One Vincentian historian notes that Delaplace used the property reparations for construction of the Church of St. Louis. Ferreux, *Histoire de la Congrégation*, 190. A French government document states that money intended for the reconstruction of the Wanghailou church was used for building materials, including an exterior clock at Zizhulin. "Biens Temporels, Indemnités de 1870."

46   Chambon, *Vie et Apostolat*, 209; and Ferreux, *Histoire de la Congrégation*, 190.

47   Chambon, *Vie et Apostolat*, 211; and Ferreux, *Histoire de la Congrégation*, 190.

48   Cordier, *Histoire des relations*, 1:388.

The year 1870 changed China. Some Chinese saw Westerners as more vulnerable than before. Qing officials, on their part, punished those deemed guilty for the violence in Tianjin, apologized in different ways, and paid out large reparations. Westerners, however, worried that Tianjin might be a harbinger of more attacks to come, recognizing it as a Chinese reaction not only to the overt presence of missionaries, churches, and foundling homes but also to the humiliating military losses that had opened the empire to Western trade. A show of force in the various ports would be a deterrent, even if only temporarily.[49]

The year 1870 changed life for Westerners in Tianjin. For security reasons, the French relocated their consulate to the foreign concession district that Britain had already inaugurated at the Black Bamboo Grove area. Vincentians also withdrew, retaining control of the Wanghailou property, maintaining the security wall, and taking measures to prevent locals from scavenging for bricks, thereby ensuring they did not accidentally or deliberately cause the façade to collapse. In addition, on its east side Vincentians buried thirteen of the victims, each grave marked with a white-marble tombstone.[50] Priests looked upon the ruins and cemetery as temporary monuments because they intended to rebuild. In the meantime, those living in the Wanghailou area had to make do with a temporary chapel for a few years until, not far away, they erected a Memorial Chapel to honor the memory of the murdered Daughters of Charity. The latter quickly rebuilt lost structures as they bravely resumed their work by opening a hospital, dispensary, and two foundling homes in the city.[51]

1.2   *The Second Wanghailou Church (1897–1900)*

Over the next twenty years, mission work in Tianjin continued "without great fervor" because of continuing tension and locals' lack of enthusiasm for the Gospel's message.[52] By the 1890s the overall situation seemed better, with Vincentians seeing Christianity as much stronger than before and ready to expand in all directions. Fr. Jean Capy said that "we still look with regret upon the dear ruins of 1870 [which] remained untouched, and our works are about

49   *The Tientsin Massacre: Being Documents Published in the Shanghai Evening Courier from June 16th to Sept. 10th, 1870, with an Introductory Narrative,* 2nd ed. (Shanghai: A.H. de Carvalho, n.d.), iii–xix.

50   Cordier, *Histoire des relations,* 1:357–359; Chambon, *Vie et Apostolat,* 217; and Ferreux, *Histoire de la Congrégation,* 189. Catholics temporarily interred the victims at the British cemetery until their transfer on 3 August.

51   "China," *Annals PF* 28 (1867): 365–366. Priests considered it a "Memorial Chapel." Corset letter, 7 August 1900, *Annals CM-E* 7 (1900): 541.

52   "Faithful Beginnings and Progress of the Faith in Maritime Chi-li, China," *Annals PF* 77 (1914): 99–100.

limited to the *Concessions* [area and the Church of St. Louis]" (italics in original). He felt that a rebuilt one at Wanghailou would serve as a mission center to promote work in the countryside and compete with Protestants then moving into the area.[53] In Beijing, Favier, now holding a high position in the vicariate, contended publicly that the Chinese had never atoned for the earlier events in Tianjin.[54] Echoing what we may interpret as a place-of-memory lament, he wrote in late 1896:

> The troubles in which France was involved at the time prevented her from visiting such atrocity with the vengeance which at any other time, would have been justly meted out to the Chinese. She was obliged, for the time, to be content with the excuses more or less sincere, offered to the President of the Republic, by an ambassador [Chonghou] sent by China—an ambassador, who in these events played the part of Pilate. *France was obliged to accept a pecuniary reparation for material damages; the necessary moral reparation being deferred to better times.* Since that period, during twenty-six years, travelers could visit the temporary monuments raised to these victims, and the ruins of the church, the façade of which, almost intact, stands out on the banks of the river as a monument attesting an *incomplete reparation*—a melancholy monument to Europeans, and even to the Chinese themselves. On beholding these sad relics, every visitor returned with a sorrowful heart, asking: "When will this magnificent church be rebuilt? When will the victims of barbarity have an honorable sepulture? When will an adequate *moral reparation* be obtained for these villainous deeds never-to-be-forgotten?"[55] (Italics added by author.)

---

53   Capy letter, 18 July 1893, *Annals CM-E* 1 (1894): 199–200. Protestant activities were of concern. The bishop of the Vicariate of Beijing and Zhili North, Jean-Baptiste Sarthou, commented that Catholics competed successfully with Protestants in the Tianjin area. Another bishop mentioned the need to "counteract Protestant influence" in Jiujiang, Jiangxi. "Report of the Missions by Rev. Father Bettemburg, ... 1894," *Annals CM-E* 2 (1895): 370–371, 375.

54   Due to Bishop Sarthou's poor health, on 12 November 1897 the pope named Favier as coadjutor and titular bishop with automatic succession upon Sarthou's death. Consecration ceremonies took place on 20 February 1898. Van den Brandt, *Les Lazaristes*, 68–69, 80.

55   By "moral reparation," he meant compensation for the lives lost and an apology. Favier letter, 25 December 1896, *Annals CM-E* 4 (1897): 224–225. He felt that the massacre was a horrible past occurrence inscribed over time with insults in the form of inadequate and delayed replies as well as lightly veiled hostile messages. In all these ways, he was reminded of—and remembered—Tianjin.

Favier understood that in 1870 war with Prussia had prevented France (and therefore the Catholic Church) from meting out proper "vengeance," but it gnawed at him that since then French ministers had twice failed to intercede.[56] With China's defeat by Japan in 1895 and Minister Auguste Gérard's successful clarification of troublesome property purchase procedures that had often stymied priests, Favier heard opportunity knocking.[57] To prepare the minister for the task, in September Favier invited him to Tianjin to see the Wanghailou ruins and memorial cemetery. One month after returning to the capital, Gérard obtained from the Zongli Yamen what Favier called an "arrangement" that was for the good of the Church, its victims, and France. Qing high officials agreed to the following: 1) a new church at Wanghailou, modeled on its predecessor with restoration of the standing façade; 2) the transfer of thirteen coffins from the cemetery to underground vaults inside the church, each to be marked with a memorial stone; 3) the erection of a white marble stele inscribed with *chijian* (here meaning erected by imperial order) and the Tongzhi emperor's decree of June 1870;[58] and 4) an imperial-style pavilion to house the stele, the latter marked with the emperor's reign title and date.[59]

Although the vicariate had never relinquished control over the Wanghailou site and hardly needed Chinese permission to rebuild or inter caskets inside

---

56   French ministers, Geoffroy in 1873 and Bourée in 1881, had attempted to reopen negotiations. Planchet [A. Thomas, pseud.], *Histoire de la mission de Pékin*, 2:686. Planchet worked in several areas, including Tianjin in 1897.

57   Property purchase procedures are mentioned in Chapter 2. More details are in my book, *Christianity in Rural China*, 102–107; and Planchet [A. Thomas, pseud.], *Histoire de la mission de Pékin*, 2:682–685. According to a historical memorial entitled the "Site of the Tianjin [Christian] Religious Case" (*Tianjin jiao'an yizhi*), missionaries took advantage of China's weakened condition following her defeat by Japan in 1895. Author's field notes, 25 September 2013. See Appendix 7 for a translation of the full text.

58   The emperor succinctly stated that Chonghou had reported on what led to the incident and that officials in Tianjin had not acted properly to prevent it. He deplored this and ordered Zeng Guofan to investigate with Chonghou, then to administer impartial justice to those involved. Cordier, *Histoire des relations*, 1:364–365. Some thought the edict insufficient; Favier found it useful enough. The longer decree of October 1870 was clear in its recognition of responsibility and specification of punishments for those held accountable, but Favier did not call for its use. *Papers Relating to the Massacre of Europeans at Tien-tsin on the 21st June, 1870* (London: Harrison and Sons, 1871), 194–195.

59   Favier letter, 25 December 1896, *Annals CM-E* 4 (1897): 226–233; Planchet [A. Thomas., pseud.], Histoire de la mission de Pékin, 2:686–687; and Ferreux, *Histoire de la Congrégation*, 191. Favier did not ask that the emperor endorse its reconstruction with a plaque inscribed with the words *chijian*. In late 1897, the German minister had demanded this for three "atonement" churches in Shandong as part of the settlement for two missionaries murdered in the province. Tiedemann, "The Church Militant," 27–28.

the church, the French minister requested it as a formality, thereby putting the Zongli Yamen in the position of having to inform officials of such and instruct them to avoid trouble.[60] Items three and four constituted concessions since an imperial statement of contrition inscribed in stone and prominently displayed had implications. First, the reigning emperor's sanction of the stele effectively linked him to his predecessor's condemnation of the lawbreakers of 1870. Second, the erection of a publicly visible open-sided pavilion with imperial-yellow roof tiles embarrassingly showed the dynasty's inability to resist another Western demand. Last, the stele and pavilion set a harmful precedent for the erection of other monuments of this sort.[61] Nonetheless, the Chinese acceded, perhaps satisfied not to pay anything more. Favier commented: "One would think that the Chinese government ... had finally concluded that it was a question of their own interest, to loyally associate themselves to us in the supreme act of reconciliation."[62]

With the deal made, Favier purchased in Beijing a huge rectangular piece of uninscribed white marble previously prepared for use by an imperial family member. Per dynastic regulations, stone carvers had decorated its top with bas-relief imperial dragons and created a tortoise base on which to mount the slab. It measured eighteen feet from the stele's top to its pedestal's bottom and six feet wide; its total weight was thirty-three thousand pounds. Favier indicates that "the cost was considerable, but it bears no comparison to the cost of transportation," with the total adding up to $6,000 or more.[63] Over six days, workers used sixty mules to pull it on custom-made wagons to the river for transfer to a barge and conveyance to Tianjin. Next to the Wanghailou church, Favier chose a high "rocky mound" fitted with proper foundation drains for placement of the stele and pavilion, most of the work completed by January 1897.[64] The elevated site topped with a tall white stone and imperial-yellow roof pavilion ensured maximum visibility from across the river.

60   Favier letter, 25 December 1896, *Annals CM-E* 4 (1897): 230–231.
61   In 1902, after an incident at Chenzhou, Hunan in which people had killed two Protestant missionaries and burned their church, authorities authorized the erection of a stone tablet. Inscribed on its top were two imperial dragons and the characters *chijian*, and just below them *yongyuan jingjie* ("an eternal admonishment"), against such and future incidents. A photograph of the tablet may be seen in Gu Changsheng, *Chuanjiaoshi yu jindai Zhongguo* (Shanghai: Shanghai renmin chubanshe, 1981), 154.
62   Favier letter, 25 June 1897, *Annals CM-E* 5 (1898): 79.
63   Favier letter, 25 December 1896, *Annals CM-E* 4 (1897): 227–228, 234–235. Favier hoped that people in Europe would make donations to cover the expense.
64   Favier letter, 25 June 1897, *Annals CM-E* 5 (1898): 73–74.

At the same time work on the stele was in progress, Favier prepared for more construction, writing that "this new edifice dedicated to Notre-Dame-des-Victoires ... [would be] rebuilt in every detail after the model of the old church of 1870." Laborers removed the foundation area of debris and cleared an interior subterranean area of "former crypts." A new area was created for the re-interment of victims' remains from the memorial cemetery. In late December 1896, Favier personally supervised removal of the caskets and the careful transfer of remains to new ones for placement inside thirteen brick vaults. They would then be covered with cut stones that served as part of the floor. Work stopped for the cold winter months, resuming in March of 1897 with repairs to the original stone perimeter foundation, its dimensions the same as before—ninety-eight feet in length by thirty-two wide, "exclusive of portico, towers, and sacristy." Next, they reinforced the façade and its towers, again remaining true to the original and "without making the least change therein." Exterior walls rose quickly, accompanied by the arrival of fourteen pillars to support a wood-beam reinforced tile roof that was more than thirty feet high. This was accomplished so that the vaults were situated "between the thirteen arches forming the lower side of the aisle; at the head of each vault a massive pilaster was erected, serving as support for the blocks of white marble bearing the name of each victim [of 1870]." Upon completion, the church's pillars were decorated in white and gray, which coordinated with the ceiling's colors, while the red walls were interspersed with the white memorials. Favier found it all visually attractive. He especially admired the altar situated in the north section. It, he said, was "surmounted by a statue of Our Lady of Victory, who has triumphantly resumed her place."[65]

By May most of the work on the Wanghailou mission compound had been completed. This included the church and to its east side the imperial stele with a pavilion as well as other structures such as a large multipurpose hall near the church's main entrance, and support buildings for clergy and staff. Workers cleared debris from the former site of the French consulate and his dwelling to create a garden for worshippers' enjoyment. Finally, workers repaired the brick wall that ran around the perimeter of the property, including the large gate on the south side near the waterfront. A French foreign ministry report of 1934 mentions that the church itself cost ten thousand taels or $14,800 (about $3,000 more than what I gave above for 1869) to build.[66]

---

65   Favier letter, 25 December 1896, *Annals CM-E* 4 (1897): 233–234; and Favier letter, 25 June 1897, *Annals CM-E* 5 (1898): 73–74. He never explains the existence of "former crypts."

66   The report indicates that it cost seven thousand taels—the number crossed out and corrected to ten thousand. "Biens Temporels, Indemnités de 1870." The dollar amounts are all at 1870 exchange rates.

Favier carefully monitored the project. In late May, he went to Beijing to coordinate personally "the program of festivities" with Minister Gérard, its dedication reserved for 21 June 1897, the twenty-seventh anniversary of its destruction. Rumormongers in Tianjin promised there would be trouble; high Chinese authorities in Beijing and Tianjin responded with preemptive measures to maintain peace. Under armed escort, Favier and Gérard departed Beijing on 19 June for the French concession at Tianjin, where the consul and Chinese officials awaited them. On Sunday, the French celebrated mass at the Church of St. Louis; as others had done in 1860 at the South Church, they chanted "*Te Deum*" in grateful thanks to God. In the early morning on the twenty-first, a delegation of important Western diplomats from Beijing, military officers, and representatives of the vicariate went by boat from the French concession to Wanghailou, the waterways patrolled by Chinese naval vessels and a French gunboat that had on board a contingent of marines. At least one top-level Qing official attended the dedication accompanied by soldiers to guard him and the area. Favier felt true gratitude for his minister's assistance in finally obtaining "moral reparation" for the 1870 incident.[67] It had not come easily or cheaply, the stele and pavilion memorial taking twenty-seven years to realize at two-thirds of the church's cost.

If Vincentians in Beijing employed a photographer to preserve images of Our Lady of Victories Church and its momentous dedication, I have not located a single print of them in the Parisian archives. However, there is a copy of a journalist's published shot of Favier with dignitaries standing in front of the stele—it is reflective of Favier's priorities and actions. Reproduced in a book on Tianjin's Christian structures is a rare photograph of the 1897 church as viewed from across the Hai River: it shows the main perimeter gate, the security wall, and the pavilion that sheltered the imperial stele.[68] Favier stated that he had modeled it after the first version and, indeed, based on a comparison of the photograph and ones from the 1870s, it appears identical.

A modern Chinese account of Tianjin labels the city as the pivot point of imperialist power in North China. Locals certainly knew this having experienced the physical and psychological wounds inflicted by the Western invasions of 1858 and 1860, the erection of a "strange" building in 1869, the creation of an exclusive concession district, and the 1897 construction of a new Wanghailou church replete with a prominent imperial stele that justified its presence. Not

---

67   Favier letter, 25 June 1897, *Annals CM-E* 5 (1898): 73, 80. Young points out that the Tianjin situation demonstrates how tightly connected the Church and France had become in China. See his *Ecclesiastical Colony*, 2–6. The minister's appearance in Tianjin at the dedication marked his last public one. He departed China on 15 July 1897. Planchet [A. Thomas, pseud.], *Histoire de la mission de Pékin*, 2:689.

68   *Tianjin lao jiaotang*, 7.

FIGURE 5.3   The second Wanghailou church and stele pavilion, 1897
            SOURCE: *TIANJIN LAO JIAOTANG*

FIGURE 5.4   Dignitaries in front of the stele pavilion, 21 June 1897. Favier is visible at
            center (white beard), second row from front.
            SOURCE: ARCHIVES CM, PARIS

surprisingly, an audience sympathetic to the antiforeign, anti-Christian Boxer movement of 1900 lived in and around Tianjin, with an estimated forty thousand of them joining up.[69] Some in the countryside explicitly blamed Catholics for dry weather and poor crops. Per a local saying, "it doesn't rain, the land has become parched; all is due to [tall] churches blocking the sky" (*bu xiayu di fa gan quanshi jiaotang zhezhu tian*).[70] In the spring, Boxers burned places of worship and homes with twelve hundred rural Catholics fleeing for their lives to the two churches in Tianjin. Later, more joined them.[71] By early June, Boxers roamed freely through the walled city's streets, effectively taking control as officials either acquiesced to or supported them. On 15 June Boxers gutted the rebuilt church, destroyed the crypts inside it, and put torches to everything. For good measure, they toppled over the imperial stele, broke it into pieces, and burned the pavilion. People called it "the Second Burning of the Wanghailou [Church]."[72] A few days later, Boxers unsuccessfully tried to enter the heavily defended foreign concession. Their siege of it lasted until a foreign military force rousted them in mid-July, afterwards using the city as a base for military preparations and reconnoitering a route to Beijing to break the Boxers' siege of the cathedral and Legation Quarter.[73]

1.3   The Third Wanghailou Church (1904–Present)

The military force that saved Catholics and Westerners in Tianjin from further loss of life and property changed the city and its residents forever. First, an occupation government ruled the city for two years and, during that time, demolished the city wall, removing for the last time any notion that it and authorities could protect the residents. Significantly, no other Chinese city suffered a similar fate.[74] Next, they attacked the suburban and rural areas that had supported

---

69   Ibid.

70   *Tianjin lao jiaotang*, 12. In general, Chinese thought that "tall buildings spelled unluckiness or misfortune" while missionaries "symbolized the power of the Christian God" through the height of sacred structures. Jeffrey W. Cody, "Striking a Harmonious Chord: Foreign Missionaries and Chinese-style Buildings, 1911–1949," *Architronic* 5, no. 3 (December 1996), 19.

71   "Missionary letter," 12 June 1900, *Annals CM-E* 7 (1900): 533–534. Altogether two thousand would take refuge inside the French Concession. Corset letter, 7 August 1900, *Annals CM-E* 7 (1900): 541.

72   Afterwards, Favier did not mention reestablishing the thirteen crypts or a stele outside it.

73   Morse, *International Relations*, 2:205–208, 215–216, 243–246.

74   Lewis Bernstein, "After the Fall: Tianjin under Foreign Occupation, 1900–1902," in *The Boxers, China, and the World*, eds. Robert Bickers and R.G. Tiedemann (Lanham, Md.: Rowman & Littlefield, 2007), 133–134, 138–139. Foreign troops also held Beijing for two years, its walls too big and lengthy to tear down.

the Boxers, iron-fist tactics designed to punish and stamp out any opposition. Third, Favier, having become the Vicariate of Beijing and Zhili North's bishop, moved assertively to build another Wanghailou church, this time not asking Chinese authorities for permission regarding its size and architectural details nor requesting officials' protection. Last, the foreign powers demanded of the dynasty an enormous indemnity, part of which was earmarked for France and, in turn, for various vicariates such as Favier's. Separate from this, additional reparations came from officials in charge of areas where Boxers had burned churches, killed Catholics, and destroyed Catholics' private property. Tianjin was one such locale.[75] Church power ascended as China's descended: Tianjin's residents had no choice but to accept, however bitter it might have been to do so, a permanent Christian and Western presence.

Workers found Wanghailou's façade heavily damaged. Salvaging what they could, they incorporated parts of it into a larger version that emerged in 1904. Without changing the structure's general appearance its face was stretched to 63 feet in width and its length grow to 147; the central tower rose to 72 feet, perhaps a little higher than the original version.[76] With removal of the city wall across the river, it looked even larger and taller than before. Two pilaster columns stretched upward from either side of the main doorway while at the second, third, and fourth levels narrow vertical windows, as before, gave it its distinctive fortress-like image. A white marble plaque, part of the façade and inscribed "N.D. DES VICTOIRES A.D. MDCCCLXIX," reminded some of its

---

75   The division of Boxer reparations called for in the 1901 protocol is not transparent. Some numbers are incomplete and others changed. In 1902, Tianjin's share was two hundred eighty thousand taels ($207,200)—the next year the number was decreased. The additional indemnities collected by local officials are hard to determine. Young, *Ecclesiastical Colony*, 290 n. 8.

76   Measurements are per blueprints used for its 2010 renovation. Author's field notes, 26 September 2016. One source indicates that when Catholics rebuilt in 1897 (actually, the year should be 1904) they extended its length and proportionally widened the façade. *Zhongguo Tianzhujiao shouce*, 18. Vincentians in Beijing and Tianjin knew details about confreres' recent projects, and this probably influenced plans for its size. Take, for instance, the cathedral built at Jiujiang. According to a newspaper article written by an attendee of the cornerstone-laying ceremony on 20 November 1895, Fr. Élisée-Louis Fatiguet, C.M., architect and procurator of the Vicariate of Jiangxi North, had designed it in fifteenth century "Ogival (Gothic) style." It would be cross shape in form and measure 177 feet in length (35 allotted for the sanctuary) and 49 wide at its center, 74 feet across at its arms. Plans included two towers, each 75 feet in height by 15 feet square in footprint. Echoing either Fatiguet or Bishop Géraud Bray, the author wrote that "when completed, [it] will compare both in beauty and style with the Catholic Cathedral of Canton." Bray letter, 2 December 1895, *Annals CM-E* 3 (1896): 196–199 and *Annales CM-F* 61 (1896): 195–198.

FIGURE 5.5   The third Wanghailou church, built 1904
SOURCE: ARCHIVES CM, PARIS

first appearance in 1869. The tall central tower topped with four white roosters sculpted from stone—a symbol of France—still projected religious and national power. Inside the tower hung a bronze bell cast by Edouard Biron in Paris (it is still there).[77] Catholics rebuilt without restoring the thirteen crypts probably because the Boxers had made sure their contents could never be recovered.[78] Nor did Favier replace the imperial stele and pavilion. This time he and vicariate leaders silently endured.

---

77   The assistant pastor and I climbed ladders inside the tower, not an easy task for either of us, and observed the bell's marking. Author's field notes, 26 September 2016.

78   The priest in charge of the interior renovations in 2010–2012 saw workers remove floor stones and dig into the soil underneath. He said that the crypts of 1897 no longer existed. Author's field notes, 8 November 2014.

Catholicism in the Tianjin area gradually gained momentum due in good part to the efforts of Vincentian priests like Vincent Lebbe, Antoine Cotta, Franz Selinka, and others who sought innovative ways to spread the Gospel, one of which was the creation of an association of the fervent; the association met periodically to share ideas and approaches with each member pledging to help convert three families per year. Emerging first at Yanshan, a rural site some distance from Tianjin, Selinka's "Association for the Propagation of the Faith" spread to three other locations. In the summer of 1911, a general meeting of the association opened at the Wanghailou church, with sixty delegates pledging support for a Chinese Catholic publication. The first issue of "Spread of Catholic Doctrine" (*Jiaoli tonggao*) appeared on 18 July with Church members paying the printing costs and making it available at no cost. Success led to another publication, dubbed "a journal of action edited by men of action."[79] The power of the printed word eventually led to a Catholic daily newspaper, *Yiohi bao* (its English title, "Social Welfare") that influenced many.[80]

In 1912, Propaganda Fide established the Vicariate of Zhili Maritime and its new bishop made the Wanghailou church his cathedral until he completed his own four years later. Through the 1920s–1940s the Wanghailou structure was buffeted by the forces of history, warlords replaced by the Japanese army and then by Communist revolutionaries. During the late 1950s government authorities closed it to religious services with Catholics living nearby watching over it. When neighborhood schoolchildren broke stained-glass windows, it caused a minor tempest between Catholics and non-Catholics that officials quickly settled, as they tolerated no disturbance of law and order.[81] In the 1960s–1970s, Red Guards turned Chinese society upside down and, in Tianjin, physically occupied all sacred structures. Government-directed historians in Tianjin did their part by publishing a handbook to remind residents of their destruction of the Wanghailou church one hundred years earlier. Filled with politically correct jargon wrapped around selectively chosen factual information, it clearly laid out the event as a patriotic reaction to foreign imperialism, the essence of which they hoped will last forever.[82] No other "[Christian] religious case" in China has generated this amount of attention.

---

79   "Faithful Beginnings and Progress of the Faith in Maritime Chi-li, China," *Annals PF* 77 (1914): 99–104.

80   "Frédéric-Vincent Lebbe," https://en.wikipedia.org/wiki/Fr%C3%A9d%C3%A9ric -Vincent_Lebbe (accessed 6 July 2016). It became a widely circulated and influential newspaper. Young, *Ecclesiastical Colony*, 141–143, 311–312 n. 85.

81   *Tianjin lao jiaotang*, 158–159.

82   *Huoshao Wanghailou*, 25–28.

A devastating earthquake in 1976 leveled the entire city of Tangshan, located not more than fifty miles north of Tianjin. The sturdily built Wanghailou church survived with only cracks and cosmetic damage, whereas at least one adjacent building collapsed. One source says that "the whole place was in a dilapidated state."[83] In 1984, the government returned the property to Catholics who restored its exterior and renovated its interior in preparation for its public reopening on 8 December 1985. The façade looks much as it did before 1949 and, overall, was and still is in good condition. Its brick walls have a patina that adds to its beauty. On top of each corner of the central tower are new, white roosters cast of concrete: once representing France, Catholics now take them to be part of a biblical story. High up at the roofline is an easily missed architectural detail—dragonhead-like stone rain spouts, eight per side, that shoot rainwater off the roof outward a few feet and away from the foundation. Most are badly weathered yet are of Chinese inspiration and of a style similar to those at the Forbidden City, the Qing Imperial Tombs, and other official Qing-era sites.[84] Over doorways there are bas-reliefs that include numerous fleurs-de-lys, symbolizing both France and Mary, Our Lady. Other motifs are those of grapes, vines, and fruits. To the northeast side of the church is a two-story building of the same brick construction that has been subdivided into rooms for use as offices, residential quarters, storage, and other purposes. On the east side is a hospital, the brick building looking comparably old—it actually dates to 1994.

Recognition of the building's historical and architectural importance came in 1988 when authorities added it to the list of national-level protected cultural sites.[85] In fact, since the Wanghailou church stood as Tianjin's most famous historic structure, the government in June 1997 made sure everyone understood its history by erecting outside the security wall on the west side a large white stone memorial entitled: "Site of the Tianjin [Christian] Religious Case" (Tianjin *jiao'an yizhi*). Outlined in eleven long lines of text are the unequal treaties that permitted its construction, the public outrage that led to its first destruction, how the West took advantage of China's weakness to rebuild it in 1897, Boxer actions, and Westerners' use of reparations to erect it again in 1904. The inscription concludes that the site represents Tianjin residents' patriotic struggles against foreign insults and their "awe-inspiring righteousness"

---

83 Jean Charbonnier, *Guide to the Catholic Church in China, 2008* (Singapore: China Catholic Communication, 2008), 63.

84 The Yongning church (discussed in Chapter 4) has spouts of a simpler design. Author's field notes, 8 October 2011.

85 *Shengdian xinmiao*, 1:19.

FIGURE 5.6   Today's church. The government memorial is visible front lower left.
            SOURCE: PHOTO BY AUTHOR, 2013

FIGURE 5.7   Government memorial: "Site of Tianjin [Christian] Religious Case"
            SOURCE: PHOTO BY AUTHOR, 2013

(*linran zhengqi*).[86] The message is not unique, but this is the only Zhili/Hebei "[Christian] Religious Case" marked by a modern-day monument.[87] Its format, a white inscribed stone, unintentionally reminds us of the 1897 stele that conveyed a very different message. The Wanghailou church is to be remembered in modern China not as Favier wanted it, but rather because it is important to government authorities' socio-historical purposes.

2   Zizhulin Jiaotang, the Black Bamboo Grove Church: St. Louis's (1872–Present)

As noted previously, in 1861 Great Britain delimited its concession district south of the walled city and adjacent to the Hai River at a location named for a kind of dwarf bamboo with a black-purple colored shaft that thrived with "wet feet," that is, roots in water-laden soil. Only a few fishermen used a rickety dock there and the boggy land had little agricultural value. Most farmers had moved on, abandoning the village named for the grove and a deteriorating Buddhist temple, the two main reminders of former activity.[88] Qing officials had no objections to the area becoming a concession district because they saw it as valueless and unhealthy terrain—a good place for the unwelcome Westerners. Soon the British opened their consulate there, the French remaining at Wanghailou.[89] The destruction of the church and consulate in 1870 led France to reevaluate its position. Safety as well as space became primary considerations, and with swelling numbers of French diplomats, merchants, and missionaries in Tianjin it made sense to move to an undisputed location, where they could erect whatever structure they wanted without Chinese interference, including barracks for the soldiers needed to defend themselves. Tianjin's foreign concession area became home to Britain, France, and seven

---

86   Author's field notes, 25 September 2013. See Appendix 7 for the text's full translation. Such sentiments are typical of the historiography that prevailed in China from the 1950s to 2000s. For example, Gu Changsheng, *Chuanjiaoshi*, 147–149.
87   Over many years of visiting former and current church sites in China, I have seen only one other marker commemorating the site of a "[Christian] religious case." Approved by the provincial government and erected by local officials, it is in a rustic place near Qingyan, Guizhou and does not include any historical explanation. There is no church nearby, only stones from the foundation of one destroyed in the 1860s. Author's field notes, 6 September 2016.
88   *Tianjin lao jiaotang*, 10–11.
89   The exact date the British built their consulate is unclear; 1861 seems the likely year. Development of the British concession area proceeded slowly even though an entrepreneurial Westerner had the Astor Hotel up and running by 1863. A modernized version of the hotel still operates at the same location.

other foreign powers, expanding over the years to more than one thousand acres (a portion of it on the opposite side of the river).[90]

In their section, the French first erected a wharf and warehouses, their "Bund"—it stretched along the river, narrower and more compact than Shanghai's famous area. They laid out a small network of roads along which they built a consular compound, hotels, shops, banks, and houses. A short street bore the name "Rue de St. Louis" in honor of King Louis IX of France, and on it, one hundred yards from the Hai River, Vincentians acquired about one and two-tenths acres of land. With Alphonse Favier as the designer, Fr. Jean-Joseph Delemasure, C.M., as the construction supervisor, and funds drawn from reparations for the Wanghailou, a sacred edifice laid out on a northwest-southeast axis emerged in 1872. One source reports its cost as ninety thousand taels ($133,200), but I am skeptical given that the one at Wanghailou had cost about one-tenth of that amount.[91] After dedication, its formal name became the Church of St. Louis (Sheng Luyi tang). Informally, many Europeans called it the French Church—local Chinese distinguished it by location and knew it as the Zizhulin jiaotang.

According to a Chinese book on Tianjin's sacred buildings, its style was "late Renaissance with Greek and Roman influences" and its orderly layout exuded harmonious openness and an elegant power, all with a vibrant feel.[92] Actually, compared with those in Beijing of this era, it was stylistically modest and had a low profile. The brick and timber building, barely two stories high, had a tiled gable roof. It covered an area of over 8,395 square feet, its length of 171 feet and width 49 feet.[93] The façade's highest point was about 65 feet from the ground, with no bell tower. An old photograph allows us to see that the façade had three entryways bordered by eight stone columns with Ionic capitals; the entablature above it demarked the first level. The second level consisted of three windows separated by eight brick pilasters that aligned with the columns below them. Above the large central window was a round design containing SL, the monogram for St. Louis. An extension of the second level consisted of a scroll design, reminiscent of those on top of Beijing's South Church, topped by a decorative square finial and cross.

---

90   Young, *Ecclesiastical Colony*, 151.
91   No citation is provided for the cost indicated in *Tianjin lao jiaotang*, 11, 165. Ninety thousand taels constitutes a large sum given its size and style, and is too high if compared to what it cost to build the one at Wanghailou just three years earlier. The Vincentians' historian in residence stated that Favier presided over the project, implying that he designed it. Planchet, *Documents sur les martyrs*, 243.
92   *Tianjin lao jiaotang*, 11–12.
93   *Tianjin lao jiaotang*, 165. I measured its width at 49 feet, using that figure to help calculate its length. Author's field notes, 27 September 2016.

FIGURE 5.8 The Church of St. Louis, late 1890s
SOURCE: FAVIER, *PÉKING*, 1897

FIGURE 5.9 Façade details, prior to restoration
SOURCE: PHOTO BY AUTHOR, 2010

During the 1890s, the church underwent improvements with the addition of a choir and "two beautiful side chapels for the Europeans." The congregation consisted mainly of Westerners with some Chinese Catholics joining them— the latter lived and worked in the French concession area. It was Tianjin's only sheltered church and became an important mission center, priests using it to support their rural activities. Vincentian brothers had their dwellings nearby, and the Daughters of Charity operated a hospital for those needing medical care.[94] These facilities proved valuable in 1900 when over two thousand Catholics, some from as far away as Baoding, took refuge there and in neighboring buildings.[95] When Boxers laid siege to the concession area, foreign consular staff members, merchants, and missionaries were ready with self-defense arrangements that allowed them to hold off the Boxers for over a month.[96] When foreign troops arrived in July, the Zizhulin jiaotang stood undamaged.

Sixty years later it took a severe beating from Red Guards, who secularized the façade by removing the cross and all religious décor, stripping the upper façade of its distinctive design, scrolls, and cross to leave behind only a plain ridgeline. They gouged out the monogram above the central window and filled the space with concrete. A few sections of the stained-glass side windows, a deep black-purple like the bamboo of the area, survived. Remnants of political slogans written on its columns, such as "[support] Mao Zedong thought," remained visible in 2010. Inside they stripped the interior of all religious adornments, only missing a few colorful stenciled designs on archways. Of all the things important to the congregation, only a large monolithic white stone altar survived. Its massive size and non-public interior location had afforded it protection.[97]

Rue de St. Louis has become Yingkou Road, one part of an area that Tianjin authorities are preserving and restoring due to its history and value for tourism.[98] Two plaques mounted on gate columns by the Tianjin city government, one in 2004 the other in 2005, announce that this is the "original Zizhulin church" and that it is under protection as an example of the "historical and stylistic architecture of Tianjin."[99] For eight years, diocesan and government leaders

94   Capy letter, 18 July 1893, *Annals CM-E* 1 (1894): 199.
95   *Tianjin lao jiaotang*, 12.
96   Cohen, *History in Three Keys*, 49, 53.
97   Author's field notes, 25 April 2010.
98   Tianjin's treaty-port era buildings are presented in Tess Johnston, *Far from Home: Western Architecture in China's Northern Treaty Ports* (Hong Kong: Old China Hand Press, 1996), 62–87.
99   Author's field notes, 25 April 2010.

FIGURE 5.10   The restored church
SOURCE: PHOTO BY AUTHOR, 2016

FIGURE 5.11   Historical plaque for Church of St. Louis
SOURCE: PHOTO BY AUTHOR, 2010

wrangled over who would pay (and what amount) for the extensive restoration the building needed. Workers finally began the task in 2013. In a building next door, a room had copies of old photographs taped to the wall alongside design instructions and a schedule for the project's different stages. In modern fashion, steel reinforced the brick walls, protected by a new roof. At the same time, old-school carpenters made custom wooden window frames using hand tools, not electric-powered saws and drills. By September 2015 workers had finished the exterior's restoration.

A year later the interior remained unfinished. On my visit in the fall of 2016, two German technicians worked at reassembling a large pipe organ imported from their home country. They had first placed it near the altar, but its size proved too large and a priest instructed them to move it near the entrance. Once they are finished doing this, decoration may proceed along with the installation of pews. Outside of and adjacent to the church, a building for use by clergy as apartments and offices stands. Unfortunately, by dint of its proximity and size it visually and spatially distracts from the excellent restoration work. Even though the Church of St. Louis is the oldest original sacred structure in the Beijing-Tianjin-Hebei area, its historical place has been literally affected on the outside by cramming another building into a small space to its side. On the inside is an equally out of place and over-size imported organ. Each, in its own way, reflects the reality of modern-day China.

3   Xikai Zongtang, the Xikai Cathedral of Tianjin: St. Joseph's
      (1916-Present)

Following the suppression of the Boxer Uprising, Catholicism began an unprecedented expansion in Zhili, one that necessitated the creation of additional vicariates to supervise the growing numbers of priests and those recently converted. As mentioned, in 1912 an area in the province's east, then part of the Vicariate of Beijing and Zhili North, became an ecclesiastical jurisdiction called the Vicariate of Zhili Maritime (twelve years later its name changed to the Vicariate of Tianjin). Its first bishop was Fr. Paul Dumond, a Vincentian. Prior to his consecration as bishop, he worked at Our Lady of Victories, learning firsthand about the earlier conflagrations, seeing its inconvenient and vulnerable location, and realizing that additional facilities could not be easily built at the site due to space limitations. Likewise, he knew that the one at Zizhulin did not have the ground space needed to expand it into a cathedral. The bishop sought a spacious site to serve as his episcopal seat, which he found on the west side of the French concession in an area called Old Xikai. After the

FIGURE 5.12   The Xikai cathedral, late 1910s
SOURCE: COURTESY LIBRARY OF CONGRESS

Boxer Uprising, France had marked it off for future expansion, waiting until the early 1910s before controversially taking control of it.[100]

French plans for the area included smooth, paved streets and modern buildings. A main boulevard would run for over one mile from near the Bund westward to its terminus at a large parcel that Dumond had purchased. The bishop had found a location that would give his cathedral maximum visibility and enhance its status. Just one year after construction began, war started in Europe, slowing funding and delaying work. Then, in 1915, Japan pushed China to accept its infamous Twenty-One Demands, their potential impact a further

---

100   Young, *Ecclesiastical Colony*, 150–158, elucidates the protracted and complicated expansion of the French concession. For a Chinese perspective, see *Tianjin lao jiaotang*, 16–18. Historical maps of Tianjin may be found at "Concessions in Tianjin," https://en.wikipedia .org/wiki/Concessions_in_Tianjin (accessed 8 July 2016).

weakening of already diminished sovereign rights. All over China, patriots re-
acted with indignation while Tianjin residents harbored hard feelings over the
French expansion of its concession and another unwanted church. They con-
sidered it an illegal landgrab and protested for naught in what became the Old
Xikai "Incident" (*shijian*). Dumond ignored the turmoil and proceeded with
his cathedral, official residence, school, hospital, convent, and other buildings.[101]
Once completed, it constituted one of the larger mission centers in North
China. In June 1916, the bishop dedicated his cathedral to St. Vincent. Tianjin's
Western community referred to it as the cathedral—most Chinese referred to
it by its location (today, the qualifier "old" is dropped).

The Xikai church is one of the most architecturally distinctive and interesting sacred structures in China. Not small by any means, it measures 197
feet in length by 98 wide at the transept; the two front towers are about 131
feet tall with the rear one 24 feet higher.[102] A plaque tells visitors it was built
"by French missionaries of the Congregation of the Mission according to
Romanesque architecture."[103] However, the church's website describes it as
Baroque.[104] Uncertainty about how to describe the style is not surprising given
its uniqueness. Contemporaries did not offer a stylistic label. Favier had influenced the style of those in North China for thirty years, but his death in 1905
and the creation of a new vicariate in 1912 gave its bishop the opportunity to
be creative, thus explaining its location, unusual orientation, and distinctive
style. Its location precluded a lay out on the line preferred by Chinese; its axis
was southwest-northeast in alignment with the street in front of it.[105] Dumond
chose to distinguish the church from others via two exterior features. First,
the walls were composed of alternating bands of red and light-yellow bricks
(imported from France) that created an eye-catching pattern. Second, three
tall towers had rounded copper-covered roofs that accentuated its verticality.

---

101   *Tianjin lao jiaotang*, 15–16.
102   These measurements are posted on the church's website: "Xikai jiaotang," http://www.tj
      -church.org/About/ (accessed 9 December 2016). I measured the façade's width at sixty-
      six feet. Author's field notes, 27 September 2016.
103   Author's field notes, 26 September 2015. A book repeats this, adding that the style is in-
      spired less by ones in Italy than by those of southern France and Spain. *Tianjin lao jiao-
      tang*, 15.
104   "Xikai jiaotang."
105   Development of the French concession put the church in line with a new street, which
      today is called Binjiang dao. Most of it is a pedestrian shopping area closed to vehicu-
      lar traffic. If walking on the street starting near the river, its prominent position can-
      not be more obvious. Author's field notes, 27 September 2016. "Xikai jiaotang," http://
      baike.baidu.com/link?url=TW20JRLaRexsVZveNVVBqPCD_BrVrfUo6LdwAgnwaQWa
      ZzPNoKl34E3ZyUQVogJ3l7SG6APMRB10jFIWznESNq (accessed 9 July 2016). The same
      article mentions that men and women used the two front aisle doors separately.

FIGURE 5.13   The cathedral during the Cultural Revolution, 1966–1976.
               The banner high on the church reads: "Exhibition by
               Tianjin Red Guards to Expose Anti-Revolutionary Religious
               Crimes."
               SOURCE: INTERNET, PUBLIC DOMAIN

For a long time it was one of the tallest buildings in the concession area—
and probably one of the most expensive, though sources do not mention
its cost.

The Xikai church and mission complex served a large surrounding area. In
the 1920s, North China suffered from severe droughts. In counties near Tianjin,
Christian and non-Christian farmers alike left their homes, some going to Xikai
because missionaries there provided some relief. Afterwards, many stayed
on in Tianjin and lived nearby. The area around it became a mostly Catholic
neighborhood.[106] In 1939, bad weather—this time too much rain—temporarily
drove people out of Tianjin. With the Xikai's grounds inundated, little could be

---

106   *Tianjin lao jiaotang*, 16.

FIGURE 5.14   View of the cathedral from Binjiang Street. The street leads from the former Bund near the Hai River to the cathedral, about one mile. The pedestrian only area is popular among residents for easy shopping, snacking, and sit-down eating.
SOURCE: PHOTO BY AUTHOR, 2013

FIGURE 5.15   Shops directly across from the cathedral's entrance
SOURCE: PHOTO BY AUTHOR, 2013

FIGURE 5.16   The cathedral's façade
SOURCE: PHOTO BY AUTHOR, 2013

FIGURE 5.17   Our Lady of China sacred grotto at the cathedral
SOURCE: PHOTO BY AUTHOR, 2013

done to help the distressed. During the 1960s, Red Guards flooded the church in a different way. Taking over the property, they defaced the façade and burned the altar, pews, and hymnals. They held numerous heavily attended gatherings there, hung banners on the building, and made it a major site of revolutionary activity, as a few photographs of that era show.

Following its return to Catholics, workers hurriedly restored the exterior and refurnished its interior. On 15 August 1980 a priest reopened it to worshippers and said mass. The church, now dedicated to St. Joseph, serves as the bishop of Tianjin's episcopal seat and a bilingual plaque at the main gate tells visitors that it is a cathedral. To the south side is a lovely sacred grotto dedicated to Mary, Our Lady of China. Farther on are two and three-story brick buildings used as offices, classrooms, and apartments that date from its earlier days. Within the compound one momentarily feels swept back in time. Walking out the gate the feeling passes as modern-day Tianjin immediately appears in the form of high-rise buildings, high-end boutiques, and high-priced coffee shops. Further on is Binjiang Street, a mile of more stores accessible only by pedestrians.

4   Other Urban Churches, Old and New

Twenty odd years after the tragic events of 1870, Catholics built a modest Memorial Chapel near the destroyed foundling home, the site of the murder of the ten Daughters of Charity. Boxers burned it but a larger replacement arose in 1903–1904. Authorities used it in the early 1950s as a children's welfare center, then later allowed a small factory to use the buildings and grounds. An urban renewal plan for the "old city" area emerged in 2006 that called for the removal of many structures, including the former chapel building. Sisters occupied the site and for three years tried to save it, even fasting in protest. They did not prevail, with heavy equipment razing the chapel in 2009.[107] The Sisters moved and resided in cramped accommodations next door to the Zizhulin church.[108] When workers began restoring it, they had to move again. Without property of their own, the Sisters requested that the government return their original site, an impossibility since it had become home to valuable high-rise apartment buildings with a river view. Instead, the government offered a location one-quarter mile away and just west of the tourist-oriented "Culture Street." There they erected a sacred structure, informally and retrospectively named

107   "'Tianjin lao jiaotang' de shuli shuwai," http://www.360doc.com/content/18/0305/11/ 32366243_734420302.shtml (accessed 25 April 2018).

108   *Zhongguo Tianzhujiao shouce*, 19.

FIGURE 5.18   Daughters of Charity Memorial Chapel, 1935
SOURCE: ARCHIVES CM, PARIS

House of Mercy to honor the Daughters of Charity of 1870 and their foundling home in Tianjin. It is dedicated to Holy Mary.[109] In 2016, the Sisters felt pressure from the city government in regard to their future use of the property and in response hung three large cloth banners on the church's exterior in protest.[110] An undercurrent of tension between Tianjin authorities, as well as some of its residents, and Catholics continues.

Two other sacred structures not often mentioned in histories of Tianjin deserve brief comment. The first is a small, former Jesuit one not far from the

---

109 Religious sisters still consider it a chapel, though by no means should this imply a small size. Its formal name is "Home of Our Lady of Victories (Sheng Mu desheng zhi jia). Priest's text message to author, 7 June 2018.

110 Author's field notes, 5 October 2015 and 26 September 2016; Priest's email to the author, 10 November 2016.

FIGURE 5.19   Memorial Chapel, today. Modeled after the previous
                one, it is larger with the tower on the opposite side.
                SOURCE: PHOTO BY AUTHOR, 2015

Church of St. Louis. Tucked away among other historic buildings, it dates to
the early twentieth century, when the Society of Jesus had a procurator and
a small staff in Tianjin to handle financial affairs and personnel matters for
the Vicariate of Zhili Southeast. Newly arrived Jesuits passing through Tianjin
on their way to assignments in Zhili/Hebei worshipped there and used its
other facilities. It is part of another, larger structure and not visible from its entrance off Yingkou Road. A priest from Xian County, the location of the Jesuits'
former headquarters, watches over it.[111] The second structure is the Sacred
Heart Church that Italians established in their concession area in the 1920s.

---

111   Author's field notes, 25 September 2013.

The hospital affiliated with it was nearby. Closed since the 1950s, the building now sits above a subway station in a popular and touristy part of Tianjin
called "Italian Town."[112] Diocesan leaders have not pursued its return because
Catholics in the area worship at Wanghailou and another place is not needed.[113]
It seems that Catholic numbers do not warrant an expensive restoration.

5   Two Early Rural Churches, Before and After

A discussion of Tianjin's historical urban churches should not distract from the
importance of those built in the countryside. After all, many Catholics lived in
rural areas and worshipped in a variety of sacred structures. Since it appears
that not a single old rural church in the greater Tianjin area has survived into
present times, observations about them can come only from historical materials without the benefit of actual visits to look them over. The story of those
at the villages (*cun*) of Shuangshu and Xiaohan helps balance the treatment
already given to the famous trio located in urban Tianjin. Prior to 1946 these
two belonged to the Vicariate of Beijing, but by distance they were closer to
Tianjin than the capital. Both are now part of Tianjin Municipality and Tianjin
Diocese—thus, their treatment here.

5.1   *Shuangshu Village*
Mid-nineteenth-century wars with foreign powers created bad impressions
that lasted for decades and directly affected mission work in eastern Zhili. In
the countryside, priests continued to minister to their flocks and add new members. The earliest church Vincentians built in this part of the province dates
to 1867 and was located at Shuangshu, Wuqing County (now one of Tianjin's
districts).[114] The place was known for having two large trees in a broad region
without many due to people desperately needing wood for construction and
kindling for cooking. Somehow the trees had flourished, providing villagers

---

112   "Concessions in Tianjin." Catholics built three sacred structures in or near Tianjin in the
      1920s and several more in the 1940s. For a list, see *Tianjin lao jiaotang*, 166–168. None of
      them has survived. At the village (*zhuang*) of Fuxin, the congregation rebuilt its church.
      Due to its location within the city, it is presently known as the Southwest-corner church
      (Xi'nanjiao jiaotang).
113   Author's field notes, 25 April 2010.
114   Information about those in Tianjin's rural areas may be found in *Tianjin lao jiaotang*,
      37–54, 168–169. The village is referred to as Shuangshu and Shuangshuzi. Archives CM,
      Paris, Folder 163-I, "Vicariat Apostolique de Pékin, État de la Mission, du 1er Juillet 1936 au
      30 Juin 1937," 134, 203.

with welcome shade from the hot summer sun and a distinctive place-name insofar as most communities bore the surname of the largest kinship group of residents.[115] When congregational numbers at Shuangshu Village multiplied to the order of several hundred, a suitable place of worship became a necessity. Over time, it grew into a mission center that included the priest's dwelling and facilities for Catholic Sisters involved in education and health care. People knew it as one of the largest and most active sites of Catholicism in Wuqing.[116]

In June 1900, Shuangshu's pastor, a French Vincentian named Fr. Émile-Jean-Baptiste Déhus, organized people to defend their homes—their valiant efforts over a day and a night failed. Boxers injured or killed many people while looting and burning. With his sacred structure in flames, Déhus fled to the village (cun) of Dabodian; there he and Catholics rallied at the church to fight off Boxer attackers for over a month.[117] Once Western forces defeated the Boxers, oral traditions have it that skilled workers used only the best materials and techniques to reconstruct the church. They completed work on it in 1902. Afterwards, its congregation and those nearby grew surprisingly fast. According to a 1904–1905 report, there were 752 Catholics in Shuangshu and another 573 divided among thirteen surrounding villages.[118]

In 1931, Catholics built a larger edifice that measured 187 feet long by 69 feet wide with an interior space of 12,884 square feet.[119] Its 164-foot-high bell tower was visible from a long distance. With a seating capacity of two thousand, it was one of North China's largest sacred structures. Shuangshu's church property, outlined by a security wall made of bricks, included the pastor's house and support buildings, a convent and related structures, and separate boys' and girls' schools, plus a variety of small miscellaneous buildings used by staff and their families. During the mid-1930s, the church had one Chinese pastor looking after the village's 935 (4 newly baptized) Catholics. In this "quasi-parish," as it was labeled, there were 1,848 (38 recently converted) Catholics living in one of eighteen village congregations (average size, about 100).[120] There were three public chapels and one private oratory, but only the large church came close to accommodating all the worshippers who came for mass or on special feast days.

---

115   A few other villages have similar names, for example, Shuangliushu (sometime called Shuangshu) in Zhuozhou and Shuangshuzi in the Xuanhua area.

116   *Wuqing xianzhi* (Tianjin: Tianjin shehui kexueyuan chubanshe, 1991), 157.

117   *Quanshi Beijing jiaoyou zhiming, juan* 11 (*Jing dong Wuqing xian*), 2–11.

118   Archives CM, Paris, Folder 163-1, "Vicariatus Apostolicus Pekini et Tche-ly Septentrionalis. Status Missionis, 1904–1905," 8.

119   The previous one's area was 9,688 square feet. *Wuqing xianzhi*, 157.

120   "Vicariat Apostolique de Pékin, État de la Mission, 1936–1937," 134–135.

In the 1950s government authorities began confiscating church property and adapting it for other uses. During the 1960s Red Guards tore down the tall tower and cross to help people forget the religion that had dominated the community and altered their vision, literally and figuratively, of the rural horizon. The building gradually fell into disuse and disappeared. Due to a resurgence of the faithful in Shuangshu and the surrounding area, Catholics started construction in 2010 of a sacred structure. The site's dimensions only allowed for an east-west axis, the chancel placed on the eastern side. The church has been completed and is dedicated to the Our Lady of the Holy Rosary (Meigui Sheng Mu).[121] The area has a strong Catholic presence that appears ready to expand further.

5.2 Xiaohan Village

Located in Tianjin's Wuqing District, Xiaohan warrants attention because a sacred structure arose there in 1870. A brief history displayed in the current church's foyer tell us that two brothers baptized in Beijing moved to the area and "many people, because their belief and teachings touched them, became Catholics." Over time it became a center of religious activity, and later a target for Boxers who killed forty-eight people and burned the church in 1900. Three

FIGURE 5.20   Xiaohan church and pastors, ca 1930s
SOURCE: ARCHIVES CM, PARIS

---

121   Literally, Our Lady of the Rose, though this is not the preferred translation. Priest's email to author, 18 August 2018; and Author's field notes, 24 April 2010.

years later, "Vincentian Fr. Vincent Lebbe personally managed the reconstruction of the church.... Its style was similar to the Wanghailou church, but its
scale was comparatively larger. Because of this there is a popular local historical saying that 'Beijing is first [in churches], Tianjin is second, and Han Village
is third.'"[122] A photograph of the village church shows an angular structure with
a tall central tower with a flat top. It had some architectural similarities with
the one at Wanghailou, except there were no side towers. At this time, Lebbe
had not become critical of churches' European style and of Western clerical
domination of the Chinese. In 1904–1905, there were 1,143 Catholics living in
the village and another 429 divided among seven other locations.[123] By the
mid-1930s, the "quasi-parish" had 3,062 Catholics (3 newly baptized) living in
twenty village congregations that were one to five miles from Xiaohan. There
were also three chapels and a like number of private oratories. Two Chinese
priests resided at Xiaohan to minister to 1,638 Catholics.[124]

The prominent church survived the war-stained period of 1937–1949 only to
have Red Guards destroy it in 1967. An elderly parish pastor led the villagers in
construction of a new one in 1988 on an east-west axis at the same site as the
former one. This structure of about seventy-seven hundred square feet in size
was, as it turned out, too small to accommodate the steadily growing Catholic
community, already several thousand in number.[125] The congregation decided
they needed a larger sacred edifice and construction of it began in 2004. On
completion a year later, it was dedicated to the Sacred Heart of Jesus (Yesu
sheng xin). People describe it as "Gothic-Roman in style, a combination of classical Western and modern Chinese cultural attributes." Its footprint measures
213 feet in length by 115 feet in width: 24,495 square feet of area able to accommodate four thousand worshippers. Its bell tower, probably rural North China's
tallest, stretches skyward for 236 feet, visible from miles away.[126] I briefly saw
its profile on the horizon as I zipped along at two hundred miles per hour on a
train going from Beijing to Tianjin. The Xiaohan congregation is proud that its
grand church is part of the area's physical and cultural landscape.

---

122 "Xiaohan cun tianzhutang jianjie" (church lobby display, 2010). Author's field notes,
     24 April 2010. Lebbe made many converts in Wuqing County. Young, *Ecclesiastical
     Colony*, 134.
123 "Vicariatus Apostolicus Pekini et Tche-ly Septentrionalis. Status Missionis, 1904–1905", 6.
124 Archives CM, Paris, Folder 163-1, "Vicariat Apostolique de Pékin, État de la mission, 1936–
     1937," 110–111.
125 In the 2008 edition of his book, Charbonnier estimates that five thousand Catholics live
     there, the largest number for any village in Tianjin Diocese. See, *Guide*, 64.
126 Its capacity seems overstated. Author's field notes, 24 April 2010.

FIGURE 5.21   Today's church at Xiaohan
               SOURCE: PHOTO BY AUTHOR, 2010

• • •

Positive and negative experiences in Tianjin illustrate the varied nature of the long-term relationship that existed between the Church, government authorities, and local people—whether they lived in the city or countryside. Priests persevered, caring for the faithful and making numerous converts, who they supported through the construction of sacred structures, some of which became vibrant mission centers. The ones at Wanghailou, Zizhulin, Xikai, and other locations demonstrate this. Information available for Shuangshu and Xiaohan for the late nineteenth and early twentieth centuries reveals the extent of Catholicism's growth in the rural areas near Tianjin. It is an important subject that will be further examined in the next two chapters.

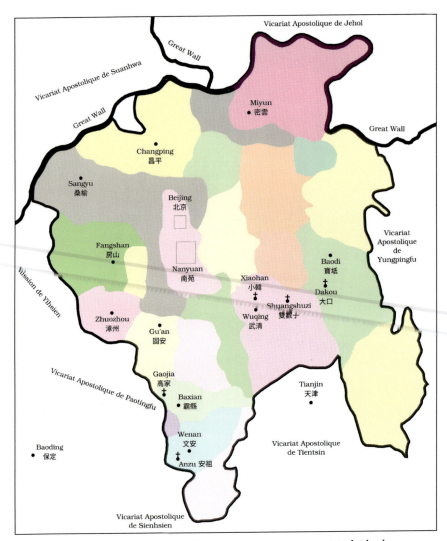

MAP 6.1   "Vicariat Apostolique de Peking," ca 1930s. Retaining its original title, the map
has been redrawn with modifications that colorfully enhance the vicariate's
ecclesiastical "district;" those relevant to this and other chapters are marked
with black circles. Likewise, select villages (with churches, note the addition of
small crosses) are included. For others places mentioned below, see map 4.1 and
map 7.1.

SOURCE: ARCHIVES CM, PARIS

Anzu (Xin); Baodi; Baoding; Baxian; Beijing; Changping; Dakou; Fangshan; Gaojia;
Gu'an; Miyun; Nanyuan; Sangyu; Shuangshuzi; Tianjin; Wen'an; Wuqing; Xiaohan;
Zhuozhou.

CHAPTER 6

Old Churches in Hebei's Small Cities, Towns, and Villages

Nine places of worship situated at various distances from Beijing offer a valuable perspective on the state of Catholicism in outlying and once mostly rural communities in Zhili/Hebei. For the sake of discussion, they are arranged into three geographic zones. First, in Hebei's northwest, are those at Xuanhua, Xiwanzi, and Xiheying, all historically and currently active sites of Christianity. They are part of modern-day Zhangjiakou Diocese, whose area is coterminous with the prefectural-level division of the same place-name. Next, in the province's center, are four old religious structures. One of them is at Anjia, the home of a rural congregation formed four hundred years ago. Another is in Baoding City, a densely populated prefectural-level municipality composed of urban, suburban, and rural space. It is also a diocese. To Baoding's northeast is Langfang (a prefectural-level unit that is not an ecclesiastical jurisdiction), and the village (*zhuang*) of Xin, which is the location of an old sacred structure. Southeast is Cangzhou, a prefectural-level municipality and diocese. Composing one part of it is Xian County, where the Jesuits had a cathedral and huge mission complex at the village (*zhuang*) of Zhangjia—the centerpiece of their vicariate from 1861 to 1946. Although the original cathedral is gone, and a grand replacement stands in its place, nearby a longstanding chapel has endured. Third, in Hebei's far south, are two time-honored religious edifices in Handan Prefectural-level Municipality, whose boundaries similarly form a diocese. Daming County is one of the municipality's rural components and in its main city there is a large sacred structure; Wu'an County is another such unit and at the village (*cun*) of Baisha there is a small church. Catholics built both about one hundred years ago. The aforementioned sites are not in the province's civil or ecclesiastical mainstream and because of this have their own important stories to tell.

1 The Northwest

During the seventeenth and eighteenth centuries, Jesuits serving the emperor in Beijing as scientists, interpreters, and artists made it possible for others to join them at one of their several churches, from which they searched Zhili for

Christians of earlier times and for new prospects. Western and Chinese missionaries often followed trade routes, convenient to use because of the roadside inns and shops that supported them. One well-worn track took them to the northwest and the walled city of Xuanhua, which served as a joint prefectural and county seat, and farther north and west into increasingly arid territories. In this relatively poor and potentially troublesome border region, the prefect and magistrate had responsibility for the basic governmental tasks of security and tax collection. They often found the maintenance of public order and fulfillment of fiscal quotas a challenge as well as the higher-level officials who constantly scrutinized their performance. The men appointed to such difficult and undesirable outposts typically had short tenures, few becoming very familiar with the locales and their residents. Generally, this proved favorable for priests who after 1724 visited illegally.

In the late 1700s, missionaries began to give the area more attention than before, building churches in and around Xuanhua and sixteen miles to the north in the border town of Zhangjiakou. Priests called the place Kalgan (after the Mongolian word for "gate"), specifically referring to the nearby Dajing Gate that controlled passage through the Great Wall into the Mongol frontier the Manchus ruled as part of their multi-ethnic Qing empire.[1] By going outside the wall, they encountered few officials, felt free to travel and preach, and gained success at small places such as Xiwanzi. Catholicism slowly spread with tiny congregations sprouting up in unexpected locations including Xuanhua Prefecture's hardscrabble southwest region, where in the mid-nineteenth century priests established a sacred structure at Xiheying Village in Yu County. That outpost steadily grew into an important mission center for Catholics and those living in the several dispersed settlements within walking distance.

The congregations at Xuanhua City, Xiwanzi, and Xiheying are historically notable for their early emergence, the attention given them by missionaries, growth in the face of imperial proscription, and survival during the sociopolitical mayhem brought by the Boxers. Catholics actively defended themselves against marauding Boxers, saving everyone they could and a few religious structures. For a few years afterwards, they quietly rebuilt and expanded, then watched as a Christian recovery surged into the mid-1930s. That decade and the next brought war and occupation as well as revolution and property

---

1   For a brief history of activities there, see "Missions of Mongolia," *Annals PF* 8 (1847): 205–208. Mongols called the place "*haalgan*," which became Kalgan to Westerners. The city was an important caravan stop on the main route into Mongolia by which tea and other goods made their way as far as Siberia. "Kalgan," http://www.britannica.com/EBchecked/topic/310134/Kalgan (accessed 9 April 2015); and "Zhangjiakou," http://en.wikipedia.org/wiki/Zhangjiakou (accessed 17 April 2015).

confiscation, followed by mass-participation political movements that collectively and deeply impacted the Church's infrastructure. During the Cultural Revolution, Chinese utilitarianism saved some churches from destruction because they were the largest, best-built structures with value to cadres, who turned them into small-scale factories, depots, medical centers, or schools. Revolutionary correctness required the occupants to strip them inside and out of religious adornments, lower the heights of façades, and dismantle bell towers or any other obvious Western architectural feature to give credence to claims that they had eliminated outside religious and imperialist symbols—a one stone kills two birds approach. Despite alternative use, over time most of the churches built before 1949 disappeared due to the development of the sites for other purposes (with a concomitant increase in value) or to fires. Consequently, only a few have survived until the present.

1.1   *Xuanhua City*

According to one account, a Jesuit priest visited Xuanhua in 1688 followed eleven years later by a confrere, and construction of the city's first church.[2] Nothing is known about its precise location, size, or style. Less than two decades after its construction, the Rites Controversy led the Kangxi emperor to look less favorably on Christianity, but this did not immediately touch the missionaries serving the Qing court in Beijing, since they were permitted to remain and maintain their sacred buildings. A few confreres continued to sneak off into the interior to visit the little pockets of the faithful they had previously stitched together. Beginning in the mid-1720s, proscription intensified, and life became hard for anyone linked to Catholicism. A chapel or oratory, part of a dwelling, survived into the early 1770s.[3] Over the remainder of the century, clandestine evangelism could not stop a steady decrease in numbers. In 1794, about sixteen hundred remained and went to annual confession.[4] Sources reveal that the Xuanhua area's congregations had survived through the efforts of Fr. Étienne Yang, S.J. He died there without the company of a confrere in 1798.[5] Thereafter, religious life barely existed because it was safer as well as

---

2   "Xuanhua tianzhutang jianjie" (Xuanhua: n.p., n.d., ca 2007), Church internal circulation material, photocopy; and *Zhangjiakou Xuanhua quzhi* (Xi'an: Sanqin chubanshe, 1998), 709.

3   J.-M. Planchet, *The Lazarists in Suanhoafu, 1783–1927*, trans. Henk de Cuijper, 41, http://sievstudia.org/wp-content/uploads/2017/06/SIEV-The-Lazarist-in-Suanghoafou-1783-1927-JM-Plancet-CM-.pdf (accessed 14 October 2017).

4   Counting those not going to confession pushes the estimated total upward to as high as three thousand for the Xuanhua area and two other places outside the Great Wall. Planchet, *The Lazarists in Suanhoafu*, 4.

5   Hubrecht, *La mission de Péking*, 72–73.

more productive for missionaries to go beyond the Great Wall to proselytize, given that officials infrequently visited the frontier settlements.

Later decades brought changes that impacted Xuanhua. As previously noted, the Holy See had established the Vicariate of Mongolia under Vincentian administration, with Mouly consecrated as the first bishop in 1842.[6] The Great Wall served as its southern boundary separating it from Xuanhua, a part of Beijing Diocese; it was also under Vincentian supervision. Mouly took on another role as diocesan administrator, a position he held from 1846 to 1856, when he relinquished it and his Mongolian bishopric for that of the Vicariate of Beijing and Zhili North, a brand-new jurisdiction that encompassed one-third of the province. Mouly's Vincentian confreres in Mongolia eventually followed him to Zhili. One of them, Fr. Matthieu Xue (his Chinese given name is not recorded), had bravely gone to Xuanhua in the late 1820s, driven from Beijing by the deteriorating circumstances of increased imperial intolerance, the closing of the North Church, and diminished financial resources. With his flock of about four hundred bemoaning his departure, he went to Xiwanzi, not returning to the Xuanhua area until 1847–1848. He then spent a lot of time at the village (*cun*) of Mengjiafen, a safe spot off the beaten track, and served as its pastor—it would be his last home. The congregation may have already had a church planned or he may have started building a new one, with the "*renzi*" floor plan—it is unclear. Before his death in 1860, he had revitalized the faith of many.[7]

As early as 1862 Bishop Mouly wanted a formal place of worship inside Xuanhua's walled city and a confrere acquired a site with a large building formerly owned by an official.[8] Construction did not start until 1869, a year after Mouly's death.[9] Fathers Alphonse Favier and Jules Garrigues, C.M., took over the project and saw to the erection of a "real church of European

---

6 Ferreux, *Histoire de la Congrégation*, 118–119; and Van den Brandt, *Les Lazaristes*, 38.
7 Regarding "*renzi*," see Chapter 3, note 104. "Xuanhua tianzhutang jianjie;" and Hubrecht, *La mission de Péking*, 206. Biographical information on Matthieu Xue (Sué) is in Van den Brandt, *Les Lazaristes*, 21. The local gazetteer notes that the Mengjiafen church was built in 1862, which means Xue could have started it. *Zhangjiakou Xuanhua quzhi*, 709. A contemporaneous French source implies that the Xuanhua mission was at Mengjiafen and dates to 1862. Three priests were assigned to it or to the area. Archives CM, Philadelphia, *Catalogue des maisons et du personnel de la Congrégation de la Mission* (Paris: n.p., 1862), 61. Also, "Tianzhujiao Xuanhua jiaoqu," http://blog.sina.com.cn/s/blog_87ca2ce40102v6dh.html (accessed 15 January 2017).
8 Planchet, *The Lazarists in Suanhoafu*, 8.
9 *Zhangjiakou Xuanhua quzhi*, 709.

FIGURE 6.1   Mengjiafen Village church, built in the early 1900s, renovated in the 1990s
SOURCE: PHOTO BY AUTHOR, 2010

style."[10] Completed in 1872 and dedicated to the Holy Cross (Sheng Shizijia), Jean-Baptiste Sarthou, expanded it seven years later by adding an extension perpendicular to the nave, the *"dingzi"* layout that allowed women to sit in the added section separate from men sitting in the main part.[11] This modification not only accommodated a local custom but also the growing body of worshippers in surrounding villages, some of whom already had chapels, notably those at the nearby village (*tun*) of Nan and (*cun*) of Shuangshuzi.[12] Jean-Marie

---

10   "Xuanhua tianzhutang jianjie." Favier arrived in north China in 1862, working and traveling with Bishop Mouly for six years. In 1870, Favier moved to Beijing. Planchet, *The Lazarists in Suanhoafu*, 10.

11   See Chapter 3, note 105.

12   In 1874, the total number of Catholics was 4,150. Planchet, *The Lazarists in Suanhoafu*, 13–14. Little information is available about the two villages. A modern-era source briefly states that a Vincentian established a church at Nan Village in 1879. Shuangshuzi is only mentioned in passing. *Xuanhua xianzhi* (Shijiazhuang: Hebei renmin chubanshe, 1993), 890. It is not to be confused with Shuangshu(zi) Village in today's Tianjin Diocese. *Quanshi Beijing jiaoyou zhiming, juan* 15 (Xuanhua, Nan), mentions Nan's and nearby villages' experiences with the Boxers, and in *juan* 17 (Xuanhua, Yuzhou, Xiheying) there is a note regarding Shuangshuzi's martyrs and a photograph of the post-1900 church.

Planchet, the Vincentian pastor at the latter, writes that by 1900 approximately ten thousand Catholics resided in the walled city of Xuanhua, in the district's six main rural congregations, and in numerous mission stations.[13] The Catholics' perspective, credible in that they typically sought help from priests when conflict with others developed, was one of peaceful, non-litigious relations with their neighbors.

Boxer activity began in the area in June 1900, which deeply troubled many residents. Pastor Gustave Vanhersecke, C.M., of Xuanhua observed that because the city's Catholics lived in different quarters it had not been possible to gather them together for a concerted defense of the church. Moreover, he felt that the numerous non-Catholics living near the building made it vulnerable, obviously implying distrust of them. Based on local accounts, as the Boxer presence in the area intensified, officials did virtually nothing to impede them or stop their posting of "incendiary placards" on the city's walls. Seeing how this had agitated people against them, the priest decided to abandon the church, convent, and foundling home for the comparative safety of Nan and Shuangshuzi, and there unite the two congregations in common defense. A small number stayed behind to protect Catholic property, cleverly putting a fake cannon in the bell tower, a ruse that made Boxers initially cautious in their approach of it. Many people headed for distant Xiwanzi, included among them Vanhersecke and Chinese confreres. The priests stayed there only several days before returning to their flocks in rural Xuanhua.[14]

At Shuangshuzi, Planchet's defensive activities consisted of acquiring guns and building barriers while another priest did the same at Nan Village. Those of smaller congregations either stayed home to protect their property or fled to the two villages, hopeful of safety there. On the fifth and sixth days of July, Boxers looted and burned in Xuanhua City. In fact, they destroyed all places of worship in the area except for the one at Xiheying. The human toll was large. Various accounts point out that most of the victims were women, children, and the elderly. They counted 85 dead in Xuanhua City, 122 in Nan Village and its three mission stations, and 56 in five other villages.[15] The total is 273, yet as precise as it may seem, certainly misses those who died either in flight or later from their wounds. One photo taken in the 1920s shows a proud group of nine

---

13   The number is possibly a rough estimate. Planchet, *Documents sur les martyrs de Pékin*, 321.

14   Ibid., 324–327, 406.

15   Planchet, *Documents sur les martyrs de Pékin*, 321–335, 363–367, 406–407; and *Quanshi Beijing jiaoyou zhiming, juan* 14 (Xuanhua cheng), 1b–3. Another source indicates that 170 from Xuanhua City died. This statistic is included in Ferreux's manuscript, not his book. General comments are in Ferreux, *Histoire de la Congrégation*, 269, 273–274.

rural women that had survived serious injuries inflicted by Boxers. Speaking in general terms, given the numerous Catholics in the area, fatalities would have been higher except for the concerted defensive efforts that stymied poorly organized Boxer units.

The Xuanhua congregation received ten thousand taels of silver ($7,400) from the vicariate's Boxer reparation funds to use in constructing a sacred structure of stone, brick, and wood.[16] (More funds came from the additional reparations that officials collected for local Catholics.[17]) A recently printed leaflet describes it as a "Gothic style double-tower structure."[18] Unmentioned is its designer, Fr. Alphonse Frédéric de Moerloose. Born in Flanders in 1858, he entered the Congregation of the Immaculate Heart of Mary in 1885, soon thereafter departing for China. After fourteen years in Gansu, he transferred to Xiwanzi in 1899 and quickly formed a friendship with Vanhersecke, telling him about his architectural background and work. De Moerloose's earliest project was a countryside church finished in 1903; this was his prior experience when he accepted his friend's request to design a large one for Xuanhua in February of that same year. Vanhersecke's bishop in Beijing (Favier) approved the plans in April and work started.[19]

During the first year of the church's construction de Moerloose often went to Xuanhua to inspect the progress because of difficulties that ranged from laying the foundation to erecting stone columns, as well as issues concerning the quality of materials and the availability of proper tools. After finding solutions, he felt confident enough in the workmanship to visit only periodically. During his varied absences Vanhersecke took charge. By June 1906, workers had finished the façade, completing the rest of the building four months later.[20] The article's authors do not mention a dedication date, but Catholics today

---

16   Missionaries built two others in the city, neither still standing. *Zhangjiakou Xuanhua quzhi,* 709.

17   The vicariate agreed in 1901 that the Xuanhua area would receive another 1.4 million taels (US $1,036,000) for destroyed property and lost lives. Materials that date to 1928 indicate that they actually received 668,700 taels (US $494,838). Archives CM, Paris, Folder 168-I-haut-a, "Accord entre les autorites de Suanhoafou et la mission Catholique."

18   "Xuanhua tianzhutang bainian daqing, 1904–2004" (Xuanhua: n.p., 2004), Church internal circulation material, pamphlet.

19   Thomas Coomans and Wei Luo, "Exporting Flemish Gothic Architecture to China: Meaning and Context of the Churches of Shebiya (Inner Mongolia) and Xuanhua (Hebei) Built by Missionary-architect Alphonse De Moerloose in 1903–1906," *Relicta* 9 (2012): 220, 223, 226.

20   Ibid., 237–239.

FIGURE 6.2 Xuanhua church, ca late 1910s–early 1920s
SOURCE: PLANCHET, *DOCUMENTS SUR LES MARTYRS DE PÉKING*

FIGURE 6.3 The current church at Xuanhua. Note the pre-wedding photo shoot in
progress at the church, front right side.
SOURCE: PHOTO BY AUTHOR, 2012

consider it to have been finished two years earlier, when workers added a cross to the building on 14 September 1904 and a priest started holding religious services.[21]

Following de Moerloose's training and predilection, a study describes it as "St. Luke style" (i.e., Flemish Gothic), hallmarks of which were its tall, thin walls, many windows, a large transept, and a geometrically decorated brick façade with tall flanking bell towers, features that imparted a sort of restructured medieval look. The front of the Xuanhua church stood out from others of the era with its steep gable roof and its large traceried window bordered by two narrow and equally vertical windows, replete with quatrefoils, lancets, and transoms. Below them was a single entryway to the sanctuary, to each side of which and slightly in front of the façade's plane were tall bell towers. The towers started with a square base and ended with pointed red roofs topped with crosses.[22] Its plan is cross-shaped positioned in the traditional Chinese manner on a north-south axis; not precisely, however, because the chancel is in the northeast and the entrance in the southwest.[23] The sanctuary measures about 154 feet long by 56 feet wide, altogether covering 9,780 square feet of interior space with a capacity for one thousand worshippers (probably standing room only). The towers dominate the exterior, rising to eighty-eight feet in height.[24] In the early 1900s, its look, location, size, and height made it a landmark.

The city's fine European-style church provided a place of worship for 892 Catholics, the largest congregation by far in the ecclesiastical Xuanhua District. A mission-status report for 1904–1905 indicates that there were eight other European-style ("properly stated") churches in the district including Xiheying's, one of the few the Boxers did not destroy (as discussed in pages that follow). A list of seven rebuilt ones includes those at Yongning (Chapter 4), Nan, Shuangshuzi, and other villages.[25] The district had sixty-four new "public chapels."[26] Prior to 1900, Vincentians had nurtured Catholicism there, and this explains its survival. Its rapid revival over the span of five years had to do with Boxer reparation money that helped fund reconstruction and influenced

---

21   "Xuanhua tianzhutang bainian daqing, 1904–2004." One gazetteer also dates it to 1904. *Zhangjiakou Xuanhua quzhi*, 709.

22   Coomans and Luo, "Exporting Flemish Gothic Architecture," 227–229, 239–248.

23   Author's field notes, 20 October 2012.

24   "Xuanhua tianzhutang jianjie;" and *Zhangjiakou Xuanhua quzhi*, 709.

25   Following plans drawn up by de Moerloose, Shuangshuzi's pastor reconstructed his sometime between 1915 and 1920. Planchet, *The Lazarists in Suanhoafu*, 19–20.

26   Archives CM, Paris, Folder 163-I, "Vicariatus Apostolicus Pekini et Tche-ly Septentrionalis. Status Missionis, 1904–1905," 26–32.

Vincentians' post-1900 modes of operation in Xuanhua City and the surrounding countryside.

Propaganda Fide redrew the Vicariate of Beijing and Zhili North's boundaries in 1926, taking its northern section to establish a vicariate under a Chinese bishop, Zhao Huaiyi—he naturally made Xuanhua his episcopal seat. The Vicariate of Xuanhua counted five "quasi-parish" churches (Xuanhua, Zhangjiakou, Nan, Shuangshuzi, and Xiheying) with nineteen places of worship scattered around the countryside.[27] Its elevated status soon led to church renovations in the city, details of which have not been preserved, though worshippers still proudly note that theirs was one of the first six vicariates in China to have a Chinese bishop and be completely under the care of native priests.[28] A decade later, the Japanese army occupied the grounds using the seminary building and the bishop's residence as offices, followed by the Chahar People's Government in the mid-1940s. Diocesan structures such as the seminary and orphanage did not survive the mid-1950s, and ten years later Cultural Revolution zealots did serious damage to the church as they converted the premises into a workshop for pre-casting concrete items. A Catholic elder told me that workers enlarged the building's front entry for trucks to access the building, unload supplies, and remove the manufactured concrete. The outline of this is faintly visible in the replacement bricks used for repairs. Abuse of the building lasted for more than a decade, a situation that could have been much worse because Red Guards demolished all the diocese's other churches except for the aforementioned and those at Shuangshuzi, Mengjiafen, and Xiheying.[29]

In early 1980, authorities returned the church to the congregation, and members hurriedly removed debris from the interior in preparation to celebrate Christmas mass in it for the first time in over two decades. Local Catholics, numbering in the three thousand plus range, generously donated the funds, materials, and labor needed to make it fully operational—some funds came from government sources.[30] Five years later, with ample resources at hand and under the direction of veteran priests relying on memory and a few old photographs, workers rebuilt the façade and towers, completely repairing its exterior. The main door was once again open and restoration efforts continued off and on. Religious roots were thick and deep, as shown by the fruit

---

27   *Xuanhua quzhi*, 709. The county history put the total at twenty-five rural churches. *Xuanhua xianzhi*, 890.

28   "Xuanhua tianzhutang jianjie."

29   Ibid. This source overlooks the one at Mengjiafen. Author's field notes, 1 May 2010.

30   *Xuanhua quzhi*, 709. Another local history gives late 1980s statistics that indicate vibrancy in the diocese's rural areas: 80 percent of the residents of each of four villages were Catholic. *Xuanhua xianzhi*, 890.

that soon emerged. By 1988, numbers reached 10,783 (5,774 women) in fifty-four villages dispersed in sixteen rural areas (*xiang*). Among the villages, four were 80 percent Catholic and nine were 30 percent.[31] Currently, there are even more churches in the greater Xuanhua area, with one suburb having several bunched unusually close together.[32]

As the city's sacred edifice approached its one-hundredth anniversary in 2004, the diocese renovated the structure with modern windows of stained glass and other improvements. A general comparison of its present-day features and its appearance in the early 1900s reveals few differences except that the tile roof is now metal and the front steps are gone. Inside, it has a beautiful wooden vaulted ceiling much as it was originally, and there are pews in the wide nave and two side aisles. Modern tastes explain the colorful stenciling added to the columns. Near the crossing on opposite sides are restored white memorial stones inscribed with information about Xuanhua's first two bishops, Zhao Huaiyi and Cheng Youxian.[33]

The Xuanhua church, large with tall octagonal towers each capped with an eye-catching red roof and cross, is uniquely beautiful and a special building in Hebei—although there are other Flemish-influenced ones in the province and in modern-day Inner Mongolia.[34] Residents consider it the city's best-preserved example of "classical" Western architecture and a website calls it "standard Gothic, Western architectural style."[35] Centrally located and on a main street not far from a busy pedestrian mall, its open, spacious front courtyard attracts locals, who go there to roller skate on the smooth concrete or use it as an urban park. It serves, too, as a popular backdrop for secular wedding photos. Xuanhua's church is a tourist attraction, featured on the front cover of a fold-up map of scenic spots published for use by visitors to the area. From its history and personal observation, it is much more than this.

1.2   Xiwanzi Village

A year after a Jesuit priest built the Xuanhua church in 1699 he began reconnoitering Mongolia. Eventually he made his way to the handful of Catholics at Xiwanzi Village, located around thirty miles northeast of Zhangjiakou City

---

31   *Xuanhua xianzhi*, 890.

32   Author's field notes, 20 October 2012.

33   "Xuanhua tianzhutang jianjie;" and Author's field notes, 20 October 2012.

34   As an example, the modern one at Shenjing Village. "Tianzhujiao Xuanhua jiaoqu."

35   "Xuanhua tianzhujiao tang," http://baike.baidu.com/item/%E5%AE%A3%E5%8C%96
      %E5%A4%A9%E4%B8%BB%E6%95%99%E5%A0%82/7058787?fromtitle=%E5%AE
      %A3%E5%8C%96%E6%95%99%E5%A0%82&fromid=15486043&fr=aladdin (accessed
      14 January 2017.

in a valley surrounded by low mountains.[36] Originally the domain of nomadic Mongols, in the 1640s Han Chinese began migrating to the area due to two main changes in Zhili. First, the recently established Qing dynasty wanted a security cordon around Beijing occupied by Manchu bannermen (soldiers and their families). This meant the expulsion of large numbers of Chinese from land they had farmed for generations. Second, sustained population growth (an empire-wide phenomenon) heightened competition for natural resources. In other words, a shortage of farm acreage had impoverished Zhili's country people, including Catholics seeking to avoid trouble, and pushed them to places like Xiwanzi that offered agricultural opportunities, forest products, and harsh winters.[37] Over a relatively short time, the area changed dramatically with open land and trees disappearing—subsistence farming became the norm.[38]

In the eighteenth century, poor Han Chinese farmers had become the majority at Xiwanzi and nearby villages, a demographic that priests took for granted. At this time and place, the critical number for a sacred structure was probably one hundred worshippers, a size reached sometime in the 1700s–1720s when Xiwanzi saw its first chapel erected.[39] Details about it are scarce, yet few rural congregations constructed European-style buildings because they would draw unwanted attention from officials. Due to the limited financial resources of priests and villagers, chapels tended to be small, one-story wooden buildings

---

36   Valère Rondelez [Long Deli, pseud.], "Xiwan shengjiao yuanliu," in *Saiwai chuanjiao shi*, ed. Gu Weiying (Taibei: Guangqi wenhua shiye, 2002), 11.

37   The observant Mouly stressed the driving forces of poverty and religious persecution as reasons for Catholics leaving Beijing and Zhili. Mouly letter, 7 March 1845, *Annales CM-F* 11 (1846): 429.

38   Évariste-Régis Huc, a half-century later, described the area's development this way: "Cultivating gradually [they] made some progress; the Tartars [Mongols] were obliged to emigrate and to push their herds somewhere else. From then on, the country's appearance changed: all the trees were pulled out, the forest disappeared from the top of the mountains, grasslands were burnt, and the farmers before long exhausted the fecundity of this land." Hubrecht, *La mission de Péking*, 201.

39   Dates for it vary. A modern-era gazetteer mentions that the first one appeared in 1700. *Chongli xianzhi* (Beijing: Zhongguo shehui chubanshe, 1995), 659. It provides a detailed list of priests and bishops, unusual in that local histories typically do not do this because they are government sponsored with a certain agenda about what to cover, resulting in brief, bland surveys of religious activities. The congregation undoubtedly provided information and through influence that came from its numbers or, more likely, friends in key positions, saw it published. Another source, Rondelez [Long Deli, pseud.], "Xiwan shengjiao yuanliu," 14–15, says the church dates to the 1720s. An online site gives the year as 1726. For this and other details, refer to "Xiwanzi tianzhujiao tang," http://baike.baidu. com/item/%E8%A5%BF%E6%B9%BE%E5%AD%90%E5%A4%A9%E4%B8%BB%E6 %95%99%E5%A0%82/10051796?fr=aladdin (accessed 16 January 2017).

made of mud walls with thatched roofs—stylistically the same as village dwellings. Such chapels did not weather well and seldom lasted for more than a decade or two before needing replacement. Xiwanzi's out-of-the way location made it a haven for those seeking to avoid arrest by officials in areas south of the Great Wall. Their presence, even if only periodic, gave the congregation reason to maintain its chapel, a factor that in turn encouraged further growth.[40]

By the mid-1780s, Vincentians had replaced the Jesuits in Beijing with a few of the newcomers venturing to this part of Mongolia in 1796 to visit three other congregations that had chapels.[41] In the difficult times of 1805, two hundred Catholics lived at Xiwanzi Village or nearby.[42] When Matthieu Xue (introduced in the Xuanhua section) reached the village in the late 1820s about one hundred remained.[43] Xue had a gift for evangelizing and dramatically increased the number of baptisms. According to the priest's estimate for the mid-1830s, 676 individuals were Catholic, out of Xiwanzi's 750 (my estimate); that is, about 120 households out of 150 (80 percent).[44] It stands out as one of only a handful of villages strewn across China's ecclesiastical landscape with most of its residents following Catholicism. Priests considered it a "Christian village."

The next stage in development came with the July 1835 arrival of a young and new-to-China Vincentian already mentioned several times, Joseph-Martial Mouly.[45] Quickly familiarizing himself with village religious life, he realized that the small chapel for the exclusive use of men and four oratories for women were insufficient.[46] He made the construction of a large, formal place of worship a priority, describing the situation in a detailed letter that is quoted

40   *Chongli xianzhi*, 659.
41   "Missions of Mongolia," *Annals PF* 8 (1847): 206; and *Chongli xianzhi*, 659.
42   Mouly letter, 12 October 1835, *Annales CM-F* 3 (1837): 52.
43   Ferreux, *Histoire de la Congrégation*, 114.
44   Ferreux, *Histoire de la Congrégation*, 114; Rondelez [Long Deli, pseud.], "Xiwan shengjiao yuanliu," 19; and *Chongli xianzhi*, 660. There may have been as many as two thousand Catholics in the greater Xiwanzi area. *The Vincentians*, vol. 3, *Revolution and Restoration (1789–1843)*, 687.
45   Mouly's work, often overlooked, helped Vincentians establish themselves in North China prior to the creation of new vicariates. He arrived at Macao in 1834, soon departing for Hubei then Xiwanzi. He served as the first bishop of the Vicariate of Mongolia and the first of Beijing and Zhili North. Mouly died on 4 December 1868 in Beijing. For his obituary, see "China. Northern Pé-tché-ly," *Annals PF* 30 (1869): 203–205. More details on him may be found in *The Vincentians*, vol. 3, *Revolution and Restoration (1789–1843)*, 690, 696–697.
46   Mouly letter, 6 November 1836, *Annals PF*, old series (1838): 399. Women's places of worship were sometimes, and probably inaccurately, referred to as chapels. Mouly letter, 9 November 1835, *Annales CM-F* 3 (1837): 151; and Gu Weiying, "Xue Madou shenfu," in *Saiwai chuanjiao shi*, ed. Gu Weiying (Taibei: Guangqi wenhua shiye, 2002), 103.

at length here because rarely do we encounter such unique and pertinent information.

> Next to Pekin, where we are not allowed to remain, this village appears to me the most desirable residence, and, to judge from our present position, promises more tranquility than we could expect to enjoy in any other part of the empire. So firmly are we now established there that in the order of our offices we follow the parochial usages of Europe.
>
> In the October of 1835, I wrote to [the Superior General] informing him that I had commenced the building of a [new] church. It is now, thank God, finished; but though the first estimate was only four, it has cost eight thousand francs [almost $1,600]. The Christians of our village and of its immediate neighbourhood, however willing, could not afford to subscribe so large an amount. Hence an appeal was made to the pious generosity of the entire Mission [of Beijing]; and so liberal were the contributions that with eight hundred francs advanced by myself we were able to cover all expenses.[47]

Contrary to some views that they were only takers and not givers to the Church, Chinese Catholics in post-1860 Jiangxi had participated in the funding of sacred structures. They did the same in Zhili and other provinces.[48] Xiwanzi's and other areas' Catholics contributed about $1,440 (90 percent) of the construction funds. This is notable because Mouly had no way of knowing how much his poor flock could or would donate, and had initially expressed uncertainty about the viability, part of which had to do with financing, of one in such a rugged setting. Members of his congregation convinced him to proceed by pointing out that, because the existing chapels did not compare favorably to the Buddhist temples, they wanted as a matter of community "face" or status a comparably respectable structure. In the words of Mouly, this

---

47   Mouly letter, 6 November 1836, *Annals PF*, old series (1838): 399–400.

48   Sweeten, *Christianity in Rural China*, 45. Anouilh, bishop of the Vicariate of Zhili Southwest, wrote that in his impoverished area priests had funded thirty churches or chapels of which "the converts have erected about twelve." Anouilh letter, 16 January 1866, *Annals PF* 28 (1867): 376. Another example is a congregation in rural Hunan that contributed about 25 percent of the total expended for the construction of its sacred structure. Navarro letter, 16 February 1866, *Annals PF* 28 (1867): 86. Bishop Delaplace took the matter of donations a step further. When a congregation requested a resident pastor, which implied there already was a church, the bishop required that Catholics give the pastor sixty taels ($89) per year. Planchet, *The Lazarists in Suanhoafu*, 28.

translated into "a suitable building for the celebration of divine worship."[49] He is indeed unusual for not only deeply understanding his congregation's religio-psychological needs but also seeing that the larger village context in which they existed made a place of worship of a certain stature necessary.

Mouly does not say that he designed and supervised the construction, but I believe he did. Likewise, he says nothing about how he acquired the building materials or found the bricklayers, carpenters, and miscellaneous workers—for economic reasons it is logical to assume they came from the vicinity. From 1835 to 1836, the jobs created by the project and its attendant expenses boosted the poor economy. Afterwards, there was more construction work, for separate school buildings for boys and girls (located in the church's outer courtyard) as well as housing for the teachers and the increasing number of staff. The mission center became the locale's largest employer.

> … The building, seventy Chinese feet long by thirty five broad, is without any doubt the largest of the kind in China.[50] In the construction the architectural rules here adopted have been strictly followed. The foundation, raised to a foot and a half over the ground, is in stone; the wall on the outside is made of handsome grey bricks, and on the inside with the exception of a brick border of three feet, is composed of clay white-washed with lime; the roof and floor are both tiled; and behind the grand altar there is reserved for the women a space of thirty feet long by twenty broad. The church stands in a court[yard], surrounded by two high walls that prevent it from being seen from the street. The entrance is by a large gate-way like to those that are seen in the houses of the rich; and through the court[yard] pathways paved in brick and lined in stone, conduct to the different doors of the church. The grand altar, in painted wood and raised on brick steps, is about eight feet long, and hence we are enabled to use without making any change the altar-cloths and fringes that formerly belonged to our altar in Pekin [at the North Church] which had been precisely of the same length. Behind the altar is a large painting of ten feet, representing the Saviour of the world, sitting on a cloud and holding a globe in his left hand; and on each side there is a painting representing, one of them, the Immaculate Conception, and the other

---

49   Mouly letter, 6 November 1836, *Annals PF*, old series (1838): 401.
50   Mouly gave the measurements as "seventy Chinese feet long by thirty-five broad." As mentioned in Chapter 4, the length of a foot (*chi*), 14.1 inches, varied.

S. Michael crushing Lucifer. The three have been executed on canvass by European artists; the frames are partly painted and partly gilt.

Though the roof is not ceiled, yet a coat of oil-varnish takes away the ugly appearance which the naked carpentry-work would otherwise present to the eye. The sanctuary, separated from the nave by a wooden railing, takes twenty feet from the length, and has the entire breadth of the church, so that we have abundant room to go through all the ceremonies. For chairs or benches which Chinese usages do not allow, we have substituted pieces of felt upon which the Faithful kneel during prayer and sit during the sermons.

At the sides of the sanctuary are two credence tables, one of which is surmounted with a painting of St. Lewis King of France, and the other with one of St. Joseph; and on the upper part of the sanctuary wall are hung four large-size medallions, representing St. John the Evangelist, St. Vincent de Paul, St. Ignatius and St. Francis Xavier: the entire six have been executed on Coroan paper by European artists. A cristal lustre placed at the entrance completes the decorations of this part of the building. In the body of the church we have ten handsome Chinese lanterns, some silk hangings with Chinese inscriptions, fifteen paintings of some merit from the pencil of one of the natives, and a profusion of inscriptions and ornamental flowers. We have reserved a choir large enough for the accommodation of forty musicians, who on festival days sing alternately with the people the usual prayers, or play pieces corresponding to the different parts of the Mass…. Our High-Mass, interrupted by the persecution of last year, has been just resumed. We have adopted the gregorian or plain chant of your European churches, which from its great similarity to their own music the Chinese very soon learn….

Our church at Pekin had been dedicated to the *Saviour of the world*; and for the new building here we adopted the same title. The ceremony of its solemn benediction and dedication took place on the 6th of August, 1836,—the day on which the festival of the Transfiguration falls. In going through this imposing ceremony I was assisted by several other Clergymen; and as it was the first time that our Christians witnessed such a scene, their surprise and delight can be more easily conceived than described….

The Chinese usage of not allowing the women and men to meet in the same church was strictly observed at Pekin, where the former had their private oratories or chapels; and the fear of scandalizing our pagan neighbours naturally suggested that the same should be done in our new settlement. It was with the view of meeting this inconvenience that I erected the already-mentioned building behind the altar, to which the women, for whose use it is exclusively destined, enter by a separate door, and where through a light bambou-grating that separates them from the sanctuary, they can see what passes at the altar without being seen themselves. By this plan I have consulted for the respect due to established usages, for the duty of hearing Mass, and for the means of facilitating the religious instruction of both sexes.[51] (Italics and variant spellings in original.)

The priest highlighted the interior's main features, indicating that the decorations were mostly Western in inspiration and executed by "European artists," albeit not bereft of Chinese touches and his accommodation of local tastes. In 1827, Xue and his confrere Fr. Joseph Han (Chinese given name unknown) had saved from Beijing's North Church sacred decorations, paintings, lanterns, Chinese ornaments, and books from the library, transporting everything to Xiwanzi.[52] Mouly does not describe the exterior, probably because of its localized appearance, but brags that its size was the largest in China and that it had a tiled roof and floor, not thatch and dirt, respectively. Its height could not have been much more than one story because the surrounding wall obscured its presence. The rectangular-shaped building probably had a simple façade with a horizontal plaque identifying it as a church, and a cross mounted at its highest point. The façade and a gabled roof projected Catholicism's and the priest's European connections while fulfilling the congregation's desire for a proper place of worship. A non-Vincentian bishop passing through on his way to Korea said, somewhat surprisingly, "it is beautiful for such a miserable village, perhaps it is too much."[53] Seldom mentioned is that with Mouly's consecration as bishop in 1842, it became his nominal cathedral. Perhaps out of deference to the South Church's long history as such, he and his confreres saw it as a village church.[54]

Mouly made a significant departure from the tradition of Chinese Catholic men and women worshipping in separate buildings by establishing different entrances to the church and, once inside, using a bamboo screen to prevent them from seeing each other during mass. Mouly aligned his on a north-south axis, and, following custom, had women sit on the west side (if facing the pews,

---

51   Mouly letter, 6 November 1836, *Annals PF*, old series (1838): 401–404.

52   Mouly letter, 9 November 1835, *Annales CM-F* 3 (1837): 150; and *The Vincentians*, vol. 3, *Revolution and Restoration (1789–1843)*, 677, 680.

53   Planchet [A. Thomas, pseud.], *Histoire de la mission de Pékin*, 2:160.

54   One study refers to it as "Mouly's cathedral." *The Vincentians*, vol. 3, *Revolution and Restoration (1789–1843)*, 687.

the right side) that Chinese considered inferior to the east.[55] Nonetheless, the
two genders were under one roof, women no longer relegated to a chapel or
oratory. This constituted an upgrade in their treatment, even though the social taboo against the mixed seating of men and women remained in place
(and will continue into modern times in rural areas).[56] The one Mouly built at
Xiwanzi is significant because it represents the permanent establishment of
Catholicism in a rural community through a variety of socio-religious and architectural adjustments. Mouly's approach explains Vincentian success in the
area. One source pegs the number of Catholics at Xiwanzi in 1851 at 989 with
almost another 1,000 spread out among more than twenty villages.[57]

Propaganda Fide transferred the Vicariate of Mongolia from the Congregation of the Mission to the Congregation of the Immaculate Heart of Mary in
1861.[58] Its first priests did not arrive from Belgium until 1865, several Vincentians awaiting them before the latter's departure to Zhili. At that time there
were approximately twenty-seven hundred Catholics divided among twenty-
six villages; one thousand resided in or near Xiwanzi. A few years later, due
to a steady growth in numbers, a larger church arose in the village.[59] Through
the next four decades, it stands out as this rugged frontier zone's largest and
most important mission center. Over time, Catholics added to the grounds a
seminary, convent, boys' and girls' schools, and a hospital, plus many support
buildings.

Given the village's Catholic majority and the faithful who lived in several
nearby hamlets, they collectively constituted a substantial community.[60] On
the eve of turmoil in the spring of 1900, 1,509 worshippers lived at Xiwanzi.[61]
Unsurprisingly, Boxers headed there with the intent of either inciting people to
act violently against their Catholic neighbors or inspiring opportunists to join
the attacks with the chance to loot. Catholics fortified the mission compound,
built barriers, and prepared supplies for all the people they anticipated would
be in need of protection. In fact, an influx of refugees from Xuanhua arrived in

---

55   This follows the *zuonan younü* (the left [is for] men, the right [is for] women) tradition
      already noted.
56   I have previously mentioned my observations of this in Jiangxi and Hebei.
57   *Chongli xianzhi*, 660.
58   *Handbook of Christianity in China, Volume Two*, 918.
59   Rondelez [Long Deli, pseud.], "Xiwan shengjiao yuanliu," 45–48.
60   Planchet, *Documents sur les martyrs de Pékin*, 325.
61   *Chongli xianzhi*, 660.

FIGURE 6.4   Xiwanzi's West Church. Catholics built it in the early 1900s as a
            "Memorial Church" in thanks for their village's survival of the Boxer
            Uprising.
            SOURCE: PRIEST'S PERSONAL PHOTOGRAPH ALBUM, COPY BY
            AUTHOR, 2010

late June. Rumored to be imminent more than once, a Boxer attack never came
as they pillaged and torched more defenseless properties.[62]

Not long after the Boxer threat faded, Catholics built the small West Church
as a memorial to commemorate their survival.[63] In 1910, the village stood out
as the most thriving of 130 congregations that peppered the countryside of the
recently formed Vicariate of Central Mongolia. The bishop resided at Xiwanzi,
and had charge of forty-five Western priests, twenty Chinese pastors, and 2,395
Catholics. In addition to the cathedral, there were two private chapels, two
seminaries, a convent, boys' and girls' schools, a foundling home, a shelter for

---

62   Rondelez [Long Deli, pseud.], "Xiwan shengjiao yuanliu," 66–68. As many as five thou-
     sand Catholics took refuge at the church. "Tianzhujiao Xiwanzi jiaoqu," http://blog.sina
     .com.cn/s/blog_87ca2ce40102wtwd.html (accessed 16 January 2017).
63   This is the printed notation on a copy of an old photograph of the church in the pos-
     session of a pastor at the village (*cun*) of Erdaogou, Zhangjiakou Diocese. Author's field
     notes, 1 May 2010.

FIGURE 6.5 Xiwanzi church, ca 1920s–1930s
SOURCE: PRIEST'S PERSONAL PHOTOGRAPH ALBUM, COPY BY AUTHOR,
2010

FIGURE 6.6 The Xiwanzi church under construction
SOURCE: PHOTO BY AUTHOR, 2012

elderly women abandoned by their families, and housing for catechumen. Xiwanzi Village's mission compound was a beehive of religious activity.[64]

Another Belgian Father and architect active in the early twentieth century, Leo de Smedt, C.I.C.M., designed and built the Cathedral of Our Lady (Sheng Mu dajiaotang) at Xiwanzi in 1922–1926. It measured 230 feet in length by 67 wide.[65] Like the one at Xuanhua, it had a steep gable façade with a large central window flanked by two tall towers. During the Civil War, contending armies fought in the area, with many people dying and the church severely damaged, then destroyed in 1946. That same year Xiwanzi became a parish (in Suiyuan Diocese) with extensive holdings of land (three hundred acres) and buildings (convent, hospital, clinics, orphanage, home for the elderly, printing office, schools, and more).[66] Sources provide few details about what happened to the congregations and their places of worship during the Cultural Revolution; they certainly fared no differently than those in other areas.[67]

To the ecclesiastical divisions that had already involved Xiwanzi, Religious Affairs Bureau authorities added one more with the creation of Zhangjiakou Diocese in 1980. They merged with it the dioceses of Xuanhua and Xiwanzi because they wanted civil and ecclesiastical boundaries to be coterminous. Thus, Zhangjiakou Prefectural-level Municipality and Zhangjiakou Diocese cover the same territory.[68] About forty-one thousand Catholics presently reside in the diocese out of Hebei's approximate total of one million. Xiwanzi's congregation remains the largest in the diocese, but it is no longer in a rural setting, having become a suburb of Chongli District City. Parishioners began working on a new, mainly self-financed church in 2003. Laid out on a north (chancel) to south (entrance) axis, it is much bigger than its predecessor though its general shape is similar to it with a tall, sharply angled façade and even taller towers.[69] Completed in 2015, it stands out as one of northern Hebei's grand sacred edifices and constitutes the fifteenth iteration of a church for the diocese—a China-wide record for a single locale.[70] It and a memorial cemetery on a

---

64   "A Model Parish of Central Mongolia," *Annals PF* 54 (1911): 133–139.
65   *Chongli xianzhi*, 665.
66   *Zhongguo tianzhujiao shouce*, 60.
67   One source states that the village's church survived. *Chongli xianzhi*, 665. Another implies that it did not make it through 1946. Coomans and Luo, "Exporting Flemish Gothic Architecture," 248. An Internet site indicates that it was destroyed in 1946. "Tianzhujiao Xiwanzi jiaoqu."
68   *Zhangjiakou Xuanhua quzhi*, 709; and "Tianzhujiao Xiwanzi jiaoqu."
69   Author's field notes, 19 October 2012.
70   Based on a count of fourteen churches from 1726 to 1936. "Xiwanzi tianzhujiao tang."

FIGURE 6.7   The recently completed church at Xiwanzi
SOURCE: PHOTO BY FRIEND OF AUTHOR, 2018

distant hillside represent Catholicism's long presence in a once backwoods area that is changing rapidly.[71]

1.3   *Xiheying Village*

In the early 1860s, a Vincentian began working in Yu Department, seventy-five dusty miles south of Xuanhua County Seat on Zhili's western border with Shanxi Province.[72] He baptized people in and near the village (*cun*) of

---

71   The Chongli area has become popular during the winter months for its ski slopes and snow-related activities. It will be one venue for the Beijing-hosted 2022 Winter Olympics.

72   It is about eighty-five miles west of central Beijing.

Nanlingluo and in 1867 built a chapel for them.[73] A confrere had more success in Xiheying, a larger village ten miles northeast of the department seat. This barren poverty-stricken area was then part of Xuanhua Prefecture as well as the Vicariate of Beijing and Zhili North (today, it belongs to Zhangjiakou Diocese and Xiheying is a town). With donations from two local men in 1871, a priest built a chapel with housing; Fr. Joseph Meng, C.M., served as the first pastor.[74] Eight years later Fr. Chen Tianyi, C.M., purchased a vacant lot that became the site for a church that still stands (the current location is in the village (*cun*) of Dongguanbao).[75] In 1881, workers built a convent for Sisters of St. Joseph on adjoining property, followed two years later by Fr. Sabin-Louis Delebarre, C.M., who during his short tenure as pastor purchased land for a cemetery, a common practice. The faithful multiplied, prompting Fr. Charles-Édouard Watson, C.M., the pastor from 1887 to 1889, to accumulate funds and materials for the construction of a church with a footprint of about thirty-three hundred square feet. A gazetteer notes that it was of "foreign style."[76] Another source reports on its continued presence and offers a photograph of how it looked in the 1920s.[77] With a convent and foundling home, it was an important mission complex for the approximately four hundred Catholic households at Xiheying and for the area's thirty village-based congregations. Catholics tersely said they led peaceful lives.[78]

The bishop assigned Fr. Emmanuel Catheline, C.M., as pastor in late April 1900, just as word of Boxer troubles arrived in the Xuanhua area. Aware of the danger, he wisely postponed his departure to the village.[79] In fact, he and others soon needed to seek temporarily refuge at Xiwanzi. Boxer activities intensified in May in a village south of Yu department city quickly impacting all the congregations. By June, Catholics, particularly those on the department's east side, felt threatened and abandoned their homes for the comparatively safe Xiheying church. Perhaps a thousand or more arrived over the span of a month. Fast thinking leaders, Fathers Dong Shouyi, C.M., and Tong Dianrong, C.M., put them to work alongside residents to reinforce the adobe walls around the property and gather provisions.[80] In July, when the Boxers attacked with spears

---

73   *Yuxian zhi* (Beijing: Zhongguo sanshan chubanshe, 1995), 681.
74   *Yuxian zhi*, 682; "Xiheying tangqu ji lishi ren shenfu jianjie." Joseph Meng's Chinese given name is unknown; he is listed under the spelling Mong in Van den Brandt, *Les Lazaristes*, 61.
75   *Yuxian zhi*, 681; and "Xiheying tangqu ji lishi ren shenfu jianjie."
76   *Yuxian zhi*, 682.
77   Planchet, *Documents sur les martyrs de Pékin*, 377.
78   *Quanshi Beijing jiaoyou zhiming, juan* 17, 1b.
79   Van den Brandt, *Les Lazaristes*, 128.
80   *Quanshi Beijing jiaoyou zhiming, juan* 17, 1b–2; and Van den Brandt, *Les Lazaristes*, 113–114, 139.

FIGURE 6.8 The Xiheying church (built in 1887), ca late 1910s–early 1920s
SOURCE: *QUANSHI BEIJING JIAOYOU ZHIMING*

and swords they repeatedly screamed "kill" (*sha*) and "burn" (*shao*) to frighten the defenders. Catholics fought fiercely for their lives with weapons similar to those wielded by Boxers except for one crucial difference: they had acquired some guns and used them effectively against the attackers.[81] Over eighteen to twenty days beginning in late July and lasting until 11 August, more than six hundred Boxers encircled the church. The guns Catholics wielded proved crucial to their successful defense.[82] Altogether, the Boxers murdered 117 people

---

81   *Quanshi Beijing jiaoyou zhiming, juan* 17, 2b–3b; and Planchet, *Documents sur les martyrs,* 378–386. Tong Dianrong recorded details in a journal about the siege and how people survived.

82   "Xiheying tangqu ji lishi ren shenfu jianjie;" *Yuxian zhi,* 681; and *Quanshi Beijing jiaoyou zhiming, juan* 17, 2–3b, 7.

in Xiheying and neighboring villages; the well-organized and tough defenders had saved many lives and the sacred structure itself. Catholics thought people were happy to have them emerge from the mission compound alive, an emotional reaction that helped in the resumption of a peaceful, normal village life.[83]

Another glimpse of Xiheying, albeit a statistical one, comes from the valuable report of 1904–1905 mentioned above. It tells us that Xiheying was one of "Xuanhua District's" seven mission "residences," which meant it had a "properly stated" church and support buildings. Its pastor looked over 2,651 worshippers divided unequally among twenty-eight congregations, fifteen of which had chapels; the one closest to Xiheying was only three miles away, the farthest sixty miles distant. A total of 497 called Xiheying home and constituted the largest group whereas the smallest had only eleven.[84] Similar numerical (and infrastructural) growth occurred over the next two decades throughout Xuanhua District, prompting the pope to form the Vicariate of Xuanhua in 1926. One gazetteer reports that before 1949 sixty-eight hundred Catholics lived in Yu County (no longer classified a department); it was approximately the same area as the former Xiheying "residence." For places of worship, they had a good one at Xiheying, three chapels in far-flung villages, and thirty-eight oratories in homes.[85] Of course, no one was safe during the war years and at different times, Japanese and liberation forces occupied Xiheying using the spacious church building and grounds to billet soldiers.

After 1949, government policies gradually constricted religious freedom, though for a few years, Catholics continued to worship publicly at worship places or privately in homes. County government authorities took over management of the foundling home in 1953, and later the various places of worship, and adjacent buildings.[86] Red Guards followed up by destroying all of Yu County's worship sites save the one at Xiheying. Diocesan leaders were imprisoned and anyone associated with Catholicism received punishments that ranged from public humiliation to torture and death. Harassment continued into the late 1970s with authorities procrastinating in the return of property or offers of compensation for that which had been destroyed. In April 1983, the government finally gave up its control of the Xiheying church building and Fr. Si Xiuli began serving as the pastor. That same year, he rededicated it to the Sacred Heart of Jesus and regularly celebrated mass. Two years later authorities returned adjacent property and the former foundling home. Per a

83   *Quanshi Beijing jiaoyou zhiming, juan* 17, 7.
84   "Vicariatus Apostolicus Pekini et Tche-ly Septentrionalis. Status Missionis, 1904–1905," 27.
85   *Yuxian zhi*, 682.
86   Ibid., 509.

FIGURE 6.9 The Xiheying church, today
SOURCE: PHOTO BY AUTHOR, 2011

gazetteer's 1988 statistics, 4,094 Catholics lived in one of 139 villages, an average of 29 per site.[87] The current pastor arrived in December 1995. He takes pride in Xiheling's long tradition of religious activity, evidenced by his written summary of notable historical events spanning one hundred plus years and list of the church's prior pastors.[88]

Via a paved road, access to the sacred structure is down a narrow, bumpy lane and via a wide iron gate added to allow car access through the security wall that surrounds about one acre of property. By habit, many people still enter via the original entryway-gate on the west side. High on it is a horizontal plaque dated 2002 with the characters for its formal name. Inside a spacious, paved courtyard are several other buildings (one with the priest's office and home, another with guest rooms for visitors). On the property's north side is a recently constructed bell tower and on the west is the original main gate. The church's south-facing façade does not have on it the characters *tianzhu-tang*, nor a plaque, nor any architectural decoration. The simple front once

---

87   *Yuxian zhi*, 682.
88   Author's field notes, 8 October 2011.

had three entryways; two are filled in with bricks, leaving only the center one usable. Directly over it is a large rose window and higher up a diamond shaped design with flowers. Four pilasters are part of the façade, each extending higher than the roofline and capped with a spire—a pleasant design that takes one's eyes skyward and helps one appreciate the beauty of its modest design. At the peak of the façade is a cross.[89] Based on a 1920s photograph of it, the only pre-PRC one available, it looks unchanged. The interior is modestly appointed with the nave divided by an aisle that leads to the altar and, centered behind it, a painting of Jesus. An image of Joseph is on the painting's east side and one of Mary on the west.

2 The Center

On the west side of the province's central section are age-old religious structures at Anjia Village, Baoding, and Xin Village. The first is one of the original sites of Catholicism in Zhili/Hebei, a village where seventeenth-century missionaries found refuge from imperial proscription and made many converts whose deep convictions have been passed down from generation to generation. At present, Anjia's residents attend mass at the village church built in 1893.[90] Approximately seventeen miles southwest of the village is Baoding, a sprawling, modern city known for being politically conservative with authorities nervously monitoring religious matters. A long list of bishops made it their episcopal seat and the current one has maintained the beautiful cathedral as a pleasant place of worship. The third one to be examined is at Xin Village, about forty-five miles east of Baoding in Langfang, a prefectural-level jurisdiction. Down jarring backroads that lead deep into the countryside is an old, archetypal rural church that makes the trip well worth the effort. In the province's center-east is a sacred edifice at the village of Zhangjia in Xian County, a rural part of Cangzhou Prefectural-level Municipality and Cangzhou Diocese.[91] Historically, it is linked to Jesuit work in Zhili/Hebei.

---

89 Ibid.
90 A priest told me that many of the village's worshippers are underground Catholics and they are a "headache" for the diocese. Author's field notes, 28 September 2013.
91 The renaming of Xianxian Diocese to Cangzhou occurred in 1981. "Cangzhou jiaoqu jianjie," Cathedral courtyard display, 2011; and Author's field notes, 17 October 2011.

2.1   *Anjia Village*

Gaspar Ferreira, a Portuguese Jesuit, arrived in Macao in the late sixteenth century. In 1604, he made his way to Beijing, a difficult trip compounded by harassment from one of his escorts and a boating accident on the Grand Canal in
which he lost much of his baggage. From 1606 to 1607 he and Diego de Pantoja,
S.J., worked in Baoding Prefecture, forming the first congregation in that area
at the village named for the extended An family whose members constituted
the majority of the residents.[92] The village (*zhuang*) of Anjia, about seventy
miles distance from the capital was a convenient overland rest stop for priests.
During times when the Qing proscribed Christianity, it was far enough from
Beijing and secluded enough to offer safe haven. By the next century, as many
as 150 people had converted. Their first chapel was a repurposed residential
dwelling that displayed on its front exterior wall a cross and a horizontal plaque
with the Kangxi emperor's "the true principle of all things" saying inscribed on
it. County functionaries destroyed the building in 1730.[93]

What religious life was like for the village's early Christians cannot be as-
certained. We may assume that they kept a very low profile and stayed out of
trouble, legal and otherwise, and for these reasons officials left them alone.
Priests went there when they could; sometimes years passed without a visit, a
situation true all over the Qing empire. In 1838, the last missionary in Beijing of
his era died and the South Church closed. Only a few others remained active.
One was Fr. João de Franca Castro e Moura, C.M., who had worked at Anjia
during the 1830s. Around 1846 he was able to build a second church, this one
with a floor plan that resembled the character for person (*"renzi"*) in order that
women could worship in the west leg or side and men the east.[94] Such a design provided separate entrances and worship sections for each gender. Each
section afforded worshippers a view of the altar, thereby eliminating the need
for the pastor to conduct duplicate services.[95]

Over the next ten years, Catholics built eight additional churches in the area,
but we have no information regarding their architectural styles.[96] In the mid
and late 1840s, Mouly visited Anjia several times while serving as administrator

---

92   *Dictionary of Ming Biography*, 461–462. One Internet site says that Matteo Ricci brought
      his religion to the area. "Xushui Anzhuang tianzhutang," http://blog.sina.com.cn/s/
      blog_87ca2ce40101qr2p.html (accessed 18 January 2017).
93   Wang Xiao-qing, "Staying Catholic: Catholicism and Local Culture in a Northern Chinese
      Village" (Ph.D. diss., University of Notre Dame, 2004), 43.
94   He arrived in Zhili in 1833 and from 1838 to 1847 held the highest positions in the Diocese
      of Beijing. He departed to Macao in 1847. Van den Brandt, *Les Lazaristes*, 31–32.
95   Wang, "Staying Catholic," 41.
96   *Xushui xianzhi* (Beijing: Xinhua chubanshe, 1997), 433.

of the Beijing Diocese and established a foundling home in the village.[97] With the formation of the Vicariate of Beijing and Zhili North in 1856 he became its first bishop, still finding the village's location convenient. A Vincentian historian writes that when Mouly made the modest village church his episcopal seat he renovated it to reflect its status as the vicariate's temporary cathedral.[98] In 1860, the bishop formally moved to Beijing's South Church with the area's mission director continuing to make the village his official home, a situation that ended in 1872 when he transferred to a sacred structure built close to Baoding City.[99] Prior to 1860, Anjia was the most important Catholic site in the prefecture, and arguably in all of Zhili.[100]

The bishop's departure did not slow religious growth, as evidenced by the construction of a larger worship place in 1886 that villagers expanded further in 1893.[101] The mission owned a total of seven acres of land upon which were several support buildings. Between two and five thousand Catholics from the Anjia area and neighboring villages fled to this site in the spring and summer of 1900. French Vincentians directed the refugees to strengthen the complex's wall and outside it to dig a moat. The priests also purchased several guns to supplement those owned by Chinese Catholics. Boxers poured into the county in June 1900, but faced a well-defended stronghold that they dared not assault until 24 July. Unsuccessful, they tried again on 4 September. Well-prepared and armed Catholics repelled them, occasionally seizing abandoned weapons. Boxers did succeed in destroying abandoned chapels and murdering the isolated and vulnerable.[102] Altogether about two thousand Catholics died.[103]

The area quickly recovered from the turmoil and numbers soon climbed steeply with the vicariate's Baoding District having ten mission "residences" (areas) with a total of 26,315 worshippers. The one at Anjia had a "properly stated" church, lodging, and many buildings for its staff and 1,166 worshippers. It included twenty-four other congregations, whose 1,172 members shared

---

97   *Bai xianshi jingji shehui diaocha, Baoding juan* (Beijing: Zhongguo dabaikequan chubanshe, 1993), 449; and *Baoding shi nanshi quzhi* (Beijing: Xinhua chubanshe, 1990), 221

98   Ferreux, *Histoire de la Congrégation*, 132–134.

99   Planchet, *Documents sur les martyrs*, 305.

100 Xiwanzi was equally important. For the period discussed, it was not part of the Vicariate of Beijing and Zhili North.

101 *Xushui xianzhi*, 433.

102 Planchet, *Documents sur les martyrs*, 306; "Report of the Boxers' Movements in the Pao-ting, during the year 1900. By Paul Dumond," 12 March 1901, *Annals CM-E* 8 (1901): 513–514; and Wang, "Staying Catholic," 45–46.

103 Fabrèques, "Notes historiques sur le district de Pao-ting-fou (Tché-li, Chine)," *Annales CM-F* 74 (1909): 674.

eighteen chapels and one oratory.[104] Incredible as it may seem, by 1909 the district had ballooned to seventy thousand Catholics.[105] Consequently, the Holy See decided in 1910 to form the Vicariate of Zhili Central, creating it from a portion taken from the Vicariate of Beijing and Zhili North. Anjia (and all of Xushui County) fell within its boundaries. Catholicism continued to grow as did the infrastructure, with workers enlarging the church again in the late 1920s.[106]

With the 1930s came the Japanese invasion of Hebei and the military occupation of Xushui County's churches, some used as field headquarters and for the garrisoning of soldiers. Others, with large red crosses painted on roofs, escaped serious damage from artillery and planes. As soon as the war against the Japanese ended, another began between the Communist and Nationalist armies. Parish priests in Anjia and other villages still said mass and in many other ways served their flocks during a time when religious activities became increasingly difficult—a major concern was how to care for all the refugees. For 1951 statistics are available for Xushui County: there were eleven villages with 2,553 Catholics, of which Anjia had the largest share, 59 percent or 1,504. Besides a fine sacred structure there were support buildings plus a cemetery— altogether the mission occupied just over five acres of land. The numerical size of the other ten congregations ranged from 36 to 179 members with the average being 105. These all had places of worship on small parcels of land.[107] The story line of the 1950s–1960s is the government's confiscation of property and arrest of priests, followed by the Red Guards' reign of terror. In Xushui County, only Anjia's church survived intact, though it had gone years without repairs and one part was on the verge of falling down.[108]

Ten years after the implementation of the 1978–1979 national policy of reform and of opening China to the world, Anjia's Catholics had renovated their sacred edifice and rebuilt three others. In addition, the government recognized eleven other locations as official sites of religious activity. Based on the Xushui County gazetteer's circa-1990 figures, there were more than ninety-two hundred Catholics spread among sixty-seven different villages. There were seventeen sites claiming more than 100 believers each, none coming close to

---

104 "Vicariatus Apostolicus Pekini et Tche-ly Septentrionalis. Status Missionis, 1904–1905," 20.

105 Fabrèques, "Notes historiques sur le district de Pao-ting-fou (Tché-li, Chine)," *Annales CM-F* 74 (1909): 674–675.

106 A modern-era plaque made of concrete and installed as part of a wall commemorates the expansion of 1927. Author's field notes, 28 September 2013.

107 "*Baoding jiaoqu liu zongtang 35 fentang jiaochan jiaoyou tongjibiao*" (report manuscript, dated 31 October 1994), 13.

108 *Xushui xianzhi*, 433.

FIGURE 6.10   The present-day church at Anjia
                SOURCE: PHOTO BY AUTHOR, 2013

FIGURE 6.11   Church façade details. At top center is the date of construction in
                Chinese by Qing reign date and Western calendar (1893). Both are
                recent additions to the façade.
                SOURCE: PHOTO BY AUTHOR, 2013

matching Anjia and its 1,750 worshippers (divided among 435 households, 4 per family on average).[109]

Now formally known as the Church of the Immaculate Conception, it is a solid, well-maintained single-story structure, its core built in the nineteenth century with several restorations and two enlargements since, the last in 1927. It is 138 feet long, 59 feet wide, and 49 feet high.[110] The chancel is in the southern section, the reverse of that traditionally preferred. Its stone foundation is slightly elevated with the same material used for the first several feet of the exterior walls and as support. Its tiled gable roof, a dusty grey color, perfectly matches the walls and façade. The bottom half of the façade is original; Catholics had to rebuild the top section due to Red Guard desecrations. There are three entryways and above the central one is a raised rhombus design that contains floral presentations; above the flanking doors are round windows, the original stained glass no longer present. Each doorway is flanked by pilasters, a total of six, which rise through the reconstructed section that supports a low, domed tower topped with a white cross. Other exterior adornments include monograms for St. Vincent in the center with Mary on one side and St. Joseph on the other.[111] They are in black with a white background and set in round rosettes, standing out as prominent features of the façade. Above these and to each side of the steeple are cast-concrete vases and a scroll-like piece with a dove. On the steeple itself are a central window with wood shutters and two slightly smaller niches, filled with Chinese characters aligned vertically. The ones on the eastern side give the construction date according to the regnal year, that is, "Guangxu 19;" the western side reads "Anno Domini 1893." Centered over the steeple and barely visible from the ground are Chinese characters identifying it as a church. Locals are proud of their church and of the fact that not far away is a Catholic cemetery—very few of the latter have survived (and even fewer pre-liberation era tombstones).[112]

2.2   *Baoding City*

During the early Qing, Baoding was an important prefecture, its walled city also serving as home for the officials of Qingyuan County. When it became the provincial capital in 1730, no other city in Zhili, except for Beijing, had so

---

109   Ibid., 434.

110   "Tianzhujiao Baoding jiaoqu," http://blog.sina.com.cn/s/blog_87ca2ce40101qr70.html (accessed 18 January 2017).

111   Inside, Mary is represented at the high altar. On her left is a side altar for Jesus and on the right is one for Joseph, who holds the young boy Jesus. Author's field notes, 28 September 2013.

112   Author's field notes, 28 September 2013.

many government offices.[113] A high concentration of officials vested in the system somewhat explains its overall conservatism and, later, its obstructionism in regard to allowing construction-minded missionaries inside the city walls. Officials worried that any concession to them would be construed as weakness and lead to further problems, of which expansion was the worst.[114] For their part, missionaries wanted to preach everywhere and knew that their presence inside cities brought them a certain status with residents. Therefore, they acquired as much property as possible either openly or surreptitiously. Mouly tried to hide his purchase of about two and six-tenths acres outside and east of the city walls near a bridge at the North Gate in the mid-1840s—building a place of worship there gave up the secret.[115] More than a decade passed before the mission district's head moved from Anjia to Baoding, establishing in 1868 or 1872 a home and a Chinese-style chapel about fifty feet long.[116] Symbolically, being near a city was better than a rural location—almost as good as being inside the city walls.

In the waning years of the century, Qing officials worried that a deterioration of law and order in Zhili might worsen so they began transferring troops from Gansu Province, stationing about four thousand outside of Baoding. In 1898, some soldiers started a ruckus at the North Gate site that escalated into violence as they physically assaulted local Catholics.[117] Fr. Paul Dumond, C.M., and a Chinese priest each suffered non-life threatening injuries, the former promptly reporting the incident to Favier of the Vicariate of Beijing and Zhili North, who then informed the French minister.[118] As it turned out, Favier did not need the minister's help and quickly settled the matter directly with Ronglu, Zhili's governor-general.[119] Ronglu readily accepted Favier's proposed exchange of the dwelling, chapel, a hovel or two, and adjacent acreage (used as a vegetable garden) in the North Gate area for the yamen once used by the Qinghe circuit intendant.[120] Well-located in the city on a busy street near the

---

113 Shijiazhuang became home to the provincial government in 1968.

114 The rural community of Anjia thus became the focal point of missionaries' activities.

115 *Baoding shi beishi quzhi* (Beijing: Xinhua chubanshe, 1991), 513; and *Bai xianshi jingji shehui diaocha, Baoding juan*, 449.

116 Planchet, *Documents sur les martyrs*, 305; Ferreux, *Histoire de la Congrégation*, 331; and Favier letter, 14 August 1899, *Annals CM-E* 6 (1899): 55.

117 For a slightly different version of the incident's cause, with Catholics as the instigators, see Young, *Ecclesiastical Colony*, 126–127.

118 Favier letter, 14 August 1899 [*sic*, 1898], *Annals CM-E* 6 (1899): 52–53; and *Baoding shi beishi quzhi*, 513.

119 Ronglu had tight connections to the Qing court and held several high positions.

120 The priest is said to have used the incident as a pretext to gain a better site. *Baoding shi nanshi quzhi*, 221.

Drum Tower, the site (Favier referred to it as a "palace," though "mansion" is more accurate) included 211 rooms with brick walls on a two and eight-tenths acre parcel. Catholics had breached the city walls and soon constructed a sacred edifice, a fact not lost on officialdom or the populace.[121]

A Chinese priest in early January of 1900 "announced the existence of the Boxers" in Xincheng County north of Baoding, providing the initial sighting of the movement in this part of Zhili.[122] However, three modern-day local histories do not include one word about the Boxer Uprising in conjunction with religious affairs in Baoding Prefecture, perhaps because a discussion of it would lead to mention of a famous "Christian village."[123] This lacuna warrants a brief side note in that present-day authorities remain unusually suspicious (almost hostile) to religious activity, especially at nearby Donglü, a village renowned for the successful actions of four thousand lightly armed Catholics who staved off forty different Boxer attacks against the fortified mission compound. Worshippers said that on one occasion they saw an apparition of Mary above the steeple as Boxers charged, and this rallied them spiritually and physically to fight hard. And, with her help, they prevailed.[124] From then onward, the village has associated itself with Mary's intervention. In recent years, religious pilgrims have been going there every year during May, the month during which the people saw her.[125] Officials do everything they can to discourage and block pilgrimage visits.[126] They, like the Boxers before them, seem

---

121   Favier letter, 14 August 1899 [sic 1898], *Annals CM-E* 6 (1899): 54–55, 58. The site was, in fact, in a select part of the city a short distance east of the Zhili governor-general's former yamen and, separately, that of the prefect. Across the street was the Lianchi shuyuan, a prestigious academy with spacious landscaped grounds. Authorities built the Zhili Provincial Library there in 1908. Author's field notes, 16 September 2016.

122   "Report of the Boxers' Movements in the Pao-ting, during the year 1900, by Paul Dumond," 12 March 1901, *Annals CM-E* 8 (1901): 511.

123   If Boxers entered a county in Zhili, its current gazetteer invariably mentions it. Baoding is an exception.

124   "Report of the Boxers' Movements in the Pao-ting, during the year 1900, by Paul Dumond," 513–514.

125   May is Mary's month and all over China (and the world) the faithful visit special sites to celebrate her. "Month of Mary," http://www.catholicculture.org/culture/liturgicalyear/ overviews/months/05_1.cfm (accessed 17 January 2017).

126   In 2010, I traveled by private car to Donglü. Several miles from the village, my driver stopped at a country-road checkpoint to register us with the police staffing it. After taking my passport and visa information, police called foreign affairs officials in Baoding. They soon arrived, firmly stating I could not continue because it was unsafe. As I waited for them to review the decision, I saw handouts on a table that warned people of superstitious and disharmonious Catholic activities, advising visitors to stay away because of

FIGURE 6.12   Baoding cathedral, 1912. The city's Drum Tower is visible on the right and
                the Zhili Provincial Library on the left.
                SOURCE: ARCHIVES CM, PARIS

to consider Donglü's church's existence as symbolizing Catholicism's survival
in the Baoding area.

Successful rural resistance did not dissuade Boxers from entering Baoding
City to torch the church in 1900. Dumond believed government officials
complicit, implying they cared only about destroying it. Indeed, the priest's
dwelling and other structures escaped the damage.[127] Numerous Catholics
survived and many converts soon joined them. A census provides a glimpse
of the Baoding mission: 1,896 Catholics formed seventeen congregations, an
average of 112 per location. The one in the city numbered 380 and had its own
European-style place of worship as well as a chapel. In the countryside, five

---

personal safety issues. Officials followed my car back to the Baoding train station, one of
them staying with me to observe my departure. Author's field notes, 10 May 2010. A local
history critically comments that underground Catholics meet illegally and have split the
Christian masses in half, a situation that harms social stability and attracts government
attention. *Baoding shi beishi quzhi*, 514.

127   Planchet, *Documents sur les martyrs*, 306, 315.

FIGURE 6.13   Today's Baoding cathedral with vendors and shops crowding its front
SOURCE: PHOTO BY AUTHOR, 2010

villages had "properly stated" churches.[128] Baoding's followers helped ensure
its reconstruction in 1905, rebuilt on the foundation of its predecessor.[129] A
French missionary laid out the axis once again on a north (chancel) to south
(entrance) line. In 1910, the pope created the Vicariate of Zhili Central with Fr.
Joseph Fabrègues, C.M., serving as its first bishop. He made the sacred edifice
at Baoding, already dedicated to St. Peter and St. Paul (Sheng Bodulu Sheng
Baolu jiaotang), his cathedral. At that time about thirty-eight priests worked
in the vicariate, watching over 255 worship places and about seventy thousand
Catholics.[130] Such explosive growth led to the formation of additional ecclesiastical jurisdictions from the new vicariate, the largest being for the counties
of Anguo and Yi.[131]

128   "Vicariatus Apostolicus Pekini et Tche-ly Septentrionalis. Status Missionis, 1904–1905," 16.
129   An on-site billboard description marks the construction year as 1905. Ferreux states it was
         in 1901. *Histoire de la Congrégation*, 331.
130   Fabrègues, "Notes historiques sur le district de Pao-ting-fou (Tché-li, Chine)," *Annales
         CM-F* 74 (1909): 675–676; and "An Apostolic Excursion in China," *Annals PF* 75 (1912): 177.
131   *Baoding shi nanshi quzhi*, 222.

At this time the church at Baoding stood out as the most important, serving the greatest number of Catholics, probably three to five thousand, of any site in central Zhili/Hebei. Limited space at the urban location curtailed infrastructural expansion and led to the purchase of property in the west gate section of the city, which became the site of a seminary, convent, and foundling home. Through the next three decades, missionaries baptized thousands of people, growth they could not sustain because of the war against Japan. In fact, during the early 1940s the vicariate had exhausted its financial resources helping the needy and refugees, a crisis that continued for the remainder of the decade.[132] After the establishment of the People's Republic, authorities moved quickly to survey Catholic assets and numbers. Using Religious Affairs Bureau materials, a report discloses that in 1951 Baoding Diocese had 121,523 Catholics living in 247 different villages, or on average 492 per location (those living in urban locations such as Baoding are not included).[133]

During the Cultural Revolution, religious services ceased in Baoding as Red Guards defaced the church's façade and gutted the interior. Authorities allowed a wood-clapper theatrical group to use it for rehearsals and performances. At this time, workers excavated earth alongside the church to build an underground air-raid shelter. Abuse, neglect, and construction took a heavy toll on the sacred structure with walls and floors cracking.[134] Its restoration began in 1980 and religious services resumed the next year. By 1988 Baoding City counted three thousand Catholics. Such numbers helped fund further restoration work.[135] In July 1993, when the government added it to the list of Hebei's protected cultural sites, diocesan leaders felt some relief in that this secured the structure's future.[136] The church sits on a busy street with its front visually and physically obstructed by a row of mercantile shops. Authorities have not returned the property because its high commercial value trumps Catholic ownership claims.

The cathedral's footprint is 178 feet long by 58 wide with a standing-room capacity of about one thousand people. White stone statues of St. Peter and St. Paul stand to each side of the three front entryways, and above them is a three-level facade of brick. Above the central doorway are the Greek letters

---

132   Ibid., 223.
133   "Baoding jiaoqu liu zongtang, 35 fentang jiaochan jiaoyou tongjibiao."
134   "Baoding tianzhujiao tang," http://wenku.baidu.com/link?url=wk8t2FjWEMlZU_Mg CQWsktrvs2V4bJWIrwdeRh4JdZokiL_ZVoHInKIIyIxc YJo7v9FjduK-sdfdblAWgizPeZzxfpl L56j8Db6oCAMXsWm (accessed 17 January 2017).
135   About thirty thousand Catholics lived in the city district in 1988. *Baixianshi jingji shehui diaocha, Baoding juan*, 450.
136   "Baoding tianzhujiao tang."

FIGURE 6.14   Façade of the Baoding cathedral
             SOURCE: PHOTO BY AUTHOR, 2013

alpha and omega in eye-catching red. Pilasters flank the east and west-side front entries and extend upward the full height of the façade. Almost sixty-six-foot-high twin towers are topped by a balustrade and dome, better viewed from across the street. At the second and third levels are recessed windows with arches that match the doorways. Aside from the characters *tianzhutang*, there are no other inscriptions or plaques on the façade. The overall appearance is familiar, and locals describe it as "classical Western architecture" in one sentence and "Roman style architecture" in another. Sitting behind it are diocesan offices and residential rooms for the bishop and priests. There is no room for expansion due to the density of surrounding commercial and residential concerns, a situation that has existed since the early 1900s.[137]

137   Author's field notes, 9 May 2010; 28 September 2013; and 16 September 2016.

2.3   Xin Village

The village of Xin was also known as Anzuxin, though few still refer to it by the longer name.[138] It is located in Langfang Prefectural-level Municipality's out of the way Wen'an County, one of those unknown or forgotten (at least by Westerners) rural locations that have a sacred structure still standing due to the support of a strongly rooted and fervent religious community. The old church is the last one in the county's southern section, maybe in the entire modern-day prefecture.[139] In 1982, Langfang was not officially a diocese and the acting bishop was never formally recognized. He died in 1996 without establishing Langfang as an independent ecclesiastical jurisdiction and with no one designated to follow him. Due to this, neighboring Baoding Diocese sent priests from Yi County to Langfang to help in the 1980s, and they made some converts. In the early 1990s, Cangzhou Diocese took responsibility for the Langfang area, proactively supporting its congregations and maintaining a presence. That diocese remains in charge of it with many people in Langfang wanting their area to be under its own bishop.[140] Langfang's struggle to define its place in the ecclesiastical hierarchy has not affected Xin Village's faithful. They have fared remarkably well in large part because of their pride in overcoming past challenges and in preserving the original building. They see in themselves the same thing that the first generation had: an "uncommon [religious] vitality" (feifan de shengming li), that is to say, very strong convictions.[141]

Missionaries first visited Wen'an County in the mid-nineteenth century, making little progress in conversions. In 1899, eight village family heads, their names still known to residents to this day, led the way by expressing interest in Catholicism. This complicated life for them as Wen'an's officials attempted to discourage their involvement with religion by imprisoning them and harassing visiting priests. A Vincentian father from a neighboring county intervened with authorities on behalf of those jailed—afterwards providing religious instruction and eventually baptizing them together with many of their family members.[142] Thereafter, they worshipped in home-based oratories. Their

---

138   "Wen'an xian Anzuxin zhuang tianzhutang," http://blog.sina.com.cn/s/blog_87ca2ce 40102v96s.html (accessed 12 January 2017).

139   During the mid-eighteenth century, Wen'an County was in the southern part of Shuntian Prefecture. Soon after the end of the dynasty, Shuntian ceased to exist, with its component civil jurisdictions administratively realigned and sometimes renamed. One part of the former Shuntian area became Langfang in 1973 and fifteen years later emerged as a prefectural-level city.

140   The diocese administers all of Langfang's districts and counties. "Cangzhou jiaoqu jian-jie," Cathedral courtyard display, 2011; and Author's field notes, 17 October 2011.

141   "Xinzhuang xinyang bainian qingdian jinian" (Xinzhuang: n.p., 1999), Church internal circulation material, pamphlet.

142   Ibid.

small numbers and the absence of a formal place of worship made it easier for them to hide from Boxers passing through in early June 1900 (they killed eleven Catholics that month).[143] A few years later the bishop of the Vicariate of Beijing and Zhili North provided a statistical glimpse of "Anzu [xin zhuang]," listed as a "residence" division in the Capital South District. At that time, 974 Catholics lived in the area's twenty-five congregations (villages). The area only had one public chapel that inexplicably was not at Xin Village, whose 176 followers made it the heaviest concentrated place.[144]

In the early twentieth century, numbers increased to the point that the congregation needed a proper place of worship, which Fr. Stéfane Léfaki, C.M., built in 1916 with financial help from the Vicariate of Beijing and Zhili North. On property acquired in the center of the village, workers constructed a building that measured eighty-two feet in length by thirty-three in width, with a bell tower fifty-nine feet high. The priest laid it out on a north-south axis with the chancel placed in the south section, probably because a north side entrance was close to the street from which worshippers arrived. He dedicated it to the Sacred Heart of Jesus. A year after construction, a flood devastated most of Wen'an County, washing away homes with adobe walls and earthen floors and leaving thousands of people starving. The well-built church stood high on a stone foundation with walls of kiln-fired bricks, a veritable island for the congregation to use for distributing food to the needy, most of whom were not fellow worshippers. People reacted with gratitude and many converted to Catholicism. By one estimate, those baptized constituted 80 percent of the village's residents.[145]

As life returned to normal, the pastor opened a village school and promoted various activities that increased physical activity and good health. From 1924 to 1934, religious work flourished among the county's ninety-nine hundred Catholics, who resided in seven towns and sixty-three villages. The average congregation had about 140 people. Xin Village's numbers increased, too, necessitating the church's 1934 expansion by an additional fifty-three feet in length and the addition of a sacristy behind the altar for a total of 4,090 square feet.[146] At its north end, workers added a second story for an organ, piano, and

143   Planchet, *Documents sur les martyrs*, 172; and "Wen'an xian Anzuxin zhuang tianzhutang."
144   "Vicariatus Apostolicus Pekini et Tche-ly Septentrionalis. Status Missionis, 1904–1905," 15; and Archives CM, Paris, Folder 168-I-a, "Vicariatus Apostolicus Pekini et Tche-ly Septentrionalis. Fructus Spirituales, 1904–1905."
145   "Xinzhuang xinyang bainian qingdian jinian;" and "Wen'an xian Anzuxin zhuang tianzhutang."
146   "Xinzhuang xinyang bainian qingdian jinian;" and "Wen'an xian Anzuxin zhuang tianzhutang."

FIGURE 6.15   The Xin Village church and pastors, ca 1930s
SOURCE: ARCHIVES CM, PARIS

other musical instruments. Eighteen columns set close together supported the roof. The interior's width was too narrow to have two side aisles. Instead, the nave's pews were centrally divided into two sections, with women facing the chancel from the west side and men opposite them. Behind the pews there was standing space. Adjacent structures added another sixty-five hundred square feet of floor space.[147] Sisters of St. Joseph established themselves in the village to care for the sick and teach at a newly opened parochial primary school.

Before the 1949 revolution, 13,130 Catholics lived in the county's 134 rural congregations and worshipped at one of its ten sacred structures.[148] In 1949, government authorities appropriated the Xin Village church for use as a military warehouse because of its ample size and good roof. Nine years later a commune took control, using it for storage because it was a well-constructed and valuable asset, the combination of which saved it from destruction. Catholics endured years of hardship with no place to worship and with the inauguration of the Cultural Revolution in 1966 were tested further in many humiliating ways. Red Guards tore down the top half of the tall tower, sold off its bell

---

147   *Wen'an xianzhi*, 628.
148   Ibid.

FIGURE 6.16   Xin Village church, today
SOURCE: PHOTO BY AUTHOR, 2011

as scrap metal, and desecrated every religious icon.[149] Although these zealots viewed it as an architectural symbol of a religion brought to China by imperialistic outsiders, the building's functional use trumped politics.

At the start of the 1980s, Wen'an County's Catholic population had shrunk to 1,410 with most concentrated at Xin and two other villages.[150] Implementation of national policies regarding religion brought hope to people as several very capable priests negotiated with authorities for the return of previously confiscated properties. In July 1985, county-level government officials agreed to return the church, attendant buildings, and the surrounding courtyard to the

---

149   "Wen'an xian Anzuxin zhuang tianzhutang."
150   *Wen'an xianzhi,* 628.

congregation, which would then have full ownership and control of the property. They immediately started raising funds for general restoration work and the reconstruction of the bell tower, both successfully completed in 1987. Since then they have added a reception room, residential quarters for the curate and his staff, a dining hall, separate schools for boys and girls, and a kitchen to prepare food for everyone. In a garden area, there is an Our Lady of China pavilion with a white statue of Mary. Altogether, they have about one acre of space to use.[151]

The church stands solidly, the largest, tallest building in the village. To Chinese its style is Gothic because there are pointed archways over the entrances. Above the central white archway *tianzhutang* is written vertically in red Chinese characters. This links the lower section with a four-sided central tower with a steep roof topped by a cross. It is easy to see from the different colored bricks the rebuilt portion. The congregation has renovated the interior, hanging a painting of Jesus (highlighting his sacred heart) behind the altar and two other paintings, one to each side. If looking toward the pews, Mary's painting is on the right side, for women sitting nearby, and on the left is St. Joseph (for the men). Judging from the many Bibles, rosaries, and personal items left on the pews between services, it is faithfully utilized as a place of worship.[152] However modest in numbers and limited their financial situation, the congregation continues to expand its facilities and use them to grow spiritually. Soon after the reopening for services, the pastor organized a women's group, children's classes, choir, and a band. At the end of the prior millennium, worshippers gathered to celebrate one hundred years (1899–1999) of religious faith and presence in the village. They jointly expressed the importance of being grateful to God for his blessings, the necessity of remembering past hardships, the struggle to achieve stability, and the need to strive for a better religious future.

2.4   Zhangjia Village

The Xian County gazetteer reports that Matteo Ricci passed through the area on his way to Beijing in the early seventeenth century. He made a few converts and confreres returned to make more, numbers that warranted two chapels in 1651 for their rural-based congregations. By the mid-eighteenth century, three thousand Christians lived there scattered among forty-two villages.[153] As previously noted, Vincentians arrived in 1785 and took over administration of Jesuit areas in China. In 1856, they gave back to the Society of Jesus

---

151   "*Xinzhuang xinyang bainian qingdian jinian;*" and Author's field notes, 9 October 2011.
152   Author's field notes, 9 October 2011.
153   *Xianxian zhi* (Beijing: Zhongguo heping chubanshe, 1995), 642.

the province's southeastern section. Stretching from north to south for about 300 miles and east to west for 75 it became the Vicariate of Zhili Southeast. Within its boundaries were three civil prefectures, five independent departments, and thirty-three counties. Due to its size and growth in the number of baptisms, the Holy See subsequently divided it several times.[154] The first bishop established himself at the village (*zhuang*) of Zhaojia in Wei County in the far south near the borders with Henan and Shandong , an imprudent decision given the area's instability and violence.[155] After Taiping military forces rampaged through the area, law and order broke down completely. An upsurge in banditry made the area unsafe and led the bishop to resettle to the north at Zhangjia Village in Xian County in 1861.[156] There he quickly began building his cathedral, completed on 2 October 1863 and dedicated to the Sacred Heart of Jesus on 28 March 1866. To commemorate its construction, the congregation erected a tall, inscribed memorial stone. Moved several times and damaged, it stands in the courtyard as testament to the Catholic experience in the area as well as the erection of its first large European-style church. A second tablet was added in 2003 and outlines the site's long history.[157]

The church was comparable in size to those in Beijing with measurements of about 164 feet in length by 69 in width. A tower dominated the façade's center much like the one at Wanghailou in Tianjin, which was finished six years later. These structures looked solid, even defensive, but the one at Zhangjia lacked side "turrets" of the kind present in Tianjin. The tower extended 108 feet from top to bottom, which in a rural setting of one-story houses exaggerated its size and height. Eye catching and even spectacular in its day, proud residents considered it "the premier church in North China" (Huabei *diyi tang*).[158] Jesuits had ample financial resources and invested in a fine sacred structure that became the epicenter of a rapidly growing mission compound based in a vicariate renowned for its numbers.

The village became home to one of the largest mission centers in Zhili with a large cathedral, a novitiate (with its own chapel), convent, hospital, publishing house, foundling homes, schools, housing for priests and support staff,

---

154   Ibid.
155   The bishop may have been attracted to Zhaojia because of its congregation, whose history dated to the early eighteenth century work of Italian Franciscans. Della Chiesa usually resided in Linqing, not far away. Professor R.G. Tiedemann, email to author, 7 October 2017.
156   It is sometimes called Zhangzhuang and Dazhang zhuang. *Xianxian zhi*, 642. Also, Tiedemann, "The Church Militant," 19.
157   Author's field notes, 18 October 2011.
158   *Xianxian jiaoqu* (Xianxian: Tianzhujiao Xianxian jiaoqu chuban, 2003), 1–2.

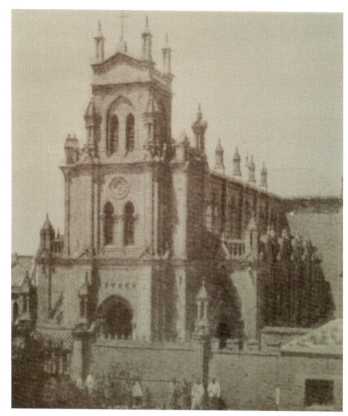

FIGURE 6.17   Zhangjia cathedral, ca 1920s. See fig. 1.4 for today's church.
                SOURCE: INTERNET, PUBLIC DOMAIN

many miscellaneous structures, and farmable land.[159] By the end of the nineteenth century, the diocese controlled from fifty to seventy-five acres of non-
contiguous land, with the largest single block at the cathedral site.[160] In a poor
part of Zhili and over a relatively short time, the vicariate had become one of
the largest landowners—and landlords, with most of its fields rented out to
farmers. Property holdings of this extent attracted Boxers to the area. A diocesan history writes that Boxer forces killed 5,153 Catholics and destroyed no
less than six hundred established places of worship in the vicariate.[161]

---

159   Author's field notes, 18 October 2011.
160   By the late 1930s and at the height of land ownership, the diocese had acquired about
       116 acres. *Xianxian jiaoqu*, 5–6.
161   Ibid., 3–4.

Like other areas, Catholicism survived the Boxer catastrophe to grow even more widespread. According to a modern-era gazetteer for Xian County, in 1903 there were thirty-five churches of which eight are described as "Sino-Western style (steep roof)," that is, Zhong Xi shi (*jianding*), and twenty-seven as "Chinese style (flat roof)," Hua shi (*pingding*). In 1925, the total had grown to sixty-six. The gazetteer's partial list of them comes with locations. More interesting to this study is the categorization by type: Western style (Xi shi tang); Chinese (Hua shi tang); and semi-Western churches (ban Xi shi tang). Irrespective of style, some are described simply as big, medium, and small.[162] This is a secular perspective that one seldom sees in print with terminology that seems well chosen and politically correct.

Due to the vicariate's size, and to make administration more efficient, the Holy See created for the southeastern territory three ecclesiastical jurisdictions, each based on a civil county: Yongnian County (apostolic prefecture, 1929, becoming a vicariate in 1935), Daming County (apostolic prefecture, 1935), and Jing County (apostolic prefecture, 1939).[163] They, and the original vicariate, had disastrous experiences during the fight against Japan, the Civil War, and the land reform periods. Catholic numbers in Xian County decreased by over half to around seventy-four hundred, distributed unequally among 135 villages (about fifty-five on average per congregation).[164] The sociopolitical mass movements of 1950–1976 took their toll, too. Red Guards damaged the cathedral, burned its library and warehouse of books, and leveled all the worship places in the countryside. As the central government moved to snuff out the zealots in 1976, they struck one last match and burned the Zhangjia cathedral.

Within three years, on Christmas Day 1979, a priest once again celebrated mass at Zhangjia Village, marking the beginning of a turnaround in fortunes as authorities returned some of their former property. In the early 1980s, about twelve thousand Catholics lived in Xian County, numbers that justified many projects.[165] Presently, rebuilding and restoration work continues side by side— there seems to be no end to construction plans. In December 2001, a beautiful cathedral opened for services. It is about the same size as its predecessor, yet architecturally different with twin towers each about 150 feet high.[166] Laid out on an east (chancel) to west (entrance) line, it is beautifully designed inside and out. In addition to it, the religious sisters' former worship place, constructed in the late nineteenth or early twentieth century, has reopened. It has an

---

162   *Xianxian zhi*, 643–644.
163   *Handbook of Christianity in China, Volume Two*, 971–976.
164   *Xianxian zhi*, 642–643.
165   Ibid., 643.
166   *Xianxian jiaoqu*, 40–41.

FIGURE 6.18   Former novitiate chapel at Zhangjia, view of its back side. It is now used
                by the Chinese Sisters of the Society of Holy Helpers.
                SOURCE: PHOTO BY AUTHOR, 2011

east-west axis with the chancel on the west side.[167] Last of all, there is an old,
recently reopened sacred structure and affiliated cemetery in the countryside
at Yuntaishan, a scenic area not far away.[168] Circumstances did not allow the
author opportunity to go there; I hope mention of it may draw interest to an
area rich in religious history and worthy of exploration.[169]

3   The South

The Vicariate of Zhili Southeast grew quickly as Jesuits returned to care for
surviving congregations, make converts, and construct numerous sacred
buildings to serve their religious needs. Two other locations provide another

---

167   Author's field notes, 17 October 2011.
168   Jesuits constructed it in 1881. Boxers torched it and Catholics rebuilt in 1903. Author's field
      notes, 17 October 2011. For information about Yuntaishan, see "Tianzhujiao Cangzhou
      Xianxian jiaoqu," http://www.xianxiancc.org/showart.asp?id=131 (accessed 6 June 2016).
169   In this regard, the following website provides an unusual amount of useful infor-
      mation and photographs: "Tianzhujiao Xianxian jiaoqu," http://blog.sina.com.cn/s/
      blog_87ca2ce40102v2pi.html (accessed 21 January 2017).

viewpoint on expansion in that vicariate. When priests built the first church in Daming County in 1872 it was about as far as you could be, 140 odd miles, from the cathedral at Zhangjia. Later, a new ecclesiastical jurisdiction emerged with the one at the county seat becoming the episcopal seat for its own bishop. That cathedral still stands. Today's Daming is part of Handan Prefectural-level Municipality, as well as of a diocese that uses the same place-name. The last stop in this chapter is about twenty miles west of Handan City in out-of-the-way Baisha, a village with a very modest sacred structure, more or less a standard model of those constructed during the first four decades of the twentieth century. Unfortunately, its future is very much in doubt due to building projects there.

3.1   *Daming City*

Antonio Caballero, o.f.m., arrived in Taiwan in 1633 and by year's end had made his way to Fujian across the straits.[170] He was the first Franciscan friar in China since the Yuan dynasty, his goal to reestablish his order on the mainland. Fluent in Chinese, he spent his life working, writing, and traveling widely. Some remember him for challenging the Jesuits' tolerant position on ancestral veneration, others for his devotion to the common people of North China among whom he proselytized successfully. In 1650 we find him in Beijing, with Schall advising him to go to Ji'nan, Shandong's capital. On the way there he passed through Daming, a combination prefectural and county seat in southeastern Zhili, staying at a poorly maintained house purchased and used earlier by Jesuits. The next year, with donations from friendly officials, he acquired another site and constructed a church dedicated to St. Francis.[171]

Only a handful of Catholics resided there and, during the decades that followed, religious life without a resident pastor proved difficult, leading most to give up their faith. In spite of this, one devout family served as the catalyst for additional conversions in 1858–1859, a situation that attracted missionaries. In 1862, two Jesuits departed from the Zhangjia cathedral in Xian County for

170   Eugenio Menegon, "Jesuits, Franciscans and Dominicans in Fujian: The Anti-Christian Incidents of 1637–1638" in *"Scholar from the West:" Giulio Aleni S.J. (1582–1649) and the Dialogue between Christianity and China*, ed. Tiziana Lippiello and Roman Malek (Brescia: Fondazione Civiltà Bresciana, 1997), 218–262.

171   *Dictionary of Ming Biography*, 24–31. One scholar is dubious that Caballero stayed in Daming because the friar was probably in Shandong at that time. In the early eighteenth century, the boundary between the Beijing Diocese under Portuguese Jesuits and Shandong under Franciscans (including parts of southeastern Zhili) was unclear. In 1805, officials took into custody a missionary carrying a map that clarified the boundary. Unfortunately, high officials in Beijing misunderstood its purpose and used it against Catholics. Professor R.G. Tiedemann, email to author, 7 October 2017.

Daming, where inside the city walls on East Street they purchased a structure for use as a combination dwelling, dispensary, and chapel.[172] They found unusual success preaching at the village (*cun*) of Dongyangshan, which eventually became almost entirely Catholic. After the two left the area, people relied on catechists and the occasional visiting priest for religious guidance. A history of the area says in an unusually critical way that the Jesuits' lack of fluency in Chinese combined with their limited understanding of culture made more conversions difficult. At the same time, it lauds a Chinese priest named Ming Jialu (S.J.?), who went to Daming in 1875 and through his eloquence and scholarship found local elite and common people receptive to his message. What had become of the dwelling-chapel building is unknown because Fr. Ming often stayed at the homes of Catholics—not an ideal arrangement for either. The growing congregation eventually purchased a site used to make and fire bricks and built a simple, one-story church alongside a residential structure. Other clergy arrived one by one to continue the work that Fr. Ming had successfully initiated.[173]

From these modest beginnings, Catholicism developed quickly in the area.[174] In the late 1870s, a missionary purchased property within the city walls near the east side of the Manzhou (Manchu) residential section for the construction of a church. By 1878 a priest had opened the first boys' school with a class of about twenty students. Meanwhile at the kiln-site property, a convent and foundling home along with support facilities took shape; added later were a girls' school, hospital, old-folks' home, garden, and cemetery. During this high-growth period, there were often five or more priests and several Sisters at Daming.[175] Such numbers allowed not only for a division of labor in supervising mission work but also for the training of catechists to help spread the Good Word into the countryside. Catholicism budded at the villages (*cun*) of

---

172   "China," *Annals PF* 28 (1867): 325–326; and *Daming xianzhi* (Beijing: Xinhua chubanshe, 1994), 620.

173   Bao Lu, *Handan Tianzhujiao shilüe* (Handan: Haixing bianjibu, 2005), 115–116; and *Daming xianzhi*, 620.

174   A priest soon moved into nearby Wei County and built a brick sacred structure "of the pointed style of architecture" (Gothic style), 108 feet long and 33 wide. "China," *Annals PF* 28 (1867): 327. A Jesuit arrived in 1876 in nearby Cheng'an County. Over the years, numbers steadily increased and in 2011 surpassed thirteen thousand, according a book written by the Cheng'an pastor. Peng Jiandao. *Xinyang ganwu* (N.p.: n.p., 2012), Church internal circulation material, book, 1–14. Priests and Catholics are generally knowledgeable of local history, yet few publicly publish their accounts because of difficulties in obtaining government authorities' approval. They work privately with Catholic or friendly printers and circulate the publications in closed circles.

175   Bao Lu, *Handan Tianzhujiao shilüe*, 116.

Qianyang and Niantou, with the former erecting its own sacred building by 1881, and the latter a few years afterwards. Both rural communities currently have active congregations.[176]

The Boxer tempest blew in from the Zhili-Shandong border area with full force in the spring of 1900. Priests and Sisters fled for their lives with lay people suffering terribly, many dying. Boxers first looted then burned the church and other property—too much destruction to describe here. In the Boxer Protocol of 1901 the Qing dynasty agreed to pay foreign powers reparations for military expenses and various property losses, mainly those suffered by missionaries. At the same time, the dynasty permitted provincial and local authorities to pay additional indemnities for the Chinese Christians killed and for the properties damaged or destroyed.[177] The county gazetteer notes that the Qing officials collected three hundred thousand taels of silver ($222,000) from twenty-seven surrounding departments and county-level jurisdictions as compensation for Catholic losses in Daming. The money proved instrumental in the construction of a sacred structure (similar to the one destroyed in the city), and modest-sized ones in several rural villages.[178] Concurrently, Catholics bought thirty-three acres of land in the northeastern suburbs for use as a mission complex that would include a church, convent, school buildings, staff housing, vegetable gardens, and a cemetery. The spacious site proved to be a good location for kilns to fire the bricks and tiles needed for various projects.[179] Rebuilt infrastructure went hand in hand with the recovery of religious activities all through the area. By 1911 there were ten thousand Catholics distributed among Daming Prefecture's seven counties and one independent department.[180]

Convert numbers in Daming City had grown by the mid-1910s to the point that the congregation needed a larger place of worship—so it acquired property owned by the government on the south side of East Street.[181] A black marble memorial erected to the west side of the church's main entrance indicates that the cornerstone was laid on 2 July 1918. Two years later workers finished construction and a priest celebrated mass. On 8 December 1921 the bishop came from Zhangjia to dedicate it formally to "Notre-Dame de la Treille," after the

---

176 *Daming xianzhi*, 621–622.

177 As noted in Chapter 1, consult Young, *Ecclesiastical Colony*, 79–82.

178 *Daming xianzhi*, 620. This was not a new policy. The Qing government had previously levied extra taxes on localities to fund reparations for damages suffered in specific areas.

179 Ibid.

180 *Handbook of Christianity, Volume Two*, 962.

181 Author's field notes, 14 September 2013.

famous cathedral in Lille, France. In Chinese it is Chong'ai zhi Mu tang, the Mother of Grace Church.[182]

In an unusual statement for government-edited local histories, one gazetteer lauds its scale and décor, stating that it is a "first rate" (*shangdeng*) church.[183] A Jesuit, Fr. Hao Jialu (French name unknown), designed it and supervised its construction. He used funds generously donated domestically and internationally, even some from the Tianjin bishopric, for construction.[184] To local people, it was Western-inspired and Gothic—and much more. First, with a size of about 13,100 square feet, it was (and still is) one of the largest in the province's southern section. Its capacious interior could accommodate more than one thousand worshippers. Its layout took the form of a cross that measured approximately 164 feet long by 80 wide.[185] It was built on a north-south axis with the chancel in the south opposite of the traditionally preferred north side.[186] The architect did this so that the façade faced the street, the direction from which most people arrived. Second, its soaring tower, reported at 138 feet high and topped by a cross, dominated the skyline.[187] Everyone in the city could see it. One account boasts that the "structure is imposing and grand, religiously dignified, even to this day [something] rarely found in China."[188]

In its day, the church stood as the flagship of a very large and active mission enterprise. To its east, workers added many residential buildings, housing for staff and visitors. Coming later were a hospital, orphanage, retirement home, and public school for girls. Across the street were a chapel, primary school classrooms, and religious education buildings for youngsters.[189] In fact, educational activities proved to be very important for the congregation and the

---

182   "The Mission of Southeast Chi-Li" (letter from Lécroart, no date), *Annals PF* 84 (1921), 87–88; and Bao Lu, *Handan Tianzhujiao shilüe*, 117. The "Mother of Grace" translation is from Charbonnier, *Guide to the Catholic Church*, 87.

183   *Daming xianzhi*, 621

184   Bao Lu, *Handan Tianzhujiao shilüe*, 117.

185   This estimate is deduced from its square footage. Author's field notes, 14 September 2013.

186   "Daming Chong'ai zhi mu jiantang bashi zhounian jinian, 1921–2001" (Daming: n.p., 2001), Church internal circulation material, pamphlet; and Author's field notes, 14 September 2013.

187   "Daming tianzhutang," https://zh.wikipedia.org/wiki/%E5%A4%A7%E5%90%8D%E5 %AE%A0%E7%88%B1%E4%B9%8B%E6%AF%8D%E5%A0%82 (accessed 9 January 2017).

188   Bao Lu, *Handan Tianzhujiao shilüe*, 117. A tourism book in my hotel room writes similarly of its large size, imposing stature, and beauty. Author's field notes, 14 September 2013.

189   The chapel is a brick building with a south-facing entrance and dates to the early twentieth century, possibly 1908. *Daming xianzhi*, 620. It is probably the former House of Mercy (Renci tang) mentioned by Bao Lu, *Handan Tianzhujiao shilüe*, 56. Even with a

FIGURE 6.19   The Daming church, ca 1930s
SOURCE: INTERNET, PUBLIC DOMAIN

community at large.[190] During the 1920 drought, and again when the Japanese invaded, many buildings sheltered refugees. In 1935, the pope created the Apostolic Prefecture of Daming and placed Hungarian Jesuits in charge of the area's thirty-seven thousand Catholics, about 40 percent of them living in or near the city.[191] Two years later, the Japanese army occupied Daming with people of all beliefs seeking refuge at the cathedral, its large grounds crowded with people. By 1940–1941, a surge in baptisms brought the area's total to forty-three thousand.[192]

After the war ended, the church served as the apostolic prefect's seat, then the bishop's when Daming became a diocese in 1946. The Communist revolution impacted the area hard in the late 1940s and early 1950s. During the implementation of land reform, Party cadres expelled Western priests and Sisters from the mission compound, followed by the dismissal of all its workers. That served merely as a precursor to the government's occupation of a large portion of the property in 1948 and, over the next two years, confiscation of the remainder. Officials pressured most Chinese priests and Sisters to leave and those that did not suffered relentless harassment. The bishop toiled in the countryside, dying there in 1950. The Cultural Revolution led to further abuses of Catholics

---

new façade, it attracts little attention due to its proximity to the cathedral. Author's field notes, 14 September 2013.

190   "On the Way to Conversion," *Cath-M Annals PF* 1, no. 1 (January 1924): 221–223.

191   Bao Lu, *Handan Tianzhujiao shilüe*, 55. The large number cited is interpreted to mean in and near Daming City. *Daming xianzhi*, 620.

192   *Handbook of Christianity in China, Volume Two*, 978.

and defilement of the sacred building, as well as the occupation or destruction of other mission property.[193] During the difficult times of the 1960s and 1970s, the cathedral became just four walls and a roof.

Neither a local historical account nor a county gazetteer directly mentions the slow post-1980 return of previously owned property to the congregation, probably due to its size and high value. It seems clear that given the current use (highest and best, in real estate terms) of the Church's former and extensive urban holdings, plus those in the northeast suburbs, Catholics may never recover all that they formerly occupied. For example, on land that once had kilns for firing bricks used to build the mission complex sits a middle school, its buildings' educational value considered more important than any potential service it might otherwise have. This general situation applies to many locales. The most important factor affecting Catholicism's influence in Daming was the number of worshippers: a 1989 count put the total at 1,710 distributed among one urban and ninety-four rural locations. The total splits equally between men and women, with the average per site at 18 (134 being the highest number for one village and 2–3 the lowest for three different villages).[194] Consequently, authorities did not see a need to return the property given these scant figures, nor did they feel that local pressure amounted to much. The diocese finally took control of the building in March 1993. It then took the congregation over a year of fund raising among a variety of nearby and distant sources before it could afford to restore it minimally. They joyfully reopened for mass on 22 August 1994. By 2001 Catholic numbers had rapidly climbed to four hundred for the city area and four thousand for the entire parish.[195] Collectively, they had the resources needed to do a full renovation of the exterior and interior, striving to attain the former sacred structure's beauty via attention to architectural details and work quality.

The church is truly a grand edifice, something all the more remarkable because it is not in a major city like Beijing or Tianjin, instead in an out-of-the-way prefectural-level city on Hebei's less-developed periphery.[196] Its architecture is intricate, and the façade is distinctive for its many planes, the northern-most of which is the tall tower's, extending from the anterior wall. The tower is framed by pilasters, its top portion a reconstruction due to Red Guards who had objected to its style and height by using sledgehammers on it. This and other destruction necessitated substantial and expensive repairs. Halfway to the

---

193   Bao Lu, *Handan Tianzhujiao shilüe*, 61–62.
194   *Daming xianzhi*, 622.
195   "Daming Chong'ai zhi mu jiantang bashi zhounian jinian, 1921–2001."
196   Ibid., for a photograph.

FIGURE 6.20   The present-day Daming church
                SOURCE: PHOTO BY AUTHOR, 2013

tower's top, a large white statue of Mary holding baby Jesus occupies a niche, obviously a replacement for the original toppled down sixty years ago. Just as in 1921, to each side of Mary is a couplet that encourages onlookers to observe that she is embracing and supporting Jesus, and to do the same.[197]

The primary entrance is through the tower's lower portion with two flanking entryways set back to the building's main plane, where it meets the gabled roof. There are two adjoining towers, each about seventy-five feet in height with spires. A most distinctive feature is the tall height of the sanctuary and its two levels of windows. Those of the lower level are almost twenty-three feet high and the ones above it ten feet.[198] Not to be ignored is the sacred grotto placed

197   *Daming xianzhi*, 620.
198   Ibid., 621.

FIGURE 6.21   Back-side view of the Daming church
SOURCE: PHOTO BY AUTHOR, 2013

behind the altar—a one-of-a-kind presentation that I have seen nowhere else. The varied architectural features convey a special look that makes it a unique example among Hebei's survivors. A travel brochure touts its special features and encourages domestic tourists to visit.[199]

3.2   Baisha Village

Located less than an hour by car west of Handan City is Baisha Village, a small place in Wu'an shi, a County-level City that is part of Handan Prefectural-level Municipality. Although the village's founding dates to the Ming dynasty, starting a decade ago it has been completely recreated with paved streets, housing, and public facilities, and its one temple rebuilt at a different location as well as renamed. Around twenty-five hundred people and a scant number of Catholics (my estimate is one hundred) call this modern village and wealthy community their home. Its oldest building is a sacred structure that dates to 1895.[200] If not for a chance meeting with the parish's senior priest, I would never have sought

---

199   Author's field notes, 14 September 2013.
200   A factual overview of the village, including photos, may be seen at a website that features some of China's scenic areas. "Wu'an shi Shucun zhen Baisha cun," http://www.hrtv.cn/zt/bsc/index.html (accessed 11 January 2017).

it out because historical records do not mention it and the modern-day Wu'an County gazetteer provides only superficial coverage. What it does say is that missionaries entered the county in the late seventeenth century, eventually making converts and building a few places of worship. Catholics are portrayed as having had bad attitudes toward their neighbors that caused conflict with them, serious anti-social criticisms.[201]

The village's own gazetteer dates Christian religious activities as starting in the 1890s, when the Zhao family took the lead.[202] In 1906, Zhao Yongqing served as the congregation's principal leader. Using funds donated by an un-named Westerner, he began planning for the construction of a church. Over a few years, he acquired two-thirds of an acre of open land for it, which when finished accommodated about 120 people; nearby workers constructed a few ancillary buildings. Nothing is said about style or décor, rather what people deemed important to include in the area's history was a complete list of lay leaders from 1899 to 2008. The list reveals that men surnamed Zhao led the congregation for almost fifty years, and probably remained influential when a resident pastor arrived in the late 1940s.[203] This group of worshippers was tiny, a small percentage of the ten thousand Catholics then in the county.[204]

By 1947, the Communists had begun instituting land reform and village cadres turned the church building into a much-needed school. The pastor, Fr. Yang Xiangtai, stayed on in Baisha during the Cultural Revolution with Red Guards subjecting him to every imaginable abuse. Somehow, he endured and returned as pastor in 1986. That same year the government opened a new village school and allowed Catholics to take possession of the church. Once again, a lay leader from the Zhao lineage helped in its management. The county gazetteer reports that in 1988 around sixty-two hundred Catholics lived in Wu'an, with eighteen lay leaders and a single priest to lead them.[205] Religious activities slowly resumed and in 1999 over one hundred people attended services, mass celebrated by a visiting priest. The village is not far from other congregations such as the one in nearby Wu'an City—the base of several priests charged with caring for those in the countryside.[206]

201   *Wu'an xianzhi* (Beijing: Guangbo dianshi chubanshe, 1990), 885.
202   *Baisha cunzhi* (N.p. [Wu'an?]: n.p., 2011), 382. Few villages publish gazetteers, and those that do tend to be comparatively wealthy with a sense of self-importance.
203   Ibid.
204   *Wu'an xianzhi*, 886.
205   Ibid. This information implies that each of the eighteen villages had a lay leader. Actually, many did not.
206   *Baisha cunzhi*, 382–383; and Author's field notes, 13 September 2013.

In 2013, the brick sacred structure sat precariously on a spot of high ground, around which excavators had leveled the land for four and five story walk-up apartment buildings occupied by families who moved there from their former farmhouses. Authorities drive the development via a master land-use plan that designates zones for residential housing, markets, public-use buildings, orchards, and annual crops—in short, a strategy on how to efficiently arrange resources in a planned community. The church no longer fits in, and authorities want to demolish it and contour the land on which it sits for more apartments buildings. Officials promise to compensate with another site and funds to rebuild, as they did for the village temple, still the lay leaders and congregation hope to avoid relocation. Worshippers are spiritually and historically attached to the building, recognizing that as a minority without agency they may be forced by officials to accept demolition, in short, to be obedient. In modern China, eminent domain seldom fails. With few options, Catholics are contending that since the village is in a scenic area of interest to domestic tourists, their place of worship should remain in place as a historical landmark.[207]

FIGURE 6.22   The Bai Village church, its unfinished setting
             SOURCE: PHOTO BY AUTHOR, 2013

---

207   Author's field notes, 13 September 2013.

FIGURE 6.23   Apartment buildings close to the church
SOURCE: PHOTO BY AUTHOR, 2013

The wall that once enclosed Baisha's church grounds is gone except for a
small portion on the east side that served as the main entrance to the grounds:
above an arched gate, Chinese characters read "Gate of Mercy" (Renci men).
Worshippers use a narrow pathway that leads around the property (about two-
thirds of an acre) to a west side courtyard and a building that serves as the
office and caretaker's room. Years ago, Catholics laid it out on a north-south
axis with an altar on the north side but without an entrance from the south
because of the building's narrow width. I estimate its size at forty-five feet long
by fifteen wide. Its capacity is reported to be 120.[208] Three entrances are on the
west side, each with an inscription in Chinese over it. From north to south they
read: "Goodness keeps the world from going astray" (*shan chu shi mi*); *tianzhutang*; and the Kangxi emperor's oft quoted "the true principle of all things."
Inside and behind the altar is a reproduction of a painting of St. Aloysius

---

208   *Baisha cunzhi*, 382.

FIGURE 6.24   The former main gate and front corner of the church
SOURCE: PHOTO BY AUTHOR, 2013

Gonzaga (Sheng Leisi Gongsage), the patron saint.[209] On his right (west side) is a smaller image of Mary and on his left one of Joseph with two rows of pews aligned with them: women and men sit on one side or the other following the traditional pattern already indicated several times.

---

209   "Jesuit Saints," https://en.wikipedia.org/wiki/Category:Jesuit_saints (accessed 19 January 2017). This village was once part of a Jesuit-directed diocese.

FIGURE 6.25   The church's interior
              SOURCE: PHOTO BY AUTHOR, 2013

This church is an excellent example of the modestly sized architecture used for sacred structures in rural communities, with most being simple rectangular brick buildings with a gable roof. Few, if any, had exterior embellishments except for a cross. Its style is noteworthy for its similarity to a notice with photograph in a 1930 religious publication that stated a Mission Chapel could be built in China for $500 or $1,000 in donations.[210] During the early twentieth century, missionaries hoped to build one for every village that had several hundred Catholics—and every congregation wanted one.

• • •

Catholicism's expansion into formerly small urban locations and rural settings is revealing. Missionaries had the usual challenges—acquiring suitable, secure sites and good construction materials for churches. In pre-1900 years, places of worship tended to be limited in size, height, and footprint because of the

---

210   *Cath-M Annals PF* 7, no. 1 (January 1930): inside back cover page and 7, no. 5 (May 1930): inside front cover page. See Chapter 2's sub-section on costs and fig. 2.8.

challenges faced and because numbers did not warrant huge buildings that neither clergy nor locals could afford. Boxers indiscriminately targeted all places of worship and Catholics tenaciously defended them, saving a few. During the post-1900 recovery, places of worship became more numerous than before, with priests using scale and style to make a religio-political power statement. The material church thus served as a strong magnet that attracted many believers. And, of course, growing congregations needed additional places of worship.

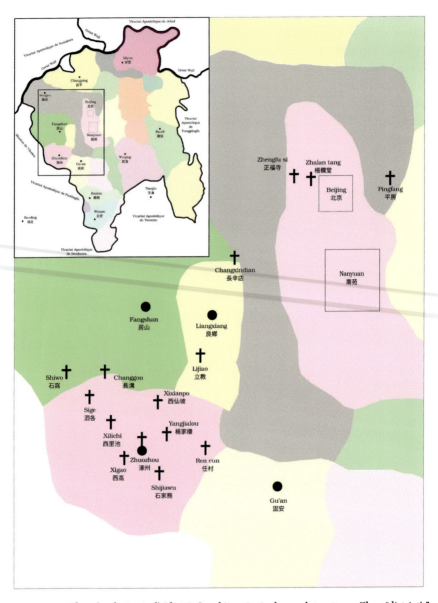

MAP 7.1   Zhuo (ecclesiastical) "district" and its principal sacred structures. Zhuo "district's"
church sites are listed below. Three nearby "districts" are each indicated by a
black circle and several place-names are added for general reference.
SOURCE: ARCHIVES CM, PARIS
Changgou (Taihe); Lijiao; Ren cun; Shijiawu; Shiwo; Sige; Xigao; Xilichi; Xixianpo;
Yangjialou; Zhuozhou.

The Churches of Rural Zhuozhou, Past and Present

The histories of old sacred structures in Beijing, Tianjin, and various parts of Zhili/Hebei provide limited amounts of data regarding the congregations that worshipped at them. Relying on rare and unusually detailed Vincentian sources affords the opportunity to closely examine development in terms of increasing numbers of Catholics and church buildings in the ordinary and bucolic locale of Zhuozhou.[1] A long two-day's walk from the capital, few missionaries gave it much attention before 1900. Change, however, seemed imminent in the 1920s when the bishop and others recognized its religious potential and took preliminary steps to make it a vicariate under Chinese priests. That this did not occur was due to the military situation, with fighting and wars soon engulfing North China. Thirty years and counting after 1949, high-level reforms gave Catholics an opportunity to begin again, yet it has not happened because diocesan leaders in Baoding have not revived former congregations nor requested the return of confiscated property. Currently in Zhuozhou there are only three weather-beaten and vacant former churches left standing, but they, and those that previously existed, deserve investigation for what they reveal about the area's religious experience, especially Catholicism's rapid growth in the countryside during the first decades of the nineteenth century.

During the early and mid-Qing periods, priests on their way to Beijing passed by Zhuozhou, a civil department that included a walled city of the same name situated thirty-five miles south of the capital.[2] Since it was part of the important prefecture of Shuntian, Qing officials carefully monitored its affairs to ensure security for the capital. For the most part, the few Catholics in the area warranted little concern. Starting in 1860, missionaries arrived at Beijing via Tianjin, then moved on to congregations already established and in need of a pastor. The bishop knew that growth would come faster if they first focused on them. The situation changed in the late nineteenth century when work began on a railroad line between Beijing and Hankou (via Baoding). By 1900, Zhuozhou had a station with a simple wooden platform situated a short

---

1 It is known by different names: Zhuozhou or Zhuo Department; Zhuoxian or Zhuo County; and Zhuozhou shi or Zhuozhou County-level City. I refer to the area as Zhuozhou, distinguishing between the entire jurisdiction and its city as needed. Materials used and context occasionally requires nominal adjustments.

2 As a department it was higher on the administrative ladder than a county. Playfair, *Cities and Towns of China*, viii, 102.

© KONINKLIJKE BRILL NV, LEIDEN, 2020 | DOI:10.1163/9789004416185_008

distance from the department seat to the southeast. Improved transportation meant that Western missionaries and Chinese priests could easily travel there by train from the capital in two hours, a convenience that mostly explains their growing presence and efforts at proselytization. According to a gazetteer, they made converts among merchants and the rural elite before establishing themselves and a place of worship inside the city walls. (There were also a few private oratories in houses located in nearby hamlets.[3]) What they had created was significantly more than just a chapel and lodging: it was a base from which to develop an infrastructure of support structures such as schools, clinics, and foundling homes—and eventually a "properly stated" church of European style. Over time, other small sites like this evolved into sprawling bustling centers of evangelical activity.

At century's end, Vincentian missionaries knew little or nothing about the Zhili-Shandong border area's antiforeignism and were caught off guard when it rapidly spread. Moving westward into Zhili, ardent Boxers attracted local people to their cause, together looting and burning Christians' homes and places of worship. By the end of May 1900, more than ten thousand Boxers had poured into Zhuozhou, easily seizing the department seat.[4] A woodblock print of the era indicates that Boxers thought that their capture of this strategic place near the capital made it "the most troublesome place in China."[5] Indeed it was for the priest, who in his haste to escape left everything behind. Boxers wasted no time stealing what they wanted and destroying his chapel. As for Catholics living in the area, they constituted just a few families per village dispersed among about twenty-five rural locales—they had no place to hide and only a few fled safely to churches in Beijing. Survivors later told missionaries about the nightmare they had endured when Boxers murdered women and children before burning their homes.[6] In addition to defenseless Christian targets, Boxers sought out the nearby railroad. Destroying it as a symbol of the foreign presence in China was one goal; another was to help cut off the capital from Qing reinforcements if the court decided to oppose the movement, a matter not then decided.[7]

As previously mentioned, following the Allied nations' military suppression of the Boxer movement, diplomats forced the dynasty to agree to pay an enormous reparation to the foreign powers, a portion of which went to the vicariates.

---

3   *Zhuozhou zhi* (Beijing: Fangzhi chubanshe, 1997), 744.

4   Cohen, *History in Three Keys*, 41–47; and Esherick, *The Origins*, 284–287.

5   *Quanfei jilüe*, comp. Qiao Xisheng (1903; reprinted, Taibei: Wenhai chubanshe, 1967).

6   *Quanshi Beijing jiaoyou zhiming, juan* 9 (Jing Xi'nan), 2b–6, 15b–26.

7   At about the same time Boxers attacked the railroad line east of Beijing to prevent foreign troops from moving into the capital to defend Christians and the Legation Quarter.

Qing provincial and local officials provided additional ("irregular") compensation to Chinese Catholics for their lost family members and destroyed property. For the Vicariate of Beijing and Zhili North, Bishop Favier reported receiving from both sources a sum in excess of 5.7 million taels ($4,218,000). This massive sum financed the reconstruction of destroyed property—and expansion in all directions.[8] The bishop sent Fr. Joseph Fabrègues, C.M., southward to the Zhuo Department City in late 1900, and he soon made his home there and opened a chapel. Within the walls he found some followers who had survived, plus some in nearby villages. By the end of 1901, he guided a flock of two or three hundred. Three years later he left to become director of the Baoding mission, leaving behind several confreres to watch over fifteen hundred Catholics in Zhuozhou and three neighboring counties. Over a few years, several mission centers opened, each having a resident priest and chapel. By 1911, the Qing dynasty's last full year, the area's Catholic population had reached forty-two hundred, and inside the city walls a church appeared.[9]

After the Qing's last emperor stepped down from the throne in early 1912, China's unity dissolved with regional and local strongmen supported by varying-sized armed forces contending for control over constantly changing domains. Sun Yat-sen directed a political movement in southern China that gradually built up the military strength needed to eliminate the warlords standing in the way of a reunified China, a deed ostensibly completed by the late 1920s. With a semblance of order restored, officials of the Republican government sought to reorganize its entire civil structure, turning administrative departments into county level units. Our place of interest became Zhuo County. Through the second and third decades of the twentieth century, Catholicism's growth continued unabated until the protracted war against the Japanese and the following four years of civil conflict brought it to a halt. Survivors endured more hardship, many apostatizing as the government consolidated power. Authorities made many provincial and local administrative adjustments to aid in governing the country. Borders were adjusted and a few place-names changed, none making the area unrecognizable. Baoding, a Prefectural-level Municipality, took charge of a county-level city jurisdiction that encompassed urban and rural zones, later renamed Zhuozhou shi. In 2010, it had over six hundred forty thousand residents living in an area of 286 square miles. Ecclesiastically, it is part of Baoding Diocese.

---

8 Young writes that in Favier's vicariate "the resulting [financial] abundance would become a key element in subsequent Catholic evangelism in the area." *Ecclesiastical Colony*, 80–81, 290 n. 8.
9 Cény letter, 16 November 1910, *Annales CM-F* 76 (1911): 207–209.

FIGURE 7.1   Zhuo County Seat church, war damaged, 1927–1928. Nationalist
              forces advancing to Beijing attacked opponents in the church area.
              SOURCE: ARCHIVES CM, PARIS

FIGURE 7.2   Church at Zhuo County Seat and pastors, early 1930s
              SOURCE: ARCHIVES CM, PARIS

1   Investigating Church Expansion into the Countryside

The Congregation of the Mission's archives in Paris preserve varied materials related to its work in China, some of which include crucial data regarding its ecclesiastical expansion. Vincentian bishops submitted annual statistical summaries of what had been accomplished, making it possible to gauge religious developments in a given vicariate over a defined period. The earliest handwritten summaries, sometimes on small pieces of easily lost paper included with letters, date to the late 1820s and are for Macao and central China. Typically, they provide an annual tally for the baptisms, confirmations, communions, confessions, marriages, and deaths of Catholics for a vicariate and, sometimes, demarcated smaller areas. Some of these were marked "mission catalogue" or just "catalogue" (Latin, *catalogus missionis* or *catalogus*) and others as "spiritual fruits" (Latin, *fructus spirituales*; French, *fruits spirituels*) summaries.[10] Whatever the name, these early nineteenth-century tallies recorded just the basics. The format evolved over time and by the late-nineteenth century, bishops used preprinted forms, some double and triple page in size, on which they filled in a growing amount of information that included an accounting of the total number of Christians, churches, chapels, and more. In the twentieth century, with Zhili/Hebei's ecclesiastical domains shrinking in territorial size, reports began to add details such as the location of congregations (village names given in Chinese) supplemented with a variety of statistics. Vincentian bishops used forms printed in Latin and French regarding "spiritual fruits," "state of the mission" (French, *état de la mission*), "reports" (French, *comptes rendus*), and "mission status" (Latin, *status missionis*).[11]

The Vicariate of Beijing and Zhili North included the capital city and for this reason assumed an importance no other ecclesiastical area could claim. With the grand North Church serving as cathedral, and with a series of experienced and influential Vincentian priests promoted to bishop, it had resources that other vicariates did not—priests, funding, infrastructure, and the power that came with them. The vicariate's success led to its division into smaller jurisdictions that priests could more efficiently administer, thereby ensuring Catholic numbers would continue to grow. Archival materials for the nineteenth and

---

10   Reports for Beijing, Macao, Jiangxi, and Zhejiang are not available for every year over the period 1820s–1840s. Archives CM, Paris, Folder 165-b, "Macao."

11   The materials went to different institutions: those in Latin to Propaganda Fide in Rome and those in French (plus a few in Latin) to the Vincentian superior-general in Paris and to the Society for the Propagation of the Faith in Lyon. Rev. John E. Rybolt, email to the author, 31 May 2011. In the Archives CM, Paris, these reports are scattered among many files.

twentieth centuries that document this pattern are generally spotty with one unexpected exception that is incredibly detailed: Zhuozhou's records. During the 1900s–1930s, no one recognized that late and slow developing Zhuozhou was any different from other rustic places with Catholic congregations. Even in the 1940s–1960s, Fr. Octave Ferreux, who had served in Beijing and Baoding as well as later researching his confreres' work for a history of the Vincentians in China, gave little attention to such localities.[12] Consequently, his book (and others) misses the huge growth in convert numbers and the full-fledged emergence of a rural Church.

The presentation below rectifies this oversight as it draws on information from four detailed "sets" of archival materials that spotlight Zhuozhou and its village-based congregations. It is the best documentation available not only for this rural area but also, as far as I know, for any locale in China. Although they are written in Latin, French, or Chinese, I give the full or abbreviated titles in English for ease of reference (notes will show each in its original language). Examined first are a set of four related and overlapping reports: one is entitled "Apostolic Vicariate of Beijing and Zhili North, Mission Status, 1904–1905;" the other three are labeled "Spiritual Fruits." All provide valuable statistical information.[13] Looked at next is a manuscript, "Project for the Division of the Apostolic Vicariate of Beijing and Formation of the Apostolic Vicariate of Zhuozhou Entrusted to Secular Native Clergy" (internally dated 1928–1931) that consists mostly of property diagrams.[14] Third is a hand-drawn map showing village locations in Chinese characters. Described as "A Complete Map of Religious Matters for Ren Village, Zhuo County," it dates to circa 1928.[15] Fourth and last is a printed report in soft-cover book format, entitled "Apostolic

---

12   He notes most rural localities only in passing with just a few marked on maps of Hebei. Ferreux, *Histoire de la Congrégation*, 72–73.

13   Archives CM, Paris. The first three are in Latin, the last in French: 1. Folder 163-I, "Vicariatus Apostolicus Pekini et Tche-ly Septentrionalis. Status Missionis, 1904–1905;" 2. Folder 168-I-a, "Vicariatus Apostolicus Pekini et Tche-ly Septentrionalis. Fructus Spirituales, 1904–1905;" and 3. Folder 164-I-b, "Fructus Spirituales, a die 15 Augusti 1904 ad diem 30 Junii 1905;" and 4. Folder 163-I, "Mission de Pékin et Tche-Ly Nord. Fruits Spirituels du 15 Août 1904 au 30 Juin 1905." Note that items one and two imply a full calendar year and items three and four each specify a ten-and-one-half month period.

14   Archives CM, Paris, Box "Lazaristes [16]," [Folder] "Vicariat de Péking, Division, 1/ Chochow, 2/ Su-kiao et Young-Ts'ing." Inside the folder is the "Projet de division du Vic. Ap. de Pekin et formation du Vic. Aps. de Chochow à confier au clergé séculier indigene." All abbreviations used in original.

15   Archives CM, Paris, Box "Lazaristes [16]," [Map] "Zhuoxian Rencun shu jiaowu quantu."

Vicariate of Beijing, State of the Mission from 1 July 1936 to 30 June 1937."[16] It includes photographs of churches and a large colored map of the "Apostolic Vicariate of Beijing" that shows their various locations.[17] A few other sources supplement these materials, none more useful than my own field notes and on-site photographs taken during visits to Zhuozhou County-level City.[18]

2 Mission Status and Spiritual Fruits, 1904–1905

We start with a forty-three-page Latin-language report, "Apostolic Vicariate of Beijing and Zhili North, Mission Status, 1904–1905" (hereafter, Mission Status), and three Spiritual Fruits summations that collectively cover a large ecclesiastical area. In Mission Status, six "districts" are given in this order: "Urban [Central] Beijing," "Capital East," "Capital South" (to be examined in detail below), "Baoding," "Xuanhua," and "Tianjin." The place-names are clear enough, though no map is attached to elucidate the exact boundaries of each. The unnamed priest assigned by the bishop to assemble the report compiled information provided by his Chinese and Western Vincentian confreres. He summarized the information provided for "Urban Beijing" and its five churches, each treated as but not called a "residence," each with one congregation. For the other five districts he added sub-categories termed "residence(s)" (*residentia, residentiæ*), followed by a listing of the affiliated congregations (*christianitates*) as identified by the village where each was located.[19] China was a mission area and as such did not have formally designated parishes, so the "residence" (usually with a sacred structure) was its equivalent—its outlying grassroots components being the congregations. For each Mission Status "residence," the first place listed is the principal village. The others appear in no

---

16   Archives CM, Paris, Folder 163-I, "Vicariat apostolique de Pékin, État de la mission, du 1ᵉʳ Juillet 1936 au 30 Juin 1937." The vicariate's name was shortened in 1924.

17   Archives CM, Paris, Folder 163-I-a, [Map] "Vicariat apostolique de Peking." Copies of it may be found in other folders.

18   Statistics on all mission organizations in China are in J.-M. Planchet, *Les mission de Chine et du Japon* (Pékin [Beijing]: Imprimerie des Lazaristes, 1916–1942). Intended to be an annual, there are several years without a publication. For who served where, see Archives CM, Philadelphia, *Catalogue des maisons de du personnel de la Congrégation de la Mission* (Paris: n.p., 1862–1940). Local gazetteers provide some information.

19   In "Fructus Spirituales, a die 15 Augusti 1904 ad diem 30 Junii 1905," "residences" are referred to as "stations of missionaries" (*stationes missionariorum*). In "Mission de Pékin et Tche-Ly Nord. Fruits Spirituels du 15 Août 1904 au 30 Juin 1905," the corresponding French terms for residences and congregations are *résidences de missionnaires* and *chrétientés*, respectively.

discernible order, with their respective distances from the main location given in Chinese *li* (one-third of a mile) increments.[20] Each table includes column headings that reveal, per congregation, the number of Catholics, and, for the year, the number of adult baptisms, confessions, communions, final rites, and the types of worship places that existed.

From the statistical categories mentioned, interest here focuses on the census of Catholics at the grassroots level and an accounting of places of worship. Within the Capital South District, six "residences" are listed as "Zhuozhou, Majiachang, Gaojia, Zhalan, Sangyu, and Anzu."[21] The area covered was large with no explanation offered for its composition. "*Residentia*" Sangyu (Chapter 4's Housangyu section) was to Beijing's west and Zhalan sat near the capital's city western wall; the other four were all south of Beijing.[22] For the entire Capital South District these are the totals: 7,754 Catholics (of which 2,414 or 31.1 percent were recent adult baptisms); 143 congregations; 6 churches; 28 public oratories (chapels); and 24 private oratories. An eye-catching statistic is the substantial number of people who had just entered the Church, a tremendous one-year growth. Within the district, there was a place of worship on average for every 134 Catholics while the average congregation was just 54 individuals.[23]

A close look at "*Residentia*" Zhuozhou reveals that of its thirty-seven congregations (each listed in French romanization accompanied by Chinese characters), about two-thirds fell within the boundaries of the civil department with the remainder in adjoining parts of the neighboring counties of Fangshan, Liangxiang, and Gu'an. Their locations ranged from one to thirty miles distant from the main site at the department seat.[24] Of the area's 1,564 Catholics, priests had made 651 (41.6 percent) adult baptisms in the year of the report.[25] Unfortunately, records do not attribute the baptisms to individual

---

20   The distances are estimates and sometimes differ with information available for 1936–1937.

21   Missionaries used Majiachang as the name of the "residence;" it was composed of twenty-nine congregations, including the village (*cun*) Majiachang. Likewise, Anzu was the name of an area with twenty-five congregations, one of which was Anzuxin Village.

22   Zhalan refers to the site of a chapel, congregation, and cemetery long affiliated with the South Church.

23   Average congregational sizes for the district's six "residences" were as follow: Sangyu, 88; Majiachang, 82; Gaojia, 56; Zhuozhou, 42; Zhalan, 41; and Anzu, 39. "Vicariatus Apostolicus Pekini et Tche-ly Septentrionalis. Status Missionis, 1904–1905, 10–15.

24   A maximum distance of about thirty miles seems to have been, with a few exceptions, the rule for other areas.

25   The percentage of recent adult baptisms are as follow: Majiachang, 31.0 percent; Gaojia, 16.4 percent; Zhalan, 18.8 percent; Sangyu, 6.8 percent; Anzu, 61.7 percent.

congregations, as is the case for other "residences."[26] In the Zhuozhou area, the sizes of congregations vary from a high of ninety-eight for those at or near the department seat to a low of twenty-five for the one at the village (*cun*) of Guashi eighteen miles away.[27] On average, there were forty-two adults per congregation.[28] Since missionaries required the baptism of both husband and wife, there were twenty-one family units per congregation.[29] Even with the inclusion of recent baptisms, Zhuozhou's average congregation size is on the low side compared to other areas within the Capital South District and the vicariate as a whole.[30]

The above accounting may be further augmented by turning to the Spiritual Fruits forms. Listed in them is a group not mentioned in the Mission Status report, Catholics' baptized children, who numbered 2,435 for the vicariate. How many children missionaries had baptized in previous years is unknown, except that for 1904–1905 we have a glimpse of the next generation. Another part of the future Church, catechumens—those studying religious doctrine before baptism—numbered twenty thousand. Taking these figures into account, an additional three children and an extra twenty-three catechumens may be added (on average) to each of the vicariate's 811 congregations. For Zhuozhou, the average size increases from forty-two to forty-five Catholics and then again to sixty-eight with catechumens counted.[31]

These statistics are significant in a larger demographic context. From what we know of Hebei's heavily populated landscape, villages were usually big. From a 1940s study of a county south of Baoding, and about eighty-five miles from Zhuo County, comes information indicating that a typical rural community may be projected at about eight hundred residents.[32] Considering

---

26   Unlike other "residences" and congregations, all adult baptisms for Zhuozhou were placed on a separate line above that of the principal location. My interpretation is that the 651 baptisms were for the entire area.

27   Since the numbers listed for the thirty-seven congregations do not reflect the 651 adult baptisms, I have increased each congregation's listed number by eighteen, on average.

28   Towards the end of the nineteenth century in Jiangxi, the number was forty-three. Sweeten, *Christianity in Rural China*, 35–36.

29   "Vicariatus Apostolicus Pekini et Tche-ly Septentrionalis. Status Missionis, 1904–1905," 10.

30   For the Capital South District, I exclude churches in urban Beijing and two city-based congregations in Tianjin from my average.

31   "Vicariatus Apostolicus Pekini et Tche-ly Septentrionalis. Fructus Spirituales, 1904–1905;" "Fructus Spirituales, a die 15 Augusti 1904 ad diem 30 Junii 1905;" and "Mission de Pékin et Tche-Ly Nord. Fruits Spirituels du 15 Août 1904 au 30 Juin 1905."

32   Sidney D. Gamble, *Ting Hsien: A North China Rural Community* (New York: Institute of Pacific Relations, 1954), 4, 19, 21–62. He gives the county's total population as 408,300 and the number of towns and villages as 454. If we roughly estimate the population of its four largest towns at fifty thousand, the average village size would be almost eight hundred.

population growth, I estimate an average-size village in Zhuo Department in 1905 at about six hundred. If correct, for those places that had a congregation of say sixty-eight people, this would have constituted about 10 percent of the residents. Whatever the exact figure, Catholics constituted a small minority in their villages and did not numerically dominate the communities in which they lived.[33] Since most locales either did not have any baptized families or had just a few, missionaries tended to refer to a community with substantial numbers as a "Christian village." The term was not meant to imply that all the residents were baptized.

The Mission Status material for Zhuozhou provides information on places of worship. In the tables is a Latin sub-heading for "churches" (*ecclesiæ*) with columns to distinguish among three types, namely, churches "properly stated" (*proprie dictæ*), "public oratories" (*oratoria publica*), and "private oratories" (*oratoria privata*). One Spiritual Fruits form in Latin specified that churches were "large ones of European construction" (*majores modo europæo constructæ*). In the French-language version they were simply called "European churches" (*églises européenes*), that is, of European architectural style. "Public oratories" were referred to as "smaller, public chapels" (*minores seu sacella publica*) in Latin and in French were "public chapels" (*chapelles publiques*). "Private oratories" were, in Latin, "oratories that are family property although used by the Christian community" (*oratoria quæ manent proprietas alicujus familiæ licet eis utatur communitas Christianorum*); in French, simply "oratories" (*oratoires*). The name shift from public oratory to public chapel reflects a minor change in hierarchical perspective, the latter more formal than the former. This point warrants emphasis: priests counted a place of worship as a church only if it were of a certain style.

All three Spiritual Fruits forms give 447 as the total places of worship in the Vicariate of Beijing and Zhili North, broken down as follows: 67 churches, 327 chapels, and 53 oratories. For the entire vicariate, there was an average of 165 Catholics per place of worship. The Capital South District had 7 churches, 28 chapels, and 24 oratories, or 131 Catholics per worship site. Within the district, Zhuozhou's numbers may surprise: zero churches, one chapel, and zero oratories. The only chapel was at the village (*cun*) of Guanzhong about twenty

---

   Gamble counted 70,034 families, making the average family size 5.8 people. He mentions that fifty-eight hundred Catholics, members of eleven hundred families, lived in the county. The average Catholic family size was 5.3 people.

33   Jiangxi Province, 1860–1900, looks similar in this respect. Sweeten, *Christianity in Rural China*, 36.

miles from Zhuo Department Seat.[34] Priests had to make do by traveling periodically to each congregation and saying mass at portable altars. This is a snapshot of Catholicism's initial expansion in one locale. The situation would soon change.

Some vicariate-wide data found in the Spiritual Fruits forms, and not listed in the Mission Status, regards the number of seminary students, boys and girls in parochial schools, and teachers. Information on foundling homes gives insight into the care of orphaned and abandoned children, as well as how many were being breast fed—and, in turn, roughly how many wet nurses were employed. Also mentioned are hospitals, dispensaries of medicine, and some figures on the treatment of infants and waifs in the community at large. Missionaries sought out and had contact with many young children that had life-threatening health issues. Consequently, there are figures on those baptized on the verge of death (French, *"enfants païens baptises à l'article de la mort"* and, Latin, *"baptismi infantium paganorum in articulo mortis"*) born to non-Catholic families. In 1904–1905, there were 6,669 such baptisms in the vicariate. Finally, missionaries' educational and philanthropic activities involved the employment of many people, for example, 1,055 teachers in the mission schools.[35] Catholicism's economic impact at the village level was substantial and an examination of it, not appropriate for these pages, would help round out the story of the Church in rural China.

3 Project for the Formation of the Vicariate of Zhuozhou, 1928–1931

The second set of materials is the "Project for the Division of the Apostolic Vicariate of Beijing and Formation of the Apostolic Vicariate of Zhuozhou Entrusted to Secular Native Clergy" (hereafter, Project for Division).[36] Its value comes from a three-page preface and loose-leaf sheets on various properties in Zhuo County that includes place-names (in French romanization and Chinese characters), some bearing the designation "parish" (*paroisse*). Diagrams show

---

34 "Vicariatus Apostolicus Pekini et Tche-ly Septentrionalis. Status Missionis, 1904–1905," 10. The report does not indicate a church or chapel for Zhuozhou Department Seat, apparently an oversight. Anzu "residence" had only one sacred structure, a chapel.

35 Salary information is not provided. Some information regarding general expenditures may be found in ledgers sent to the Vincentians' motherhouse in Paris.

36 "Vicariat de Péking, Division, 1/ Chochow, 2/ Su-kiao et Young-Ts'ing;" "Projet de division du Vic. Ap. de Pekin et formation du Vic. Aps. de Chochow à confier au clergé séculier indigene."

churches and other buildings, each numbered and briefly described. Property lot measurements are also given. The process of vicariate division itself had already occurred several times, typically with an investigation into C.M.-owned assets—that is, real and business personal property (in modern terminology), its value, and what would be transferred.[37] The assessment is unique for its thoroughness concerning an entire county.

The substantial numerical progress and the trend of entrusting them to native clergy led Propaganda Fide in 1926 to form ecclesiastical areas under Chinese bishops.[38] Stanislas-François Jarlin, C.M., the Vicariate of Beijing and Zhili North's bishop from 1905 to 1933, stands out as a leading proponent of growth, admitting as many Church members as fast as possible, even allowing priests to provide financial assistance as an incentive. Take, as an example, the village (*cun*) of Guzhuangtou in Zhuo County whose count of 21 Catholics a few years after the Boxers had increased to 2,766 thirty-two years later.[39] According to a retrospective account by a local man, a flood in 1917 destroyed the county's crops with the vicariate taking advantage of the situation to flex its considerable financial power by paying poor, needy people of all ages to convert. Enticed by other benefits such as free education for children, as many as 80 percent of them claimed affiliation. "Why do I want to convert? For the three silver dollars," went one popular saying.[40] A Catholic confirms this: "[Whether you] believed in the religion or not, [you got] three silver dollars."[41]

Consequently, the number increased from almost seventy-four thousand to several hundred thousand during his episcopate.[42] Such success led the

---

37 This matter was important in the creation of areas under Chinese clergy. Young, *Ecclesiastical Colony*, 239–241.

38 Xuanhua is an example of one previously mentioned.

39 "Vicariatus Apostolicus Pekini et Tche-ly Septentrionalis. Status Missionis, 1904–1905," 10; and "Vicariat apostolique de Pékin, État de la mission, 1936–1937," 202.

40 Dong Jinhe, "Guzhuangtou jiao'an neimu," *Zhuozhou wenshi ziliao* 2 (May 1988): 129–130. This village is located about six miles southeast of the county seat. In the mid-1930s, Guzhuangtou was also the name of one of Zhuo's "quasi-parishes," which included a total of twenty congregations, three chapels, and 2,766 Catholics (54 recently baptized). Guzhuangtou Village itself had a chapel and 186 Catholics (26 newly baptized)—included with the totals given. "Vicariat apostolique de Pékin, État de la mission, 1936–1937," 83.

41 *Zhuozhou gongan zhi* (Shijiazhuang: Hebei renmin chubanshe, 1992), 137.

42 Planchet, without commenting on the methods used, lauds Jarlin for increasing convert numbers in his jurisdiction from 73,920 in 1905 (for all the areas that were part of his vicariate for that year) to 400,000 in 1933 (in a vicariate smaller in size due to divisions). See his *Les missions de Chine*, 108. "Vicariat apostolique de Pékin, État de la mission, 1936–1937," 204, puts the total at 267,899. Jarlin sought to convert people by any and all means available. This included building schools to teach religion and using catechists to offer money to those willing to go through the process leading to baptism. Lebbe thought the

bishop in the late 1920s to support planning for the creation of two vicari-ates, one with an episcopal center located at the Zhuo County Seat, with its boundaries encircling the adjacent counties of Fangshan, Liangxiang, and Gu'an.[43] To help the proposed vicariates, he would transfer property. He in-structed priests in the counties involved to inventory Church-owned land, buildings, and business personal property.[44] Based on the documents pre-served in the Vincentians' archives, it seems only priests in Zhuo County such as Fr. Eugène-Gustave Castel, C.M., forwarded materials to Beijing.[45] At the North Church, Fr. Dominique-François Saint-Martin, C.M., organized the incom-ing information, most of his paperwork bearing the date October 1928 with amendments in pencil continuing over the next three years.

Saint-Martin stopped work on the project in 1931 because the Holy See de-cided not to create the two vicariates. Fortunately left behind is a thorough sur-vey that warrants our attention. According to its introductory pages, 21 priests and 189 catechists watched over 69,013 Catholics (in 1924), out of 582,318 people residing in the proposed vicariate's four-county area. They had use of twelve residences, eleven churches, and twenty-five public and seventy private ora-tories (locations not provided). For Zhuo County, ten of the church sites can be determined as well as the year each opened, noted parenthetically: Zhuo County Seat (1901); Ren Village (1911); Changgou Town (1914); Xigao Village (1916); Sige Village (1916); Lijiao Village (1916); Xilichi Village (1917); Xixianpo Village (1917); Shiwo Village (1922); Shijiawu Village (1922).[46] For the Project for Division, Saint-Martin's revised and amended property diagrams elucidate

---

bishop went too far in offering grants, the process being commercialized with catechists becoming cash recruiters—even using non-believers to help them find people willing to convert. A harsh critic, Lebbe called it "evangelization by millet." Propaganda Fide learned of Jarlin's approach in the early 1920s and instructed him to stop giving money to those recently baptized. Jarlin told his priests to terminate the practice and monitor the process of conversion. For Zhuo County of the 1920s–1930s, the figures do not show an actual slowdown in convert numbers. Young, *Ecclesiastical Colony*, 181–182, 220. A priest (born in Hebei and ordained in 1956) said he knew that earlier in Zhuo County and other areas priests "gave money to people to convert, but they did not become true Catholics and later left the Church." Author's field notes, 26 September 2011. The existence of "rice Christians" (as likely as it seems) cannot be directly verified nor can their numbers be determined.

43   The other vicariate was to be based at the principal city of Wen'an County and would encompass a four-county territory.

44   Similar details for Wen'an are unavailable.

45   Either priests did not collect information for the other counties or no one preserved it.

46   The list and year of establishment comes from "Vicariat apostolique de Pékin, État de la mission, 1936–1937," 57–89. Xilichi, Xixianpo, Shiwo, and Shijiawu are all villages (*cun*); the others have been previously mentioned.

the general scope of religious activity in the county and allow for a tightly focused view of specific congregations such as those at the county seat, Lijiao (Chapter 4), Changgou (Chapter 6), and Ren and Shijiawu Villages.

Most county-level gazetteers include maps, as is the case for two that are part of the Zhuo County's Republican-era edition. One shows the county's various towns and villages and the other shows the county seat's main streets and its prominent places (and by deduction the occupants). Two Church-owned sites, separated by an east-west oriented lane, are plainly indicated.[47] The Project for Division supplements this view with a plot map and diagram that zooms in close to reveal the buildings at each site. The northern one included the church, and was an irregular square parcel surrounded by a security wall with these boundary dimensions: north, 320 feet; east, 410 feet; south, 340 feet; and west, 360 feet. Its footprint came to three and four-tenths acres, almost as large as the county government's site. The property consisted of two halves, one with two large structures used as schools for boys (called "Castel's school") and two small support buildings. The other half had three small and three large buildings, the latter marked as the priest's "residence" (dwelling), "former public oratory" (chapel), and "church." Besides housing for the pastor and guests, there were offices and meeting rooms. The former chapel, built on an east-west axis, was divided into twelve rooms. The church was laid out on an east-west axis with the chancel in the eastern part. A gatehouse on the security wall's south side served as the main entry to the grounds. To the lane's south was the other Catholic site, occupied by the Sisters of St. Joseph. Their property consisted of lodging, support buildings, a school, and housing for girl students. The gazetteer map shows a hospital at this location, which was on a parcel of one and two-tenths acres.

The vicariate stood out as one of the county seat's most prominent, if not richest, occupants. During the late 1920s, the Nationalist army heavily damaged the church and other buildings as it moved against warlord forces that blocked their move to take Beijing. Given the turmoil of the period, the bishop did not receive any compensation. Of great importance to work in the area, missionaries used vicariate funds to quickly repair the damages.

Project for Division material allows a close look at religious infrastructure and the degree to which Catholicism had physically penetrated the countryside. At Shijiawu, about four miles to the county seat's southeast, one of the

---

47   *Zhuoxian zhi* (N.p.: n.p., 1936).

涿 縣 城 圖

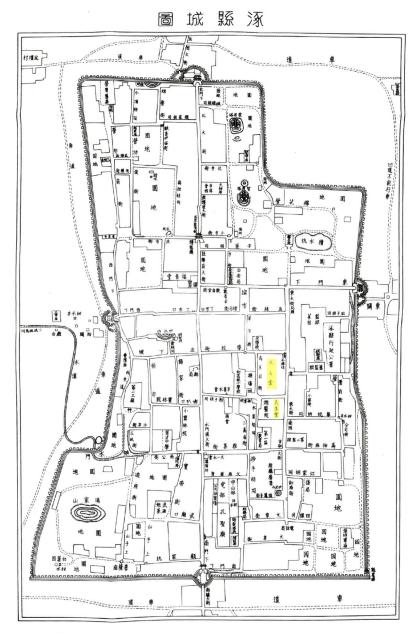

MAP 7.2   The Zhuo County Seat and its important places, 1936. Two spacious Catholic
sites (highlighted) are not far from county government offices to the northeast.
SOURCE: *ZHUOXIAN ZHI*

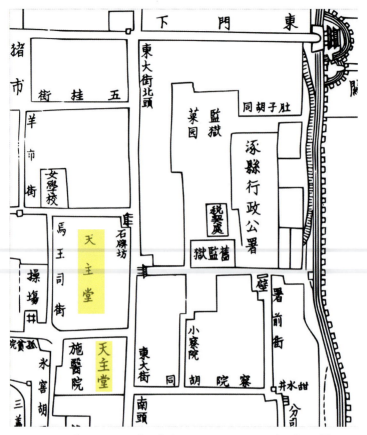

MAP 7.3   Close-up view of Catholic property sites. Note the charitable
           hospital on the west side of the southern parcel.
           SOURCE: *ZHUOXIAN ZHI*

last sacred structures to be built in Zhuo County arose in 1922.[48] Based on a
plot diagram, a priest built the church (on a north-south line, the chancel in
the northern part), residential quarters, three support buildings, and a small
school building for boys that included dormitory rooms. A security wall surrounded a rectangular lot of one and one-tenth acres. Not far away was a small
school for girls with limited housing for them. In 1905, only 11 Catholics lived
in Shijiawu; by 1937 the "residence's" number had grown to 3,701 (including
192 new baptisms, constituting 5.2% of the total) spread among twenty-eight
village-based satellite congregations (average size, 132). Such phenomenal

---

48   It was actually in Bei (North) Shijiawu, not Nan (South) Shijiawu. Both are on the gazet-
      teer's map and local people usually distinguish between the two places.

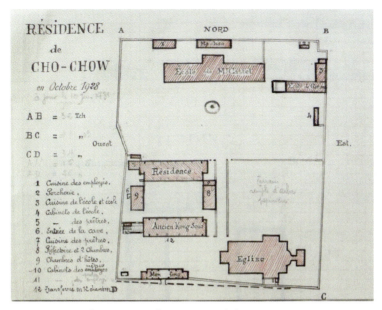

FIGURE 7.3 Site diagram I, "residence" center of Zhuo County, 1928. Key
structures include the church (*eglise*), and former chapel (*ancien
kong-souo*).
SOURCE: "PROJECT FOR DIVISION"

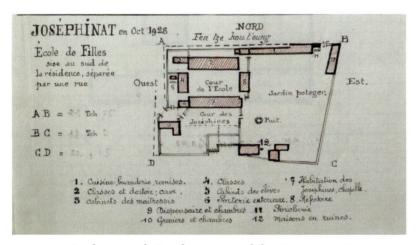

FIGURE 7.4 Site diagram II, the Josephinate center of Zhuo County, 1928. Key structures
include the Sisters' residential building and chapel (center, left).
SOURCE: "PROJECT FOR DIVISION"

FIGURE 7.5 Shijiawu church and pastor, ca 1930s
SOURCE: ARCHIVES CM, PARIS

growth led to the construction of three public oratories (chapels) and eight private oratories, or on average, one for every 308 Catholics.

People and buildings survived the 1940s–1950s only to see Catholicism's decline start in the '60s and continue into the future. At the site today, trash and debris are strewn everywhere with the long-ago-defaced church building looking fragile and forlorn.[49] Without a congregation to protect and perhaps one day restore the premises, it faces an uncertain future.

Xigao, located less than three miles from the county seat, provides another glimpse of the area. In 1904–1905, the congregation of thirty-five people did not have a chapel or oratory. Only eleven years later, it had its own brick-made place of worship laid out on a north-south axis. Within a decade there was a mission compound one and two-tenths acres in size with several support buildings. During the mid-1930s, the village had 646 converts (17 were recent baptisms) with another 5,607 distributed among thirty-two nearby ones (average size 175), with one chapel and one private oratory to serve those living as far

---

49   Author's field notes, 23 September 2011.

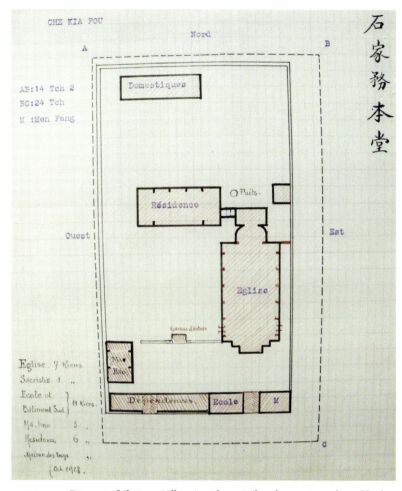

FIGURE 7.6   Diagram of Shijiawu Village "residence." Church is center right and laid
            out on a north-south axis.
            SOURCE: "PROJECT FOR DIVISION"

away as sixteen miles from the church. The congregation and its facilities faced
the same difficulties as Shijiawu—and the same fate, dwindling numbers and
structural deterioration.

In the autumn of 2011, Xigao's church stood alone to one side of a dirt lane
covered with ears of corn drying under a bright sun. Neighbors wanting the
extra space had long ago demolished its security wall and support structures.
Without a roof, the sturdy building has not weathered well with its interior
walls showing sun and water damage. The fresco on its north (chancel side)

FIGURE 7.7 Current condition of the Shijiawu church
SOURCE: PHOTO BY AUTHOR, 2011

FIGURE 7.8 Xigao Village church, ca 1930s
SOURCE: ARCHIVES CM, PARIS

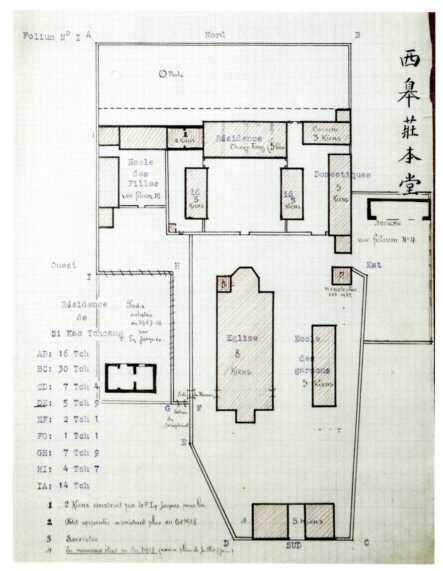

FIGURE 7.9   Diagram of Xigao Village "residence"
       SOURCE: "PROJECT FOR DIVISION"

FIGURE 7.10   Xigao church, today
                SOURCE: PHOTO BY AUTHOR, 2011

wall, a red sun and yellow rays (suggesting "the East is Red"), is faded, and
political tributes to Mao Zedong are barely readable, visual remnants of the
Cultural Revolution nobody cares about anymore. Without repairs, its days
are numbered.

4   Congregations in the Ren Village Area

The third document set consists of an oversized page labeled "A Complete
Map of [Catholic] Religious Matters for Ren Village, Zhuo County" (hereafter,
Ren Village Map), which dates to the late 1920s and comes from the hand of a
Chinese priest with personal knowledge of the area.[50] Located about ten miles
east of the county seat, Ren Village was the site of the area's second sacred
structure. The village was placed at the center of a simple ten-by-ten grid of
squares, which allowed for the detailed organization of map information covering an approximately sixteen square mile area of the county's eastern sector.
Clearly written in Chinese are 111 villages and towns. Ren Village Map shows

50   [Map] "Zhuoxian Rencun shu jiaowu quantu." Judging from the calligraphy, the writer
        was literate in the language.

FIGURE 7.11   Ren Village church and pastor, ca 1930s
SOURCE: ARCHIVES CM, PARIS

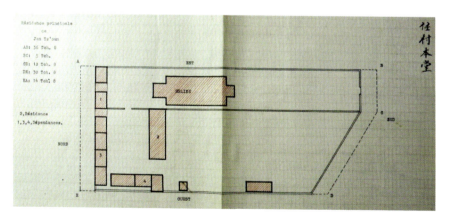

FIGURE 7.12   Diagram of Ren Village "residence." Church is top center.
SOURCE: "PROJECT FOR DIVISION"

marketplaces, their staggered and recurring ten-day schedules crucial to the economic life of rural China. In some provinces, priests had attempted to locate churches at market sites to take advantage of the regular flow of people that would make for easy contact with Catholics and prospective converts alike. Surprisingly, Ren was not a market town. It was on the map due to its congregation and place of worship there.

Mission Status and Spiritual Fruits documents for 1904–1905 do not list a congregation at Ren Village though it probably had a few Catholics. By 1911 it had enough recent converts to warrant a church (laid out on a north-south axis) with the later addition of four support buildings, based on a plot diagram preserved in the Project for Division materials. The congregation had a small girls' school nearby, education being an important component of mission work. A wall, about 982 feet in total length, surrounded the main site's buildings. The irregularly shaped site occupied one acre of land, a large footprint indeed in a densely populated venue of high-value farmland. As mentioned, Ren Village Map shows the area's numerous communities and that only four of them had a chapel. Catholics had built these four in a quadrant around the church, their distances ranging from one to four miles away from it.[51] This approach aided religious growth in the area during the 1920s–1930s.

5   Vicariate of Beijing, State of the Mission, 1936–1937

A Lazarist Press publication in French, bearing the translated title "Apostolic Vicariate of Beijing, State of the Mission from 1 July 1936 to 30 June 1937" (hereafter, State of Mission) constitutes the fourth and last set of materials consulted for this chapter.[52] Its fragile and yellowed pages provide locale-by-locale statistics in the greatest detail preserved for any section of Hebei Province for any era. It contains photographs of pastors and bucolic churches, the only source in the Vincentians' archives to do so. With the Sino-Japanese War beginning in July 1937, it stands out as the fullest and probably final accounting of mission work for the area. Within its 208 pages, we find the vicariate divided into seven "districts" as follows: "[Urban Central] Beijing," "Capital South," "Zhuo County," "Capital North," "Capital East," "Yongqing County," and "Suqiao."[53] Three of the

---

51 One of the chapels was at the village (*zhuang*) of Magong; twenty-two Catholics lived there in 1904–1905. Shuangliushu (sometimes shortened to Shuangshu) was not mentioned in the 1904–1905 report. In 1928, Shuangliushu had a chapel on a small parcel about one-sixth acre in size. Eight years later 214 worshipped at its chapel.

52 "Vicariat Apostolique de Pékin. État de la Mission, 1936–1937."

53 "[Urban Central] Beijing," not called a district, was in fact treated as one. Suqiao is a town in Wen'an County.

district names are the same as those used in the 1904–1905 Mission Status, their geographic areas changed somewhat. They and four new ones (two with county-level names), reflect the substantial jurisdictional and ecclesiastical alterations made to the vicariate via reorganization. A color map attached to State of Mission shows the vicariate divided into counties with district centers and "residences" marked with red crosses.

State of Mission synopsis pages indicate that in the vicariate there were 267,899 Catholics, of whom 3,666 were newly baptized adults (a 1.4 percent increase for 1936–1937). They were scattered among 2,150 congregations (average size, 125) and worshipped at 635 different locations (counted as 60 churches, 223 public oratories or chapels, and 352 private oratories). On average, there was one place of worship for every 422 Catholics. Like Mission Status, this report provides essential information in columns that list the seven districts, each with its "residences," and the number of Christians, adult baptisms, confessions, communions, final rites, and worship places for each location. Listed on other pages are the component units that made up a "residence" area, affording a good indication of religious activity at the congregational (village) level in Zhuo County.

Of the vicariate's seven ecclesiastical district divisions, Zhuo County had the largest number of Catholics, 65,520 (1,104 or 1.7 percent being recent converts). They were split between 434 congregations with the average size being 151. The congregations had 114 places of worship (12 churches, 45 public oratories or chapels, and 56 private oratories), that is, on average 1 for every 575 Catholics. Zhuo County "district" was composed of eighteen sub-areas, each designated a "quasi-parish" (*quasi-paroisse*)—an often-used term in State of Mission.[54] Provided for each in no discernible order is a village place-name (that is, the congregation) in French romanization and Chinese characters. Following each name are the same columns and headings twice mentioned above.

One "quasi-parish" carried the name Zhuo County, that is, the walled city and those living adjacent to it. Altogether, 5,533 Catholics lived in the area (including 3 new adult baptisms) split up among twenty-nine congregations (average size, 191). A priest had built one sacred edifice inside the city walls, and, as discussed with regard to Project for Division, it was the centerpiece of a large mission compound. Three had a public oratory or chapel and four had private oratories, with the congregation's size and its distance from the county seat being determining factors. The largest one was within the city walls and numbered 1,265; the next largest was 471 and less than one-third of a mile away;

---

54 In State of Mission, districts (also referred to as "residences") are composed of "quasi-parishes," which in turn are made up of village-based congregations (*chrétientés*). Regarding mission areas terms, see Chapter 2, notes 10, 19, and 92.

the third largest was 418 and the same distance away; and the fourth largest was 370, about two miles distant, with its own chapel. The smallest consisted of only seventeen people and was two miles outside the city, with neither a chapel nor private oratory.

The Ren Village "quasi-parish" had a total of 3,767 believers (31 recently baptized) distributed unequally among twenty-seven congregations (average size, 140). At the village there was a church for use by 363 people (one of whom was a new convert). Others were naturally drawn there and to the pastor. Within two miles there were eight congregations with a combined total of 1,191 Catholics. If, for the sake of argument, they all worshipped at this church, then the area's other 2,576 followers had only two chapels and two private oratories available to them (an unusually high average of 644 per place of worship). In terms of distance, the closest one to the church was a mile away and the farthest ten miles. The second largest consisted of 291 Catholics and was five miles distant while the smallest had 38 and was four miles away; both were without a chapel or oratory. On Ren Village Map, twenty-six of the twenty-seven congregations mentioned in State of Mission can be pinpointed.[55]

From the statistics, it is clear that the surge in conversion to Catholicism occurred after the termination of the Boxer Uprising. Without annual statistics, it is difficult to monitor growth except to observe that increases continued until the mid to late 1920s, judging by the plan to create a new vicariate. As mentioned, the last church arose in 1922, but a substantial chapel at the village (*cun*) of Yangjialou was built in 1928. By 1936–1937, according to State of Mission data, there had been a 1.4 percent rise in adult baptisms in the vicariate and 1.7 percent increase in the ecclesiastical district of Zhuo County. The change over thirty years is impressive, one impact being that the vicariate could not build sacred structures fast enough. In the district, only twelve of the eighteen "quasi-parishes" had a "properly stated" church. Funding certainly was one explanation for this and the availability of pastors another. A statistical summary of China missions for 1935–1936 names twenty-three clergy in Zhou County or one priest for every 2,855 Catholics.[56]

Fast growth had come with shallow roots, given the government's successful post-1949 efforts to eradicate Catholicism and the fact that most of its infrastructure disappeared from the area. A 1951 survey found 10,097 Catholics distributed among ninety-six Zhuo County villages or, on average, about 105 per congregation. The next year authorities contended that an unspecified

---

55   On a modern map of Zhuozhou, twenty-two of the twenty-seven villages can be found.
56   Another source confirms the total and by deduction the other numbers. *Les Missions de Chine, 1935–1936* (Shanghai: n.p., 1937), 67–68.

number called themselves followers only because of monetary gifts received. Those aside, supposedly 53 percent were of "indifferent" (*lengdan*) faith.[57] By 1964 Catholics numbers had declined to 2,940 with authorities labeling one-third as either simply "of the faith" (*xin*) or "ardent" (*reqing*) believers and two-thirds as "indifferent." Likewise, places of worship dropped from a high of 114 in 1937 to 13.[58] To be sure, an exact count of oratories as well as those remaining Catholic is impossible because many people had to worship secretly to avoid government attention that would lead to personal and family complications or disadvantages for the next generation.

At present, there are few overt signs of Catholic activity and no indication of a religious recovery in either urban or rural Zhuozhou.[59] It is not surprising to learn that residents know something about the area's formerly vibrant Catholic history and physical presence. At Xilichi Village, the former site of a mission center (it also a "residence") and large sacred structure (in the mid-1930s used by twenty-three congregations with a total of 2,593 people), a non-Catholic man told me that his father and grandfather had been baptized. He proudly repeated a locally held (but erroneous) belief that the village's church "had been larger than those in Beijing." To him it was a real and important place due to his family's connection and memory of it.[60] Whether or not people's knowledge about their prior connections to Catholicism will lead to regrowth in Zhuozhou will depend in good part on priests aware of and sensitive to their history.

State of Mission's old photographs are indeed a treasure that preserve a visual record of Zhuozhou's rural churches, which have either disappeared or remain in poor, unrestored condition, such as the ones at Changgou, Shijiawu, and Xigao, or, for comparison, the restored one at Lijiao. While details about the construction of them (architect, materials, costs, etc.) are unknown, it is a reasonable presumption that the vicariate, through the district's Western director, made design decisions for and funded each endeavor. He probably consulted neither his Chinese confreres (they had become the majority) nor the congregations worshipping at them. For ten of the thirteen "properly-stated" European-style sacred structures for which there are photographs we may observe that the most commonly built ones either had a tower as part of the

---

57   *Zhuozhou shi gongan zhi*, 138–139.
58   *Zhuozhou shi gongan zhi*, 140. Another gazetteer notes that through a process of raising political awareness, many Catholics apostatized. *Zhuozhou zhi*, 744. (Of the area's thirteen *jiaotang*, per State of Mission information, seven were churches and six were chapels.)
59   A small number of Protestants have a church. Author's field notes, 23 September 2011.
60   The man happily took a copy of an old photograph of the church that I had with me. Author's field notes, 23 September 2011.

façade or twin towers. (Further parsing of the architectural styles is made in Chapter 8.) I venture that Chinese Catholics found the repeated architectural styles used (with some variation in the details of individual churches) customary and to their liking.

The present-day city of Zhuozhou warrants a few supplementary comments. Getting there is an easy trip from Beijing by train with its station, as before, conveniently close by. The city walls and narrow streets are gone, replaced by smooth boulevards filled with battery-powered motorbikes silently darting here and there. A Kentucky Fried Chicken franchise attracts customers, its parking area jammed tight with numerous electric and some pedal-type two wheelers together with a few cars. None of the Catholic-owned buildings mentioned above still stand, nor are the former properties in the hands of one owner. An elementary school with a spacious playground occupies part of the former mission compound. Through the years, local people have built apartment buildings and small businesses on all sides, erasing former boundary lines, and for this reason (highest and best use) have increased the properties' current values, a factor that one day will complicate negotiations for compensation to the diocese. In other words, physical evidence of Catholicism's once thriving presence is important. A few in the city worship at home-based oratories, just as the first ones did over one hundred years ago. More to the point, the diocese has not initiated negotiations with authorities for return of its former property because the negligible number of Catholics does not warrant the expense of opening, maintaining, and staffing a formal sacred structure. The bishop in Baoding has no current plans for the locality.[61]

• • •

Catholicism's numerical growth in rural Zhuozhou came with "properly stated" churches and infrastructural expansion. The special materials at hand provide hard-to-find statistical information and particulars that have made it possible to trace priests' work in a cluster of villages for a limited geographical area in Hebei. Fleeting as it may be, we have had a peek into religious life at the local level. Congregations over a thirty-year period in the early twentieth century averaged about one hundred persons in size. A minority in their communities, they did not exist independently of the non-Catholic kith and kin living around them and the communities of which they remained a part—demographic and cultural realities important for understanding the Church's place in the countryside.

---

61   This is based on conversations with the bishop. Author's field notes, 15–16 September 2016.

The Catholic Legacy

Old churches are the lens used here to view Catholicism's establishment, travails, growth, and legacy in one part of China during a span of four hundred plus years. Such a choice in optics imparts a Vincentian tint because of their active efforts over a long period and large area. From 1785 onward in Beijing, Tianjin, and Zhili/Hebei, Congregation of the Mission priests played a crucial role in constructing and reconstructing sacred structures, in building and rebuilding the Church. The role they played in this has been documented and discussed, as has how their actions illustrated era-specific developments. We have seen thriving congregations and places of worship in these three areas—most people aware of their former Vincentian connections and the role played by the Congregation of the Mission as well as by other societies and orders. The assessment presented here takes into account that the past is well connected to current times.

1   The Importance of Churches

Matteo Ricci initially considered using a Chinese design for his first formal church, then changed his mind. He decided, and later missionaries agreed, that churches should have distinctive architectural features, that is Euro-Catholic ones, to distinguish them from the gathering places commonly associated with China's so-called "Three Religions" (*sanjiao*): Buddhism, Daoism, and Confucianism. No one, not even a casual observer, would then confuse a church with a temple or hall. The earliest ones missionaries constructed in Beijing were unequivocally European looking brick-walled structures standing prominently in residential neighborhoods composed of small, low-level wooden buildings. That two dynasties found missionaries' expertise crucial in making astronomical calculations and calendars gave Catholics a status that allowed them some immunity, in modern parlance, to zoning restrictions and building regulations. It helped, too, that the first two Qing monarchs personally found Christianity intriguing, leading the Kangxi emperor to declare ipso facto that the North Church of 1702 had been "built by imperial order." These words, displayed on a plaque and mounted on the façade, implied his approval of its style. The honor had been bestowed in a specific way, a fact that did not

© KONINKLIJKE BRILL NV, LEIDEN, 2020 | DOI:10.1163/9789004416185_009

stop missionaries from seeing it as an opportunity to take architectural liber-
ties in the construction of churches in the capital and, later, in the countryside.
They used churches' materiality to their advantage in proselytizing.

The early eighteenth century proscription of Christianity lasted into the
middle decades of the nineteenth century, when a variety of factors made
enforcement of it difficult. In southeastern China, Western merchants had
opened a marketplace filled with Chinese suppliers of tea and silks and, later,
one with an abundance of customers for opium. Missionaries arriving by ship
from Europe used Macao as a base before taking advantage of the porous border to venture illegally into China. Intrepid Vincentians like Évariste-Régis Huc
traveled over one thousand miles across China to Xiwanzi to meet his confrere
Joseph-Martial Mouly and observe his work. The rural congregation there had
worshipped initially in oratories, daily used rooms in small dwellings, and then
in a house adapted into a chapel. Such an approach drew minimal attention
from local authorities. As Catholic numbers and confidence grew, they eventually wanted a proper sacred structure, which Mouly found the funds to build in
1836. By village standards, it was large and substantial with a stone foundation
and tile roof. It stood out for its size, quality of construction, and style, the first
of many European-looking ones constructed there. For both priests and congregations, a church gave them a sense of respectability and spiritual comfort,
making it clear to neighbors that they followed certain beliefs. In many places over a long period, priests used a Western design template that Catholics
saw not only as an architectural statement (these were not temples or kinship
halls) but as a declaration of having chosen a non-Chinese religious path.

Another aspect, a religio-political one, deserves mention. By the 1850s–
1860s, with proscription over and Catholics multiplying, missionary budgets
expanded and funds poured into projects that reflected wealth and power
such as the one supervised by Alphonse Favier in 1868 at Gaojia Village. He
and other confident priests declared their treaty-given right to be in any small
city or hamlet, and the congregation's right to worship in a sacred structure
that could stylistically be whatever they wanted. Tall, well-built rural churches
dominated neighborhoods of low-slung shoddy houses, their towering bell
towers visible from miles away.[1] And, if not seen, the periodic pealing of bells
reminded Catholics of worship and non-Catholics of their presence. According

---

1   In the interior, missionaries initially built chapels and other buildings "on the model of local
    dwellings." *Handbook of Christianity in China, Volume Two*, 736. The Vincentian record for
    Zhili/Hebei indicates that this was the case only when it was a temporary solution for quickly
    establishing a place of worship. As soon as circumstances allowed, and finances permitted,
    they constructed large European-style sacred structures.

FIGURE 8.1   Dakou Village church, Vicariate of Beijing, ca 1930s
            SOURCE: ARCHIVES CM, PARIS

FIGURE 8.2   Shiyaozi Village church, Zhangjiakou Diocese
            SOURCE: PHOTO BY AUTHOR, 2012

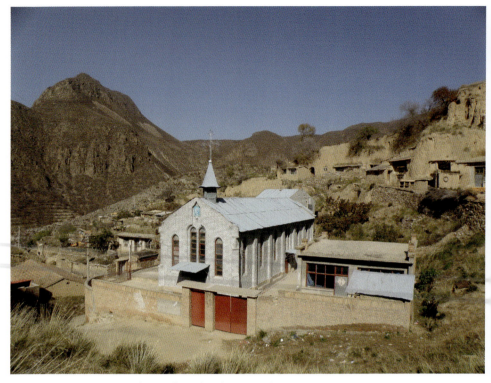

FIGURE 8.3   Huangtuliang Village church, Zhangjiakou Diocese
SOURCE: PHOTO BY AUTHOR, 2012

to an early twentieth century Scheutist missionary working in a northern border area adjacent to Zhili, "churches were the most important buildings of such
[rural] settlements: their crosses [and towers] expressed the religious identity
of the inhabitants and above all the success of the mission."[2] The statement
could have easily been made by a Vincentian, who would have agreed that the
religious aspect was explicit and the political portion (the mission's right to be
there) implicit. In the early twenty-first century, restored old and new churches still project special meanings. For Catholicism's followers, being Catholic
is spiritual and religious, as well as deeply personal. Suspicious government
authorities, however, view it as more than this and monitor worshippers when
they gather for mass or go on group pilgrimages.

---

2   Towers, in particular, stood out "as a radiant symbol of a successful [Catholic] Scheutist vil-
    lage" and as a counterstatement to Buddhist pagodas. Coomans and Luo, "Exporting Flemish
    Gothic Architecture," 229, 250.

We may wonder what Catholics think about their past and present situations. Many are very aware of their history and know the names of famous Western missionaries such as Ricci and certain nineteenth and twentieth century Vincentian bishops like Favier. They are cognizant, too, of the eighteenth-century controversy over the religio-cultural significance of ancestral rites that involved the pope, emperor, and Jesuits; the problems it caused; and another emperor's proscription of Christianity. Ignoring all of this, Catholics proudly display the imperially bestowed *wan you zhen yuan* on church façades and interpret it to mean "the true source of everything [is found in God]." They find the words to be religiously inspirational.[3] On another level, congregations preserve their history via stone memorials to those killed because of their religious affiliation, such as the one at Yongning for those murdered during the Boxer period. Posted in church lobbies are displays with narratives recounting their good and bad experiences. Diocesan and parish sponsored pamphlets and books provide historical information as well. Catholics have a good sense of their past role and a broad understanding of their place in modern China's rise.[4] They accomplish this through a reading of their own religious history and its intertwined politics, mostly without a persecution complex. This is an imperative when, as many are aware, the Party-State "constantly changes reality and history to its own favor."[5]

2   "Properly Stated" Churches

Vincentian bishops annually tallied for Paris and Rome the places of worship in their vicariates and treated only those of European style as "properly stated" churches. In their reports, they did not distinguish among them in design or architectural terms, though priests occasionally and privately might refer to them as Gothic. They did not need to go into details because Vincentians mostly hailed from France, with the images of those churches at home deeply imprinted on their minds. However, they did not attempt to replicate exactly

---

3   It is well-known as the Kangxi emperor's statement and, as such, there is some implied association with imperial greatness.

4   Regarding Chinese Protestants, one study finds them lacking in historical consciousness. Ryan Dunch, "Protestant Christianity in China Today: Fragile, Fragmented, Flourishing," in *China and Christianity: Burdened Past, Hopeful Future*, ed. Stephen Uhalley, Jr. and Xiaoxin Wu (Armonk, N.Y.: M. E. Sharpe, 2000), 207–208.

5   "Seven Questions: Ai Weiwei," *Time*, 23 October 2017, 112. He is a famous contemporary artist and prominent (non-Catholic) activist.

French ones, which were typically tall intricate structures with stone vaults and flying buttresses. Vincentians (and those of other religious associations) preferred a variety of simple edifices in Western style. A study of Scheutist missionaries in China sums it up nicely: they built "medieval looking churches, because that was the style that expressed their [national] identity."[6] The same may be said for Vincentians, who prior to 1949 made the design decisions for their congregations, which accepted (and presumably agreed with) the choices made.[7] After 1979, with missionaries long gone, Chinese Catholics chose to rebuild churches as close as possible to their former appearance, giving special attention to their façades. They also built new ones in the same general Western styles as before. In Hebei, people have had the choice of constructing sacred structures of any style from Chinese-influenced to post-modern, but the type brought to them by Vincentians years earlier predominates.

Another point about the "properly stated" old churches of this study is that the survivors are almost all post-1900 buildings; notable exceptions are Tianjin's 1872 Church of St. Louis, Beijing's 1888 North Church, and several in rural areas.[8] Many rebuilt after the Boxer destruction copied previous versions and those renovated after 1979 modeled their façades, using photographs and good memories, on their last undamaged iterations. The façade is particularly important because, as pointed out at the study's outset, it is the congregation's public face in building form. Unlike human countenances, the façades of "properly stated" churches came in four general architectural styles, and each of Beijing's four historic sacred edifices (North, South, East, and West Churches) illustrates this. Using a typology based on Beijing's does not mean that other churches were specifically modeled on them.[9] Rather, it helps reveal

---

6   Coomans and Luo, "Exporting Flemish Gothic Architecture," 225–227, 246–249.

7   A Catholic priest born in Hebei in 1926, told me that "church style was what Vincentian priests wanted. They built with the [European] traditional steeple or bell tower wanting it to look like a church, not a house or temple." He expressed no opinion about liking or disliking the style, instead stating three times that Chinese Catholics (of the pre-1949 era) "did not dare disobey their priests in that there was a great distance [in relationship] between them [because] the status of priests was too high." Among the elderly, such sentiments are common. Author's field notes, 26 September 2011.

8   Xiheying's dates to 1889, Anjia's to 1893, Baisha's to 1895, and one at Zhangjia possibly to the late nineteenth century. A few more pre-1900 ones will surely be found in rural areas.

9   There are two exceptions to this statement. Yongning's "Little North Church" obviously refers to the one in Beijing with which it has a few architectural similarities. Similarly, the "Minor South Church (Xiao Nantang)" at the village (*cun*) of Xihulin in Beijing's suburbs reminds people of its urban version. *Beijing Tianzhu jiaohui*, item entitled "Xihulin Sheng Mu wuranyuanzui jiaotang."

the variety of types within a particular style, and the fact that for missionaries different façades were a "compromise between what was wanted and what was possible to erect."[10] The examples provided below include a number enclosed by parentheses that refers to the chapter in which it is discussed and where there are illustrations.

Urban Sites	Rural Sites

1) Flat façade, primarily of a single plane, with no bell tower. (Façades range from relatively plain to complex; lower costs made them the most popular sub-style.)

Urban Sites	Rural Sites
South Church (3)	Housangyu (4)
Zizhulin (5)	Xiheying (6)
	Anjia (6)
	Baisha (6)

2) Façade with one bell tower whose front side merges with the building's main plane, or the tower is attached to the façade's central section. (More expensive than flat façades yet commonplace.)

Urban Sites	Rural Sites
West Church (3)	Xin (6)
Nangangzi (3)	Pingfang, Lijiao (4);
	Zhuozhou area (7)[11]

3) Façade with two towers or tower-like additions that exceed the façade's highest center point. (The extra materials and labor to build upward add to construction costs.)

Urban Sites	Rural Sites
North Church (3)	Baoding (6)
St. Michael's (3)	Xiwanzi (6)
Xikai (5)	Zhangjia (6)
Xuanhua (6)	Zhuozhou area (7)[12]

---

10 Missionaries made compromises based on workers' expertise, available materials, size, design aesthetics, and the total cost. Cody, "Striking a Harmonious Chord," 24–25.

11 Those of this style were at Zhuozhou City and at the villages of Xigao, Xixianpo, Jen, Lijiao, Sige, and Xilichi.

12 Those of this style were at the town of Changgou and at the villages of Shiwo and Shijiawu.

4) Façade with three towers, the center one usually the tallest. (The most intricate design, and, depending on particulars, the most expensive.)

East Church (3)   Xiaohan (5)
Wanghailou (5)

To accentuate the point, "properly stated" churches meant, by missionaries' definition, only those of European style. Historical materials, photographs, and extensive travels in Beijing and Tianjin Municipalities as well as in Hebei led me to these churches.[13] Vincentian missionaries simply did not build a blended type or style. Today, a church looks like, according to a priest working in a rural area outside Beijing, what the parishioners want—in this case, a simple façade with a tower.[14] It should be added that the style may be what the pastor or his bishop wants. After making a pilgrimage to a post-1980 church in Shanxi Province famous for its incorporation of Qing-era imperial design features, a Hebei priest came away impressed that it exemplified Catholicism's indigenization. When he asked for permission to model a parish sacred structure after it, his bishop told him it would be too expensive to build.[15] Even though size and stylistic details impact the financial side of things, it appears compromise may be possible. Following a familiar profile, the entry gate and front of a post-1980 rural church in Dingxing County (central Hebei) suggests another option by adding modest Chinese design features and bright paint colors, especially red. These appear to be neither extravagantly appointed nor expensive. In 2018, the congregation remodeled the façade, retaining its distinctively traditional style

---

13 This is not to deny the existence of Sino-Western and Chinese style churches in the area under study or in other areas in China. Vincentians built one in Jiangxi with a distinctive southern flair at the village (*cun*) of Pinglushang near Ganzhou City, sometime in the 1910s–1920s. Other religious groups did the same in their vicariates. The Foreign Missionary Society of Paris erected one in Guiyang City, Guizhou in 1850. Twenty-five years later, they replaced it with an elaborate façade that incorporated colorful minority designs. Known to residents as the North Catholic Church, it still stands. *Guiyang bei tianzhutang* (Guiyang: n.p., n.d.), Church internal circulation material, book; and Author's field notes, 5 September 2016. The Catholic Foreign Mission Society of America adapted Chinese temples' features for use on churches starting in the 1920s even though it increased the costs. Jean-Paul Wiest, *Maryknoll in China: A History, 1918–1955* (Armonk, N.Y.: M. E. Sharpe, 1988), 281–286.

14 Author's field notes, 30 September 2011.

15 The priest implicitly agreed on the economics. He did observe that it was sometimes too easy to emphasize outside appearance and ignore a congregation's deep faith. Peng Jiandao, *Xinyang ganwu*, 222. "Expensive" is always a relative term. Prior to 1949, "indigenous style" churches cost more than others. Cody, "Striking a Harmonious Chord," 23.

FIGURE 8.4 Shizhu Village church, Dingxing County, Baoding Diocese
SOURCE: PHOTO BY FRIEND OF AUTHOR, 2016

gate that is part of the surrounding wall. Except for the gate, it seems more like
the types Vincentian missionaries once preferred, and which continue to be
favored by Hebei's varied congregations.[16]

---

16   Photograph taken at the village (*cun*) of Shizhu in 2016. "Dingxing Shizhu cun tianzhu-
     tang," http://blog.sina.com.cn/s/blog_87ca2ce40102vyd5.html (accessed 15 June 2017).
     Inevitably, economic growth will further alter rural Hebei and as residents become
     wealthier their tastes may change. Prosperous Shanghai stands out for its large number of
     churches, many of them having contemporary designs. *Jinri Tianzhujiao Shanghai jiaoqu*
     (Shanghai: Tianzhujiao Shanghai jiaoqu Guangqishe chubanshe, 2000).

FIGURE 8.5 The Shizhu church after recent renovations
SOURCE: PHOTO BY FRIEND OF AUTHOR, 2018

3   Interpreting Churches

Prior to 1949 Catholicism had firmly established itself, but not without controversy. Missionaries proceeded aggressively, measuring progress by the number of places of worship they built among "pagans," the conversion of whom
proved to be limited due to Chinese opposition to their proselytization techniques and activities. Ordinary Chinese castigated their Catholic neighbors for
using priests to intervene unfairly in disputes or lawsuits that often had more
to do with matters of everyday life than religion.[17] They thought Catholics
acted like opportunists, whether in seeking help or receiving a handout, and
smeared them as "rice Christians" and "wannabes," or even worse considered

---

17   Sweeten, *Christianity in Rural China*, 3–7.

them walking "dead devils" (*sigui*)—those devoid of all morality and deserving of death.[18] Traditional Chinese elites for their part saw missionaries as power-hungry rivals determined to erode their influence over local society via judicial interventions or involvement in philanthropic and educational activities. Non-Catholics generally felt victimized.[19] Consequently, self-contained incidents, that is, "[Christian] religious cases," sometimes became larger-scale occurrences with opponents burning churches and giving Christians the option of apostasy or death. Qing officials and Western diplomats tried to settle cases as tension mounted.

In the early twentieth century, a few priests realized that Catholicism had barely survived a near catastrophe with the Boxer Uprising, and, if it wanted to move forward, would need to revise its approach to proselytization. Vincent Lebbe, C.M., an impressionable young man, arrived in China in 1901 to witness personally the suffering that people had just experienced and learn of the Vincentians' huge infrastructural losses.[20] He gradually formulated a critical view of Catholicism's past work in China, opining that missionaries had for too long dominated religious life by putting a foreign imprint on architecture, art, congregational activities—virtually everything. Even worse than Western priests' domination of the Church hierarchy was their treatment of their Chinese confreres as mere supporters, not equals.[21] The pope agreed and dispatched Archbishop Celso Costantini to China as apostolic delegate. During his stay (1922–1933), he observed a foreign-led Church with foreign-looking sacred edifices and icons that affected, he believed, the very way Chinese people related to Catholicism. To thrive spiritually in China, he believed missionaries had to adapt by first having Chinese bishops take over the vicariates and home-grown priests replace Western missionaries. Under native leaders, places of worship would then change to mirror architecturally and aesthetically Chinese

---

18   Cohen, *History in Three Keys*, 164. The term is found in Chinese materials included in *The Cause of the Riots in the Yangtze Valley*, 6 and "Picture VI."

19   Western missionaries and Chinese Catholics almost always saw themselves as the victims and claimed as such in yamen courts. An examination of many "[Christian] Religious Cases," including Tianjin's, leads one scholar to wonder how the Christian concept of "exhorting people to do good" caused widespread indignation. In the conflict that occurred, he asks: "Who were the defendants?" The answer, from one politically correct Chinese perspective, is that Western missionaries and Chinese Christians caused problems and should be held accountable. Gu Changsheng, *Chuanjiaoshi*, 126–155.

20   From the mid-nineteenth century, Vincentians (and others) had emphasized the construction of churches and an infrastructure to support them. Chapter 1, notes 3 and 5.

21   Young, *Ecclesiastical Colony*, 180–184.

CHAPTER 8

tastes.[22] Over time, Catholicism would then be fully integrated into China's cultural and physical landscape.

This was the direction that Costantini, Lebbe, and others wanted to go.[23] The process formally began in 1926, when the pope created three vicariates—one was at Xuanhua—each was led by a Chinese bishop. Western missionaries stayed active as the numbers of Chinese priests began to increase, most working in rural areas. They participated in a religious resurgence that had begun after the Boxers, with numbers reaching unprecedented heights as Chinese pastors established "quasi-parishes." Delayed by the Sino-Japanese War, the stage had been set for China to leave, in 1946, its mission stage for a regularized place and role within the Church. Many dioceses were formed, their transition to another stage of development halted by the rise of "New China" and its leaders' thirty-year agenda of mass movements directed against perceived remnants of harmful feudal thinking and outside influences. During this time, the Vatican's role in Chinese Catholic affairs virtually disappeared.

Since the 1980s, the Catholic Patriotic Association has in conjunction with government authorities returned former churches (and other properties) to diocesan control. In doing so, they dictated neither how congregations could renovate them nor what should be the style of new ones. During this crucial transitional time, why did conservative sociopolitical forces that saw churches as symbols of cultural imperialism not demand that they assume a different look? Moreover, why did other authorities identify some older ones as being part of China's cultural heritage, attaching to them plaques that gave them a special status and implied protection? One answer may be that authorities overestimated their ability to control public opinion during a time when a robust economy has given people more and more personal choices. Tastes and fads have proved problematic, as evidenced by the many non-baptized couples that seek out old and new churches as backdrops for wedding photographs—arrangements made by studios that pay for access.[24] Brides and grooms worry less about cost than aesthetics and the creation of special memories. Several

---

22 Frederick C. Dietz, "Chinese Christian Art," *Cath-M Annals PF* 10, no. 5 (May 1933): 145–146. Costantini did not explain how Chinese Catholics would compensate the various vicariates (that is, the congregations and orders) for their enormous property investments, which included large mission centers with sturdy sacred structures, residential housing for priests and staff, schools, foundling homes, clinics, and hospitals. Nor did Costantini take into consideration what ordinary people of that time might want their churches to look like, a point brought up by Professor R.G. Tiedemann, email to the author, 7 October 2017.

23 Young, *Ecclesiastical Colony*, 224–232.

24 Author's field notes, 17 October 2011.

brides have told me that they are there because churches are "beautiful," a subjective view given without qualification.[25] To them, churches are an aesthetic part of their heritage; if they are aware of what people once considered them to represent, they do not care.[26]

Congregations are comparatively more aware than the public at large of Catholicism's past ties to the West's invasion of China. Individuals know something about their parish churches' origins via bulletin boards and commemorative pamphlets that give historical details and reproduce old photographs. Authors of these materials typically and proudly describe them as "Gothic" and "Western style," not concerned about what message this might convey. Use of such terms seems to suggest a lingering influence in that it is close to missionaries' former definition of a "properly stated" church. Another trend is to say that current ones are of a harmoniously combined or "blended Chinese-Western style" (Zhong Xi hebi shi) even though they look similar to the purported Gothic ones. This may be a nominal adjustment suggesting that politically-correct labels matter. Years ago, Costantini wanted the construction of churches in a "Sino-Christian" style.[27] The archbishop assumed this is what the Chinese of his day wanted—he, of course, had no way to foresee what future generations would prefer. Contrary to his view that its architecture needed to change for Catholicism to flower in China, congregations with "old" style sacred structures are flourishing.[28]

---

25   Author's field notes, 30 September 2007; 23 September 2008; 16 October 2008; and 17 October 2011.

26   Millennials and the next generation are only vaguely aware that the Chinese government tries to keep certain issues (e.g., imperialism and Chinese sovereignty) historically current to generations unaffected by them. If authorities can politicize the discourse on unequal treaties to help define and redefine the Chinese nation's past, then I would ask: how are people supposed to reconcile Christianity's perceived place in the treaties and accusations of cultural imperialism, with its actual physical and spiritual place in modern Chinese society? Tension results from the contradiction. One scholar's ideas regarding the role of the treaty system in this is relevant. Wang, *China's Unequal Treaties*, 124–129, 135–138.

27   Coomans, "A pragmatic approach to church construction in Northern China," 105.

28   This is true in Hebei and other provinces. In the early nineteenth century, Vincentians worked in Hubei before withdrawing to focus on other areas. Franciscans took charge of the province, later giving over one part to the Missionary Society of St. Columban. One of its priests remarked that "it seems that the Roman Catholic communities [congregations] in Hanyang, small, struggling, yet remarkably sturdy, are the fruit of the Columban mission there." Collins, *The Splendid Cause*, 135. The Hanyang area's churches and vibrant congregations indicate more success than what he suggests. Author's field notes, 13–14 September 2016.

4   Places of Memory

Becoming unencumbered, as much as it is possible, from various assumptions about churches makes it possible to move in another direction and consider how they occupy the mind as memories—whether as general physical places of religious practices or as the specific sites of events, both subject to the influences of time and interpretation. In different ways, memories constitute an important part of human existence. They are important to individuals and communities of individuals not to mention institutions and governments. No matter the context, memories are in constant flux, some convincingly genuine, some unverifiable. Given their mutable, subjective, even ephemeral form they are difficult to grasp. Connecting them to certain places or sites such as churches is one way to parse their importance.

Take, for instance, places of memory that are tied to nation-building, the sites that occupy mental space and activate some groups' civic feelings about a nation's formative moments and its people's patriotic feelings about them. In France, the Bastille, and in America, Boston Harbor have automatic meanings with people intuitively recognizing their revolutionary context and importance. Likewise, in the emergence of modern China, locations, events, and memories have been conflated. Most Chinese immediately recognize what is meant when certain years and places are alluded to such as 1860 Beijing's Summer Palace (Yuanmingyuan demolished by Anglo-French imperialists attacking China), 1870 Tianjin's Wanghailou church (burned by Chinese protesting the West's political-cultural invasion), and 1937 "Rape of Nanjing" (Japanese soldiers' brutal treatment and mass murder of civilians). The Tianjin case of 1870 was particularly difficult to resolve because Chinese had reacted to what they thought was missionaries' cruel treatment of children. Westerners remembered it as a "massacre," as an example of barbaric Chinese behavior. Bishops and diplomats deemed the dynasty's indemnification for lost property and lives insufficient and demanded "moral reparations" in the form of punishments for the perpetrators, formal apologies, a rebuilt church, and an imperially sanctioned public memorial inscribed to indicate Chinese culpability. Qing officials begrudgingly assumed accountability, not hesitating to castigate missionaries for their *moral responsibility* (my words and italics) in precipitating conflict that often led to violence. A place of memory may be subject to different interpretations.

Chinese still call it the "Tianjin [Christian] Religious Case," general details of which are known by many with help from textbooks, scholarly publications, political tracts, and government sources. Nationalistic and patriotic lessons have replaced moral embellishments, as can be seen in the stone monument sitting to the side of the Wanghailou church. Erected by Tianjin authorities in 1997, it is the only one of its kind in China. It provides a modern, official Chinese perspective on what happened and why. Clearly, the Tianjin government considers the monument valuable in sustaining the site as a public place with educational value. Online informational sites and blogs in Chinese keep memories of Tianjin religio-political events current. Bloggers acting as amateur historians plagiarize all the same sources (and each other) to highlight how missionaries caused trouble and how the patriotic masses defended themselves—and China. Internet censors have no reason to interfere with the electronic reinforcement of these active memories.

Tianjin's Catholics are certainly conscious of past and present opinions regarding 1870 (and 1900) and find silence to be an effective defense. A low profile is helpful as well. Wanghailou church is situated in Tianjin's central area at a busy intersection near "Culture Street" and its popular souvenir shops. Visits by camera-toting domestic tourists are discouraged, and problems minimized, by keeping the main gate closed and locked between times when religious services are held. It seems that Wanghailou's priests have opted to be careful. They know that just one mile away religious sisters and authorities are embroiled in a property dispute over the site of their Memorial Chapel (to the 1870 incident). Non-Catholics are aware of and have been influenced by these controversies. Those of the millennial generation, unlike others at churches I have visited, stay away. Not once have I observed a bride and groom using either it or Wanghailou's publicly accessible façade as a backdrop for photographs.

Each sacred structure has its own history and associated memories. Take, for examples, Tianjin's Xikai church, which had a divisive—albeit non-violent— beginning as part of the French concession's expansion, and Beijing's East Church, which has a long history including destruction by Boxers in 1900. The two share a discernible connection to Catholicism's forced presence, the Xikai one often criticized online as epitomizing Church aggression. It is easier to see that Internet articles and blogs treat churches as remnants of Western imperialism than it is to gauge their influence on specific situations. Why has one of the East Church's adjoining buildings been tagged with anti-religious graffiti, and not others elsewhere?[29] Putting negative images of them aside, these two have other things in common. Both sit prominently near or at the end of long, broad streets that serve as pedestrian shopping areas. Various retail stores attract thousands of locals and domestic tourists who generate huge revenues, with real estate values skyrocketing. For the churches, heavy foot traffic has been good (exposing non-believers to religious space) and bad (subjecting the

---

29   Author's field notes, 27 October 2011.

sanctuary to camera-toting and snack-eating visitors). The Xikai church, which
has a security wall, and the East Church, which does not, keep doors open during the day. At each, docents welcome countless numbers of visitors cheerfully
answering questions and dispersing literature. The East one is a popular venue
for wedding photographs; Xikai's is not.

Two other factors deserve mention. First, neither the Xikai nor the East
Church has a government-sponsored monument explaining its history, like at
the Wanghailou church. The government is cognizant that it is unnecessary
to single out every example in order to sustain a "collective memory of the
Chinese past" that legitimizes its (and the Party's) position.[30] Second, and this
is increasingly important, domestic tourists, most of whom are not Catholic,
go to urban centers like Beijing and Tianjin and visit not only historic sites
like former imperial palaces and old churches but also post-1949 memorials,
museums, and malls. In the process, they take away a jumble of impressions
with few going home with holiday memories that revolve around past national
shames and mass political movements: people understand why the government stresses such matters. When on holiday, most want to see interesting
places and go to good restaurants—in short, have a nice time. According to
one study, famous places of memory (old churches included) imbued with
State-oriented narratives are thus subject to a counter-position or perspective
that is based on apolitical, personal experiences.[31]

At lesser-known rural churches that few tourists visit, congregations keep
religious memories alive in significant ways. Chapter 4 told of a family at
Jiahoutuan who lived through mass movements and the Cultural Revolution,
somehow preserving a 1920s-era tattered book on Catholic experiences during
the Boxer period. The book is no longer hidden, has been mimeographed, and
is proudly shared. It is noted that in the 1960s, Yongning's Catholics buried a
stone tablet inscribed with the names of people that had died in 1900. The
marker has been placed at a prominent place close to the church's main entrance. The book and marker are reminders of prior hardships and of events
worthy of remembrance. Other congregations have preserved photographs to
serve as further proof of their history. Online blogs post copies of these photographs, some made from the 1936–1937 report referred to in Chapter 7's discussion of Zhuozhou.[32] Catholics in rural areas know how to survive and how

30   The Chinese Communist Party's need to have "legitimacy and patriotic credentials" has
      changed over time and continues to do so. Wang, *China's Unequal Treaties*, 138.
31   Marc Andre Matten, ed. *Places of Memory in Modern China: History, Politics, and Identity.*
      (Leiden: Brill, 2012), 7.
32   One blog focuses on those in Langfang and is unusually thorough in terms of outlin-
      ing a history of the area's various churches supported by photos of former and current

to preserve their faith. Add to that the power of living memories associated with the Church and churches. Rites of baptism, marriage, and death are life events emotionally imprinted on the participants and, as such, constitute an important individual-level discourse that will be preserved in private journals and biographies.

5   Our Lady of China

Any discussion of Catholicism in China must note Mary's venerated place. In the early 1600s, Ricci opened a women's chapel in Beijing dedicated to her, the start of a gradually increasing emphasize on her so as to aid proselytization during that century and the next. In the nineteenth century, Vincentians played a prominent part in showing her religious place. Bishop Mouly wrote and published in 1859 a Chinese-style bound book entitled "Divine Mary's Holy Month" (*Sheng Mu sheng yue*). His Vincentian successors deemed the contents so important that they reprinted it in four subsequent editions.[33] At about the same time across the world at Lourdes, French country people had just established a shrine to the Blessed Virgin Mary, which the pope formally approved in 1862. Six years later a Jesuit priest built a shrine dedicated to her at Sheshan (Shanghai), the chapel associated with it shortly thereafter replaced by a basilica.[34] Louis-Gabriel Delaplace worked in China for thirty-eight years and actively promoted Mary to the faithful whenever he visited congregations. He did this in Henan, Jiangxi, and Zhejiang (1846–1870) and, especially, in the Vicariate of Beijing and Zhili North, which he led as bishop from 1870 until his death fourteen years later.[35] Like Mouly, he authored and disseminated publications in Chinese concerning "Our Lady of Mount Carmel, the Sacred Heart of Mary and the Holy Rosary." Worship of Mary became easier at the North Church when the bishop had a tall altar dedicated to her.[36] Catholics everywhere, especially women, were steadily attracted to Mary.

---

ones. "Langfang tianzhutang," http://blog.sina.com.cn/s/blog_71ea7d850102xlcd.html (accessed 13 January 2017).

33   Priests republished it in 1891, 1903, 1923, and 1928. Van den Brandt, *Catalogue des principaux ouvrages*, 18.

34   "History of the Shrine to Our Lady of Sheshan," http://www.fides.org/en/news/14510#.WKY_gBH2zok; "Sheshan Basilica," https://en.wikipedia.org/wiki/Sheshan_Basilica; and "Our Mother of Sheshan," https://en.wikipedia.org/wiki/Our_Mother_of_Sheshan (all accessed 20 February 2017).

35   Van den Brandt, *Les Lazaristes*, 51–52.

36   Chambon, *Vie et Apostolat*, 266–267.

In Zhili, the first and most important site dedicated to Mary arose not far from Baoding at Donglü Village. During the 1860s Vincentian priests had opened a chapel for the approximately fifty converts living there. More success came in the early to mid-1890s when Stanislas-François Jarlin raised the number to about six hundred, with more in neighboring communities. By 1897 Donglü had a small sacred structure and its own pastor. A few years later, with Boxers on the horizon, he organized about one thousand Catholics at the church in defense of life and property. A large, well-armed Boxer force repeatedly attacked them over two months in 1900. One day during these desperate times, Catholics reported seeing a woman dressed in white hovering over the steeple. Deciding that an apparition of Mary had come to protect them, they resolved to fight hard to save their church and village. According to later Catholic accounts, when Boxers withdrew in August they reported having seen her, and that this had caused them to hold back their attacks.[37]

In 1901, grateful worshippers of Donglü, believing that Mary's spiritual intervention had been instrumental in saving them, replaced the existing small church with a larger one dedicated to her.[38] The pastor, Louis Giron, C.M., helped channel their faith by commissioning a Chinese Catholic to compose a painting of Mary holding Jesus as a child, which he hung behind the altar. The congregation knew it as the "Portrait of the Queen of Donglü, Holy Mary" (Donglü zhi hou Sheng Mu xiang). Seven years later in 1908, René Flament, C.M., became pastor and ordered a new version by a French artist, who presented the figures with Chinese countenances and wearing imperial-style robes. It replaced the first portrait. Above it was written, "Holy [Mary,] Mother of God, Queen of Donglü, pray for us" (Tianzhu Sheng Mu Donglü zhi hou *wei women qi*).[39] Jarlin later served as the Vicariate of Beijing and Zhili North's bishop and authorized it as an invocation to be "repeated ... at the end of all common prayers."[40] The village's fame quickly spread far and wide with other Catholics establishing various shrines to Mary.[41]

---

37   J.M. Tremorin, "Pilgrimages to Our Lady of Tong-Lu: The 'Lourdes' of China," *Cath-M Annals PF* 10, no. 5 (May 1933): 142–144; and *Jingli Donglü shengmu shihua* (Baoding: Baoding jiaoqu mu'enmeiti zixun zhongxin, 2012), 14–18.

38   The European-style structure measured 180 feet long by 51 wide with twin towers each 75 feet high. Japanese troops destroyed it in 1941. *Jingli Donglü shengmu shihua*, 36–37.

39   *Jingli Donglü shengmu shihua*, 37–42. Ferreux refers to her as "Notre-Dame de Tong-Lu" in his *Histoire*, 421–424; and "Dong-Lu Shrine," https://www.udayton.edu/imri/mary/d/dong-lu-shrine.php (accessed 20 February 2017).

40   Tremorin, "Pilgrimages," 143.

41   Most notably people at Housangyu believed that Mary helped save them from the Boxers and established a shrine for her. Presently, almost every Catholic church in Beijing, Tianjin, and Hebei has a courtyard sacred grotto dedicated to Mary. Author's field notes, various dates, 2005–2018.

FIGURE 8.6 "Donglü, Altar of Our Lady of China"
SOURCE: PLANCHET, LES MISSIONS DE CHINE, 1935

东闾圣母像
绘于1901年

东闾圣母像
绘于1908年

中华圣母像

东闾圣母像绘于1992年

FIGURE 8.7 Our Lady, four presentations. Clockwise, starting upper left, "Our Lady of Donglü, painted in 1901;" "Our Lady of Donglü, painted in 1908;" "Our Lady of Donglü, painted in 1992;" and "Our Lady of China."

SOURCE: *JINGLI DONGLÜ SHENG MU SHIHUA*

FIGURE 8.8 A popular version of Our Lady of China
SOURCE: XIKAI CATHEDRAL GIFT SHOP,
PHOTOGRAPHIC COPY BY AUTHOR, 2016

In recognition of the trend, Church leaders at a Shanghai bishops' synod in 1924, announced the consecration of the Chinese people to the Blessed Virgin Mary. The bishops selected a painting almost identical to the 1908 version in Donglü that would personify her under a unifying title, "Our Lady of China" (Zhonghua Sheng Mu). In 1928, the pope formally approved use of the image and four years later made Donglü an official Marian shrine site.[42] With attention to Mary growing, and her connection to a well-established and centrally located congregation firmly established, the bishop of the Vicariate of Baoding thought Donglü should become an official pilgrimage site.[43] Archbishop

---

42   It is one of two, the other being Our Lady, Help of Christians at Sheshan, Shanghai.
43   The practice of visiting a special place as an act of devotion or veneration belongs to Chinese-Buddhist and Christian traditions. For the latter, it is traceable back to historic

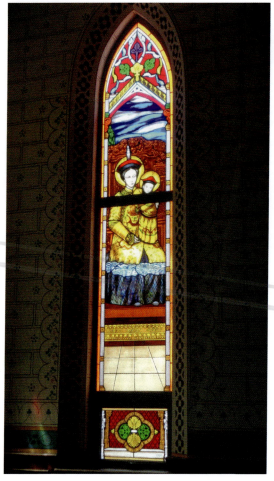

FIGURE 8.9 New stained-glass of Our Lady of China,
Beijing's North Church
SOURCE: PHOTO BY AUTHOR, 2018

Costantini wanted to see Catholicism sinicized and fully agreed because both
the Church and Chinese would benefit. The pope decided that since May was
already Mary's month, this would be the best time for people to celebrate her
through devotional pilgrimages.[44] People had already established a tradition

_____

      sites in the Holy Land devoted to Jesus and some later ones in Europe. Naquin and Yü,
      Pilgrims and Sacred Sites in China, 499–564, give several examples.

44   The pope later added to the liturgical calendar a feast day in May for Our Lady of China.
      In 1973, it became the day preceding the second Sunday of May.

FIGURE 8.10   Donglü Village church, today. The history of Catholicism at the Donglü church,
with special attention to events of 1900, is inscribed on white stone slabs
located to each side of the main entrance.
SOURCE: PHOTO BY AUTHOR, 2013

FIGURE 8.11   Pavilion for "Queen of Donglü"
              SOURCE: PHOTO BY AUTHOR, 2013

of going to the Donglü shrine before the first "official" pilgrimage occurred on 7 May 1929, when over thirty priests and an estimated ten thousand Catholics from hundreds of congregations participated. The next year it was fifteen thousand; then twenty-five thousand the following year.[45] In 1936, thirty-five thousand believers went there.[46] These were sizable numbers for a community of four thousand to handle (even though Catholics composed 80 percent of the residents and it was the Vincentians' largest "Christian village" in Hebei).[47] They somehow accommodated everyone.

The Donglü pastor announced in 1938 that pilgrimages would not take place that year, and, in fact, they stopped for the duration of the Sino-Japanese and Civil Wars. After the 1949 revolution, authorities began closing churches and curtailing visits to all religious shrines. Forty years passed before Donglü's Catholics began building a church that the bishop dedicated to Our Lady in 1992.[48] Reestablishment as a pilgrimage site did not come as easily. The area's authorities tolerated worship at the same time not wanting an influx of pilgrims, who were seen as potentially dangerous outsiders participating in non-sanctioned activities. Government control proved difficult as Catholics have gained confidence about publicly practicing their faith as improved modes of transportation and higher wages made travel a practical option. Pilgrimage to Donglü quickly gained popularity, and it once again became Hebei's, if not China's, most famous site, with numerous Catholics from all over visiting. In May 1995, an estimated fifty thousand people gathered there to honor Mary. The next year, Baoding's Public Security Bureau requested help from the army to stop outsiders from visiting, an effort that had limited success. Thousands still go during the month of May, even though police set up checkpoints on the main routes and only allow residents to pass through. Locals and veteran visitors know the side roads and guide pilgrims to Donglü. People make the trip for a variety of devotional and personal reasons, some even quietly advocating greater religious freedom.[49] Whatever the reason for going to Donglü, many believe Mary saved the village in 1900 and residents consider her "Our Lady of China, Queen of Donglü." These sentiments are part of the Catholic history

45   Tremorin, "Pilgrimages," 143.
46   Ferreux, *Histoire de la Congrégation*, 424.
47   Tremorin, "Pilgrimages," 143.
48   It took three years to build due to its size (222 feet long, 59 wide, and 141 high) and cost. *Zhonghua Shengmu chaoshengdi* (Donglü: n.p., ca 2013), Church internal circulation material, pamphlet.
49   In the Baoding section of Chapter 6, I mentioned my own experience. For the personal account of a pilgrimage from Daming to a site in Henan Province, see Bao Lu, *Handan Tianzhujiao shilue*, 157–160.

proudly inscribed on the white marble that is prominently part of the church's front exterior wall on either side of the main entrance.[50]

Pilgrims visiting Donglü hold that Mary watches over not just them, rather she truly cares for everyone. Our Lady of China pilgrimage sites dot China with myriads of people visiting them annually, even in remote areas.[51] For those that do not make the trip, almost every urban and rural church has an inside altar for Mary, as well as a small outside pavilion or sacred grotto dedicated to her.[52] Such devotion has brought a certain amount of commercialization, which is a global phenomenon. At pilgrimage shrines (or in nearby church gift shops) Catholic and non-Catholic vendors sell religious accessories, such as popular card-size reproductions of Mary and one that is a colorful hologram. This is pointed out because religious beliefs expressed in a tangential, material way are relevant and part of the context.[53] The Vincentians' role in nurturing the development of a vibrant Marian movement within Hebei, which has now spread to almost every province, will forever be part of their legacy.

6   Looking Ahead

The administrative director of the Eastern Qing Mausoleums once told me that fire prevention was his primary concern for the various imperially constructed buildings, some dating back to the seventeenth century, under his care.[54] A related issue is maintenance, made difficult by the toll of time and of busloads of domestic tourists routinely ignoring rules that prohibit on-site smoking and eating. Indeed, one way or another, all historic structures are vulnerable. In July 2014, the Ningbo cathedral in Zhejiang built by Vincentians in 1872, suffered heavy damage, its roof and interior consumed by flames. Across the world in April 2019, flames engulfed Notre Dame in Paris. The façade, walls, and main towers of each, fortunately, did not fall. Ningbo's congregation has already rebuilt because of its religio-historical importance and stature while in France

---

50   Local Catholics carefully distinguish details of "their" portrait of her from that of Our Lady of China. *Jingli Donglü shengmu shihua*, 72–76; and *Zhonghua shengmu chaosheng-di.* Author's field notes, 28 September 2013.

51   For a list of major shrine sites, go to "Shrines in China," https://www.udayton.edu/imri/mary/s/shrines-in-china.php (accessed 10 January 2017).

52   Not frequently mentioned is that the one at Lourdes has been an inspiration. An exception to this is a display at the sacred grotto at the Xikai church. Author's field notes, 27 September 2016.

53   Investigating the things that grow out of religious practices is a complicated subject, a focal point of material religion studies.

54   Author's field notes, 19 September 2007.

massive donations have allowed for planning of what will be a multi-year restoration project. The troubling issue of how to protect the world's historic churches remains. In China, the danger is not just fire but economic development (private and public projects) that leads to the encroachment of commercial buildings onto high-value religious property—Beijing's East Church a case in point. Planned growth and zoning may also threaten a rural church's existence, as has occurred at Baisha Village.

Unique to China is the situation regarding sacred structures the government confiscated and has not returned to Catholics' control. To illustrate, on the spacious grounds of a large public hospital in Zhengding is the site of the city's first chapel, built in the 1860s.[55] Vincentians added other buildings and by the mid-1920s had constructed a large cathedral there.[56] Currently devoid of religious icons, the building is in good condition and used for storage or sometimes as an auditorium. Outside it there is a small stone memorial erected to honor several Vincentian priests who perished during a Japanese attack in 1937.[57] There are also unreturned properties such as the dilapidated and vacant churches at Changgou, Shijiawu, Xigao, and other villages. For diocesan leaders, ownership of real estate in a locality is of economic and logistic advantage because it is a place where they may easily return and reopen a church. Once congregations reemerge, this will happen. And, with the trend in nearby areas being one of growth and expansion, it may occur relatively soon. Already hundreds of congregations have either reopened former churches or built new ones, some in the suburbs of Beijing and Tianjin, most in Hebei's rural areas. In one of Xuanhua City's outlying neighborhoods several churches stand not far from one another, each recently built in a general style that people find familiar (and consider Gothic). Whatever stylistic label is applied, these churches are not out of place; instead they are a part of the locale's religious life and the province's cultural setting. Whether old or new, urban or rural, churches reflect Catholic spirituality in China.

---

55   The site had buildings once used by the Jiaqing emperor during a visit and has been described as an "imperial palace." The bishop of the Vicariate of Zhili Central converted part of one building into a chapel and later a church. He considered Chinese cession of the property a significant statement regarding Catholicism's right to be there as defined by treaty and imperial edicts. Anouilh letter, 16 January 1866, *Annals PF* 28 (1867): 369–370.

56   De Moerloose designed the cathedral. Coomans and Luo, "Exporting Flemish Gothic Architecture," 229.

57   Author's field notes, 8 May 2010.

Chinese Catholics, Estimates

TABLE A1.1 Chinese Catholics, estimates (with added information)

Year	China	Zhili/Hebei (entire province)	Beijing[1]
c. 1600	1,000	100	0
c. 1700[2]	200,000	23,000	2,000
c. 1800	200,000[3]	20,000[4]	700[5]
c. 1900	600,000–720,000[6]	126,000–150,000[7]	25,000[8]
c. 1950	3,400,000[9]	800,000[10]	50,000
c. 2000	8,000,000[11]	750,000	50,000[12]
At present	9,000,000–12,000,000[13]	1,000,000–1,500,000[14]	75,000–100,000[15]

1 This includes those living close to but outside the walled city through 1950, which thereafter may be termed "suburbs." Post-1950 figures are for the municipality of Beijing.

2 For 1700 and 1800 and only Zhili, see *Handbook of Christianity in China, Volume One*, 385–386. I have rounded off dates and numbers.

3 *Handbook of Christianity in China, Volume Two*, 214.

4 In 1785, according to one estimate, about fifteen thousand Catholics lived in Zhili. Planchet [A. Thomas, pseud.], *Histoire de la mission de Pékin*, 1:27. By the early 1800s, the scattered Christian population of the Beijing Diocese ranged from approximately forty to fifty thousand, about half of whom lived in Zhili and Beijing. Kenneth Scott Latourette, *A History of Christian Missions in China* (London: Society for the Promotion of Christian Knowledge, 1929), 183; and *Handbook of Christianity in China, Volume Two*, 116.

5 My estimate for 1800 is based on Mouly who wrote that in 1787 there were 900 Christians in "la ville de Pékin" and in 1836 not more than 350. Mouly letter, 6 November 1836, *Annales CM-F* 4 (1838): 52–53. Mouly letter, Nov. 6, 1836, *Annals PF*, old series (1838): 398.

6 Latourette, *History of Christian Missions in China*, 537; and *Handbook of Christianity in China, Volume Two*, 239.

7 *Handbook of Christianity in China, Volume Two*, 962. It relies on the figures given by Joseph de Moidrey, *Carte des préfectures de Chine et de leur population chrétienne en 1911* (Chang-hai [Shanghai]: Imprimerie de la Mission Catholique, Orphelinat de T'ou-sè-wè, 1913), 4. Cordier, *Histoire des relations*, 3:472, cites the lower number for 1879. According to

Favier, prior to the Boxer Uprising there were forty-seven thousand Catholics in his vicariate with twenty thousand of them dying in 1900. Alphonse Favier, *The Heart of Pekin: Bishop A. Favier's Diary of the Siege May–August 1900*, ed. J. Freri (Boston: Marlier & Co., 1901), 2, 15. However, in a letter to the Holy See written in 1901, Favier counted six thousand Catholic victims. Young, *Ecclesiastical Colony*, 80. Since he sought reparations for the smaller number, it may be assumed to be the more accurate of the two. In 1911, the figure for the Vicariate of Beijing and Zhili North was approximately one hundred fourteen thousand Catholics with sixty-four thousand residing in Shuntian Prefecture, which encompassed the capital.

8   *Handbook of Christianity in China, Volume Two*, 962. We may note that the number of Catholic deaths during the Boxer period will never be known exactly, and that in the years following 1900 there was a tremendous increase in conversions to Catholicism (see Chapter 7). My estimates for Zhili and Beijing take this into consideration.

9   *Handbook of Christianity in China, Volume Two*, 522.

10   *Handbook of Christianity in China, Volume Two*, 978. For the Vincentian areas of Hebei, approximately four hundred and forty-five thousand, per Ferreux, *Histoire de la Congrégation*, 507–508.

11   This figure is for those affiliated with the "official Church." *Handbook of Christianity in China, Volume Two*, 815. It possibly and mistakenly includes those of the "unofficial Church."

12   Based on the 8 million figure, these are my estimates for Hebei and Beijing Municipality. For the early 2000s, the Beijing Diocese put its number at fifty thousand. *Beijing Tianzhu jiaohui*, item entitled "Beijing jiaoqu Mi'e'er Fu Tieshan zhujiao jinmu ershiwu zhounian."

13   Estimates range widely. The Pew Center puts the 2011 total at 9 million with 5.7 million belonging to the "official Church." The Holy Spirit Study Centre in Hong Kong uses a 12 million figure for 2012 without further breakdown. It suggests that since that year the number may have declined. "Catholic Church in China," https://en.wikipedia.org/wiki/Catholic_Church_in_China (accessed, 16 February 2018); and "The Decline of China's Catholic Population and its Impact on the Church," http://www.asianews.it/news-en/The-decline-of-China%E2%80%99s-Catholic-population-and-its-impact-on-the-Church-38373.html (accessed 16 February 2018). According to another source, there are from 9 to 10.5 million Church members. "Statistics of the Catholic Church in China (2016)," *China Church Quarterly* 106 (May 2017): 3.

14   "Hebei," https://en.wikipedia.org/wiki/Hebei (accessed 23 March 2017); and "Catholic Church in China," https://en.wikipedia.org/wiki/Catholic_Church_in_China (accessed 16 February 2018).

15   This is my estimate.

Additional Ecclesiastical Divisions for Zhili/Hebei

TABLE A2.1 Apostolic Vicariate of Beijing and Zhili North (formerly, Apostolic Vicariate of Zhili North and Apostolic Vicariate of Beijing), 1899–1946

Year	Area	Name
1899	Northeastern part detached from A.V.	A.V. of Zhili East; name changed to A.V. of Yongping, 1924; diocese, 1946
1910	West-central part detached from A.V.	A.V. of Zhili Central; name changed to A.V. of Baoding, 1924; reduced area becomes diocese, 1946
1912	Eastern part detached from A.V.	A.V. of Zhili Maritime; named changed to A.V. of Tianjin, 1924; diocese, 1946
1926	Northern part detached from A.V.	A.V. of Xuanhua; diocese, 1946

TABLE A2.2 Apostolic Vicariate of Baoding (formerly, Apostolic Vicariate of Zhili Central), 1924–1946

Year	Area	Name
1924	Southern part detached from A.V.	Apostolic Prefecture (A.P.) of Li County, 1924; becomes A.V. of Anguo, 1929; diocese, 1946
1929	Western part detached from A.V.	Independent Mission; becomes A.P. of Yi County, 1936

© KONINKLIJKE BRILL NV, LEIDEN, 2020 | DOI:10.1163/9789004416185_011

TABLE A2.3 Apostolic Vicariate of Zhengding (formerly, Apostolic Vicariate of Zhili Southwest), 1924–1946

Year	Area	Name
1929	Southern part detached from A.V.	A.P. of Zhao County, becomes A.V., 1932; diocese, 1946
1933	Far southern part detached from A.V.	A.P. of Xunde, 1933; becomes A.V., 1944; diocese, 1946

TABLE A2.4 Apostolic Vicariate of Xian County (formerly, Apostolic Vicariate of Zhili Southeast), 1924–1946

Year	Area	Name
1929	Southwestern part detached from A.V.	A.P. of Yongnian; becomes A.V., 1933; diocese, 1946
1935	Far southern part detached from A.V.	A.P. of Daming; diocese, 1946
1939	Southeastern part detached from A.V.	A.P. of Jing County; becomes A.V., 1945; diocese, 1946

Currency Exchange Rate Estimates

Year[1]	China	France	Great Britain	U.S.
1698	N/A	14.33 *livres*	1 gold guinea[2]	N/A
1700	1.0 tael[3]	5.0 *livres*[4]	£0.38[5]	N/A
1775	1.0 tael	7.5 *livres*[6]	£0.33–0.38[7]	N/A
1792			£0.28	$1.25[8]
1836	1.0 tael	Ff 7.0[9]	£0.28	$1.39[10]
1843		Ff 25.0	£1.0[11]	N/A
1854	1.0 tael		£0.33[12]	$1.48[13]
1870	1.0 tael	Ff 5.0[14]	£0.33[15]	$1.48
1884	1.0 tael		£0.28[16]	$1.26
1894	1.0 tael		£0.16[17]	$0.72
1899[18]	1.0 tael	Ff 3.6[19]		$0.78
1901[20]	1.0 tael	Ff 3.75	£0.15	$0.74

1 By year and country for which information is available and relevant to this study. Extrapolations are made to arrive at dollar amounts (with a few unavoidable inconsistencies).

2 In 1698, one gold guinea was set at 21 shillings (s.) 5 pence (d.), that is, 14.33 French *livres*. "Currency Converter," http://www.pierre-marteau.com/currency/converter/eng-fra.html (accessed 15 November 2016).

3 A tael or Chinese *liang* (ounce) equaled 37.5 grams of silver. One source states that it was precisely 37.783 grams of silver. (In fact, the weight varied slightly over time and place.) Hosea Ballou Morse, *The Trade and Administration of China* (1908; reprint, 3rd rev. ed., New York: Russell & Russell, 1967), xv. For a long period during the Qing, 1.0 tael was valued at 1,000 copper cash (coins), but starting in the nineteenth century the ratio changed and, depending on the locale and year, the copper cash value increased to 1,250 or more. Western traders often paid in Spanish silver dollars, which I do not include because the Chinese and missionary sources used do not mention them.

4 The valuation of 1.0 tael at 5.0 *livres* comes from a priest's letter dated 9 December 1700, cited in Bornet, "Les anciennes églises ... Pei-t'ang [part 1]," 122.

5 The exchange rate was £1.0 to 13.3 *livres*. "Currency Converter."

6 A missionary wrote in 1775 that 1.0 tael exchanged for 7.5 *livres*. Bornet, "Les anciennes églises ... Nant'ang [part 1]," 503. In 1795, the French *franc* (Ff) replaced the *livre* at 1:1.

7 The pound to tael conversion rate can be generally set at 1:3, but varied slightly, according to available records of transactions that took place at Guangzhou in 1772. Hosea Ballou Morse, *The Chronicles of the East Asian Company Trading to China, 1635–1834*, 5 vols. (Oxford: Clarendon Press, 1926), 1:x, 165–168.

© KONINKLIJKE BRILL NV, LEIDEN, 2020 | DOI:10.1163/9789004416185_012

8   The U.S. Mint was founded in 1792. In that year, £1.0 converted to $4.47. "Dollar-Pound Exchange Rate from 1791," https://www.measuringworth.com/datasets/exchangepound/result.php (accessed 27 December 2016).

9   A priest in North China reported in 1836 that the value of 1.0 tael was Ff 7.0. Mouly letter, 6 November 1836, *Annales CM-F* 2 (1836): 58–59. For the same year, a priest in Jiangxi writes that 1,000 copper cash were valued at Ff 5.0. Ly letter, 4 April 1836, *Annales CM-F* 2 (1836): 88, 90. This would have put the value of 1.0 tael at 1,400 cash.

10 During the 1820s–1830s in South China, 1.0 tael was valued at $1.39. Frederic D. Grant, Jr., "The April 1820 Debt Settlement between Consecqua and Benjamin Chew Wilcocks" in *Americans and Macao: Trade, Smuggling, and Diplomacy on the South China Coast*, ed. Paul A. Van Dyke (Hong Kong: Hong Kong University Press, 2012), 77, 187 n. 11.

11 The pound extrapolation is possible for 1843–1853 using figures found in "Report of the Receipts ... 1842," *Annals PF* 4 (1843), 136; and "Annual Report, 1853," *Annals PF* 15 (1854): 107.

12 A published letter from Yunnan Province includes an editorial comment that the exchange rate was 1.0 tael to British 6s. 6d. (that is, £0.325). Chauveau letter, 1 December 1854, *Annals PF* 17 (1856): 99.

13 A recent study gives these numbers for 1864: the value of 1.0 tael was 6s. 8d. or $1.65. Smith, *The Qing Dynasty*, 411. It seems, from the rates for other years, that the relative value of the dollar was actually $1.48, perhaps less.

14 Leboucq letter, 18 January 1870, *Annals PF* 31 (1870): 282. Also mentioned in "Southern Pe-tche-li," *Annals PF* 32 (1871): 116. In Zhejiang in 1872, a Vincentian wrote that "200 sapecs [copper cash]" equals "1 franc" (that is 1,000 cash were valued at Ff 5.0). "China, Vicariate-Apostolic of Tche-kiang," citing Barbier letter, 5 September 1872, *Annals PF* 37 (1876): 34.

15 One source gives the value at 1.0 tael to 6s. 8d. (that is, £0.33). Morse, *Trade and Administration of China*, xv. For 1879, see Henry Yule and A.C. Burnell, *Hobson-Jobson: A Glossary of Colloquial Anglo-Indian Words* (London: John Murray, 1903): 888. Cited by Dilip K. Basu, "Chinese Xenology and the Opium War: Reflections on Sinocentrism," *Journal of Asian Studies* 73, no. 4 (November 2014): 931.

16 Morse, *Trade and Administration*, xv.

17 Ibid. The dollar amounts for 1870, 1884, and 1894 are extrapolated.

18 According to an editorial note added to a priest's letter from southern Jiangxi, the official franc to dollar rate varied from Ff 5.0 to less than Ff 3.0 for $1.00. Peres letter, 30 December 1893, *Annals CM-E* 3 (1896): 51. I add this to emphasize, as mentioned, the many regional variations in exchange rates.

19 In Beijing in 1899, 1.0 tael was valued at Ff 3.6. "La vie en Chine," *Annales CM-F* 44 (1899): 475. For 1894, Smith, *The Qing Dynasty*, 411, equates 1.0 tael to 3s. 2d. [or $0.78, by extrapolation].

20 The September 1901 protocol between China and various foreign powers provided terms for the settlement of claims resulting from the Boxer Uprising. Article 6 (a), provides the following currency exchanges rates: 1.0 customs (*haiguan*) tael was set at: Ff 3.75; 3s. 0d.; and $0.742.

The South Church's Stelae

There are two stelae at the South Church, the first erected in 1657 by order of the Shunzhi emperor, the second placed there by the Kangxi emperor in 1692. Sculpted according to traditional Chinese format, each consisted of three parts: 1) a base in the shape of a tortoise with a mortise on top of the back; 2) a separate rectangular body (with a tenon on its bottom for insertion into the mortise)—it is this part that was inscribed; and 3) a top or head that was part of the body, which had a bas-relief of two coiled dragons surrounding an inscription in Chinese seal script and Manchu stating the stele was "commissioned [and established] by order of the emperor" (yu zhi).[1] The stele of 1657 stood in front of the church on the east side of the main entrance with the inscription of the stele's principal side facing southward. Although similar stelae from the period were not covered by an open-sided pavilion with a yellow-tile roof, this one was, perhaps part of the emperor's gift but more likely added by missionaries to showcase and protect the stele.

The state of the stelae today gives no hint of their previous appearance. Both are missing the tortoise base and the body of each is in poor condition; the Chinese inscription of the 1657 stele is mostly readable (half of its top is broken off and gone) while the 1692 one is entirely unreadable (and its top is completely missing). Centuries and the elements only partially explain the current condition of each. Man-inflicted damage is another reason. In 1900, Boxers torched the pavilions, fire inflicting the stone surface with minor cracks that during subsequent winters filled with moisture and froze, thereby affecting the inscriptions. Sixty-seventy years later, Red Guards occupied the church grounds, destroyed the rebuilt pavilions, and toppled each stele's body from its base. Using sledge hammers, they broke it into smaller pieces for removal. They completely destroyed the stone tortoises and nothing of them remains. Today, the stelae's bodies are encased in a brick wall just to the east and west of the church's

---

1 I estimate the monument's total height to have been about eight or nine feet tall, including the tortoise base, by less than three feet wide. Based on a rubbing made of the stele's inscription (body and top), the two parts measured about seven feet. Zhu Pingyi, "Jinshimeng," 394. Compared to stelae of the same era, it was shorter, smaller, and thus less expensive. I base this on my extensive examination of numerous stelae of the 1650s–1700s in Liaoning Province and at the Qing Eastern Tombs. Author's field notes, various dates, 2001–2005. Imperial stelae of the Kangxi emperor's mid and late reign became taller and more refined. However, his gift of 1692 matched the one of 1657, to show respect for his father.

© KONINKLIJKE BRILL NV, LEIDEN, 2020 | DOI:10.1163/9789004416185_013

FIGURE A4.1   Stele of 1658 at Yongling, Liaoning Province. It is
               similar in general format but not bas-relief to the one
               erected a year earlier at the South Church.
               SOURCE: PHOTO BY AUTHOR, 2006

entrance, with a thick plexiglass cover added for protection. Nearby (in Chinese) are brief explanations of the inscription's content that focus on Schall.[2]

The East Stele

If the 1657 stele still stood in its original place facing south, its Manchu inscription would be seen as beginning vertically on the body's western edge and finishing in the

---

2   Author's field notes, 30 September 2007.

FIGURE A4.2   The current condition of the South Church stele of
1657. It has not fared well and about one-third of the
inscription is unreadable. A thick plexiglass covering
now affords some protection.
SOURCE: PHOTO BY AUTHOR, 2007

center. It was read from top to bottom and left to right, with the last of its sixteen lines
near the slab's center marking the date of its imperial bestowal to the church.[3] As far as
I know, no one has published the Manchu text, nor has it been translated. Its Chinese

---

3   Manchus considered the west side superior to the east, thus the arrangement of the inscriptions. Alan Richard Sweeten [Shi Weidong, pseud.], "Cong Qing huangjia lingmu kan Manzu
zaoqi de fazhan tedian," *Ouya xuekan* 8 (December 2008): 264–267. For additional background on this, see Alan Richard Sweeten, "The Early Qing Imperial Tombs: From Hetu Ala
to Beijing," in *Proceedings of the North American Conference on Manchu Studies*, ed. Stephen
Wadley (Wiesbaden: Harrassowitz, 2006), 61–102.

counterpart consists of fourteen unpunctuated vertical lines, also read from top to bottom but starting on the eastern side, with its final line, the date, situated in the center. The presentation is balanced and representative of early Qing stelae. I rely on Huang Bolu for the Chinese text, which he punctuated.[4] Willem Grootaers also published the Chinese inscription in 1944, following the stele's line by line layout.[5] His translation into French leaves considerable room for improvement. My version provides some clarifications and different interpretations. I have personally inspected the stele and note some of my observations.

Chinese Text[6]

［御］製[7]

易序卦。革而受之以鼎。革之象曰。澤中有火。革。君子以治歷明時。鼎之象曰。木上有火鼎。君子以正位凝命。是以帝王膺承歷數。協和萬邦。所事者。皆敬天勤民之事。而其要莫先於治歷。定四時以成歲功。撫五辰而熙庶績。使雨暘時若。民物咸亨。道必由之。矧開創之初。昭式九圍。貽謀奕葉。則治歷明時。固正位凝命之先務也。

粵稽在昔。伏羲制干支。神農分八節。皇帝綜六術。顓頊命二正。自時厥後。堯欽歷象。舜察璣衡。三統迭興。代有損益。見於經傳。彰矣。而其法皆不傳。若夫漢之太初。唐之大衍。元之授時。俱號近天。元歷尤為精密。然用之既久。亦多疏而不合。蓋積歲而為曆。積月而為歲。積日而為月。積分而為日。凡物與數之成於積者。不能無差。故語有之曰。銖銖而稱之。至石必謬。寸寸而度之。至丈必差。況天體之運行。日月星辰之升降遲疾。未始有窮。而度以一定之法。是以久則差。差則敝而不可用。凡歷之立法雖精。而後不能無修改。亦理勢之必然也。

自漢以還。訖於元末。修改者七十餘次。創法者十有三家。至於明代。雖改元授時歷為大統之名。而積分之術。實仍其舊。洎乎晚季。分至漸乖。朝野之言。僉云宜改。而西洋學者。雅善推步。於時湯若望航海而來。理數兼暢。被薦召試。設局授餐。奈眾議紛紜。終莫能用。

歲在甲申。朕仰承天眷。誕受多方。適當正位凝命之時。首舉治歷明時值典。仲秋月朔。日有食之。特遣大臣。督率所司。等臺測驗。其時刻分秒起復方位。獨與若望豫奏者。悉相符合。及乙酉孟春之望。再驗月食。亦纖毫無爽。豈非天生在斯人。以待朕創制立法之用哉。

朕特任以司天。造成新歷。勒名時憲。頒行遠邇。若望索習泰西之教。不婚不宦。祗承朕命。勉受鄉秋。涖曆三品。仍賜以通微教師之名。任事有年。益勤厥職。都

4 Huang Bolu, *Zheng jiao feng bao*, 27b–29.

5 Willem A. Grootaers, "Les anciennes églises de Pékin: Nant'ang, texte et traduction des steles du Nant'ang." *Bulletin catholique de Pékin* 31 (1944): 586–593.

6 The original used traditional characters without punctuation. For ease in reading, I have divided the text into paragraphs.

7 The character in brackets is based on my reading of the original stele's broken top. Author's field notes, 30 September 2007.

城宣武門內向有祠宇。素祀其教中所奉之神。近復取錫賚所儲。而更新之。朕巡幸
南苑。偶經斯地。見神之儀貌。如其國人。堂牖器飾。如其國制。問其几上之書。
則曰。此天主教之說也。
夫朕所服膺者。堯舜周孔之道。所講求者。精一執中之理。至於玄笈貝文。所稱道
德楞嚴諸書。雖嘗涉獵。而旨趣茫然。況西洋之書。天主之教。朕素未覺閱。焉能
知其說哉。但若望入中國。已數十年。而能守教奉神。肇新司宇。敬慎蠲潔。始終
不渝。孜孜之誠。良有可尚。人臣懷此心以事君。未有不敬其事者也。朕甚嘉之。
因賜額名曰。通微佳境。而為之記。
銘曰。大圜在上。周迴不已。七精之動。經緯又理。庶續百工。於焉終始。有器有
法。爰觀爰紀。惟此遠臣。西國之良。測天治歷。克彈其長。敬業奉神。篤守弗
忘。乃陳儀象。乃構堂皇。事神盡虔。事君盡職。凡爾疇人。永斯矜式。
順治十有四年歲在丁酉二月朔日

English Translation[8]
Commissioned [and established] by order of the Emperor

A *Book of Changes* exegesis writes that after the *ge* [hexagram symbol] is the *ding* [hexagram].[9] The *ge* form indicates fire in the lake, that is, transformation. [Due to this,] wise men formulated calendars suitable for the seasons. The *ding* form shows fire above wood, that is, stability. [Because of this] the wise man rectifies positions to secure [Heaven's] destiny. Therefore, the sovereign took his place in governing the world and that which he accomplished complied completely with Heaven's will for the people's welfare. In doing this, the most important matter was to formulate a calendar that differentiated the four seasons to ensure agricultural harvests would accumulate.[10] [Calendar officials] followed natural patterns so that the knowledge of favorable weather for crops would bring material wealth and social stability. It was crucial to do this. Moreover, in the [country's] beginning, moral standards and laws were made

8   My thanks to Drs. Zhao Zifu and Wang Shuo as well as Mr. Stephen Ford for their input. I follow the original as closely as possible with the minimal addition of bracketed words. Inserted italics, quotation marks, parentheses, and paragraph breaks are for clarification. Several footnotes are used to provide additional relevant information. Given that the inscription reflects the emperor's subjective view of past affairs and Schall, his words and syntax leaves, in places, ample room for interpretation. According to a study of stelae inscriptions, especially those on the tombstones of missionaries buried in Beijing, typically there are two sections: the first "a record of events" (*zhi*) and the second "additional words of praise" (*ming*). Malatesta and Gao, *Departed, Yet Present*, 109. Although the 1657 stele is not of the funerary type, the inscription reads similarly, and its last section is set off by the character *ming*, which I translate as "epigraph."
9   The emperor refers to the Book of Changes (*Yijing*) specifically citing one of its many supplemental works, the *Yi xu gua* [*zhuan*].
10   This calendar was much more than a list of days and months, it was an astronomical guide and agriculture-oriented almanac.

clear to everyone, and were passed down through the generations. [The sovereign] ordered a calendar that illuminated the seasons, firming up the urgent matter of rectifying positions and securing [Heaven's] destiny.

In examining the past, Fuxi instituted the system of cyclical heavenly stems and earthly branches; Shennong divided the year into the eight periods; Huangdi assembled six kinds of astronomical knowledge; and Zhuanxu assigned two standards [of timekeeping].[11] Afterwards, Yao decreed calendrical symbols and Shun used astronomic instruments. During the three early historical periods [calendrical] changes occurred; [with them] there were gains and losses.[12] Classical books clearly recorded this but not how all of it was accomplished. As for the Han's Tai chu [calendar], the Tang's Da yan [calendar], and the Yuan's Shou shi [calendar], all were adequate. The Yuan dynasty's calendar was especially precise, but after long use it manifested many inaccuracies. In fact, through the accumulations of years a calendar is formed; of months years are formed; and of minutes days are formed. That is, all things and amounts that are added together, in the end, cannot be without error. Hence there is a saying: ["]measure by tiny fractions and a picul of grain will certainly be wrong. Use inches and a yard will surely be inexact.["][13] Moreover, in the movements of heavenly bodies where the rising and setting as well as the speed of the sun, moon, and stars are incessant, estimates by a fixed method over a long time will be deficient and deficiencies will lead to uselessness. Whatever the calendar, although accurate at its inception, it cannot continue in use without corrections. This is a certainty.

From the Han until the late Yuan dynasty, innovators from thirteen schools modified the calendar more than seventy times. During the Ming, although the Yuan's Shou shi [calendar] was renamed the Da tong [calendar], in fact, the calculation methods were as before. By the late Ming, the calendar had gradually become imprecise with officials and people wanting it revised. Western scholars were talented as well as innovative, and, at that time, Adam Schall had already crossed the seas to come here. Proficient in natural science and mathematics, he was recommended to the court then awarded an official position with salary. Since high officials' opinions about him varied, he was not utilized.[14]

In the *jiashen* year [1644] I received Heaven's benevolence and became China's sovereign, a time when I appropriately rectified positions to secure [Heaven's] destiny. The first thing I did was to revise the calendar. On the first day of the eighth lunar month, there was to be a solar eclipse so I specially dispatched high officials, together

---

11   That is, ways to mark the start of a new, lunar year. His approach involved observing meteorological phenomena and farming seasons.

12   The Xia, Shang, and Zhou periods.

13   This saying appears in chapter 23 in *Shuo yuan* (*Garden of Stories*), compiled by Liu Xiang (77–6 BCE). My thanks to Mr. Stephen Ford for this reference.

14   Officials doubted his knowledge of astronomy and calendar making.

with those of the inspectorate office, to the observatory to monitor it. The exact time and position of the sun corresponded to what Adam [Schall] had calculated and written beforehand in a memorial to me.[15] In the *yiyou* year [1645], on the fifteenth day of the first lunar month, there was to be an eclipse of the moon. Again, he did not err even slightly. How can it not be that Heaven produced such a person to serve me by making a calendar?

I appointed [Adam Schall] to supervise the Directorate of Astronomy and compose a new calendar, which was called Shi xian and promulgated everywhere. Adam follows a Western religion and has not married or [previously] served as an official. Only out of consideration to me, has he reluctantly taken a position of the third official rank. I have also bestowed on him the stylistic title Religious Master who Comprehends the Mysteries.[16] He has served for years, working dutifully and diligently. Inside the capital's Xuanwu Gate there has for a long time been a sanctuary [that is, a church with a residence] within which is a revered image of his religion's deity. Recently, he has used the accumulated savings of the court's monetary gifts [to him] to renovate it. When I go on imperial tour to Nanyuan, I occasionally go there. I have seen the deity's statue, which looks like his countrymen, and the main building, its windows as well as its decorations, which are like those of his country. I once asked about books on a table and he answered that they were about Catholicism.

As for me, I usually follow the principles of Yao, Shun, [the Duke of] Zhou, and Kong [Confucius], striving for sincerity of action to attain the middle way [to perfect social harmony]. As for abstruse Daoist and Buddhist writings such as the *Dao de* [*jing*], *Leng yan* [*jing*], and other books, I read them cursorily without fully understanding.[17] Regarding Western books and those on Catholicism, which I have not perused, how could I comprehend their religious tenets! However, Adam has been in China for decades, following his faith, honoring his deity, and building a new sanctuary. He has steadfastly and continuously maintained his beliefs and displayed the deepest sincerity. His goodness is to be esteemed. If people and officials had the same heart in serving their sovereign, there would be no one acting disrespectfully. I deeply commend him and because of this I bestow a plaque that reads: a beautiful place to comprehend the mysteries, and the words of this inscription.

Epigraph. In the great heavens above, the rotations are incessant. The sun, moon, and planets are all in motion, woven together by coherent principles of the natural

---

15   The emperor uses only Schall's Chinese given name, a highly personal gesture that speaks of their friendly relationship.

16   Tong wei jiao shi has also been translated as "The Master of Mystery" and "Religious Teacher who Comprehends the Mysterious." Malatesta and Gao, *Departed, Yet Present*, 36, 133.

17   The *Leng yan jing* is also known as the Śūraṅgama Sūtra, a Mahayana text. Mr. Stephen Ford provided this information.

world. Let those who work in astronomy always fulfill their duties, use instruments and models, and make meticulous observations and records. There is this official [Adam Schall] from a faraway place, an outstanding talent from the West who has surveyed the heavens and composed a calendar, whose strong point is his strenuous efforts. Still he faithfully serves his deity and maintains his beliefs, displaying the images of his deity and building a grand hall [for worship]. Piously he serves his deity and dutifully serves his sovereign. All those involved in astronomy will forever see him as their exemplar.

The Shunzhi reign, fourteenth year, second month, first day [15 March 1657]

The West Stele

Today, this stele is not much more than a rectangular-shaped block of heavily weathered stone, but it still has symbolic value and historical importance because the Shunzhi emperor's successor gave it to the South Church. The Kangxi emperor reigned for sixty-one years as one of the Qing's most able rulers and his attitude and position towards Catholicism greatly affected its development over this period. Initially, not only did the Kangxi emperor help in the North Church's establishment but he also allowed other churches to remain open and missionaries to care for them as well as their worshippers. The 1692 stele's inscription cites memorials by two Western priests and several Chinese officials, who point out the contributions made by Catholic missionaries and that they, as well as their religion, had helped not hurt the empire. The emperor's endorsement of the memorials, effectively an imperial policy not to hinder Catholicism, became known to Westerners as the "Edict of Toleration."

The Chinese inscription is about twice the length of the one of 1657. With only a few words written by the emperor himself, it is devoid of expressions of personal feelings like those made by the Shunzhi emperor. Again, Huang Bolu and Grootaers each provide the Chinese text in punctuated format and the latter a translation into French.[18] I neither reproduce the Chinese text nor translate it since there is a recent in-depth study of it by Nicolas Standaert entitled "The 'Edict of Tolerance' (1692): A Textual History and Reading."[19]

---

18   Huang Bolu, *Zheng jiao feng bao*, 113b–114b; and Grootaers, "Les anciennes églises de Pékin: Nant'ang, texte et traduction des steles du Nan-t'ang," 593–599.
19   *In the Light and Shadow of an Emperor: Tomás Pereira, SJ (1645–1708), the Kangxi Emperor and the Jesuit Mission in China*, ed. Artur K. Wardega and António Vasconcelos de Saldanha (Newcastle upon Tyne: Cambridge Scholars Publishing, 2012), 308–358.

The North Church's Stelae

Of Beijing's four original churches, only the South Church had imperially bestowed stelae until 1888, when, with the completion of the North Church at its new location, stelae with protective pavilions appeared. To the church's main entrance on the south, one stood on the east and the other on the west. According to Chinese tradition, east was the superior of the two sides and that is where the most important inscription was placed (facing south).[1] In the various materials regarding the negotiations for the church's transfer and construction, the erection of a stele or stelae inscribed with the imperial edict approving the matter is only briefly mentioned.[2] Church authorities (led by Favier) wanted the stelae for two principal reasons: first, their presence gave the sacred structure an authoritative cachet not just visually but also politically, insofar as an imperial edict was being presented to the public; and second, other inscriptions would preserve something about the North Church's illustrious history and explain how the church came to be at this location, naming the people involved.[3]

The stelae at the North Church were larger and taller than those then standing at the South Church but were of the same format: a stone tortoise base; a body or rectangular slab for the inscription; and a top that was part of the body, composed of deep bas-relief coiled dragons and a short inscription labelling it.[4] The North Church's stelae survived the Boxer era unscathed, but Red Guards heavily damaged the pair during the Cultural Revolution. Of the original stone body that stood on the east side, only a portion of the top remains, its other pieces either buried or hauled away from the premises. Today's stelae's bodies and inscriptions date to the 1980s.

---

1   As previously discussed, Chinese and Manchus had different views on the matter of which side was superior. That said, sometimes it is difficult to understand the rationale for the placement and orientation of certain stelae.
2   See the Chinese text of the inscription that was on the north side of this stele (English translation, item number four). The text does not state how to inscribe and display the edict. High court officials, however, would have insisted that the edict be presented in Chinese on the eastern stele and Manchu on the western one, both facing south to accord with post-1644 Qing custom in China. The additional inscriptions, those on the two stelae's north side, are not mentioned in Chinese texts, and their inclusion must have been decided by the bishop or Favier. Cordier provides a translation of an agreement that states "the decree will be inscribed on a stele sheltered by a roof of yellow tiles and placed at the entrance to the new church." Cordier, *Histoire des relations*, 2:611. It appears that at some point location was also discussed.
3   See Chapter 3, note 174.
4   I estimate its height to be seventeen to eighteen feet (from the surface on which the tortoise sits to the stele's very top. Both appear to be of the same dimensions.

© KONINKLIJKE BRILL NV, LEIDEN, 2020 | DOI:10.1163/9789004416185_014

FIGURE A5.1   The North Church's stele, ca late 1880s. View of east side, looking north.
SOURCE: FAVIER, *PÉKING*, 1897

The East Stele, Front (Southern) Face

On the main (south) side of the east stele's face is where the important inscription displayed in Chinese is found. It is the Guangxu emperor's edict regarding the church's move to and construction at this site. Although the Chinese inscription has been published, it has not been previously translated into English.[5] For the most part, the edict and other stele inscriptions at the North Church have been ignored. They, however, importantly recount the negotiation of the church's destruction at one site, and reconstruction at another, which satisfied certain figures like the Empress

5   The Grand Council forwarded a copy of the edict to the Zongli Yamen. See *JWJAD*, IV/1/106, 108b–109. The punctuation reproduced here is that amended by the series' editors. Cordier published a French translation of the edict that has slight textual differences (*Histoire des relations*, 619–621). I also rely on the replica stele's inscription.

FIGURE A5.2   The top of the stele on the west side. This is all
               that remains of the original. The other stele had
               the same bas-relief.
               SOURCE: PHOTO BY AUTHOR, 2007

Dowager Cixi. Yet it was really a moot victory for the Qing court because ownership, and the symbolic gain that came with it, had cost a large sum of silver. It was also a dubious triumph for the Vincentians, who left a privileged location next to the Forbidden City while acquiring a larger site that could accommodate more facilities. With a sizable subsidy in hand, missionaries built a substantial security wall around the property to protect their steadily expanding physical assets. In 1900, that wall helped save the church from destruction at the hands of the Boxers and protected the several thousand Catholics who found safety there. Today, although the North Church grounds are less than half of what they once were, the sacred structure is Beijing's cathedral and, as such, is well maintained. During 2016–2018 it closed for mostly interior renovations with minor attention given to the two pavilions near the church's main entrance.

FIGURE A5.3   Today's replica stele, east side
SOURCE: PHOTO BY AUTHOR, 2018

Chinese Text

上諭[6]

光緒十二年十一月初七日

奉上諭。李鴻章奏鹽池口教堂与教士定議遷移。并與駐京公使商定互送照會一摺。覽奏均悉。西安門內鹽池口教堂於康熙年間欽奉諭旨准令起建。迄今百數十年。該教士等仰戴朝廷怙冒深仁。咸知安靜守法。

上年修理南海等處工程。為慈禧端佑康頤昭豫莊誠皇太后頤餘頤養之所。西南附近一帶地勢尚須擴充。該處教堂密邇禁苑。經李鴻章派英人敦約翰前赴羅瑪商酌。並令稅務司德璀琳與教士樊國樑訂約遷移。議於西什庫南首地方申畫界址。給資改

---

6   The two characters were inscribed on the stele's top part. I have added paragraph breaks to
     the text.

造。該教士復聲明。改建之堂以五丈高為度。比較舊建之樓減低三丈有餘。鐘樓亦斷不令高出屋脊。議定後。樊國樑又赴羅馬告諸教會總統費雅德。據覆文歷敘感激中朝覆幬保護之忱。有激發天真。圖報萬一等語。情詞尤為肫懇。

李鴻章現復與公使恭思當互相照會。亦據覆稱。無不依照辦理。和協邦交。深知大體。實堪嘉許。此事既據李鴻章詳細商定。均無異詞。即著照所請行。其改造經費亦著分期撥給。俾資營建。餘均照議辦理。

候補道恩佑於創辦之初奉委出力。著交軍機處記名。遇缺題奏。主教達里布誠信報效。教士樊國樑英人敦約翰遠涉重洋。不辭勞瘁。達里布著賞給二品頂戴。樊國樑著賞給三品頂戴。敦約翰著賞給三等第一寶星。樊國樑敦約翰並著各再加賞銀二千兩。由李鴻章發給。稅務司德璀琳領事林椿往來通詞。始終奮勉。德璀琳著賞換二品頂戴。林椿著賞給二等第三寶星。其餘出力之英商怭克等。著李鴻章查明奏請獎勵。

該衙門知道。欽此。

English Translation

Imperial Edict

The Guangxu reign, twelfth year, eleventh month, seventh day [2 December 1886], imperial edict: Li Hongzhang memorialized that he and [Catholic] missionaries had agreed on the Canchikou [Catholic] church's move and that he and the [French] minister in Beijing had decided to send a joint communication for full [imperial] review. [The communication stated that] over one hundred years ago, during the Kangxi reign, an edict permitted construction of the Canchikou church that is located inside the Xi'an Gate. Missionaries respected the court, relied on its great benevolence, and were peaceful as well as law abiding.

Last year, in a project to renovate the Nanhai area for the Empress Dowager Cixi's personal use, several places were found to the southwest where there was space suitable to expand. A church was nearby, which is [now] prohibited to be there, beside the [Western] Park. Li Hongzhang sent John Dunn, a Briton, to go to Rome to deliberate [with Catholic authorities] on the matter; he also ordered the [Tianjin] Commissioner of Customs, Gustav Detring, to reach an agreement on moving the church with the missionary, Alphonse Favier. They discussed [moving the church to] the southern part of the Xishiku area as well as boundaries and the allocation of funds for its reconstruction. That missionary stated that the new church would be limited to five *zhang* [sixty feet] in height and compared to the old church tower would be lower by three *zhang* [thirty-six feet] or more, plus the bell tower would not be higher than the building's ridgeline. After making the agreement, Favier went to Rome to inform the Congregation of the Mission's Superior General, Antoine Fiat. According to [their] reply, they were grateful for the court's sentiments of protection and glad to have a plan, which they expressed with feelings of sincerity.

Li Hongzhang and the [French] minister sent a communication that again stated it would be handled as such for mutually amicable relations; they knew that acting for the general interest was commendable. This matter, according to Li Hongzhang's detailed consultations, is as stated and will be implemented accordingly. The funds for the relocation [of the church] will be paid in installments so that the construction may proceed; everything will be handled as decided.

The expectant Dao[tai], Enyou, from the start of construction, worked very hard and his name will be submitted to the Grand Council for promotion, when there is an opening. Bishop Françoise Tagliabue has truly repaid us with kindness. The missionary, Favier, and the Briton, Dunn, have traveled far and not shirked hardship. Tagliabue is bestowed with the hat emblem of the second official rank, and Favier with the hat emblem of the third official rank.[7] Dunn is bestowed with the distinction of the double dragon order's first division, third class. Favier and Dunn are each awarded two thousand taels of silver, which will be given to them by Li Hongzhang. The [Tianjin] Commissioner of Customs, Detring, and the [French] consul [at Tianjin], Paul Ristelhueber, participated in the discussions and from start to finish were diligent. Detring is bestowed with the second official rank and Ristelhueber is bestowed with the distinction of the double dragon order's third division, second class.[8] Li Hongzhang can memorialize for awards to others, like the British merchant, Alexander Michie, who acted vigorously [for a resolution].

The office [involved] is informed [of the imperial edict]. Respect this.

The East Stele, Back (Northern) Face

The inscription on the back or northern side recapitulates the agreement to transfer the church from Canchikou to Xishiku made between Li Hongzhang, assisted by the Tianjin Commissioner of Customs, Gustav Detring, and Alphonse Favier. The agreement is included in a communication that Detring sent to the Zongli Yamen in which he also briefly explained what had led to this point.[9] Including this long inscription makes little sense except that missionaries wanted their account preserved and displayed publicly.

---

7 The emblems, sometimes called buttons, adorned the top of officials' hats. H.S. Brunnert and V.V. Hagelstrom, *Present Day Political Organization of China*, trans. A. Beltchenko and E.E. Moran (1912, reprint, Taipei: Book World, 1963), 966. Of spherical shape, a little over one inch in diameter, they were made of various precious materials and part of a silver filigree piece designed for its attachment and display. The description is based on one for the fourth official rank that I acquired in Changsha, Hunan. Author's field notes, 11 September 2016.

8 For information on Qing official ranks and decorations, refer to Brunnert and Hagelstrom, *Present Day Political Organization of China*, 499, 507.

9 *JWJAD*, IV/1/113, 112b–114b. I also rely on the replica stele's inscription.

Chinese Text[10]

照澤商定天津稅務司德璀林。北堂教士樊國樑。為商議移讓北堂在西什庫改建。酌擬辦法。恭呈鈞鑒。仍應祇候大清國大皇帝。大羅馬大教皇。御覽批准。謹遵奉行事。計共五端。詳列於後。

一。自光緒十三年正月一日起。以二年為限。凡北堂仁慈堂地基房屋及樹木等。均於限內交付。除傢具外。一概不准移動損壞。

二。應請於本年十一月初一日。將西什庫內南邊地方酌給三分之二。丈量四至。交與北堂主教收管。該地現有樹木若干。一併交付。不可折損移動。

三。查北堂地方係康熙年間蒙聖祖仁皇賞給教士等居住。並派員相助起建大天主堂。又頒發敕建天主堂金字匾額。中外同深欽感。今因朝廷欲廣禁地。　教士等遵敕移讓。復蒙賞西什庫內地方另為建堂。朝廷厚澤深仁。後先一轍。教士等尤深感激。應請奏明。按照康熙年間辦法。明降諭旨。俾中外咸知。教士永遠遵守。則仰荷恩寵益無涯涘。

四。如蒙查照康熙年間成發辦理頌發諭旨。教士等於西什庫新堂成後。當照南堂式。恭刊詔旨於碑。護以黃亭。以漢白玉製匾。以照誠敬。至在西什庫建造大堂。自地至樑以五丈高為度。鐘樓亦斷不令高出屋脊。

五。此次在西什庫改建北堂。教士等甚願官家按照北堂仁慈堂原代為蓋造。房屋一切均照原式。是為最要。如官家不肯照樣代辦。祇得由教士等畫圖自行起造。此項工料銀兩。應請於付西什庫地方時付給三分之一。遇六個月再付一次。又六個月付訖。分作三次。為時十八個月。似較輕便。按此次另建北堂仁慈堂。工料等項實需用至四十五萬餘金。奉中堂諭令核減。教士等於無可減之中勉力酌減銀十萬兩。計共需庫平銀三十五萬兩。次係格外報效。

伏祈亮察。再北堂所有百鳥堂內禽獸及一切古董物件。鐘樓內風琴喇叭等。樊教士願請教皇吩示。概行報效奉送中國國家。

光緒十二年四月二十六公共商定畫押[11]

以上所議各條款均經
大清國大皇帝
大羅馬大教皇
大法國伯理錫天德
聖味增爵會總統費雅德

先後　　　批准實行

English Translation

In accordance with the discussions between the Tianjin Customs Commissioner, Gustav Detring, and the North Church Missionary, Alphonse Favier, it has been agreed that the North Church will be moved to Xishiku for reconstruction. We have drafted

---

10　Paragraph breaks have been included.

11　This line and the six that follow it were not part of the copy received by the Zongli Yamen.

the methods for doing so and have respectfully presented them for perusal. It remains for the Qing emperor and the pope in Rome to review and approve, then for [the agreement] to be implemented. Altogether there are five items, which are presented in detail below.

1. Starting on the Guangxu reign's thirteenth year, first month, first day [24 January 1887], there will be a two-year time limitation for the full transfer of the North Church and Hall of Mercy [Orphanage, their] grounds, buildings, trees, and so on. Except for furniture, all else is prohibited from being moved or damaged.

2. It is requested that on the eleventh month, first day of this year [26 November 1886] two-thirds of the Xishiku's southern area, measured out on all sides, be handed over to the North Church bishop for his control. That area currently has a certain number of trees that will all be given over and will not be damaged or moved.

3. It has been determined that during the Kangxi years the North Church property had been granted to the missionaries as a residence. [He] also dispatched officials to help in the construction of a large Catholic church, and awarded a plaque [inscribed] in golden letters that ["]the church was built by imperial order.["] Chinese and foreigners all had great admiration [for this] and were touched. Today, because the court wants to expand into a prohibited area, missionaries have complied with an imperial order to move [from there]; they will receive another location within the Xishiku area to build a church. Throughout this, the court has been generous and kind. The missionaries have been deeply grateful and requested that it be clearly reported as such. According to how it was handled during the Kangxi years, an edict will be promulgated so that Chinese and foreigners alike will be informed. Missionaries will eternally comply and admire how such [imperial] kindness benefits them.

4. In compliance with the handling of the Kangxi era edict, after completion of the new church at Xishiku and in accordance with the style of the South Church, missionaries may have the [current] edict inscribed on a stele. It will be protected by a yellow [-tile roof] pavilion. [Additionally, an inscribed] plaque of white marble will reflect [our] sincerity. Regarding the construction of the large church at Xishiku, from ground-level to the top beam, it will not exceed five *zhang* [sixty feet] and the bell tower will not exceed the height of the building's roof ridgeline.

5. In the rebuilding of the North Church at Xishiku, missionaries agree that the [construction] supervisor will follow the original style of the North Church and House of Mercy [Orphanage]: this is most important. If the supervisor is not willing to do it this way, then there is no choice but for the missionaries to draw up their own designs. The project's cost for labor and materials will be requested at the time of the North Church's [start] and one third will be paid. After six months, a further payment; after another six months, payment in full. The division into three periods and over eighteen months will be convenient. This time the construction of the North Church and House of Mercy [Orphanage] will cost up to four hundred fifty thousand taels for labor and materials. The grand secretary requested that it be reexamined and reduced.

Missionaries, while not wanting to do so, were able to decrease the amount by one hundred thousand taels. The total comes to three hundred fifty thousand taels. This results from [our] exemplary kindness and has been acknowledged. It is hoped, in regard to the North Church's collection of birds and small animals, all of its antiques, and the bell tower's musical instruments that Favier will request the pope for instructions that they be given to China as compensation.[12]

The Guangxu reign, twelfth year, fourth month, twenty-sixth day [29 May 1887], jointly agreed and signed.

Without exception, each item above has been discussed and approved.

The Qing Emperor

The Pope

The French President

The Congregation of the Mission, Superior General, Antoine Fiat,

Successively approved for implementation.

The West Stele

Red Guards broke the west side stele's original body and top into three large sections with one part still on the ground not far from the modern-day replacement. Presently, the front (southern) side's top is inscribed in Manchu and reads "*dergi hese*," the equivalent of "*shang yu*" in Chinese, that is, "imperial edict."[13] Below it is a Chinese inscription entitled "a record of the [North] Church's transfer" (*qianjian tianzhutang beiji*), and a statement indicating that Vincentian missionaries composed it. I do not provide the inscription or a translation because the content offers no new information. To summarize, it briefly mentions early missionaries and Catholicism in China followed by a short chronology of the negotiations leading up to the church's transfer. Workers put the replacement body in place during the 1980s with the Manchu text side improperly facing north instead of south. (As mentioned in note 2 above, it must be the Guangxu emperor's edict.[14]) If turned to the south, it would then be displayed properly per Qing imperial custom. Human error explains the unconventional presentation in place today.

---

12   Fr. Armand David, C.M., arrived in Beijing in 1862. His interest in nature took him all over China as he assembled a collection of birds, animals, and plants. Vincentians kept part of his collection in a building on the grounds of the North Church. Chang, *Empress Dowager Cixi*, 176; and Van den Brandt, *Les Lazaristes*, 67–68.

13   My thanks to Professor Mark C. Elliott for the transliteration and translation. He notes that the Manchu script "is modern" looking and includes an error with "*hese*" miswritten as "*kese*." Email to author, 3 February 2018.

14   The Chinese text is in Tong Xun, *Jidujiao yu Beijing jiaotang wenhua* (Beijing: Zhongyang minzu daxue chubanshe, 1999), 275–276.

The West Church's Stone Tablets

Inside the church's main entrance just before the nave are two inscribed stone tablets embedded into the walls at eye-level. One is inscribed in traditional Chinese characters that are colored white for enhanced visibility on the black stone. That text is unpunctuated and presented in vertical lines read from top to bottom and right to left. Below it has been converted into a horizontal format with traditional-style punctuation. The Latin text is presented all in capital letters with the use of many abbreviations. It is also a white inscription on black stone. Both date to 1913.

Chinese Text

改建聖母聖衣堂碑記

繄維聖教永存。眥生洪濟。數千年帲幪幹興誠。大主之仁慈靈佑在焉。遣使會司鐸德理格。於一千七百二十三年。獨輸鉅資。購置斯基。恭建聖母七苦堂一座。一千八百一十一年。適清嘉慶間。聖教蒙難。全堂被毀。迨至一千八百六十七年六月。主教孟幕理。重為構筑。宏工鉅制。規模一新。詎意一千九百年六月十五日。遭拳匪之禍。本堂金司鐸遇害。臺宇院落。一炬無遺。一千九百十二年。仁愛會脩女博郎西耶氏復捐資新峽。更易今名。落成之日。北京林主教飭勒石以志顛末云爾。

西曆一千九百十三年二月　勒石

English Translation

A Record of Our Lady of Mt. Carmel Church's Reconstruction

Catholicism is eternal and has given the multitudes great blessings. God mercifully protected us over the millennia and through good as well as bad times. Teodorico Pedrini, C.M., in 1723 accumulated the funds to buy this site and build a church dedicated to the Seven Sorrows of Holy Mary. In 1811, during the Jiaqing emperor's reign, Catholicism endured difficulties and the church was completely destroyed. Later, in June 1867, Bishop Mouly rebuilt it in a grand, new style. Unexpectedly, on 15 June 1900 amid the Boxer catastrophe Pastor Doré was killed and the church totally destroyed. In 1912, Sister Branssier of the Daughters of Charity [gave money] to rebuild [the church] with its name changed to Our Lady of Mt. Carmel. On the day of its completion, Bishop Jarlin of Beijing had this stone engraved with its history.

Engraved, February 1913, Western calendar

© KONINKLIJKE BRILL NV, LEIDEN, 2020 | DOI:10.1163/9789004416185_015

Latin Text

D. O. M.[1]

TEODORICUS PEDRINI. PRESB. CONGR. MISS., INFANTIUM IMPERATORIS KANGHSI PRÆCEPTOR, AN. DOM. 1723 HUNC FUNDUM PROPRIO ÆRE EMIT, IN EOQUE ECCLESIAM SUB AUSPICIIS SEPTEM DOLORUM B.M.V.DEO DEDICAVIT, QUÆ TEMPORE PERSECUTIONIS KIATSING (1811) FUNDITUS EST DESTRUCTA.[2]

POSTEA A.D. 1867, ILL. DD. MOULY, C.M., HIC NOVUM SACRUM ÆDIFICAVIT. QUOD DIE 15 JUNII 1900 BOXORES FLAMMIS TRADIDERUNT, DUM PAROCHUM ECCLESIÆ MAURITIUM DORE, C.M. SACERDOTEM CRUDELITER TRUCIDANT.[3]

TANDEM, ANNO DOMINI 1912 LARGITATE BENEMERITÆ ROSALIÆ BRANSSIER, SOCIETATIS PUELLARUM CARITATIS, TERTIA HÆC ECCLESIA SUB TITULO B.M. DE MONTE CARMELO ÆDIFICATA EST. IN QUORUM MEMORIAM ILL. DD. JARLIN, C.M., VIC. AP PEKINESIS, HUNC LAPIDEM EREXIT.

English Translation

See the Chapter 3 section on the fourth West Church.

---

1 Sometimes translated "To God Most Good and Most Great." Malatesta and Gao, *Departed, Yet Present*, 18.
2 Line ending with blank space, per the original.
3 Same as note 2.

The Government Memorial at Tianjin's Wanghailou Church

Alphonse Favier went to considerable expense and trouble to have a large inscribed stele, protected by an open-sided pavilion, erected at the Wanghailou Church in 1897. He wanted Tianjin residents to be aware that the imperial government acknowledged its responsibility for the destruction of the first church in 1870 and had approved its reconstruction twenty-seven years later. Both the church and the stele represented Catholicism's presence and power not only in Tianjin but in all of China. Exactly one hundred years later, Tianjin authorities established a stone monument adjacent to the Wanghailou church, its purpose being to remind everyone of the sociopolitical importance of the events that occurred at the site. The implied message is clear: although Catholicism and churches remain in China, the masses, through their People's Government, now have power.

Chinese Text[1]

天津教案遗址

望海楼始建于1773年，是清帝巡视天津的驻跸之所。第二次鸦片战争后，法国取得在天津辟租界，建教堂的特权。1862年，　清政府将望海楼及楼房崇禧观15亩土地租予法国传教士。法国在望海楼设领事馆。并于1869年在崇禧观旧址建天主教堂，俗称望海楼教堂。

1870年，津城屡发丢失儿童事，引起天津人民的警觉。据拐卖儿童罪犯武兰珍，张栓供认，其行径受望海楼教堂教民王三指使。舆论哗然，群情义愤，天津街巷遍见反洋教揭帖。

是年6月21日，天津知府张光藻，知县刘杰押解武兰珍等到教堂与王三指证，众多群众齐集教堂向法籍神甫谢福音抗议。法国领事丰大业带其秘书西蒙到通商衙门，持枪威逼清政府官员镇压群众。返途遇刘杰，又向刘杰开枪，群众怒不可遏，殴毙丰大业，西蒙和谢福音，烧毁教堂和法国领事馆。复将隔河仁慈堂及附近多处英，美讲书堂焚毁，打死传教士，洋人20人。此即震惊中外的天津教案。

中日甲午战争后，法国乘机威逼清政府于1897年重建教堂。1900年义和团运动中再次被焚。1904年法国用 "庚子赔款" 修复。

1　The original is in simplified characters and includes the punctuation marks used, but not the paragraph breaks.

© KONINKLIJKE BRILL NV, LEIDEN, 2020 | DOI:10.1163/9789004416185_016

天津教案系我市人民反抗外侮，维护民族尊严的爱国斗争，展现了中国人民的凛然正气，在中国近代史上占有重要地位。为弘扬爱国主义精神，特将天津教案遗址辟为爱国主义教育基地，让人民世代牢记这一历史。

天津市河北区之民政府 1997年6月

English Translation

Site of the Tianjin [Christian] Religious Case

Wanghailou was first established in 1773 and is the place where the Qing emperor stayed while on imperial tour in Tianjin. After the Second Opium War, France acquired in Tianjin the right to establish a concession area and build churches. In 1862, the Qing government leased Wanghailou and the [adjoining] Chongxi temple buildings, [altogether] fifteen *mu* of land, to French missionaries. France set up its consulate at Wanghailou.[2] In 1869, at the old site of the Chongxi temple [missionaries] erected a church, commonly called the Wanghailou church.

Within the walled city in 1870, repeated matters involving missing children aroused the people of Tianjin's vigilance. According to the confessions of the kidnapper-criminals Wu Lanzhen and Zhang Shuan, they had acted on the instructions of Wang San, a Catholic of the Wanghailou church. Public opinion was in an uproar and the masses were morally incensed. Appearing everywhere in Tianjin's streets and lanes were posters that opposed the foreign religion.

That year, on 21 June, Tianjin Prefect Zhang Guangzao and Magistrate Liu Jie led the criminals Wu Lanzhen and others to the church to testify against Wang San. The masses, in a great crowd, had gathered at the church to protest against the French priest, Claude Chevrier. [Meanwhile] French Consul Henri-Victor Fontainer, accompanied by his chief secretary [Mr.] Simon, went to the Superintendent of Trade's office, brandishing a gun to coerce Qing officials into suppressing the masses.[3] On the way back [to the consulate], Fontainer encountered and shot his gun at Liu Jie. The masses [who saw this] boiled over with anger and beat to death Fontainer, Simon, and Chevrier; then they burned the church and French consulate. They also burned the Catholic orphanage located along the river [across from the church], as well as several British and American churches in the area, killing missionaries and foreigners, twenty in total. This is the Tianjin [Christian] Religious Case that shocked China and the West.

After the Sino-Japanese War of 1894–1895, France took the opportunity to force the Qing government to [permit] reconstruction of the [Wanghailou] church in 1897.

---

2   About two and one-half acres.

3   At that time, Chonghou was Superintendent of Trade for the Northern Ports, that is, those opened by treaty to trade with Westerners. *Eminent Chinese*, 209.

During the Boxer Movement in 1900 it was again burned. In 1904, France used "Gengzi [Boxer] Reparations" to restore it.[4]

The Tianjin [Christian] Religious Case is our city people's patriotic struggle to maintain our national dignity by resisting foreign insults. It developed into the Chinese people's awe-inspiring righteousness and has an important place in modern Chinese history. To honor the spirit of Chinese patriotism, [we] especially support the Tianjin [Christian] Religious Case site as a base for patriotic education, one that will allow [future] generations of people to remember well this history.

The People's Government of Hebei District, Tianjin City, June 1997

---

4   "Gengzi [nian]" refers to 1900—thus, the Boxers.

Glossary

Who and what to include in the form of Romanizations using the *pinyin* system and simplified Chinese characters is a subjective decision based on two main factors: importance to the narrative, and the ease with which the Chinese may be determined. Accordingly, I do not give the Chinese names of historical figures and Western priests because such information is not vital here and is available in *Eminent Chinese*, Van den Brandt's *Les Lazaristes*, and other sources. Nor do I include the Chinese for well-known place-names, commonly used words and terms, or people mentioned in passing.

Anjia (zhuang)　安家(庄)
Anjia zhuang tianzhutang　安家庄天主堂
Anzhuang　安庄
Anzu (nanzhuang)　安族(南庄)
Anzuxin (zhuang)　安族辛(庄)

Baidu baike　百度百科
Baisha (cun)　白沙(村)
ban Xi shi tang　半西式堂
Beijing Sheng Lujia yishu　北京圣路加艺术
biandou　匾斗
biane　匾额
bi min da de bao zhong wai　庇民大德包中外
bu xiayu di fa gan quanshi jiaotang zhezhu tian　不下雨地发干全是教堂遮住天

can'an　惨案
Canchikou (tang)　蚕池口(堂)
Changgou (zhen)　长沟(镇)
Changxindian (cun)　长辛店(村)
Cheng Youxian　程有献
Chen Tianyi　陈天义
chi ci tong wei jia jing　敕赐通微佳境
chijian　敕建
chijian tianzhutang　敕建天主堂
Chong'ai zhi Mu tang　宠爱之母堂
chongjian　重建
Chongxi guan　崇禧观
Chu Deming　楮德明

chu chuang　初刱

cunzhi　村志

Dabodian (cun)　大薄店(村)

Dakou (tun)　大口(屯)

da maozi　大毛子

Dazhang (zhuang)　大张(庄)

de jiao chun cun　德教春存

dibao　地保

difang dang'anguan　地方档案馆

difangzhi　地方志

diji shi　地级市

dingzi　丁字

Dongguanbao (cun)　东关堡(村)

Dongjiaominxiang tang　东交民巷堂

Donglü (cun)　东闾(村)

Donglü zhi hou Sheng Mu *xiang*　东闾之后圣母像

Dong Shouyi　董守义

Dong xuan zi　洞玄子

Dongyangshan (cun)　东杨善(村)

duilian　对联

Erdaogou (cun)　二道沟(村)

er maozi　二毛子

Fangshengchi　放生池

feifan de shengming li　非凡的生命力

Fei Libo　斐理伯

Fu Tieshan　傅铁山

Fuxin (zhuang)　富辛(庄)

fuyin tang　福音堂

Gao Jiali　高嘉理

Gaojia (zhuang)　高家(庄)

Gao Rohan　高若翰

Gete fuxing　哥特复兴

Gete shi　哥特式

gongsuo　公所

Guangxu *shisan nian chijian tianzhutang*　光绪十三年敕建天主堂

Guanzhong (cun)　观中(村)
Guashi (cun)　瓜市(村)
guguai　古怪
Guzhuangtou (cun)　古庄头(村)

Hao Jialu　郝嘉禄
Helou jiaotang　河楼教堂
Housangyu (cun)　后桑峪(村)
Huabei *diyi tang*　华北第一堂
Huangtuliang (cun)　黄土梁(村)
Hua shi tang　华式堂
hui wo dong fang　惠我东方
huoshao Wanghailou　火烧望海楼

Jiahoutuan (cun)　贾后疃(村)
Jiajiatuan (cun)　贾家疃(村)
jianding　尖顶
jiao'an　教案
Jiaoli tonggao　教理通告
jiaotang　教堂
jiaotang wenhua guangchang　教堂文化广场
jing tian　敬天
Jiudu　九都
Jiushi tang　救世堂

Konghuaying (cun)　孔化营(村)

lengdan　冷淡
Lianchi shuyuan　连池书院
libai tang　礼拜堂
Lijiao (cun)　立教(村)
Li Jichang　李际昌
Lingjia (cun)　凌家(村)
linran zhengqi　凛然正气
Luoma shi　罗马式

Magong (zhuang)　马公(庄)
Majiachang (cun)　马家场(村)
Meigui Sheng Mu　玫瑰圣母

Mengjiafen (cun)   孟家坟(村)
ming   铭
Ming Jialu   明嘉禄

Nanganzi Tianzhujiao tang   南岗子天主教堂
Nanlingluo (cun)   南绫罗(村)
Nantun   南屯
Nanyuan   南苑
neibu ziliao   内部资料
Niantou (cun)   埝头(村)
Nihewan (cun)   泥河湾(村)
Niumu (tun)   牛牧(屯)

paifang   牌坊
pailou   牌搂
pingding   平顶
Pingfang (cun)   平房(村)
Pinglushang (cun)   平路上(村)
Pu'ai jiaotang   普爱教堂

Qianyang (cun)   前扬(村)
Qiku Sheng Mu tang   七苦圣母堂
Qintian jian   钦天监
qi san chang zhi men kai sheng mie si   启三常之门开生灭死
quzhi   区志

Renci men   仁慈门
Renci tang   仁慈堂
Rencun   任村
renzi   人字
renzi tang   人字堂
reqing   热情

Sancha hekou   三岔河口
Sangyu (cun)   桑峪(村)
sanjiao   三教
shan chu shi mi   善除世迷
shangdeng   上等
shang fu hong xun guan gu jin   尚父宏勳冠古今
shang yu   上谕

sha yang guizi xian sha Faguo guizi　杀洋鬼子先杀法国鬼子

Sheng Boduolu　圣伯多禄堂

Sheng Boduolu Sheng Baolu (jiaotang)　圣伯多禄圣保禄 (教堂)

Sheng Leisi Gongsage　圣类思公撒格

Sheng Mi'e'er tianzhutang　圣弥 (米) 额 (厄) 尔天主堂

Sheng Mu dajiaotang　圣母大教堂

Sheng Mu desheng tang　圣母得胜堂

Sheng Mu desheng zhi jia　圣母得胜之家

Sheng Mu lingbao tang　圣母领报堂

Sheng Mu shan　圣母山

Sheng Mu shengyi tang　圣母圣衣堂

Sheng Mu sheng yue　圣母圣月

Sheng Mu tang　圣母堂

Sheng Mu wuranyuanzui tang　圣母无染原罪堂

Shengnü Xiaodelan tang　圣女小德兰堂

Sheng Ruose tang　圣若瑟堂

Sheng Ruose xiunühui chuxueyuan　圣若瑟修女会初学院

shengshan　圣山

Sheng Shizijia tang　圣十字架堂

Sheng Weizengjue　圣味增爵

Sheng xin tang　圣心堂

Shenjing (zhen)　深井 (镇)

shijian　事件

Shijiawu (cun)　石家务 (村)

Shitai tang　世泰堂

Shiwo (cun)　石窝 (村)

Shiyaozi (cun)　石窑子 (村)

Shizhu (cun)　石柱 (村)

Shuangliushu (cun)　双柳树 (村)

Shuangshu (cun)　双树 (村)

Shuangshuzi (cun)　双树子 (村)

Sige (zhuang)　四 (泗) 各 (庄)

sigui　死鬼

Si Xiuli　司修礼

Suqiao (zhen)　苏桥 (镇)

Taihe (zhuang)　太和 (庄)

Tianjin jiao'an　天津教案

Tianjin jiao'an yizhi　天津教案遗址

Tianjin minjiao zishi　天津民教滋事

Tianzhu　天主
tianzhujiao tang　天主教堂
Tianzhu Sheng Mu Donglü zhi hou wei women qi　天主圣母东闾之后为我们祈
tianzhutang　天主堂
Tong Dianrong　佟殿荣
tong wei jia jing　通微佳境
Tong wei jiao shi　通微教师
tong xuan jia jing　通玄佳境
Tong xuan jiao shi　通玄教师

Wanghailou　望海楼
Wanghailou jiaotang　望海楼教堂
Wanghailou tianzhutang　望海楼天主堂
Wanghai si　望海寺
wan you zhen yuan　万有真源
Weiji baike　维基百科
Weizengjue tang　味增爵堂
wu shi wu zhong xian zuo xing sheng zhen zhu zai　无始无终先作形声真主宰

xiang　乡
xianji shi　县级市
xianzhi　县志
Xiao Beitang　小北堂
Xiaodelan shengtang　小德兰圣堂
Xiaohan (cun)　小韩(村)
xiao jiaotang　小教堂
Xiao Nantang　小南堂
xiao tianzhutang　小天主堂
Xigao (zhuang)　西高(庄)
Xiheying (cun, zhen)　西和营(村,镇)
Xihulin (cun)　西湖林(村)
Xikai　西开
Xikai zongtang　西开总堂
Xilichi (cun)　西里池(村)
xin　信
Xi'nanjiao jiaotang　西南角教堂
xinggong　行宫
Xin (zhuang)　辛(庄)
Xishiku　西什库

Xi shi tang   西式堂
Xiwanzi (cun, zhen)   西湾子(村, 镇)
Xixianpo (cun)   西仙坡(村)
xuan jen xuan yi yu zhao zheng ji da quan heng   宣仁宣义聿照拯济大权衡

yang guizi   洋鬼子
Yangjialou (cun)   杨家楼(村)
Yang Xiangtai   杨祥太
Yang Yuxiu   杨玉秀
ye luo gui gen   叶落归根
Yesu junwang (tang)   耶稣君王(堂)
Yesu sheng xin tang   耶稣圣心堂
yidao   驿道
yingbi   影壁
Yishi bao   益世報
Yongning (cun, zhen)   永宁(村, 镇)
yongyuan jingjie   永远警戒
Youjia (cun)   游家(村)
Yuntaishan   云太山

Zhalan (tang)   栅栏(堂)
Zhangjia (zhuang)   张家(庄)
Zhang Yuanlin   张元林
Zhaoge (zhuang)   赵各(庄)
Zhao Huaiyi   赵怀义
Zhaojia (zhuang)   赵家(庄)
Zhao Yongqing   赵永清
Zhengfu si   正福寺
zhi ba jing zhi du lian chen cheng zhen   制八镜之度炼尘成真
Zhonghua Sheng Mu   中华圣母
Zhong Xi hebi shi   中西合璧式
Zhong Xi shi   中西式
Zhu Deming   褚德明
Zhuo xian Ren cun shu jiaowu quantu   涿县任村属教务全图
zhuwei xinyou zhimingzhe zhi mu   诸位信友致命者之墓
Zizhulin   紫竹林
Zizhulin Tianzhujiao tang   紫竹林天主教堂
Zongli (geguo shiwu) yamen   总理(各国事务)衙门
zuonan younü   左男右女

Bibliography

Anderson, Aeneas. *A Narrative of the British Embassy to China, in the Years 1792, 1793, and 1794.* London: J. Debrett, 1795.

Annales de la Congrégation de la Mission. Paris: Congrégation de la Mission, 1834–1963.

Annales de l'Oeuvre de la Sainte-Enfance. Paris: Bureau central de l'Oeuvre, 1846–1912.

Annals of the Congregation of the Mission. Baltimore and New York: Congregation of the Mission, 1894–1925.

Annals of the Propagation of the Faith. Old series (without vol. no.), Paris: Society for the Propagation of the Faith, 1838–1839; New series (with vol. no.), London: Society for the Propagation of the Faith, 1840–1923.

"Apostolic Prefect." https://en.wikipedia.org/wiki/Apostolic_prefect. Accessed 17 July 2017.

"Apostolic Vicariate." https://en.wikipedia.org/wiki/Apostolic_vicariate. Accessed 17 July 2017.

"Architecture and Furnishings." http://www.kencollins.com/glossary/architecture.htm. Accessed 15 October 2015.

Archives of the Congregation of the Mission, (Eastern Province) Philadelphia.

Archives of the Congregation of the Mission, (Maison-Mère) Paris, France.

Aubert, Marcel. *Gothic Cathedrals of France and their Treasures.* London: Nicholas Kaye, 1959.

Bainian endian: Jinshi zhi guang 百年恩典: 津世之光 (A hundred years of blessings: Tianjin's glory). Tianjin: Yishi bianjishi bianji chuban, 2012.

Baisha cunzhi 白沙村志 ([Hebei, Wu'an County] Baisha Village gazetteer). N.p. [Wu'an?]: n.p., 2011.

Bai xian shi jingji shehui diaocha, Baoding juan 百县市经济社会调查保定卷 (An investigation into the economy and society of one hundred counties and cities, Baoding chapter). Beijing: Zhongguo dabaikequan chubanshe, 1993.

Baldacchino, Georges. "Relevé global des dossiers sur la chine." Revised 2013. http://famvin.fr/Congreg_Mission/ARCH_Invent_PDF%2026_08_09/ARCH_Chine%20Mais_Mere.pdf. Accessed 10 November 2016.

"Baoding jiaoqu liu zongtang 35 fentang jiaochan jiaoyou tongjibiao" 保定教区六总堂35分堂教产 教友统计表 (Statistical table of Baoding diocese's [rural] six main churches [and] thirty-five affiliated churches, property, and Catholics). Report manuscript, dated 31 October 1994.

Baoding shi beishi quzhi 保定市北市区志 ([Hebei] Baoding City, north area gazetteer). Beijing: Xinhua chubanshe, 1991.

Baoding shi nanshi quzhi 保定市南市区志 ([Hebei] Baoding City, south area gazetteer). Beijing: Xinhua chubanshe, 1990.

"Baoding Tianzhujiao tang" 保定教主教堂 (The Baoding Catholic church). http://
wenku.baidu.com/link?url=wk8t2FjWEMlZU_MgCQWsktrvs2V4bJWIrwde
Rh4JdZokiL_ZVoHInKIIyIxcYJo7v9FjduK-sdfdblAWgizPeZzxfplL56j8Db6oCAMXs
Wm. Accessed 17 January 2017.

Bao Lu 保禄. *Handan Tianzhujiao shilüe* 邯郸天主教史略 (Brief history of Catholicism
at Handan). Handan: Haixing bianjibu, 2005.

"Basilica of Notre-Dame-des-Victoires, Paris." http://en.wikipedia.org/wiki/Basilica_
of_Notre-Dame-des-Victoires,_Paris. Accessed 12 January 2015.

Basu, Dilip K. "Chinese Xenology and the Opium War: Reflections on Sinocentrism."
Journal of Asian Studies 73, no. 4 (November 2014): 927–940.

Baum, Julius. *German Cathedrals*. New York: Vanguard Press, 1956.

Becker, Émile. *Un demi-siècle d'apostolat en Chine, le Révérend Père Joseph Gonnet de la
Compagnie de Jésus*. 3rd ed. Ho-kien-fou: Imprimerie de la Mission, 1916.

"Beijing." https://en.wikipedia.org/wiki/Beijing. Accessed 14 May 2017.

Beijing chengshi dituji 北京城市地图集 (Beijing city atlas). Beijing: Dizhi chubanshe,
2008.

"Beijing de jiaotang: Housangyu cun Tianzhujiao tang" 北京的教堂: 后桑峪村天主
教堂 (Bejing's churches: the Housangyu Village Catholic church). http://blog.sina
.com.cn/s/blog_494d86ef01019p73.html. Accessed 23 January 2017.

Beijing shi Mentougou quzhi 北京市门头沟区志 (Beijing Municipality, Mentougou
District gazetteer). Beijing: Beijing chubanshe, 2006.

Beijing Tianzhu jiaohui 北京天主教会 (The Catholic Church in Beijing). Compiled by
Beijing Tianzhu jiaohui bianjihui. Beijing: Zhongguo minzu sheying yishu chubanshe, 2004.

"Beijing Yongning Tianzhujiao tang misa shijian" 北京永宁天主教堂弥撒时间
(Beijing's Yongning Catholic church mass times). http://bj.bendibao.com/tour/
20151123/208900_3.shtm. Accessed 13 May 2016.

"Beitang jianjie" 北堂简介 (A brief introduction to the North Church). Church courtyard display, 2007.

Beny, Roloff, and Peter Gunn. *The Churches of Rome*. New York: Simon and Schuster,
1981.

Bernstein, Lewis. "After the Fall: Tianjin under Foreign Occupation, 1900–1902." In *The
Boxers, China, and the World*, edited by Robert Bickers and R.G. Tiedemann, 133–146.
Lanham, Md.: Rowman & Littlefield, 2007.

Bickers, Robert. *The Scramble for China: Foreign Devils in the Qing Empire, 1832–1914*.
London: Penguin, 2012.

Bierchane, Joseph. "Urbanisme et églises chinoises." *Églises d'Asie* 5 (November 2008):
66–73.

Bishop, Kevin. *China's Imperial Way: Retracing an Historical Trade and Communication
Route from Beijing to Hong Kong*. Hong Kong: Odyssey, 1997.

Bony, Jean. *French Cathedrals*. Boston: Houghton Mifflin, 1951.

Bornet, Paul. "La chapelle votive de la Vierge au cimetiere de Chala." *Bulletin catholique de Pékin* 34 (1947): 440–448.

Bornet, Paul. "Les anciennes églises de Pékin: notes d'histoire, le Pei-t'ang [part 1]." *Bulletin catholique de Pékin* 32 (March 1945): 118–132.

Bornet, Paul. "Les anciennes églises de Pékin: notes d'histoire, le Pei-t'ang [part 2]." *Bulletin catholique de Pékin* 32 (April 1945): 172–187.

Bornet, Paul. "Les anciennes églises de Pékin: notes d'histoire, le Pei-t'ang [part 3]." *Bulletin catholique de Pékin* 32 (May 1945): 239–245.

Bornet, Paul. "Les anciennes églises de Pékin: notes d'histoire, les anciennes églises Russes." *Bulletin catholique de Pékin* 32 (1945): 339–349, 391–401.

Bornet, Paul. "Les anciennes églises de Pékin: notes d'histoire, Nant'ang [part 1]." *Bulletin catholique de Pékin* 31 (October 1944): 490–504.

Bornet, Paul. "Les anciennes églises de Pékin: notes et histoire, Nant'ang [part 2]." *Bulletin catholique de Pékin* 31 (November 1944): 527–545.

Bornet, Paul. "Les anciennes églises de Pékin [notes et histoire,] Nan'tang [part 3]." *Bulletin catholique de Pékin* 32 (1945): 22–31.

Bornet, Paul. "Les anciennes églises de Pékin: notes d'histoire, le Si-t'ang." *Bulletin catholique de Pékin* 32 (1945): 293–300.

Bornet, Paul. "Les anciennes églises de Pékin: notes d'histoire, Tongt'ang." *Bulletin catholique de Pékin* 32 (1945): 66–74.

Bornet, Paul. "Les anciennes églises de Pékin: supplément." *Bulletin catholique de Pékin* 32 (1945): 246–251.

Bosker, Bianca. *Original Copies: Architectural Mimicry in Contemporary China.* Honolulu: University of Hawai'i Press, 2013.

Boyd, Andrew. *Chinese Architecture and Town Planning, 1500 B.C.–A.D. 1911.* Chicago: University of Chicago Press, 1962.

Brockey, Liam Matthew. *Journey to the East: The Jesuit Mission to China, 1579–1724.* Cambridge, Mass.: Belknap Press of Harvard University Press, 2007.

Brunnert, H.S., and V.V. Hagelstrom. *Present Day Political Organization of China.* Translated by A. Beltchenko and E.E. Moran. 1912. Reprint, Taipei: Book World, 1963.

"Cangzhou jiaoqu jianjie" 沧州教区简介 (A brief introduction to Cangzhou diocese). Cathedral courtyard display, 2011.

Catalogue des maisons et du personnel de la Congrégation de la Mission. Paris: n.p. (or various publishers), 1862–1940.

"Catholic Church in China." https://en.wikipedia.org/wiki/Catholic_Church_in_China. Accessed 16 February 2018.

"Catholic Church with Walled Courtyard Garden in Beijing," Yudin Collection, Library of Congress. https://www.loc.gov/item/2011660670. Accessed 28 March 2016.

Catholic Missions and Annals of the Propagation of the Faith. New York, N.Y.: Society for the Propagation of the Faith, 1924–1935.

The Cause of the Riots in the Yangtse Valley: A "Complete Picture Gallery." Hankow: n.p., 1891.

Chambon, Octave, ed. *Vie et Apostolat de Monseigneur Louis-Gabriel Delaplace*. Auxerre: Octave Chambon, Imprimeur, 1892.

Chang, Jung. *Empress Dowager Cixi: The Concubine Who Launched Modern China*. New York: Anchor Books, 2014.

Charbonnier, Jean. *Guide to the Catholic Church in China, 2008*. Singapore: China Catholic Communication, 2008.

Chaves, Jonathan. *Singing of the Source: Nature and God in the Poetry of the Chinese Painter Wu Li*. Honolulu: University of Hawaii Press, 1993.

Chen, Hui-Hung. "Encounters in Peoples, Religions, and Sciences: Jesuit Visual Culture in Seventeenth Century China." Ph.D. diss., Brown University, 2004.

Child, Mark. *Discovering Church Architecture*. Oxford: Shire Publications, 2008.

China in the Sixteenth Century: The Journals of Matthew Ricci: 1583–1610. Translated by Louis J. Gallagher. New York: Random House, 1942.

Chongli xianzhi 崇礼县志 ([Hebei] Chongli County gazetteer. Beijing: Zhongguo she-hui chubanshe, 1995.

"Christianity in China." *Christian History & Biography* 98 (Spring 2008): 6–34.

Chu, Cindy Yik-yi, ed. *Catholicism in China, 1900–Present: The Development of the Chinese Church*. New York: Palgrave Macmillan, 2014.

"Church of the Gesù." http://en.wikipedia.org/wiki/Church_of_the_Ges%C3%B9. Assessed 9 May 2015.

"Church in Peking," Yudin Collection, Library of Congress. https://www.loc.gov/item/2002715463/. Accessed 28 March 2016.

Clark, Anthony E. "China Gothic: Indigenous Church Design in Late-Imperial Beijing." *History Faculty Scholarship*. Paper 10. Spokane, Wash.: Whitworth University, 2015. http://digitalcommons.whitworth.edu/historyfaculty/10. Accessed 28 October 2016.

Clark, Anthony E. "Rape, Baptism, and the 'Pig' Religion: Chinese Images of Foreign Missionaries during the Late Nineteenth Century." In *Beating Devils and Burning Their Books: Views of China, Japan, and the West*, edited by Anthony E. Clark, 43–81. Ann Arbor, Mich.: Association for Asian Studies, 2010.

Clark, Anthony E. "Vincentian Footprints in China: The Lives and Legacies of François-Régis Clet, C.M. and Jean-Gabriel Perboyre, C.M." *Vincentian Heritage Journal* 32, no. 1 (Spring 2014). http://via.library.depaul.edu/vhj/vol32/iss1/3. Accessed 23 November 2015.

Clunas, Craig. *Pictures and Visuality in Early Modern China*. London: Reaktion Books, 1997.

Cody, Jeffrey W. "Striking a Harmonious Chord: Foreign Missionaries and Chinese-style Buildings, 1911–1949." *Architronic* 5, no. 3 (December 1996): 1–30.

Cohen, Paul A. "The Anti-Christian Tradition in China." *Journal of Asian Studies* 20, no. 2 (February 1961): 169–180.

Cohen, Paul A. *China and Christianity: The Missionary Movement and the Growth of Chinese Antiforeignism, 1860–1870.* Cambridge, Mass.: Harvard University Press, 1963.

Cohen, Paul A. "Christian Missions and Their Impact to 1900." In *The Cambridge History of China.* Vol. 10, *Late Ch'ing, 1800–1911, Part 1,* edited by John K. Fairbank, 543–590. Cambridge: Cambridge University Press, 1978.

Cohen, Paul A. *History in Three Keys: The Boxers as Event, Experience, and Myth.* New York: Columbia University Press, 1997.

Collard, Maurice. *Les Martyrs de Tien-Tsin.* Paris: Libraire-Éditions A. Giraudon, 1926.

Collins, Neil. *The Splendid Cause: The Missionary Society of St Columban, 1916–1954.* Dublin: The Columban Press, 2009.

"Concessions in Tianjin." https://en.wikipedia.org/wiki/Concessions_in_Tianjin. Accessed 8 July 2016.

Coomans, Thomas. "A pragmatic approach to church construction in Northern China at the time of Christian inculturation: the handbook 'Le missionnaire constructeur', 1926." *Frontiers of Architectural Research* 3 (2014): 89–107.

Coomans, Thomas. "Indigenizing Catholic Architecture in China: From Western Gothic to Sino-Chrisitian Design, 1900–1940." In *Catholicism in China, 1900–Present: The Development of the Chinese Church,* edited by Cindy Yik-yi Chu, 125–146. New York, N.Y.: Palgrave Macmillan, 2014.

Coomans, Thomas, and Wei Luo. "Exporting Flemish Gothic Architecture to China: Meaning and Context of the Churches of Shebiya (Inner Mongolia) and Xuanhua (Hebei) Built by Missionary-architect Alphonse De Moerloose in 1903–1906." *Relicta* 9 (2012): 219–262.

Cordier, Henri. *Histoire des relations de la Chine avec les puissances occidentals, 1860–1900.* 3 vols. 1901–1902. Reprint, Taipei: Ch'eng-wen Publishing Co., 1966.

Corsi, Elisabetta. "Pozzo's Treatise as a Workshop for the Construction of a Sacred Catholic Space in Beijing." In *Artifizi della metafora: saggi su Andrea Pozzo,* edited by Richard Bösel et al, 232–243. Roma: Artemide, 2011.

Criveller, Gianni, and César Guillén-Nuñez, eds. *Portrait of a Jesuit: Matteo Ricci, 1552–1610.* Macau: Macau Ricci Institute, 2010.

"Currency Converter." http://www.pierre-marteau.com/currency/converter/eng-fra.html. Accessed 15 November 2016.

"Daming Chong'ai zhi Mu jiantang bashi zhounian jinian, 1921–2001" 大名宠爱之母建堂八十周年纪念 1921–2001 (In commemoration of the eightieth anniversary of the establishment of Daming's Mother of Grace Church, 1921–2001). Daming: n.p., 2001. Church internal circulation material, pamphlet.

"Daming tianzhutang" 大名天主堂 (The Daming Catholic church). https://zh .wikipedia.org/wiki/%E5%A4%A7%E5%90%8D%E5%AE%A0%E7%88%B1%E4 %B9%8B%E6%AF%8D%E5%A0%82. Accessed 9 January 2017.

Daming xianzhi 大名县志 ([Hebei] Daming County gazetteer). Beijing: Xinhua chubanshe, 1994.

David, Armand. *Abbe David's Diary: Being an Account of the French Naturalist's Journeys and Observations in China in the Years 1866 to 1869*. Translated and edited by Helen M. Fox. Cambridge, Mass.: Harvard University Press, 1949.

David, Armand. *Journal de mon troisième voyage d'exploration dans l'empire Chinois*. 2 vols. Paris: Librairie Hachette, 1875.

DeAndreis Rosati Memorial Archives, DePaul University Library, Chicago.

"The Decline of China's Catholic Population and its Impact on the Church." http:// www.asianews.it/news-en/The-decline-of-China%E2%80%99s-Catholic-populati on-and-its-impact-on-the-Church-38373.html. Accessed 16 February 2018.

De Groot, J.J.M. *The Religious System of China, Its Ancient Forms, Evolution, History and Present Aspect, Manners, Custom and Social Institutions Connected Therewith*. 6 vols. 1892–1910. Reprint, Taipei: Ch'eng Wen Publishing Co., 1976.

De Groot, J.J.M. *Sectarianism and Religious Persecution in China: A Page in the History of Religions*. 2 vols. 1903–1904. Reprint (2 vols. in 1), Taipei: Literature House, 1963.

D'Elia, Pasquale M. *Le Origini dell'arte Cristiana Cinese (1583–1640)*. Roma: Reale Accademia D'Italia, 1939.

"Demographics of China." https://en.wikipedia.org/wiki/Demographics_of_China. Accessed 13 April 2017.

Devine, W. *The Four Churches of Peking*. London: Burns, Oates & Washbourne, 1930.

Dictionary of Ming Biography, 1368–1644. Edited by L. Carrington Goodrich. 2 vols. New York: Columbia University Press, 1976.

"Dingxing Shizhu cun tianzhutang" 定兴石柱村天主堂 (Shizhu Village, Dingxing, Catholic church). http://blog.sina.com.cn/s/blog_87ca2ce40102vyd5.html. Accessed 15 June 2017.

"Dollar-Pound Exchange Rate from 1791." https://www.measuringworth.com/datasets/ exchangepound/result.php. Accessed 27 December 2016.

Dong Conglin 董丛林. *Long yu shangdi: Jidujiao yu Zhongguo chuantong wenhua* 龙与上帝: 基督教与中国传统文化 (The dragon and god: Christianity and traditional Chinese culture). Beijing: Xinzhi sanlian shudian, 1992.

Dong Conglin 董丛林. *Yanzhao wenhua de jindai zhuanxing* 燕赵文化的近代转型 (The modern evolution of North China [Hebei] culture). Shijiazhuang: Hebei jiaoyu chubanshe, 2000.

Dong Jinhe 董金和. "Guzhuangtou jiao'an neimu" 古庄头教案内幕 (The inside story of the Guzhuangtou [Christian] religious case). *Zhuozhou wenshi ziliao* 2 (May 1988): 129–133.

"Dong-Lu Shrine." https://www.udayton.edu/imri/mary/d/dong-lu-shrine.php. Accessed 20 February 2017.

Dunch, Ryan. "Protestant Christianity in China Today: Fragile, Fragmented, Flourishing." In *China and Christianity: Burdened Past, Hopeful Future*, edited by Stephen Uhalley, Jr. and Xiaoxin Wu, 195–216. Armonk, N.Y.: M. E. Sharpe, 2000.

Dutton, Michael, Hsiu-ju Stacy Lo, and Dong Wu. *Beijing Time*. Cambridge, Mass.: Harvard University Press, 2008.

Eastman, Lloyd E. *Family, Field, and Ancestors: Constancy and Change in China's Social and Economic History, 1550–1949*. New York: Oxford University Press, 1988.

Eminent Chinese of the Ch'ing Period. Edited by Arthur W. Hummel. 2 vols. 1943–1944. Reprint (2 vols. in 1), Taipei: Ch'eng-wen Publishing, 1970.

Entenmann, Robert. "Chinese Catholic Clergy and Catechists in Eighteenth-Century Szechwan." In *Images de la Chine: le Contexte Occidental de la Sinologie Naissante*, edited by Edward J. Malatesta and Yves Raguin, 389–410. Paris: Institute Ricci—Centre d'Études Chinoises, 1995.

Entenmann, Robert. "The Establishment of Chinese Catholic Communities in Early Ch'ing Szechwan." In *Echanges culturels et religieux, entre la Chine et l'Occident*, edited by Edward J. Malatesta, Yves Raguin, and Adrianus C. Dudink, 147–161. Paris: Institute Ricci—Centre d'Études Chinoises, 1995.

Esherick, Joseph W. *The Origins of the Boxer Uprising*. Berkeley: University of California Press, 1987.

The Face of China as Seen by Photographers & Travelers, 1862–1912. Philadelphia: Philadelphia Art Museum—Aperture, 1978.

Fairbank, John K. "Patterns Behind the Tientsin Massacre." *Harvard Journal of Asiatic Studies* 20, no. 3/4 (December 1957): 480–511.

Fang Hao 方豪. *Zhongguo Tianzhujiao shi renwuzhuan* 中国天主教史人物传 (Biographies of figures in Chinese Catholic history). 1967. Reprint, Shanghai: Tianzhujiao Shanghai jiaoqu Guangqi she, 2003.

Fangshan quzhi 房山区志 ([Beijing] Fangshan District gazetteer). Beijing: Beijing chubanshe, 1999.

Fangshan xianzhi 房山县志 ([Hebei] Fangshan County gazetteer). N.p: n.p., 1928.

Favier, Alphonse. *The Heart of Pekin: Bishop A. Favier's Diary of the Siege May–August 1900*. Edited by J. Freri. Boston: Marlier & Co., 1901.

Favier, Alphonse. *Péking: histoire et description*. Péking [Beijing]: Imprimerie des Lazaristes au Pé-t'ang, 1897; "2nd edition," Lille: Société de Saint Augustin, Desclée, de Brouwer et Cie, 1900; and "nouvelle edition," Paris: Desclée, de Brouwer et Cie, 1902.

Favier, Alphonse [Fan Guoliang 樊国梁, pseud]. *Yanjing kaijiao lüe* 燕京开教略 (A short history of the Church in Beijing). N.p.: n.p., 1905. Reprinted as *Lao Beijing naxie shi'er: sanpin dingdai yang jiaoshi kan Zhongguo* 老北京那些事儿: 三品顶戴洋教士看中国 (Old Beijing matters: a foreign missionary of the third civil rank looks at China). Beijing: Quanguo baijia chubanshe, 2010.

Ferreux, Octave. *Histoire de la Congrégation de la Mission en Chine (1699–1950)*. Paris: Congrégation de la Mission, 1963. Published as vol. 127 of *Annales de la Congrégation de la Mission*.

Ferreux, Octave [Fan Guoyin 樊国阴, pseud]. *Qianshihui zai Hua chuanjiao shi* 遣士会在华传教史遣 (History of the Congregation of the Mission in China). Translated by Wu Zongwen. Taibei: Huaming shuju, 1977.

"First Services Held in Sacred Heart Church." *Turlock Journal*, 31 October 2009. Reprint of article from the *Turlock Tribune*, 25 October 1929.

Fortune, Robert. *A Journey to the Capitals of Japan and China*. London: John Murray, 1863.

Franklin, J.W. *The Cathedrals of Italy*. London: B. T. Batsford, 1958.

Frankl, Paul. *Gothic Architecture*. Revised by Paul Crossley. New Haven: Yale University Press, 2000.

"Frédéric-Vincent Lebbe." https://en.wikipedia.org/wiki/Fr%C3%A9d%C3%A9ric -Vincent_Lebbe. Accessed 6 July 2016.

Gamble, Sidney D. *Ting Hsien: A North China Rural Community*. New York: Institute of Pacific Relations, 1954.

Gernet, Jacques. *China and the Christian Impact: A Conflict of Cultures*. Translated by Janet Lloyd. Cambridge: Cambridge University Press, 1990.

Gewurtz, Margo S. "The 'Jesus Sect' and 'Jesus Opium': Creating a Christian Community in Rural North Honan, 1890–1912." In *The Chinese Face of Jesus Christ*. Vol. 2, edited by Roman Malek, 685–705. Nettetal: Institut Monumenta Serica and China-Zentrum Sankt Augustin, 2003.

Golvers, Noel. *The Astronomia Europaea of Ferdinand Verbiest, S.J. (Dilligen, 1687): Text, Translation, Notes and Commentaries*. Nettetal: Steyler Verlag, 1993.

Grant, Frederic D. Jr. "The April 1820 Debt Settlement between Consecqua and Benjamin Chew Wilcocks." In *Americans and Macao: Trade, Smuggling, and Diplomacy on the South China Coast*, edited by Paul A. Van Dyke, 73–94. Hong Kong: Hong Kong University Press, 2012.

Grootaers, Willem A. "Les anciennes églises de Pékin: Nant'ang, texte et traduction des steles du Nant'ang." *Bulletin catholique de Pékin* 31 (1944): 586–599.

"Guanyu luoshi Yongning Tianzhujiao jiaohui fangchan yijian de baogao" 关于落实永天主教教会房产意见的报告 (A report on carrying out the opinion [rendered for compensation] for the Catholic congregation's property). Compiled by Yanqing xian minzhengju. 20 June 1985. Church internal circulation material, photocopy.

Gu Changsheng 顾长声. *Chuanjiaoshi yu jindai Zhongguo* 传教士与近代中国 (Missionaries and modern China). Shanghai: Shanghai renmin chubanshe, 1981.

Guillén-Nuñez, César. "The Façade of St. Paul's, Macao: A Retable-Façade?" *Journal of the Hong Kong Branch of the Royal Asiatic Society* 41 (2001): 131–188.

Guillén-Nuñez, César. *Macao's Church of Saint Paul: A Glimmer of the Baroque in China.* Hong Kong: Hong Kong University Press, 2009.

Guillén-Nuñez, César. "Matteo Ricci, the Nantang, and the Introduction of Roman Catholic Church Architecture to Beijing." In *Portrait of a Jesuit: Matteo Ricci, 1552–1610*, edited by Gianni Criveller and César Guillén-Nuñez, 101–128. Macau: Macau Ricci Institute, 2010.

Guillén-Nuñez, César. "Rising from the Ashes: The Gothic Revival and the Architecture of the 'New' Society of Jesus in Macao and China." In *Jesuit Survival and Restoration: A Global History, 1773–1900*, edited by Robert A. Maryks and Jonathan Wright, 278–298. Leiden: Brill, 2015.

Guiyang bei tianzhutang 贵阳北天主堂 (Guiyang's North Catholic Church). Guiyang: n.p, n.d. Church internal circulation material, book.

Guo Maogong 郭懋功. "Tianzhujiao Nancheng jiaoqu shimo" 天主教南城教区始末 (The Catholic diocese of Nancheng, from beginning to end). *Nancheng wenshi ziliao* 1 (December 1985): 81–87.

Gu Weiying 古伟瀛. "Xue Madou shenfu" 薛玛窦神父 (Fr. Matthew Xue). In *Saiwai chuanjiao shi* 塞外传教史 (A history of Catholic missions beyond the Great Wall), edited by Gu Weiying, 95–124. Taibei: Guangqi wenhua shiye, 2002.

Gu Yulu 顾裕禄. *Zhongguo Tianzhujiao de guoqu he xianzai* 中国天主教的过去和现在 (Chinese Catholicism's past and present). Shanghai: Shanghai shehui kexueyuan chubanshe, 1989.

"Hai River." http://en.wikipedia.org/wiki/Hai_River. Accessed 22 April 2015.

Halbwachs, Maurice. *The Collective Memory.* Translated by Francis J. Ditter, Jr. and Vida Yazdi Ditter. New York: Harper & Row, 1980.

Handbook of Christianity in China, Volume One: 635–1800. Edited by Nicolas Standaert. *Handbook of Oriental Studies*, vol. 15/1. Leiden: Brill, 2001.

Handbook of Christianity in China, Volume Two: 1800 to the Present. Edited by R.G. Tiedemann. *Handbook of Oriental Studies*, vol. 15/2. Leiden: Brill, 2010.

"Hebei." https://en.wikipedia.org/wiki/Hebei. Accessed 23 March 2017.

Hebei ji zhoubian tiqu gonglu licheng dituce 河北及周边地区公路里程地图册 (Maps of highway routes in Hebei and surrounding districts). Beijing: Dizhi chubanshe, 2012.

Hebei sheng dituce 河北省地图册 (Maps of Hebei Province). Beijing: Xingqiu ditu chubanshe, 2010.

Hickey, Edward John. "The Society for the Propagation of the Faith: Its Foundation, Organization and Success (1822–1922). Ph.D. diss., The Catholic University of America, 1922.

"History of the Shrine to Our Lady of Sheshan." http://www.fides.org/en/news/14510#. WKY_gBH2zok. Accessed 20 February 2017.

The Horizon Book of Great Cathedrals. Edited by Jay Jacobs. New York: American Heritage Publishing, 1984.

Hsiang, Paul Stanislaus. *The Catholic Missions in China during the Middle Ages (1294–1368)*. 1949. Reprint, Cleveland: John T. Zubal, 1984.

Hsü, Immanuel C.Y. *The Rise of Modern China.* 6th ed. New York: Oxford University Press, 2000.

Huang Bolu 黃伯禄, comp. *Zheng jiao feng bao* 正教奉褒 (In praise of Catholicism). Shanghai: Cimu tang, 1894.

Hubrecht, Alphonse. *La mission de Péking et les Lazaristes.* Péking [Beijing]: Imprimerie des Lazaristes, 1939.

Huc, Évariste-Régis. *The Chinese Empire, Forming a Sequel to the Work "Recollections of a Journey through Tartary and Thibet."* Translated by Mrs. Percy Sinnett. 1854. Reprint, Port Washington, N.Y.: Kennikat Press, 1970.

Huc, Évariste-Régis. *Le Christianisme en Chine, en Tartarie et au Thibet. 4 vols.* Paris: Gaume Frères, Libraires-Éditeurs, 1857–1858.

Huc, Évariste-Régis. *Christianity in China, Tartary, and Thibet.* 3 vols. London: Longman, Brown, Green, Longmans, & Roberts, 1857–1858.

Huc, Évariste-Régis. *L'empire Chinois, faisant suite à l'ouvrage intitulé: "Souvenirs d'un voyage dans a Tartarie et le Thibet."* 2nd ed. Paris: Librairie de Gaume Frères, 1856.

Huc, Évariste-Régis and Joseph Gabet. *Souvenirs d'un voyage dans la Tartarie, le Thibet, et la Chine pendant les années 1844, 1845 et 1846.* 2 vols. Paris: A. LeClère & Cⁱᵉ, 1850.)

Huc, Évariste-Régis and Joseph Gabet. *Travels in Tartary, Thibet and China, 1844–1846.* 2 vols. Translated by William Hazlitt. New York: Dover Publications, 1987.

Hucker, Charles O. *A Dictionary of Official Titles in Imperial China.* 1975. Reprint, Taipei: SMC Publishing, 1995.

Huoshao Wanghailou—1870 Tianjin renmin fan yangjiao douzheng 火烧望海楼——一八七0年天津人民反洋教斗争 (Burning the Wanghailou [church]—the 1870 struggle of the Tianjin people against foreign religion). Edited by Tianjin lishi yanjiusuo and Tianjin shihua bianxiezu. Tianjin: Tianjin renmin chubanshe, 1973.

Irigoin, Alejandra. "A 'Trojan Horse' in Daoguang China?: Explaining the Flows of Silver (and Opium) in and out of China." *LSE Economic History Department Working Papers* 173, no. 13 (January 2013): 1–34. http://mpra.ub.uni-muenchen.de/43987/. Accessed 10 November 2016.

Jantzen, Hans. *High Gothic: The Classic Cathedrals of Chartres, Reims, and Amiens.* Translated by James Palmes. Princeton: Princeton University Press, 1984.

"Jesuit Saints." https://en.wikipedia.org/wiki/Category:Jesuit_saints. Accessed 19 January 2017.

"Jiahoutuan jiaotang xingshuai shi" 贾后疃教堂兴衰史 (A history of the Jiahuotuan church's rise and fall). Jiahoutuan: n.p., n.d. (ca 2009). Church internal circulation material, pamphlet.

"Jiahoutuan tianzhutang" 贾后疃天主堂 (The Jiahoutuan Catholic church). http://blog.sina.com.cn/s/blog_87ca2ce40102vkow.html. Accessed 25 January 2017.

Jiangxi sheng dituce 江西省地图册 (Maps of Jiangxi province). Shanghai: Zhonghua ditu xuehui zhiban, 1993.

Jiaowu jiao'an dang 教务教案档 ([Zongli yamen] Archives on [Christian] religious cases). Series I, 1860–1866, 3 vols.; Series II, 1867–1870, 3 vols.; Series III, 1871–1878, 3 vols.; Series IV, 1879–1886, 3 vols.; Series V, 1887–1895, 4 vols.; Series VI, 1896–1899, 3 vols.; Series VII, 1900–1911, 2 vols. Taibei: Zhongyang yanjiuyuan, jindai shi yanjiusuo, 1974–1981.

Jingli Donglü Sheng Mu—shihua (Saluting Our Lady of Donglü—a history) 敬礼东闾圣母—史话. Baoding: Baoding jiaoqu mu'enmeiti zixun zhongxin, 2012.

Jinri Tianzhujiao Shanghai jiaoqu 今日天主教上海教区 (The Catholic church in Shanghai today). Shanghai: Tianzhujiao Shanghai jiaoqu Guangqishe chuban, 1995.

Jinri Tianzhujiao Shanghai jiaoqu 今日天主教上海教区 (The Catholic church in Shanghai today). Shanghai: Tianzhujiao Shanghai jiaoqu Guangqishe chubanshe, 2000.

Johnston, Tess. *Far from Home: Western Architecture in China's Northern Treaty Ports.* Hong Kong: Old China Hand Press, 1996.

Johnston, Tess. *God & Country: Western Religious Architecture in Old China.* Hong Kong: Old China Hand Press, 1996.

Johnston, Tess. *The Last Colonies: Western Architecture in China's Southern Treaty Ports.* Hong Kong: Old China Hand Press, 1997.

"Kalgan." http://www.britannica.com/EBchecked/topic/310134/Kalgan. Accessed 9 April 2015.

Kang Zhijie 康志杰. *Shangzhu de putaoyuan—E xibei mopanshan Tianzhu jiaoshequ yanjiu (1634–2005)* 上主的葡萄园—鄂西北磨盘山天主教社区研究 (1634–2005) (God's vineyard—a study of Hubei's northwestern Catholic district of Mopanshan). Xinzhu: Fujen daxue chubanshe, 2006.

King, Gail. "Note on a Late Ming Dynasty Chinese Description of 'Ricci's Church' in Beijing." *Sino-Western Cultural Relations Journal* 20 (1998): 49–51.

King, Michelle T. *Between Birth and Death: Female Infanticide in Nineteenth-Century China.* Stanford: Stanford University Press, 2014.

Kritzman, Lawrence D. "Foreword: In Remembrance of Things French." In *Realms of Memory: Rethinking the French Past.* Vol. 1, *Conflicts and Divisions*, edited by Pierre Nora, ix–xiv. New York: Columbia University Press, 1996.

Kwok, Pui-lan. *Chinese Women and Christianity, 1860–1927.* Atlanta: Scholars Press, 1992.

Laamann, Lars P. *Christian Heretics in Late Imperial China: Christian Inculturation and State Control, 1720–1850*. New York: Routledge, 2006.

Lam, Sui-ky Anthony. "The Decline of China's Catholic Population and its Impact on the Church." http://www.asianews.it/news-en/The-decline-of-China%E2%80%99s-Catholic-population-and-its-impact-on-the-Church-38373.html. Accessed 16 February 2018.

"Langfang tianzhutang," 廊坊天主堂 (Langfang Catholic churches). http://blog.sina.com.cn/s/blog_71ea7d850102xlcd.html. Accessed 13 January 2017.

"Lao zhaopian," 老照片 (Old photographs). http://www.360doc.com/content/13/0204/17/2280746_264220367.shtml. Accessed 11 November 2015.

"L'art Chrétien Chinois." *Dossiers de la Commission Synodale* 5, no. 5 (May 1932): 403–524.

Latourette, Kenneth Scott. *A History of Christian Missions in China*. London: Society for Promoting Christian Knowledge, 1929.

Leonard, Jane Kate. *Controlling from Afar: the Daoguang Emperor's Management of the Grand Canal Crisis, 1824–1826*. Ann Arbor, Mich.: Center for Chinese Studies, University of Michigan, 1996.

"Lijiao cun li de tianzhutang" 立教村里的天主教堂 (Lijiao Village's Catholic church). http://blog.sina.com.cn/s/blog_69cda1bf01017pmu.html. Accessed 26 January 2017.

Li, Lillian M. *Fighting Famine in North China: State, Market, and Environmental Decline, 1690s–1990s*. Stanford: Stanford University Press, 2007.

Lin Jizhong 林基中, comp. *Yan xing lu quan ji* 燕行录全集 (A complete collection of records of travels in northern Hebei). Hancheng: Dongguo daxue chubanbu, 2001.

Lin Wenhui 林文慧. *Qingji Fujian jiao'an zhi yanjiu* 清季福建教案之研究 (Research into Fujian [Christian] religious cases of the Qing period). Taibei: Taiwan shangwu yinshuguan, 1989.

Lin Zhiping 林治平. *Jindai Zhongguo yu Jidujiao lunwen ji* 近代中国与基督教论文集 (Papers on modern China and Christianity). Taibei: Yuzhouguang chubanshe, 1981.

"List of Largest Cities Throughout History." http://en.wikipedia.org/wiki/List_of_largest_cities_throughout_history. Accessed 29 October 2014.

Litzinger, Charles A. "Patterns of Missionary Cases Following the Tientsin Massacre, 1870–1875." *Papers on China* 23 (July 1970): 87–108.

Litzinger, Charles A. "Rural Religion and Village Organization in North China: The Catholic Challenge in the Late Nineteenth Century." In *Christianity in China: From the Eighteenth Century to the Present*, edited by Daniel H. Bays, 41–52. Stanford: Stanford University Press, 1996.

Litzinger, Charles A. "Temple Community and Village Cultural Integration in North China: Evidence from 'Sectarian Cases' (*chiao-an*) in Chihli, 1862–1895." Ph.D. diss., University of California, Davis, 1983.

Liu, Qinghua. "The Beitang Collection in Ningxia and the Lazarist Mission Press in the Late Qing Period." In *History of the Catholic Church in China: From Its Beginning to the Scheut Fathers and 20th Century. Unveiling Some Less Known Sources, Sounds and Pictures*, edited by Ferdinand Verbiest Institute, 419–442. Leuven: Ferdinand Verbiest Institute K.U. Leuven, 2015.

Liu Qingyu 刘青瑜. *Saiwai kugeng: jindai yilai Tianzhujiao chuanjiaoshi zai Neimenggu de shehui huodong ji qi yingxiang* 塞外苦耕: 近代以来天主教传教士在内蒙古的社会活动及其影响, 1865–1950 (Tough tilling beyond the Great Wall: the social activities and influence of Catholic missionaries in modern times, 1865–1950). Hehehaote: Neimenggu daxue chubanshe, 2011.

Liyi shouce, 2014 礼仪手册, 2014 (Handbook of liturgical rites, 2014). N.p.: Zhejiang sheng Tianzhujiao jiaowu weiyanhui, 2013.

Lü, Lingfeng. "Eclipses and the Victory of European Astronomy in China." *East Asian Science, Technology and Medicine* 27 (2007): 127–145.

Lü Shiqiang 吕实强. *Zhongguo guanshen fanjiao de yuanyin, 1860–1874*, 中国官绅反教的原因, 1860–1874 (The origin and cause of the anti-Christian movement by Chinese officials and gentry, 1860–1874). Taibei: Zhongyang yanjiuyuan jindai shi yanjiusuo, 1966.

Malatesta, Edward J., and Gao Zhiyu, eds. *Departed, Yet Present: Zhalan, the Oldest Christian Cemetery in Beijing*. Macau and San Francisco: Instituto Cultural de Macau and Ricci Institute, University of San Francisco, 1995.

"Martyrs de Tien-tsin." http://eventail.pagesperso-orange.fr/martyrs/martyrse.html. Accessed 9 October 2015.

Mathews' Chinese-English Dictionary. Rev. American ed., 1943. Reprint, Taipei: n.p., 1963.

McInerney, Athanasius. "The Spanish Franciscans in the Province of Kiangsi, China, during the Years 1685–1813." Master's thesis, St. Bonaventure University, 1945.

Menegon, Eugenio. "Jesuits, Franciscans and Dominicans in Fujian: The Anti-Christian Incidents of 1637–1638." In *"Scholar from the West:" Giulio Aleni S.J. (1582–1649) and the Dialogue between Christianity and China*, edited by Tiziana Lippiello and Roman Malek, 218–262. Brescia: Fondazione Civiltà Bresciana, 1997.

Menegon, Eugenio. "Yongzheng's Conundrum: The Emperor on Christianity, Religions, and Heterodoxy." In *Rooted in Hope: China—Religion—Christianity*, edited by Barbara Hoster, Dirk Kuhlmann, and Zbigniew Wesolowski, 311–336. Sankt Augustin: Institut Monumenta Serica, 2017.

Mentougou quzhi 门头沟区志 ([Beijing] Mentougou District gazetteer). Beijing: Beijing chubanshe, 2006.

Mémoires de la Congrégation de la Mission. 3 vols. Paris: La Procure de la Congrégation de la Mission, 1911–1912.

Meyer, Jeffrey F. *The Dragons of Tiananmen: Beijing as a Sacred City.* Columbia, S.C.: University of South Carolina Press, 1991.

Meynard, Thiery [Mei Qianli 梅谦立, pseud]. *Beijing jiaotang ji lishi daolan: Beijing Yesuhui zuji daoyouce* 北京教堂及历史导览: 北京耶稣会足迹导游册 (A tour of Beijing churches and history: a guidebook to the footprints of Beijing Jesuits). Beijing: Shangzhi bianze guan, 2007.

Ming Xiaoyan 明晓艳 and Jean-Paul Wiest [Wei Yangbo 魏扬波, pseud]. Lishi yizong— Zhengfu si Tianzhujiao fendi 历史遗踪—正福寺天主教墓地 (Historical traces— Zhengfu si, the Catholic cemetery). Beijing: Wenwu chubanshe, 2007.

Missions de Chine, 1935–1936, Les (Shanghai: n.p., 1937).

Moidrey, Joseph de. *Carte des préfectures de Chine et de leur population chrétienne en 1911.* Chang-hai [Shanghai]: Imprimerie de la Mission Catholique Orphelinat de T'ou-sè-wè, 1913.

Moidrey, Joseph de. *La hiéarchie Catholique en Chine, en Corée et au Japon (1307–1914).* Chang-hai [Shanghai]: Imprimerie de l'Orphelinat de T'ou-sè-wè, 1914.

"Month of Mary." http://www.catholicculture.org/culture/liturgicalyear/overviews/ months/05_1.cfm. Accessed 17 January 2017.

Morelli, A. *Notes d'histoire sur le vicariat de Tcheng-ting-fou, 1858–1933.* Pei-p'ing [Beijing]: Imprimerie des Lazaristes, 1934.

Morse, Hosea Ballou, *The Chronicles of the East Asian Company Trading to China, 1635– 1834.* 5 vols. Oxford: Clarendon Press, 1926.

Morse, Hosea Ballou. *The International Relations of the Chinese Empire.* 3 vols. 1910– 1918. Reprint (3 vols. in 2), Taipei: n.p., n.d.

Morse, Hosea Ballou. *The Trade and Administration of China.* 1908. Reprint, 3rd rev. ed., New York: Russell & Russell, 1967.

Mungello, D.E. *The Catholic Invasion of China: Remaking Chinese Christianity.* Lanham, Md.: Rowman & Littlefield, 2015.

Mungello, D.E. *The Forgotten Christians of Hangzhou.* Honolulu: University of Hawaii Press, 1994.

Mungello, D.E. *The Spirit and the Flesh in Shandong, 1650–1785.* Lanham, Md.: Rowman & Littlefield, 2001.

"Nangangzi Tianzhujiao tang" 南岗子天主教堂 (The Nangangzi Catholic church). http://baike.baidu.com/view/1434159.htm. Accessed 28 February 2012.

"Nangangzi Tianzhujiao tang jianjie" 南港子天主教堂简介 (A brief introduction to the Nangangzi Catholic church). Church courtyard display, 2008.

"Nangangzi Tianzhujiao tang jianjie" 南港子天主教堂简介 (A brief introduction to the Nangangzi Catholic church). http://2008.people.com.cn/GB/22192/116781/118467/ 118479/7008345.html. Accessed 28 February 2012.

"Nantang jianjie" 南堂简介 (A brief introduction to the Nantang). Church courtyard display, 2009.

Naquin, Susan. *Peking: Temple and City Life, 1400–1900*. Berkeley: University of California Press, 2000.

Naquin, Susan, and Chün-fang Yü, eds. *Pilgrims and Sacred Sites in China*. Berkeley: University of California Press, 1992.

Needham, Joseph. *History of Scientific Thought*. Vol. 2 of *Science and Civilisation in China*. Cambridge: University Press, 1956.

"New Advent, Catholic Encyclopedia." http://www.newadvent.org/cathen/09193a.htm. Accessed 15 October 2015.

Nora, Pierre. "General Introduction: From *Lieux de mémoire* to *Realms of Memory*." In *Realms of Memory: Rethinking the French Past*. Vol. 1, *Conflicts and Divisions*, edited by Pierre Nora, xv–xxiv. New York: Columbia University Press, 1996.

Nora, Pierre. "Introduction to Volume 1: Between Memory and History." In *Realms of Memory: Rethinking the French Past*. Vol. 1, *Conflicts and Divisions*, edited by Pierre Nora, 1–23. New York: Columbia University Press, 1996.

Novelli, Luigi. *Shanghai: Religious Buildings*. Shanghai: Haiwen Audio-Video Publishers, 2003.

"Our Lady of Mount Carmel." https://en.wikipedia.org/wiki/Our_Lady_of_Mount_Carmel. Accessed 13 April 2016.

"Our Mother of Sheshan." https://en.wikipedia.org/wiki/Our_Mother_of_Sheshan. Accessed 20 February 2017.

Papers Relating to the Massacre of Europeans at Tien-tsin on the 21st June, 1870. London: Harrison and Sons, 1871.

Peng Jiandao 彭鉴道. *Xinyang ganwu* 信仰感悟 (Faith realized). N.p.: n.p., 2012. Church internal circulation material, book.

Peng Jiandao 彭鉴道. *Zhongguo chuanjiaoshi* 中国传教士 (China missionaries). Hong Kong: Zhongguo guoji chubanshe, 2010.

Pfister, Louis. *La hierarchie catholique en Chine, en Corée et au Japon*. Changhai [Shanghai]: Imprimerie de l'Orphelinat de T'ou-sè-wè, 1908.

Planchet, J.-M. [Jean-Marie]. *Documents sur les martyrs de Pékin pendant al persécution des Boxeurs*. Pékin [Beijing]: Imprimerie des Lazaristes, 1923.

Planchet, J.-M. *Guide du touriste aux monuments religieux de* Pékin. Pékin [Beijing]: Imprimerie des Lazaristes, 1923.

Planchet, J.-M. [A. Thomas, pseud.]. *Histoire de la mission de Pékin*. 2 vols. Paris: Imprimerie de la Presse Française, 1923–1925.

Planchet, J.-M. *Le cimetière et la paroisse de Tcheng-fou-sse, 1732–1917*. Pékin [Beijing]: Imprimerie des Lazaristes, 1918.

Planchet, J.-M. *Le cimetière et les oeuvres Catholiques de Chala, 1610–1927*. Pékin [Beijing]: Imprimerie des Lazaristes, 1928.

Planchet, J.-M. *Les Lazaristes à Suanhoafu*. Pékin [Beijing]: Imprimerie des Lazaristes, 1927.

Planchet, J.-M. *Les Missions de Chine et du Japon*. Pékin [Beijing]: Imprimerie des Lazristes, 1916–1942.

Planchet, J.-M. *The Lazarists in Suanhoafu, 1783–1927*. Translated by Henk de Cuijper. http://sievstudia.org/wp-content/uploads/2017/06/SIEV-The-Lazarist-in-Suang hoafou-1783-1927-JM-Plancet-CM-.pdf. Accessed 14 October 2017.

Playfair, G.M.H. *The Cities and Towns of China: A Geographical Dictionary*. 2nd edition. 1910. Reprint, Taipei: Ch'eng Wen Publishing Co., 1971.

Poole, Stafford. *A History of the Congregation of the Mission, 1625–1843*. N.p.: n.p., 1973. Church internal circulation material, book.

Prache, Anne. *Cathedrals of Europe*. Ithaca: Cornell University Press, 1999.

Preston, Diana. *The Boxer Rebellion: The Dramatic Story of China's War on Foreigners that Shook the World in the Summer of 1900*. New York: Walker & Co., 2000.

Price, Frank Wilson. *The Rural Church in China: A Survey*. New York: Agricultural Missions, 1948.

Qingji jiao'an shiliao 清季教案史料 (Historical materials on [Christian] religious cases during the [late] Qing). Edited by Gugong wenxian guan. 2 Parts. Peip'ing [Beijing]: n.p., 1937 and 1941.

Qingmo jiao'an 清末教案 (Late Qing [Christian] religious cases). Edited by Diyi lishi dang'anguan. 3 vols. Beijing: Zhonghua shuju, 1996–1999.

Qing zhongqianqi Xiyang Tianzhujiao zai Hua huodong dang'an shiliao 清中前期西洋天主教在华活动档案史料 (Archival materials on the activities in China of Catholicism in the early and mid-Qing). Edited by Diyi lishi dang'anguan. 4 vols. Beijing: Zhonghua shuju, 2003.

Quanfei jilüe 拳匪纪略 (A brief account of the Boxers). Compiled by Qiao Xisheng 侨析生. 1903. Reprint, Taibei: Wenhai chubanshe, 1967.

Quanshi Beijing jiaoyou zhiming 拳时北京教友致命 (Beijing's Catholic fatalities during Boxer times). 18 *juan*. Beijing: Jiushi tang, 1920–1931.

Ren Yanli 任延黎. *Zhongguo Tianzhujiao: Jichu zhishi* 中国天主教: 基础知识 (Chinese Catholicism: basic information. Beijing: Zongjiao wenhua chubanshe, 2005.

Rite of Dedication of a Church and an Altar. N.p.: International Committee on English in the Liturgy, 1978. http://www.liturgyoffice.org.uk/Resources/Rites/RDCA.pdf. Accessed 15 June 2018.

Ronan, Charles E., and Bonnie B.C. Oh, eds. *East Meets West: The Jesuits in China, 1582–1773*, Chicago: Loyola University Press, 1988.

Rondelez, Valère. *La chrétienté de Siwantze: un centre d'activité missionaire en Mongolie*. Siwantze: Van Roey, 1938.

Rondelez, Valère [Long Deli 隆德里, pseud.]. "Xiwan shengjiao yuanliu" 西湾圣教源流 (The origins of Xiwan's sacred religion). In *Saiwai chuanjiao shi* 塞外传教史 (A history of Catholic missions beyond the Great Wall), edited by Gu Weiying, 9–94. Taibei: Guangqi wenhua shiye, 2002.

"Sacred Heart Cathedral (Guangzhou)." http://en.wikipedia.org/wiki/Sacred_Heart_Cathedral_(Guangzhou). Accessed 14 March 2015.

"Sainte-Trinité, Paris." http://en.wikipedia.org/wiki/Sainte-Trinit%C3%A9,_Paris. Accessed 5 March 2015).

"Saint Michael in the Catholic Church." https://en.wikipedia.org/wiki/Saint_Michael_in_the_Catholic_Church. Accessed 6 April 2106.

Sandhaas, Joseph A. *Catholic Peking! A Guide to Modern and Historic Places of Interest to Catholics*. Peiping [Beijing]: Catholic University Press, 1937.

"Sangyu jiaotang jianjie" 桑峪教堂简介 (A brief introduction to the Sangyu church). Housangyu: n.p., n.d. (ca 2009). Church internal circulation material, pamphlet.

Séguy, Marie-Rose. "A propos d'une peinture Chinoise du cabinet des estampes a la bibliothèque nationale. *Gazette des beaux-arts* 88 (December 1976): 228–230.

"Seven Questions: Ai Weiwei." *Time*, 23 October 2017, 112.

Shengdian xinmao 圣殿新貌 (The contemporary form of Chinese Catholic churches). 3 vols. Beijing: Zhongguo qingnian chubanshe, 2003.

Shengtang fengcai 圣堂风采 (The elegance of Chinese Protestant churches). 5 vols. Beijing: Zhongguo qingnian chubanshe, 2003.

"Sheshan Basilica." https://en.wikipedia.org/wiki/Sheshan_Basilica. Accessed 20 February 2017.

"Shrines in China." https://www.udayton.edu/imri/mary/s/shrines-in-china.php. Accessed 10 January 2017.

Simson, Otto von. *The Gothic Cathedral: Origins of Gothic Architecture and the Medieval Concept of Order*. 3rd ed. Princeton: Princeton University Press, 1988.

Skinner, G. William. "Introduction: Urban and Rural in Chinese Society." In *The City in Late Imperial China*, edited by G. William Skinner, 253–273. Stanford: Stanford University Press, 1977.

Spence, Jonathan D. *God's Chinese Son: The Taiping Heavenly Kingdom of Hong Xiuquan*. New York: W. W. Norton & Co., 1996.

Spence, Jonathan D. *The Search for Modern China*. New York: W. W. Norton & Co., 1990.

Standaert, Nicolas. "The 'Edict of Tolerance' (1692): A Textual History and Reading." In *In the Light and Shadow of an Emperor: Tomás Pereira, SJ (1645–1708), the Kangxi Emperor and the Jesuit Mission in China*, edited by Artur K. Wardega and António Vasconcelos de Saldanha, 308–358. Newcastle upon Tyne: Cambridge Scholars Publishing, 2012.

"Statistics of the Catholic Church in China (2016)." *China Church Quarterly* 106 (May 2017): 3.

Stauffer, Milton T. *The Christian Occupation of China: A General Survey of the Numerical Strength and Geographical Distributon [sic] of the Christian Forces in China Made* by the Special Committee on Survey and Occupation China Continuation Committee, 1918–1921. Shanghai: China Continuation Committee, 1922.

Staunton, George. *An Authentic Account of an Embassy from the King of Great Britain to the Emperor of China.* 2 vols. London: W. Bulmer and Co. for G. Nicol, 1797–1798.

Sweeten, Alan Richard. "Catholic Converts in Jiangxi Province: Conflict and Accommodation." In *Christianity in China: From the Eighteenth Century to the Present*, edited by Daniel H. Bays, 24–40. Stanford: Stanford University Press, 1996.

Sweeten, Alan Richard. *Christianity in Rural China: Conflict and Accommodation in Jiangxi Province, 1860–1900.* Ann Arbor: Center for Chinese Studies, University of Michigan, 2001.

Sweeten, Alan Richard [Shi Weidong 史维东, pseud.]. "Cong Qing huangjia lingmu kan Manzu zaoqi de fazhan tedian" 从清皇家陵墓看满族早期的发展特点 (Early Manchu development characteristics as seen from the Qing imperial tombs). *Ouya xuekan* 8 (December 2008): 262–276.

Sweeten, Alan Richard. "The Early Qing Imperial Tombs: From Hetu Ala to Beijing." In *Proceedings of the North American Conference on Manchu Studies*, edited by Stephen Wadley, 61–102. Wiesbaden: Harrassowitz, 2006.

Sweeten, Alan Richard. "The Mason Gunrunning Case and the 1891 Yangtze Valley Anti-missionary Disturbances: A Diplomatic Link." *Zhongyang yanjiuyuan, Jindai shi yanjiusuo jikan* 4, pt. 2 (December 1974): 843–880.

Sweeten, Alan Richard. "The *Ti-pao*'s Role in Local Government as Seen in Fukien Christian 'Cases,' 1863–1869." *Ch'ing-shih wen-t'i* 3, no. 6 (December 1976): 1–27.

Sweeten, Alan Richard. "A Village Church in Jiangxi: Christianity in One Rural Locale from the Late Ming to the Late Qing." In *Tradition and Metamorphosis in Modern Chinese History: Essays in Honor of Professor Kwang-Ching Liu's Seventy-fifth Birthday*, edited by Yen-p'ing Hao and Hsiu-mei Wei, 1155–1172. 2 vols. Taipei: Institute of Modern History, Academia Sinica, 1998.

"Taihe zhuang tianzhutang" 太和庄天主堂 (The Taihe Village Catholic church). http://blog.sina.com.cn/s/blog_87ca2ce40102vkox.html. Accessed 26 January 2017.

"Thérèse of Lisieux." https://en.wikipedia.org/wiki/Th%C3%A9r%C3%A8se_of_Lisieux. Accessed 1 April 2016.

Thevenet, Jacqueline, ed. *Joseph Gabet, Évariste Huc: Lettres de Chine et d'ailleurs, 1835–1860.* Paris: Les Indes Savants, 2005.

Tianjin lao jiaotang 天津老教堂 (Tianjin's old churches). Compiled by Tianjin shi dang'an guan, Yu Xueyun, and Liu Lin. Tianjin: Tianjin chubanshe, 2005.

"'Tianjin lao jiaotang' de shuli shuwai" '天津老教堂'的书里书外 ('Tianjin's old churches'—[information from] inside and outside the book). http://www.360doc.com/content/18/0305/11/32366243_734420302.shtml. Accessed 25 April 2018.

"Tianjin Massacre—Chonghou's Report." http://www9.georgetown.edu/faculty/spendelh/china/TJ700623.htm. Accessed 4 February 2013.

"Tianjin Wanghailou jiaotang de jianjie" 天津望海楼教堂的简介 (A brief introduction to the Tianjin Wanghailou church). https://zhidao.baidu.com/question/7144 26023923780045.html?qbl=relate_question_0&word=wanghailoujiaotangduoda. Accessed 26 November 2016.

Tian Qu 天衢 (The Quzhou [Zhejiang] Catholic church). Quzhou: Zhejiang sheng Quzhou shi Fushan tianzhutang, 2011.

"Tianzhujiao Baoding jiaoqu" 天主教保定教区 (The Catholic diocese of Baoding). http://blog.sina.com.cn/s/blog_87ca2ce40101qr70.html. Accessed 18 January 2017.

"Tianzhujiao Beijing zong jiaoqu" 天主教北京总教区 (The Catholic diocese of Beijing). http://blog.sina.com.cn/s/blog_87ca2ce40101pjcj.html. Accessed 23 January 2017.

"Tianzhujiao Cangzhou Xianxian jiaoqu" 天主教沧州献县教区 (The Catholic diocese of Cangzhou, Xian County. http://www.xianxiancc.org/showart.asp?id=131. Accessed 6 June 2016.

Tianzhujiao Wenzhou jiaoqu zongtang xiujian ji jiaotang zhengti dingsheng kaigong qingdian: xiangguan ziliao huibian 天主教温州教区总堂修建暨教堂整体顶升开工庆典：相关资料汇编 (Renovation of the Wenzhou parish Catholic cathedral and celebration of the start of the church work: a compilation of interrelated materials. Wenzhou: n.p., 2012. Church internal circulation material, report.

"Tianzhujiao Xianxian jiaoqu" 天主教献县教区 (The Catholic diocese of Xian County). http://blog.sina.com.cn/s/blog_87ca2ce40102v2pi.html. Accessed 21 January 2017.

"Tianzhujiao Xiwanzi jiaoqu" 天主教西湾子教区 (The Catholic diocese of Xiwanzi). http://blog.sina.com.cn/s/blog_87ca2ce40102wtwd.html. Accessed 16 January 2017.

"Tianzhujiao Xuanhua jiaoqu" 天主教宣化教区 (The Catholic diocese of Xuanhua). http://blog.sina.com.cn/s/blog_87ca2ce40102v6dh.html. Accessed 15 January 2017.

Tiedemann, R.G. "Christianity and Chinese 'Heterodox Sects:' Mass Conversion and Syncretism in Shandong Province in the Early Eighteenth Century." *Monumenta Serica* 44 (1996): 339–382.

Tiedemann, R.G. "Christianity in a Violent Environment: The North China Plain on the Eve of the Boxer Uprising." In *Historiography of the Chinese Catholic Church: Nineteenth and Twentieth Centuries*, edited by Jeroom Heyndrickx, 138–144. Leuven: Ferdinand Verbiest Foundation, K. U. Leuven, 1994.

Tiedemann, R.G. "The Church Militant: Armed Conflicts between Christians and Boxers in North China." In *The Boxers, China, and the World*, edited by Robert Bickers and R.G. Tiedemann, 17–41. Lanham, Md.: Rowman & Littlefield, 2007.

Tiedemann, R.G. [Di Deman 狄德满, pseud.]. *Huabei de baoli he konghuang: Yihetuan yundong qianxi Jidujiao chuanbo he shehui zhongtu* 华北的暴力和恐慌：义和团运动前夕基督教传播和社会冲突 (Violence and fear in north China: Christian missions and social conflict on the eve of the Boxer Uprising). Nanjing: Jiangsu renmin chubanshe, 2011.

Tiedemann, R.G. "Rural Unrest in North China, 1868–1900: With Particular Reference for South Shandong." Ph.D. diss., University of London, 1991.

The Tientsin Massacre: Being Documents Published in the Shanghai Evening Courier from June 16th to Sept. 10th, 1870, with an Introductory Narrative. 2nd ed. Shanghai: A. H. de Carvalho, n.d.

Tongxian zhi 通县志 ([Hebei] Tong County gazetteer). Beijing: Beijing chubanshe, 2003.

Tong Xun 佟洵. *Jidujiao yu Beijing jiaotang wenhua* 基督教与北京教堂文化 (Christianity and Beijing church culture). Beijing: Zhongyang minzu daxue chubanshe, 1999.

Van den Brandt, Joseph. *Catalogue des principaux ouvrages sortis des presses des Lazaristes à Pékin de 1864 à 1930.* Pékin [Beijing]: H. Vetch, 1933.

Van den Brandt, J. [Jospeh]. *Les Lazaristes en Chine, 1697–1935: notes biographiques.* Pei-p'ing [Beijing]: Imprimerie des Lazaristes, 1936.

Vanderstappen, Harrie. "Chinese Art and the Jesuits in Peking." In *East Meets West: The Jesuits in China, 1582–1773*, edited by Charles E. Ronan and Bonnie B.C. Oh, 103–126. Chicago: Loyola University Press, 1988.

Vauchez, André. "The Cathedral." In *Realms of Memory: The Construction of the French Past.* Vol. 2, *Traditions*, ed. Pierre Nora, 37–68. New York: Columbia University Press, 1997.

Verhaeren, Hubert G. *Catalogue de la bibliothèque du Pé-t'ang.* 1949. Reprint, Paris: Les Belles Lettres, 1969.

The Vincentians: A General History of the Congregation of the Mission. 6 vols. Hyde Park, N.Y.: New City Press, 2009–2016. Vol. 1, Luigi Mezzadri and José María Román, *From the Foundation to the End of the Seventeenth Century (1625–1697)*; Vol. 2, Luigi Mezzadri and Francesca Onnis, *The Eighteenth Century to 1789*; Vol. 3, John E. Rybolt, *Revolution and Restoration (1789–1843)*; Vol. 4, John E. Rybolt, *Expansion and Reactions (1843–1878)*; Vol. 5, John E. Rybolt, *An Era of Expansion (1878–1919)*; Vols. 6A and 6B, John E. Rybolt, *Internationalization and Aggiornamento, (1919–1980)*.

Vitruvius: The Ten Books on Architecture. Translated by M.H. Morgan. New York: Dover Publications, 1960.

Wang, Dong. *China's Unequal Treaties: Narrating National History.* Lanham, Md.: Lexington Books, 2005.

Wang, Lianming. "Church, a 'Sacred Event' and the Visual Perspective of an 'Etic Viewer': An 18th Century Western-style Chinese Painting Held in the Bibliothèque nationale de France." In *Face to Face: The Transcendence of the Arts in China and Beyond.* Vol. 1, *Historical Perspective*, edited by Rui Oliveira Lopes, 370–397. Lisbon: Centro de Investigacöes Estudos em Belas-Artes, 2014. https://materiale-textkulturen .academia.edu/LianmingWang%E7%8E%8B%E5%BB%89%E6%98%8E. Accessed 19 October 2016.

Wang Lianming 王廉明. "Zhenghua Tianxing: Lang Shining dui Beijing tianzhu-tang de gongxian" 正画天形: 郎世宁对北京天主堂的贡献 (Depicting paradise: Guiseppe Castiglione's contributions to Beijing churches). *Gugong wenwu yuekan* 393 (December 2015): 30–37.

Wang, Lianming and Francesco Maglioccola [Ma Fangji, pseud.]. "The Architectural Drawings of an Eighteenth Century Jesuit Church (Nantang) in Beijing: Analysis and Reconstruction." In *Le Vie dei Mercanti. S.A.V.E. Heritage: Safeguard of Architectural, Visual and Environmental Heritage*, edited by Carmine Gambardella. Naples: La scuola di Pitagola editrice, 2011. https://materialetextkulturen.academia.edu/Lian mingWang%E7%8E%8B%E5%BB%89%E6%98%8E. Accessed 19 October 2016.

Wang Minglun 王明论, comp. *Fanyangjiao shuwen jietie xuan* 反洋教书文揭帖选 (A selection of anti-Christian writings). Ji'nan: Qilu shushe, 1984.

Wang Xiao-qing. "Staying Catholic: Catholicism and Local Culture in a Northern Chinese Village." Ph.D. diss., University of Notre Dame, 2004.

Wells, Williams S. *The Middle Kingdom: A Survey of the Geography, Government, Literature, Social Life, Arts, and History of the Chinese Empire and Its Inhabitants.* Rev. ed. 2 vols. New York: C. Scribner's Sons, 1883.

"Wen'an xian Anzuxin zhuang tianzhutang" 文安县安祖辛庄天主堂 (The Anzuxin Village, Wen'an County, Catholic church). http://blog.sina.com.cn/s/blog_87ca2ce40102v96s.html. Accessed 12 January 2017.

Wen'an xianzhi 文安县志 ([Hebei] Wen'an County gazetteer). Beijing: Zhongguo she-hui chubanshe, 1995.

Wenzhou Tianzhujiao jianshi 温州天主教简史 (A brief history of Catholicism in Wenzhou). Wenzhou: Tianzhujiao Wenzhou jiaoqu, n.d. Church internal circula-tion material, pamphlet.

Wiest, Jean-Paul. "The Building of the Cathedral of Canton: Politics, Cultural, and Religious Clashes." In *Religion and Culture: Past Approaches, Present Globalisation, Future Challenges—International Symposium Organised by the Macau Ricci Institute* and the Instituto do Oriente (Lisbon), Macau, November 28th–29th 2002, 231–252. Macau: Macau Ricci Institute, 2004.

Wiest, Jean-Paul. "Catholic Activities in Kwangtung Province and Chinese Responses, 1848–1885." Ph.D. diss., University of Washington, 1977.

Wiest, Jean-Paul. *Maryknoll in China: A History, 1918–1955.* Armonk, N.Y.: M. E. Sharpe, 1988.

Wilkinson, Endymion. *Chinese History: A Manual, Revised and Enlarged.* Cambridge, Mass.: Harvard University Asia Center, Harvard-Yenching Institute, 2000.

Willeke, Bernward. "Fray Manuel del Santisimo Sacramento, the Last Franciscan in Kiangsi, China. *Franciscan Studies* 26, no. 2; n.s. 5, no. 2 (June 1945): 175–196.

Witek, John D. "Understanding the Chinese: A Comparison of Matteo Ricci and the French Jesuit Mathematicians Sent by Louis XIV." In *East Meets West: The Jesuits in*

China, 1582–1773, edited by Charles E. Ronan and Bonnie B.C. Oh, 62–102. Chicago: Loyola University Press, 1988.

"Wu'an shi Shucun zhen Baisha cun" 武安市淑村镇白沙村 (Baisha Village, Shucun Town, Wu'an City). http://www.hrtv.cn/zt/bsc/index.html. Accessed 11 January 2017.

Wu'an xianzhi 武安县志 ([Hebei] Wu'an County gazetteer). Beijing: Guangbodianshi chubanshe, 1990.

Wu, Hung. *Remaking Beijing: Tiananmen Square and the Creation of a Political Space.* Chicago: University of Chicago Press, 2005.

Wuqing xianzhi 武清县志 ([Hebei] Wuqing County gazetteer). Tianjin: Tianjin shehui kexueyuan chubanshe, 1991.

Wu Shengde 吴盛德, and Chen Zenghui 陈增辉, eds. *Jiao'an shiliao bianmu* 教案史料 编目 (Bibliography of historical materials on [Christian] religious cases). Peip'ing [Beijing]: Yanjing daxue, 1941.

Xianxian jiaoqu 献县教区 ([Hebei] Xian County diocese). Xianxian: Tianzhujiao Xianxian jiaoqu chuban, 2003.

Xianxian zhi 献县志 ([Hebei] Xian County gazetteer). Beijing: Zhongguo heping chubanshe, 1995.

"Xiaohan cun tianzhutang jianjie" 小韩村天主堂简介 (A brief introduction to the Xiaohan Village Catholic church). Church lobby display, 2010.

"Xiheying tangqu ji lishi ren shenfu jianjie" 西和营堂区及历史任神父简介 (A brief introduction to [Hebei's] Xiheying parish and a historical list of appointed priests). Xiheying: n.p., n.d. Church internal circulation material, photocopy.

"Xikai jiaotang" 西开教堂 (The Xikai church). http://baike.baidu.com/link?url=TW20 JRLaRexsVZveNVVBqPCD_BrVrfUo6LdwAgnwaQWaZzPNoKl34E3ZyUQVogJ3 l7SG6APMRB10jFIWznESNq. Accessed 9 July 2016.

"Xikai jiaotang" 西开教堂 (The Xikai church). http://www.tj-church.org/About/. Accessed 7 March 2012.

"Xinzhuang xinyang bainian qingdian jinian" 辛庄信仰百年庆典纪念 (Commemorating a celebration of one hundred years of faith in Xin Village). Xinzhuang: n.p., 1999. Church internal circulation material, pamphlet.

"Xiwanzi Tianzhujiao tang" 西湾子天主教堂 (The Xiwanzi Catholic church). http:// baike.baidu.com/item/%E8%A5%BF%E6%B9%BE%E5%AD%90%E5%A4% A9%E4%B8%BB%E6%95%99%E5%A0%82/10051796?fr=aladdin. Accessed 16 January 2017.

"Xizhi men tianzhutang" 西直门天主堂 (The Xizhi Gate Catholic church). http://baike .baidu.com/view/764328.htm?fromtitle=%E8%A5%BF%E5%A0%82&fromid=581 4456&type=syn. Accessed 21 October 2016.

"Xizhi men tianzhutang" 西直门天主堂 (The Xizhi Gate Catholic church). http:// baike.baidu.com/link?url=866ut-Z4lacbFogA14D5PhJb2EINaRl9cz95zEKxJFk

BhxlLNSBNhP-etap63WOAOnTIFovOfPT1FIs4r5XFzA89ziAZd2PiO1aF0QGMepqz
os1l6eVjRupZXpFkZQwoh69i7nOie1HwPxsLHL5-xk. Accessed 13 April 2016.

"Xuanhua Tianzhujiao tang" 宣化天主教堂 (The Xuanhua Catholic church). http://
baike.baidu.com/item/%E5%AE%A3%E5%8C%96%E5%A4%A9%E4%B8%BB%
E6%95%99%E5%A0%82/7058787?fromtitle=%E5%AE%A3%E5%8C%96%E6%9
5%99%E5%A0%82&fromid=15486043&fr=Aladdin. Accessed 14 January 2017.

"Xuanhua tianzhutang bainian daqing, 1904–2004" 宣化天主堂百年大庆, 1904–2004
(The centennial celebration of Xuanhua's Catholic church, 1904–2004). Xuanhua:
n.p., 2004. Church internal circulation material, pamphlet.

"Xuanhua tianzhutang jianjie" 宣化天主堂简介 (A brief introduction to Xuanhua's
Catholic church). Xuanhua: n.p., n.d. (ca 2007). Church internal circulation material, photocopy.

Xuanhua xianzhi 宣化县志 ([Hebei] Xuanhua County gazetteer). Shijiazhuang: Hebei
renmin chubanshe, 1993.

"Xushui Anzhuang tianzhutang" 徐水安庄天主堂 (The An Village, Xushui, Catholic
church). http://blog.sina.com.cn/s/blog_87ca2ce40101qr2p.html. Accessed 18 January 2017.

Xushui xianzhi 徐水县志 ([Hebei] Xushui County gazetteer). Beijing: Xinhua chubanshe, 1997.

Yan, Kejia. *Catholic Church in China.* Beijing: Wuzhou chuanbo chubanshe, 2004.

Yan Kejia 晏可佳. *Zhongguo Tianzhujiao jianshi* 中国天主教简史 (A brief history of
Chinese Catholicism). Beijing: Zongjiao wenhua chubanshe, 2001.

Yang, Mayfair Mei-hui. "Spatial Struggles: Postcolonial Complex, State Disenchantment,
and Popular Reappropriation of Space in Rural Southeast China." *Journal of Asian
Studies* 63, no. 3 (August 2004): 719–755.

Yang Qingyun 杨靖筠. *Beijing Tianzhujiao shi* 北京天主教史 (A history of Catholicism
in Beijing). Beijing: Zongjiao wenhua chubanshe, 2009.

Yanqing xianzhi 延庆县志 ([Beijing] Yanqing County gazetteer). Beijing: Beijing chubanshe, 2006.

"Yongning tianzhutang" 永宁天主堂 (The Yongning Catholic church). http://baike
.baidu.com/link?url=QU94hk3c_FNEpl8oQYra1Lhf7zDuAdOtSJSHOZoYc9ClG8t
WKKhcAliSdRnmoojdxhGiegYeOZXoHQKRNBQPbSHU4r_U1058hboS2WQNsO
EooXdIDhyTNm-sW6OSgRDr. Accessed 24 January 2017.

Young, Ernest P. *Ecclesiastical Colony: China's Catholic Church and the French Religious
Protectorate.* Oxford: Oxford University Press, 2013.

Yule, Henry and A.C. Burnell. *Hobson-Jobson: A Glossary of Colloquial Anglo-Indian
Words and Phrases, and of Kindred Terms, Etymological, Historical, Geographical and
Discursive.* London: John Murray, 1903.

Yu Sanle 余三乐. *Zaoqi Xifang chuanjiaoshi yu Beijing* 早期西方传教士与北京 (Early
Western missionaries and Beijing). Beijing: Beijing chubanshe, 2001.

Yu Sanle 余三乐. *Zhong Xi wenhua jiaoliu de lishi jianzheng: Ming mo Qing chu Beijing Tianzhu jiaotang* 中西文化交流的历史见证: 明末清初北京天主教堂 (Historical evidence on Sino-Western cultural exchange: Beijing Catholic churches in the late Ming and early Qing). Guangzhou: Guangdong renmin chubanshe, 2006.

Yuxian zhi 蔚县志 ([Hebei] Yu County gazetteer). Beijing: Zhongguo sanshan chubanshe, 1995.

Zang Lihe 藏励和 et al, comps. *Zhongguo gu jin diming dacidian* 中国古今地名大辞典 (A dictionary of China's ancient and current place names). 1932. Reprint, Taibei: Taiwan shangwu yinshuguan, 1973.

"Zhangjiakou." http://en.wikipedia.org/wiki/Zhangjiakou. Accessed 17 April 2015.

Zhangjiakou Xuanhua quzhi 张家口 宣化区志 ([Hebei] Zhangjiakou Xuanhua District gazetteer). Xi'an: Sanqin chubanshe, 1998.

Zhang Li 张力 and Liu Jiantang 刘鉴唐. *Zhongguo jiao'an shi* 中国教案史 (A history of [Christian] religious cases). Chengdu: Sichuan sheng shehui kexue yuan chubanshe, 1987.

Zhang Qiyun 张其昀, comp. *Zhonghua minguo ditu ji* 中华民国地图集 (National atlas of China). 2d ed. 5 vols. Taibei: Guofang yanjiuyuan, 1964–1967.

Zhongguo Tianzhujiao shouce 中国天主教手册 (Directory of the Catholic Church in China). 6th ed. Shijiazhuang: Xindeshe, 2006.

Zhonghua Sheng Mu chaoshengdi 中华圣母朝圣地 (Sacred pilgrimage site for Our Lady of China). Donglü: n.p., ca 2013. Church internal circulation material, pamphlet.

Zhou, Tailiang, and Li Hui. *Catholic Church in China*. Translated by Zhou Tailiang. Beijing: China Intercontinental Press, 2005.

Zhouban yiwu shimo 籌辦夷務始末 (Complete record of the management of barbarian affairs). 1930. Reprint (8 vols.), Taibei: Tailian guofeng chubanshe, 1971.

Zhu Pingyi 祝平一. "Jinshimeng—'Yuzhi tianzhutang beiji' yu Qingchu de Tianzhujiao" 金石盟—"御制天主堂碑记" 与清初的天主教 (An inscriptive union—"the imperial commissioned stele's inscribed record for the Catholic church" and early Qing Catholicism). Zhongyangyanjiu yuan, Lishi yuyan yanjiusuo 75, no. 2 (June 2004), 389–421.

Zhuoxian zhi 涿县志 ([Hebei] Zhuo County gazetteer). N.p.: n.p., 1936.

Zhuozhou shi gongan zhi 涿州市公安志 ([Hebei] Zhuozhou public security gazetteer). Shijiazhuang: Hebei renmin chubanshe, 1992.

Zhuozhou zhi 涿州志 ([Hebei] Zhuozhou gazetteer). Beijing: Fangzhi chubanshe, 1997.

Index